USE IT ALL

USE IT ALL

The Leftovers
COOKBOOK

BY

JANE MARSH DIECKMANN

Illustrations by Peter Kahn

 THE CROSSING PRESS / Trumansburg, New York 14886

For all of you out there—young and old—who have given your encouragement, ideas, support, and love, not to mention your recipes! And for one in particular, who in a lasting way has shared with me all my special pleasures.

Typesetting by Martha J. Waters

Library of Congress Cataloging in Publication Data

Dieckmann, Jane M.
   Use it all.

   1. Cookery (Leftovers) I. Title
TX740.D53   641.5   81-15215
ISBN 0-89594-061-1   AACR2
ISBN 0-89594-062-0 (pbk.)

Contents

Introduction viii
   General Hints ix
   Ingredients xi
   Procedures xii

Apples 1
   Applesauce 8
Apricots 13
   Dried 13
   Fresh 16
Asparagus 18
Avocados 20

Bananas 22
Beans (Green and Wax) 29
Beef 34
Beets 38
Berries 41
   Black Raspberries 41
   Blackberries 42
   Blueberries 44
   Red Raspberries 47
   Strawberries 47
Bread 48
Broccoli 52
Buttermilk 55

Cabbage 63
Cake and Cookies 66
Carrots 67
Cauliflower 76
Celery 77
Cereals 79
   All-Bran, Krispies, Flakes, Chex 80
   Cooked Cereals 83

Cheese 88
Cherries 93
Chestnuts 96
Chicken 100
Coconut 105
Coffee 110
Corn 113
Cottage Cheese 116
Cranberries 121
Cream Cheese 126
Cucumbers 130
Currants 136
    Fresh 136
    Dried 137
Dates 139
Eggnog 143
Eggplant 146
Eggs 149
    Egg Yolks 150
    Egg Whites 151
Evaporated Milk 155
Fish 159
Grains 161
Granola 166
Grapefruit 171
Grapes 173
Ham 176
Jams, Jellies, Marmalades 181
Lamb 187
Leeks 190
Legumes 192
Lemons 198
Lima Beans 200
Livers 202
Melons 206
Mushrooms 208
Noodles and Pasta 211
Nuts 215
Onions 223
Oranges 227
Parsley 228
Peaches 230

Pears 235
Peas 239
Peppers 241
Pineapple 244
Plums 248
Pork 252
Potatoes 255
Pumpkin 261

Raisins 268
Rhubarb 272
Rice 277
Ricotta 281

Sour Cream 286
   Dairy Sour Cream 288
Sour Milk 290
Spinach 294
Squash 299
   Summer Squash 299
   Winter Squash 300
Sweet Potatoes 303

Tea 306
Tomatoes 308
   Tomato Juice 316
Tuna 319
Turkey 323

Veal 329

Wine 331

Yogurt 339

Zucchini 344

Appendix 354
   Basic Recipes 354
   Substitutions and Equivalents 360
   Basic Measures 361
   Baking Pans 362

Index 363

Introduction

*—Overheard at the Ithaca Farmers' Market:
"With the price of food these days, we don't
throw anything away. We simply can't af-
ford to."*

How often have you opened your refrigerator and looked at some small
amount of leftover roast, or cottage cheese, or dairy sour cream, or boiled potatoes? How often have you wished you could use it up simply, economically, and
tastefully? If you are a person who does not want to throw out the overripe bananas, the three ears of cooked corn on the cob, the dry bread, or the abundance
from your vegetable garden or apple tree, the following collection is for you.

We all know about the problems of world hunger and food supply, and from
our position of affluence we should feel some responsibility about not wasting a
commodity upon which human life depends. But in addition to moral, ethical
and humane considerations, it is simply stupid from an economical viewpoint to
throw away food. I realize that the truly efficient, well-organized housewife or
the mother with ravenous adolescent boys should have little food left over and
would certainly *never* have overripe bananas. But many of us are not well organ-
ized or always efficient, and even with the best planning, certain foodstuffs sometimes are not eaten up. And many of us, like Ado Annie, "just cain't say no"
when someone hands us a bag of winter pears, or a basket of tomatoes, or a quantity of large zucchini. Such a collection of recipes as I have put together should
be helpful in dealing with these problems.

My intention is to make the cooking quick and easy. I realize that certain
tasks do take time (removing the meat from the turkey carcass, for example).
But I have tried to keep the recipes simple and the preparation time short. I per-

sonally do not enjoy spending hours putting together an elaborate gourmet meal. I am convinced that a very good meal can be quickly, economically, and easily prepared.

Many recipes may seem low in fat—this is intentional, as I have had to cook for a missing gall bladder for many years; besides, I find cutting out fat is a good way to keep the weight down. After all, who needs it? If you find a certain lack of salt in the recipes, feel free to add more. I do not like salt myself and feel that it is not particularly healthful. You may want to add more pepper and other seasonings. But proceed with caution. Too little is better—and more easily remedied—than too much.

A word of warning—this is not a book for anyone learning how to cook. I have given few explanations of cooking terms nor have I provided detailed instructions for making yeast bread, tricky sauces, or a delicate cake. Any general, all-purpose cookbook will explain these procedures, often with helpful illustrations. It will also supply definitions of any terms you do not understand. I do frequently use three French cooking terms that have really become a part of our language: sauté—to cook in a small amount of fat; purée—to blend (usually in a food mill, processor, or blender) until very smooth; crepe—a thin pancake, one that can be served as a dessert or as a main or side dish when filled with meat or vegetables and covered with sauce.

The collection is set up as an encyclopedia, so that if you have some food you want to use up, you simply look under that food. Recipes using apples, for example, will appear under Apples. At the end of the section on apples, there is a list of recipes that use apples and appear elsewhere in the book. A general index gives recipes in the usual categories. I have tried to group the recipes in each section in order of importance. To my mind, the best way to use buttermilk is to bake with it; therefore the breads come first in the buttermilk section. My favorite and most used recipes are indicated by three stars (☆☆☆).

My special thanks go to my artist friend who illustrated the book and to many other friends who have offered recipes and suggestions and who simply had faith. I have used no names, but each of you should know who you are and that I am grateful. Certain recipes have previously appear in *The Grapevine,* published weekly in Ithaca; I am happy to be associated with that publication. My family have cheerfully swallowed many experiments and have served as patient and helpful judges. I am most grateful to them.

General Hints

Don't throw away any of the following:

dill pickle juice: Make bread out of it (see under Cucumbers).

fruit syrup from canned or frozen fruits: Use it for flavoring puddings and mixed fruit bowls, for liquid in gelatin desserts and salads, for thinning salad dressings, for cooking fresh fruits (pears, plums, cranberries, tart apples). Or make a sauce: Save the syrup until you have 2 cups (you can freeze it until you have collected enough). Add 1 tablespoon each butter and lemon juice and heat until bubbly; then thicken with 1 tablespoon cornstarch or 2 tablespoons flour (blended with a small amount of cold water). Cook until thickened and clear. Serve warm over ice cream, gingerbread, puddings, sponge cake, pancakes.

lemon and orange rinds: After you have squeezed the fruit for juice, save the rinds in a plastic container or bag in the refrigerator until you have enough to make it worth your while. Then grate and store in a tightly covered container (I use baby food jars) in the freezer until needed for your next cake, tea bread, or dessert.

vegetable stock: Keep a jar in your refrigerator or freezer and pour the stock right in. Add this stock to soup or use it in cream sauce (you can substitute stock for water when making milk from instant milk powder—the result is much more nutritious and tasty). The strong flavors (broccoli, cauliflower, cabbage, onions) you should keep by themselves for appropriate uses.

potato water: Add to soup, sauces. Or, better still, use it for making bread.

meat juices, pan juices, scrapings: Pour into a jar, and then deglaze the roasting pan; add a little hot water, put the pan over a low heat, and scrape. What you get up is the best part, excellent in gravies, stews, soups, sauces, casseroles. Don't worry about the fat; as the juices cool, it will rise to the top and congeal. You can scrape it off; use it for cooking, if you like. If you have a lean dog, you can feed the fat to him; he'll love you for it.

vegetables: Add them to the soup jar, make a vegetable salad, put them in a casserole with a cheese-flavored cream sauce.

old lettuce leaves: Put them in some boiling water (also true for raw vegetable trimmings, bean ends, mushroom pieces, wilted carrots and spinach, celery and green onion tops), add vegetable broth powder; when all is cooked, purée in the blender and eat as soup or add to the soup pot. You will be surprised at the excellent flavor all these remains have.

leftover green salad: Make an almost instant, delicious, finely flavored soup. Heat 1 tablespoon oil in a skillet, slice in a small potato (peeled or not, as you wish); when it is cooked, add a green onion or two, any leftover raw or cooked vegetables, and sauté gently for a few minutes. Then stir in 1 to 2 cups chicken broth, vegetable stock, or a combination. Add the salad remains, dressing and all, a dash of a favorite herb (try basil, oregano, rosemary, dill). Simmer about 10 minutes. Pour everything into the blender and whirl until smooth. Taste and adjust the seasoning. Serve with seasoned croutons (which you have made from leftover dry bread).

small amounts of greens: Wash, drain well, keep in a plastic bag in the refrigerator. They will stay crisp this way several days, and you can put them in salad as needed.

baked potato skins: Scrape out the potato, butter the skins a little, add salt and pepper, and cut in strips if you like. Bake at 400 degrees or broil until brown and crisp. *Watch them!* Serve hot as an hors d'oeuvre or crumble them into soup or salad.

Don't forget the basic dishes to which you can add leftover foods; pilaf, quiche, soufflé, omelette, timbale, hash, noodle or rice casserole, soup.

Use your freezer. You can store leftover meat and stock, cooked vegetables and stock, mushrooms (cooked), bread, cake, cookies. I store chicken livers in a plastic container until I have enough to cook with. You can freeze milk, buttermilk, cream, sour cream, cottage cheese, hard cheeses, yogurt; they will not be so appetizing when thawed, but do bake and cook with them. Don't freeze hard-boiled eggs (the whites become tough and rubbery), fried foods or boiled potatoes (they become soggy), uncooked vegetables, dishes with mayonnaise, or custards.

Ingredients

flour: I mean general all-purpose white flour. If you want to sift it before you measure, please do so. I never do any more (getting old and lazy, I guess). Also I am using more whole wheat pastry flour (and whole wheat bread flour in breads) for baking and less white flour. Do try this yourself; just remember that delicate cakes and cookies that should be light and white will not be so if you use whole wheat flour. It *is* heavier and makes a darker baked product. In breads and cookies, you can substitute equal amounts of rolled oats or wheat germ for flour. Don't substitute more than one-quarter of the total amount. Yes, I do use level measurements.

sugar: I use brown sugar more than white; I like the taste better. The quantities indicated are level measures, firmly packed. 10X sugar is confectioners' sugar. I am working on substituting honey or molasses for sugar in many recipes. I urge you to try it. Keep in mind that a baked product with honey will be moister, will bake faster, and will have a heavier texture. Don't try to reduce the sugar in any recipe in this book; I have already done so.

baking powder: All recipes are for double-acting sodium-based baking powder. In my next collection, this may not be so. With some kind help, I am working on making my own tartrate-based baking powder.

salt and pepper: As you will guess, I am not fond of either of these. Do add more if you like. And do grind your pepper fresh if you possibly can.

herbs: The recipes call for dry herbs, because they are so much more readily available year round (the exception is parsley, which you should use fresh any time you can). One teaspoon dried herbs, crushed, is roughly equivalent to one tablespoon fresh minced herbs.

butter/margarine: I use at least half butter, and the rest margarine. If the recipe really requires all butter, it will be indicated; the same is true for unsalted (sweet) butter. I use margarine in almost all breads. Have butter and margarine at room temperature for mixing.

yeast: This means baking yeast. One package dry yeast equals one tablespoon. You can use yeast cakes if you like (one cake equals one package dry yeast); I prefer dry yeast, it is easier to measure, to vary measurements, and to dissolve. Nutritional (or brewers) yeast is available in health food stores.

plain gelatin: One envelope equals one tablespoon.

eggs: If the recipe calls for separated eggs, beat the whites first, if possible; then use the same beaters for the yolks. It is all right if some white gets into the yolk, but not vice versa. Eggs should be at room temperature for mixing, and especially for beating.

Procedures

Most recipes say to preheat the oven before you even start mixing ingredients. In some cases, this is fine, but in many instances, it is wasteful. So when a recipe of mine says to bake at 375 degrees, this means in an oven *preheated* to 375. You should turn on the oven ahead of time, yes—but try not to heat it any longer than necessary. When you are baking bread, set the oven hotter than the temperature indicated; as you put the bread in the oven (gently and carefully so it won't fall—this does take time), the oven will lose some heat. It is important that the bread (or cake) starts to bake at the correct temperature. So judge accordingly and allow for oven heat loss. Don't forget to change the temperature setting after the baking has begun.

I use teflon bread and cake pans and cookie sheets; I almost never grease them. Most cookies have lots of shortening in them anyway, which should be sufficient. If you don't have teflon (or other non-stick) bakeware, do by all means grease the loaf pans for your breads, the tins for bar cookies and cakes, and the cookie sheets, especially if the batter or dough contains little or no shortening.

I hope this collection will be useful. Not only can you save on your budget, but you can have the immense satisfaction of putting it all together—creatively and without waste. *Bon appétit!*

JMD
Ithaca, New York
January 1981

Apples

What a wonderful way to begin! Apples are one of the most versatile fruits that we have and, thanks to modern refrigeration methods, we can enjoy them all year. Living as we do in an apple-growing region, my family and I can eat fresh apples all the time and enjoy many different varieties.

Apples can be fried: slice or cube them and fry in some margarine or bacon fat with some brown sugar sprinkled over the top. Cook gently until brown and tender; serve with sausage or crisply fried bacon. Baked apples are easy to prepare; select large, squat ones, tart and flavorful. You can fill them with raisins or dates or sausage. Consult a general cookbook for procedure. Apples also are delicious in fruit salads and mixed fresh fruit compotes. And, of course, you can make applesauce; a section on that follows.

☆☆☆ HUGUENOT TORTE

This recipe comes from the American South. It puffs up while baking, leaving a crunchy top that looks collapsed.

3 eggs	1/4 teaspoon salt
2 cups sugar	1 1/2 cups chopped tart apples
6 tablespoons flour	1 1/2 cups chopped pecans
3 teaspoons baking powder	1 1/2 teaspoons vanilla

Beat the eggs with an electric mixer until very frothy and lemon colored. Add the other ingredients in the order given. You can use walnuts instead of pecans, but pecans are much better. Pour into a large (15 x 10), *well-buttered* pan. Bake at 325° about 45 minutes. Cut in squares and remove with a turner. It will be hard to get neat servings; don't worry, so many really good desserts fall apart anyway. Top with whipped cream or vanilla ice cream.

☆☆☆   This symbol indicates my favorite and most used recipes.

APPLE NUT TORTE

This light dessert is very easy to make.

1 egg	1 teaspoon baking powder
1 teaspoon vanilla	1/4 teaspoon salt
1/4 cup white sugar	2 cups peeled, cut-up apples
1/2 cup brown sugar	1/2 cup chopped walnuts
1/2 cup flour	1/2 cup raisins (optional)

Preheat the oven to 350°. Beat the egg and vanilla until light and lemon colored. Beat in the sugars and blend well. Sift the dry ingredients; fold into the egg mixture. Then fold in the apples, walnuts, and raisins. If the apples are bland in taste, add a little lemon juice. Pour into a well-greased 8-inch square pan, or 9-inch pie pan. Bake 35 to 40 minutes, until lightly colored. This is better served warm and is very good with vanilla ice cream. If you keep it until the next day, it will sink, but it's still very good.

APPLE HARVEST CAKE

If you have a fluted tube pan (12-cup size), use it for this cake and the result will be beautiful. Whether your pan is fluted or not, be sure to grease it very well, using about 1 tablespoon of shortening, even if it is teflon coated.

1 1/4 cups flour	1/2 teaspoon baking soda
1 cup whole wheat flour	3/4 cup cooking oil
1 cup brown sugar	1 teaspoon vanilla
1/2 cup white sugar	3 eggs
1 tablespoon cinnamon	2 cups peeled, *finely* chopped apples
2 teaspoons baking powder	3/4 cup chopped nuts
1/2 teaspoon salt	

Sift the dry ingredients, except the brown sugar, into a large mixer bowl. Stir in the brown sugar. Combine the oil, vanilla, and eggs; beat well. Blend them into the dry ingredients and beat 3 minutes at medium speed.

By hand, stir in the apples and nuts. Pour into the prepared pan and bake at 325° for 50 to 60 minutes, or until toothpick inserted in the center comes out clean. Cool upright in pan 15 minutes; turn onto a serving plate and cool slightly.

Make a confectioners' sugar glaze (see the Appendix) and spoon over the cake.

☆☆☆ HONEYED FRUIT CRUMBLE

I make this dessert more often than any other. You can combine other fruits with the apples. Try blueberries, the combination I make most often, or cranberries or plums. If you like, add some chopped nuts to the apples and/or to the topping.

3 cups (or more) sliced apples	1/4 cup brown sugar
2 tablespoons lemon juice	1/4 teaspoon salt
1/4 cup honey	1/8 teaspoon *each* cinnamon
1/2 cup whole wheat flour (graham	and nutmeg
is best)	1/4 cup butter/margarine, softened
1/4 cup wheat germ	

Slice the apples into a 10-inch pie pan or other baking dish (I often don't measure them, I just fill the dish with apples); sprinkle the lemon juice over and then drizzle the honey over that. Mix the remaining ingredients together with your fingers until crumbly. Spread evenly over the fruit. Bake at 375° about 40 minutes, or until the topping is browned and the fruit is soft. Serve with cream or vanilla ice cream.

Note: Other toppings can be found under Cranberries, Peaches, and Plums.

APPLES IN CUSTARD

A lovely, light pudding, low in calories.

2 apples, pared, cored, sliced	pinch of salt
1/4 cup water	1 teaspoon vanilla
2 eggs	1 1/2 cups skim milk
3 tablespoons brown sugar	ground nutmeg

Combine the apples and water in a small saucepan. Simmer, covered, until just tender, about 5 minutes. Place in the bottom of a deep 1-quart baking dish. Beat eggs lightly with the sugar, salt, and vanilla; stir in the milk. Pour over the apples in the baking dish. Grate some nutmeg over the top. Place the dish in a pan of hot water, to the depth of 1 inch.

Bake at 325° about 50 minutes, or until set. Cool. Refrigerate until ready to serve.

CARAMEL APPLE PUDDING

3/4 cup flour
1/2 cup sugar
1 teaspoon baking powder
1 teaspoon cinnamon
1/4 teaspoon salt
1/2 cup milk

1 1/2 cups coarsely chopped apples
1/2 cup chopped almonds *or* walnuts
3/4 cup brown sugar
1/4 cup butter/margarine
3/4 cup boiling water

Sift the dry ingredients into a bowl. Stir in the milk, apples, almonds. Spread in a greased 1 1/2-quart casserole or 8-inch square pan.

Combine the brown sugar, butter, and boiling water; stir until the butter melts. Pour over the batter. Bake at 375° for 40 to 50 minutes. Serve warm.

PRALINE APPLE PIE

2 1/2 cups sliced apples
1/3 cup granulated sugar
1/4 teaspoon nutmeg
1/4 teaspoon cinnamon
9-inch pie shell, unbaked

2 tablespoons honey
1/2 cup brown sugar
2 tablespoons butter
1 egg, beaten
1/2 cup pecan pieces

Combine the apples, sugar, and spices. Put in the pie shell. Bake at 400° for 15 minutes. Mix the honey, brown sugar, and butter; bring to a boil. Remove from the heat; add the egg and nuts and mix well. Take the pie from the oven and pour this mixture over the top. Return to the 400° oven for 10 minutes; then reduce the heat to 325° and bake 25 to 30 minutes longer, or until the pie is set and the apples are soft. Serve warm.

APRICOT-APPLE PIE

1/2 cup dried apricots
1/2 cup water
4 medium tart apples
1 cup sugar
1/4 cup flour

1/4 teaspoon ground nutmeg
dash of salt
pastry for 9-inch pie, double crust
2 tablespoons butter

Cut the apricots in quarters (wet scissors work wonders). Combine the apricots and water, heat to boiling, cover, and simmer 5 minutes. Peel and dice the apples (you should have 4 cups); combine with the apricots in a large bowl. Mix the sugar, flour, nutmeg, and salt and sprinkle over the fruit; toss lightly to mix. Spoon into the prepared pie shell; dot with butter. Make a lattice top, brush the strips with milk and sprinkle lightly with sugar, if you wish.

Bake at 400° for 40 minutes, until pastry is golden and pie is bubbly.

BUTTERY APPLE SQUARES

An unusual layered dessert that is somewhat inbetween a cake and a bar cookie.

2 cups Rice Krispies	1/2 cup milk
1 1/2 cups flour	5 cups sliced apples
1/2 teaspoon salt	3/4 cup sugar
1/2 cup butter/margarine	2 tablespoons flour
1 egg, separated	1 tablespoon butter

Crush the cereal into fine crumbs. Sift the flour and salt; mix with the crumbs. Cut in the butter/margarine until the mixture resembles coarse corn meal. Combine the egg yolk and milk; beat well. Add to flour mixture and stir only until combined. Pat one-half in the bottom of a 9-inch square baking pan. Cover with the sliced apples. Combine the sugar and 2 tablespoons flour and sprinkle over the apples. Dot with 1 tablespoon butter. Roll out the remaining dough to fit the pan; place over the apples. Beat the egg white slightly and brush over the crust.

Bake at 375° about 45 minutes. While still warm, frost with Honey Glaze or a confectioners' sugar glaze (see the Appendix). Cut into squares. Serve warm or cold.

☆☆☆ APPLE BROWNIES

This is one of the easiest bar cookie recipes there is.

1/2 cup margarine	1/2 cup chopped walnuts
1/4 teaspoon salt	1 cup flour
1 egg, beaten	1/2 teaspoon baking powder
1 cup sugar	1/2 teaspoon baking soda
3 medium apples, pared and diced	1/2 teaspoon cinnamon
or 1/2 cup applesauce	

Cream the margarine with the salt; add the egg and sugar and beat well. Stir in the apples and nuts, then the dry ingredients. Blend well. Bake in an 8-inch square pan at 350° about 40 minutes. Cool and cut in squares.

APPLE DROP COOKIES

2 cups flour
1 teaspoon baking soda
1/2 teaspoon salt
1 teaspoon cinnamon
1/2 teaspoon cloves
1/2 teaspoon allspice
1/2 teaspoon nutmeg

1 cup finely chopped walnuts
1 cup raisins, chopped
1 cup finely chopped unpeeled red
  apple
1/2 cup butter/margarine
1 cup brown sugar
1 egg
1/4 cup apple cider *or* apple juice

Sift the dry ingredients into a large bowl; stir in the walnuts, raisins, and apple. Cream the butter, sugar, and egg until light and fluffy. Add the juice and beat until combined. Stir in the flour mixture and blend well. Drop by heaping teaspoonfuls, 2 inches apart, on greased cookie sheets. Bake 8 minutes at 400°, or until golden brown. If desired, glaze cookies while they are still hot with Light Butter Frosting (see the Appendix).

◆

APPLE PANCAKES

1 cup buckwheat flour
1 cup white flour
4 teaspoons baking powder
1/2 teaspoon salt
1/2 teaspoon cinnamon

1 egg, beaten
2 cups milk
1/4 cup melted shortening *or* oil
3/4 cup peeled, grated apple

Sift the dry ingredients. Add remaining ingredients and stir until smooth. Bake on a hot griddle, turning once. Serve with Cider Sauce (see the Appendix).

APPLE FRUIT LOAF

You might try this fresh apple and fruit bread for afternoon tea.

1 cup brown sugar
1/2 cup oil
2 tablespoons sherry
1 teaspoon vanilla
1 cup raisins
1 cup coarsely cut candied fruit
1 cup chopped nuts

1 cup dates, cut fine
1 1/2 cups coarsely shredded apples
2 teaspoons baking soda
2 cups flour
1/2 teaspoon salt
1/4 teaspoon cinnamon
1/4 teaspoon nutmeg

In a large bowl, mix together the sugar, oil, sherry, and vanilla. Stir in the raisins, candied fruit, nuts, and dates. Mix the apples with the soda and stir them in. Sift the dry ingredients into the wet mixture and blend thoroughly. Pour into a greased and floured loaf pan (9 x 5) and bake at 350° for 1 hour and 25 minutes, or until done. Cool in pan about 3 minutes, then turn out on a rack to cool.

Variation: For a simpler apple-nut bread, omit the raisins, candied fruit, dates, and nutmeg.

PARADISE JELLY

This jelly is as beautiful and perfect as its name.

9 sour apples
6 quinces

1 pound cranberries
sugar

Cut apples in eighths; discard stem and blossom ends. Quarter quinces, discard core, chop fine. Combine the fruits in a large pot, adding enough water to show through the top layer. Boil until the fruit is soft; strain through a jelly bag. Allow 1 cup sugar per 1 cup juice. Follow the rule for jelly under Black Raspberries.

Applesauce

Applesauce is the best way to use up spotted, sometimes tired, often free (part of nature's bounty) apples. If you or your friends have a tree that drops apples all over the place, try them alone—or combined with commercially grown apples—in applesauce. When my older daughter was a very little girl, she one day whispered in a confiding tone to my mother that I made applesauce with part rotten apples and part good apples. To which my mother said, equally confidingly, that she used *all* rotten apples.

There are two methods for making applesauce. You can peel the apples first, slice them, add a little water, and stew until tender. Then mash with a fork and sweeten. I find it simpler to remove the stems, cores, and seeds (and—if you are using "rotten" apples—also the worms, wormholes, rotten spots); then slice the apples into a large pot. Add just enough water to keep them from sticking. The amount of water needed depends on the water content of the apples you are using (older apples need more water than younger ones). It is better to use less water than more. Cook until the apples are mushy. Put them through a food mill, sweeten to taste (I use brown sugar—it's marvelous), add some cinnamon if you like. Cool. You can freeze applesauce for later use.

You can serve applesauce warm or cold; with whipped cream, ice cream, custard, pudding, or yogurt; combined with sweet or sour cherries, raspberries, raisins, chopped dates, stewed fruits (cranberries or rhubarb are particularly good).

Hot applesauce topping over pound cake and vanilla ice cream makes an unusual quick dessert: Combine 2 cups applesauce, 1 teaspoon cinnamon, a dash of nutmeg, 1/4 cup brown sugar, and 1 teaspoon lemon juice. Heat until very warm and the sugar is dissolved.

APPLESAUCE CORN BREAD

Serve this hot with lots of butter.

1 cup whole wheat flour	1 cup buttermilk
1 cup white flour	1 cup molasses
2 cups cornmeal	3/4 cup applesauce
1/2 teaspoon salt	3/4 cup raisins
1 teaspoon baking soda	

Mix the flours, cornmeal, salt, and soda in a large bowl. Add buttermilk and molasses and beat with a spoon until smooth. Fold in the applesauce and raisins. Spread in a greased 9-inch square pan. Bake at 350° for 35 minutes. Cut in squares.

APPLESAUCE BREAD

This is very spicy and has the added pizazz of a topping.

1 1/4 cups applesauce
1 cup sugar
1/2 cup oil
3 tablespoons milk
2 cups flour
1 teaspoon baking soda

1/2 teaspoon baking powder
1/2 teaspoon cinnamon
1/4 teaspoon nutmeg
1/4 teaspoon allspice
1/2 cup chopped nuts

Mix together the applesauce, sugar, oil, and milk. Sift the dry ingredients and add to the applesauce mixture. Stir in the nuts. Pour into a greased 9 x 5 loaf pan. Sprinkle with Cinnamon Topping (see the Appendix). Bake at 350° for 1 hour.

Variations:
Cardamom: Omit the topping, reduce applesauce to 1 cup and beat in 1 egg; substitute 1/2 teaspoon cardamom for the nutmeg and allspice.
Fruit-Nut: Omit the topping, increase the nuts to 1 cup and add 1/2 cup mixed candied fruit.

APPLESAUCE CAKE

I have tried many recipes for applesauce cake; this is my favorite.

1/2 cup butter/margarine
1 cup sugar
1 egg
1/2 cup bran flakes
1 cup applesauce
1 1/2 cups flour

2 teaspoons baking powder
1/4 teaspoon baking soda
1/4 teaspoon cloves
1/2 teaspoon cinnamon
1/4 teaspoon salt
1 teaspoon vanilla

Cream the butter and sugar. Add the egg and beat well. Stir in the bran flakes and applesauce. Sift the dry ingredients together and add to the creamed mixture. Stir in the vanilla. Pour into a greased 9-inch square pan and bake at 375° for 30 to 40 minutes.

Cool and frost with Light Butter Frosting (see the Appendix).

HONEY AND SPICE CUPCAKES

Here is a change from the usual chocolate-vanilla cupcake combination.

1/3 cup butter/margarine	1 teaspoon baking soda
1/2 cup brown sugar	1/2 teaspoon salt
1 egg	1/4 teaspoon nutmeg
3/4 cup applesauce	1 cup rolled oats
1 1/2 cups flour	1/2 cup milk
1 teaspoon cinnamon	

Cream butter with sugar and beat in the egg and applesauce. Sift together the flour, cinnamon, soda, salt, and nutmeg. Combine with the rolled oats. Blend dry ingredients into creamed mixture alternately with milk, beginning and ending with dry ingredients. Pour the batter into greased medium-sized muffin cups, filling each about three quarters full. Bake at 375° about 20 minutes. Cool.

Spread Honey Glaze (see the Appendix) over the tops of the cupcakes. Sprinkle with coconut if desired. Makes 12 cupcakes.

OATMEAL SAUCERS

Applesauce cookies made with oatmeal are the best, in my view.

2/3 cup butter/margarine	1 1/2 cups flour
1 cup sugar	1 1/2 teaspoon baking powder
1 egg	1/2 teaspoon salt
3/4 cup applesauce	1 cup rolled oats
1 tablespoon grated orange rind	3/4 cup chopped walnuts
2 teaspoons orange extract	

Cream the butter and sugar. Add the egg and mix well. Stir in applesauce, orange rind, and extract. Sift the flour, baking powder, and salt; stir in the rolled oats and walnuts and add all this to the creamed mixture. Drop by tablespoons on a greased cookie sheet. Bake at 400° for 12 minutes. Cool. If desired, frost with Orange Glaze (see the Appendix).

☆☆☆ APPLESAUCE SPICE SQUARES

One of the top ten bar cookies in my recipe collection. They are moist and have a tendency to get moldy if you leave them too long; so freeze some and take them out as needed. These go very well with applesauce or with pumpkin custard.

1 cup flour	1 scant cup sugar
1 cup rye flour	1 egg
1 teaspoon baking soda	1 1/2 cups applesauce *or* 3/4 cup
3/4 teaspoon cinnamon	applesauce and 3/4 cup mashed
1/4 teaspoon cloves	pumpkin
1/4 teaspoon nutmeg	1/2 cup dark raisins
dash of salt	1/2 cup light raisins
1/2 cup butter/margarine	1/2 cup chopped walnuts *or* soy grits

Sift the dry ingredients together and set aside.

Cream the butter and sugar; beat in the egg. Add the flour mixture alternately with the applesauce (or applesauce-pumpkin combination) and blend well. Stir in the raisins and nuts. Pour into a 15 x 10 pan. Bake 25 minutes at 350°. Cool and sprinkle with 10X sugar, if desired. Cut in squares.

APPLESAUCE FUDGE SQUARES

A delicious, brownie-like combination.

2 squares baking chocolate	2/3 cup applesauce
1/2 cup butter/margarine	1 cup flour
2 eggs, beaten	1/2 teaspoon baking powder
1 cup sugar	1/4 teaspoon baking soda
1 teaspoon vanilla	1/4 teaspoon salt

Heat the chocolate and shortening together until just melted. Add the eggs and blend well. Stir in the sugar, vanilla, and applesauce. Sift the dry ingredients and stir them in last.

Pour into an ungreased 9-inch square pan. Bake at 350° for 35 to 40 minutes. Cool and cut into squares.

COLONIAL APPLE CUSTARD

This pudding is very easy to make. It can be eaten as a side dish with meat, or for dessert with a topping of light cream or yogurt.

1 tablespoon melted butter	**3 eggs, beaten**
1 cup applesauce	**1/4 teaspoon salt**

Butter four custard cups. Combine the remaining butter with the applesauce, eggs, and salt. Pour into the cups. Place them in a pan of hot water and bake about 30 minutes at 350°. Serve this hot or cold.

HEXENSCHNEE

An airy, easy, and unusual German dessert (the name means witches' snow). I serve it with crisp spice cookies.

2 cups applesauce, divided	**2 tablespoons cold water**
1 envelope plain gelatin	**4 egg whites, beaten stiff**
1 teaspoon vanilla	**whipped cream**

Heat 1/2 cup of the applesauce. Dissolve the gelatin in the water; when softened, stir into the hot applesauce and blend until the gelatin is dissolved. Add the vanilla to the remaining 1 1/2 cups applesauce and combine with the gelatin mixture. Fold in the egg whites. Chill thoroughly. Top with chopped candied ginger or toasted sliced almonds, if you like. Serve with unsweetened whipped cream.

Other recipes using apples: Vermont Blueberries (Berries); Apple Bread Pudding (Bread); Baked Carrots and Apples, Apple-Carrot-Orange Salad (Carrots); Three Fruit Topping (Jams, Jellies, Marmalades); Pineapple-Orange Sauce (Pineapple); Apple-Plum Compote (Plums); Raisin Apple Betty (Raisins); Apple Oatmeal Muffins (Sour Cream); Apple Streusel Coffee Cake (Sour Milk); Sweet Potato Rice Pudding; Sherry Pork Chops, Sliced Baked Apples (Wine).
The various curry dishes (see Index) use apples; so do many cranberry recipes. Plum Cake and Pflaumenkuchen (Plums) can be made with apples.

Other recipes using applesauce: Banana Applesauce Cake; Oatmeal Spice Squares (Cereals).

Apricots
Dried

Apricots are *the* deluxe dried fruit, from the point of view of both taste and price. Sometimes when I open a box, I stew only part of them and bake with the remainder.

APRICOT BAVARIAN CREAM

Here is one of the real gourmet recipes in this collection. It should be velvet smooth, and is guaranteed to melt in the mouth. If you have a lovely cut-glass bowl, here is the dessert to put in it.

1 cup cooked apricots, drained	1 teaspoon lemon juice
2 cups juice (from apricots)	1 1/2 tablespoons plain gelatin
2 eggs, separated	1/2 cup cold water
3/4 cup sugar	1 cup whipped cream

The apricots should be cooked without sugar; drain the liquid into a cup and add enough water to make the 2 cups juice. Put it in the blender container with the egg yolks, sugar, cooked apricots, lemon juice. Blend until completely smooth. Pour into a saucepan and bring to a boil.

In the meantime, soften the gelatin in the water. Take the hot fruit mixture from the stove, add the gelatin, and stir until completely smooth. Chill until mixture begins to thicken. Beat the egg whites stiff and fold them in. Then fold in the whipped cream. Pour into a bowl. Chill until firm.

APRICOT KISEL

Here is a version of a standard German dessert called *Rote Gruetze* (see under Currants). It is delicious served ice-cold with whipped cream.

1/2 cup dried apricots, cut up	4 teaspoons sugar
1 1/2 cups water	2 tablespoons potato starch *or* cornstarch

Cook the apricots in the water until tender, then whirl in the blender until smooth. Stir in the sugar. Dissolve the potato starch in a small amount of cold water and stir it into the fruit. Cook, stirring constantly, until the mixture thickens and clears. Pour into dishes and chill completely.

GOLDEN FRUIT BREAD

This will make one 9 x 5 loaf, or three 7 1/2 x 3 1/2 loaves.

1 1/2 cups All-Bran	**1 1/2 cups flour**
1/2 cup sugar	**3 teaspoons baking powder**
1 cup finely cut dried apricots	**3/4 teaspoon salt**
or **raisins** *or* **dates** *or* a	**2 eggs**
combination	**1/3 cup oil**
1 1/2 cups boiling water	**additional sugar** *or* **cinnamon/sugar**

Measure the All-Bran, sugar, and fruit (my favorite mixture is 2 parts apricots, 1 part each raisins and dates) into a large mixing bowl. Pour the boiling water over the mixture, stir well, and let stand until most of the moisture is absorbed.

Sift together the flour, baking powder, and salt. Set aside.

Beat the eggs and add with the oil to the All-Bran mixture. Add the flour mixture, stirring only until combined.

Spread in greased pans, sprinkle with additional sugar. Bake at 350° about 55 minutes for the large pan, about 45 to 50 for the smaller pans. Cool thoroughly before slicing.

APRICOT WALNUT BREAD

A quickly prepared loaf. The apricots give it a lovely bright color.

2 cups biscuit mix (see Appendix)	**1/2 to 3/4 cup finely cut dried apricots**
1 cup rolled oats	**1 cup coarsely chopped walnuts**
3/4 cup sugar	**1 egg, beaten**
1 teaspoon baking powder	**1 1/4 cups milk**
1/4 teaspoon salt	

Stir together the first five ingredients. Mix in the apricots and walnuts. Combine the egg and milk, add to the dry ingredients, and beat hard for 30 seconds. Pour into one 9 x 5 pan or three #2 cans, well greased. Bake at 350° for 1 hour for the large pan, 45 minutes for the cans.

BRANDIED APRICOTS AND RAISINS

Here is a rich, fruity sauce to spoon over ice cream, custard, or sponge cake. Packed in decorative containers, it makes an attractive and unusual gift.

1 cup dried apricots	1 cup sugar
1/2 cup golden raisins	1 three-inch piece stick cinnamon
1 1/2 cups water	1/2 cup brandy

Cut the apricots in half, and combine them with the raisins and water in a medium-size saucepan. Let stand 10 minutes for the fruits to soften.

Stir in the sugar, add the cinnamon stick. Bring to a boil over medium heat, simmer 5 to 10 minutes, or until apricots are soft but not mushy. Cool slightly. Stir in the brandy. Pack into containers and store in the refrigerator for at least a week. Serve warm. Makes 3 1/2 cups.

APRICOT-PINEAPPLE BARS

1/3 cup soft butter/margarine	1/4 teaspoon baking soda
1/2 cup brown sugar	1/2 teaspoon salt
1 cup flour	3/4 cup rolled oats

Combine these ingredients (it is easiest to wade in with your hands). Press about two-thirds of the mixture into a greased 9-inch square pan. Spread with the filling (below). Top with the remaining mixture. Bake at 350° about 25 minutes. Cool. Cut into bars.

APRICOT FILLING

There are many other desserts in which this filling can be used: turnovers, fruit roll, filled pastries, pie (with a lattice top).

1 1/2 cups cooked apricots	1/4 cup hot water
1/2 cup sugar	1/2 cup chopped nuts
2 slices pineapple, chopped	

The apricots should be cooked until plump; then chopped. Combine them in a saucepan with the other ingredients except the nuts. Simmer about 10 minutes, until thick. Cool. Stir in the nuts (walnuts are best). Makes 2 cups.

☆☆☆ APRICOT BARS

This is my favorite bar cookie, one that should really get four stars.

2/3 cup dried apricots	1/4 teaspoon salt
1/2 cup butter/margarine	1 cup brown sugar
1/4 cup granulated sugar	2 eggs
1 1/3 cup flour, divided	1/2 teaspoon vanilla
1/2 teaspoon baking powder	1/2 cup chopped nuts

Rinse the apricots and cover with water. Boil 10 minutes. Drain, cool, and chop. Preheat the oven to 350°. Mix the butter/margarine, granulated sugar, and 1 cup flour (use part whole wheat, if you have it) until crumbly. Press in an 8-inch square pan, and bake 20 minutes.

Sift the remaining 1/3 cup flour with the baking powder and salt. Beat the eggs, gradually beat the brown sugar into them; mix in the flour mixture, then the vanilla, nuts, and apricots. Spread over the baked layer.

Return to the oven and bake 30 minutes longer. Cool in pan. Cut into bars, and, if you like, sprinkle with or roll in 10X sugar. I never have.

Fresh Apricots

After years during which most of us had no idea what a fresh apricot looked like, this marvelous fruit has appeared in the markets, and in good quantity. Apparently a hardy strain has been developed for growing in Northern states. Here are a few ideas for preparing apricots. Of course, you can stew them as you would most fresh fruit. You can add them to your fruit compote or stewed apples. The plum cakes and peach desserts are all good with apricots.

APRICOT STUFFING

This dressing has a delicate, spicy taste. It is especially good for duck or goose.

2 tablespoons oil	1 cup fresh orange juice
1/2 cup sliced mushrooms	1/2 teaspoon summer savory
1 small onion, chopped	generous pinch of mace
3 tablespoons minced parsley	generous pinch of cinnamon
3 cups cooked brown rice	1/4 teaspoon salt
1 cup chopped apricots	2 tablespoons nutritional yeast
1/2 cup finely chopped celery	

Heat the oil and sauté the mushrooms, onion, and parsley. Combine the remaining ingredients in a large bowl and blend in the sautéed vegetables.

APRICOT KUCHEN

1 1/2 cups flour	1 egg
2 teaspoons baking powder	1/2 cup milk
1/4 teaspoon salt	1/2 cup butter/margarine, melted
1 cup sugar, divided	apricots
	1/2 teaspoon cinnamon

Sift the flour, baking powder, salt, and 1/2 cup sugar into a bowl. Beat the egg well, mix in the milk and butter. Stir these ingredients gently into the flour mixture. Spread in a greased 8-inch square pan.

Remove the pits from the apricots, cut them in quarters, and arrange them, sharp edges down, on the batter in parallel rows. Combine the remaining 1/2 cup sugar with the cinnamon and sprinkle this over the top. Bake at 375° about 25 minutes, or until the apricots are tender and the cake is crusty.

APRICOT-ORANGE JAM

This beautiful jam has the advantage of not requiring any stirring-over-the-hot-stove.

3 pounds apricots, pitted	3 cups sugar
3 thick-skinned oranges	

Preheat the oven to 225°. Put the apricots and oranges (remove the seeds) through a meat grinder or process in the food processor. Stir in the sugar; taste the jam and add more sugar, if you like. Pour all this in a shallow roasting pan, and bake it for 4 or more hours, stirring from time to time. Pour into sterilized jars and seal with paraffin.

Other recipes using apricots: Apricot-Apple Pie (Apples), Snowballs (Dates), Holiday Bread (Eggnog); Plum-Apricot Party Dessert. Raisin Apple Betty (Raisins) has a variation for stewed apricots. Apricot-Orange Tea (Tea) uses apricot nectar, as does Holiday Bread (Eggnog).

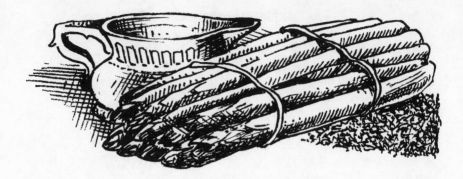

Asparagus

When I was growing up, I can remember the true arrival of spring—the appearance of fresh asparagus and fresh strawberries. A favorite luncheon was very simple—steamed asparagus, arranged on buttered toast, with more butter, lemon juice, and grated cheese on top.

Asparagus is best prepared with a light touch. Remove the tough ends, and then cook it as little as possible by steaming, or cut it in diagonal slices and stir-fry it.

ASPARAGUS ROULADES

18 stalks asparagus
6 slices boiled or baked ham
2 minced green onions

1 cup seasoned cream sauce (see
 the Appendix)
grated cheese
bread crumbs

Steam the asparagus until just tender, or use leftover cooked asparagus. Arrange 3 stalks on each slice of ham, sprinkle with the onions, roll, and place seam-side down in a shallow baking dish. Pour the cream sauce over the top, sprinkle with grated cheese and bread crumbs, and bake at 350° about 20 minutes, until completely hot, bubbly, and browned. Serves 3.

ASPARAGUS TIMBALES

One of the best ways of dressing up leftover food is the timbale. This dish isn't served very much in our country, heaven knows why. It is a wonderful and easy combination of vegetables and/or meats and eggs. It is somewhat similar to the soufflé, but less rich and less problematical.

20 cooked asparagus tips *or*
  1 cup finely cut-up cooked
  asparagus
1 1/2 cups warm milk
4 beaten eggs

1/2 teaspoon salt
1/2 teaspoon paprika
1 tablespoon chopped parsley
lemon juice

Arrange the asparagus tips, points down, in 4 deep custard cups or a 7-inch ring mold, all well greased. (If you use the cut-up asparagus, you can either put it in the bottom of the cups or mold, or fold it into the custard as the last step.) Combine the remaining ingredients and pour this mixture over the asparagus. Fill about 2/3 full. Place the cups or mold on a rack in a pan of hot water. The water should come up as high as the filling in the molds. Bake at 325° about 30 minutes, or until firm. Invert on hot platter and serve with hollandaise sauce or hot cheese sauce. Serves 4.

ASPARAGUS SUPREME

This makes a very elegant and lovely-colored party vegetable dish.

1 1/2 pounds asparagus
1 cup milk
3 tablespoons butter
2 tablespoons flour
1 cup grated cheese
dash tabasco sauce *or* 1 teaspoon
  worcestershire

1/4 teaspoon salt
2 tablespoons fresh minced parsley
3 hard-boiled eggs, sliced
1/2 cup toasted almonds, chopped
buttered bread crumbs

Prepare and steam the asparagus gently until just tender. Make a cream sauce with the milk, butter, and flour; cook, stirring, until thick and smooth. Add the cheese and seasonings to the sauce and cook until blended. Stir in the parsley. In a greased casserole (13 x 8 is good), make two layers of asparagus, sliced eggs, sauce, and almonds. Cover with the bread crumbs and bake, uncovered, at 350° for 30 minutes. Serves 6 to 8.

Other recipes using asparagus: Slim Spinach Soup has a variation for asparagus.

Avocados

Avocados discolor very rapidly, so any slices you want to add to your salad (and they will make it deluxe) should be brushed with lemon juice, or marinated. To prepare an avocado (which is ripe when the imprint of your thumb stays when you squeeze it gently), cut it in half the long way, carefully, and take out the pit. Cut in quarters and peel each section, as needed.

AVOCADO SOUP

This is ridiculously simple to make. You can adjust proportions according to your supply. Serve this soup very cold.

1 avocado, peeled and pitted
2 cups vegetable or chicken stock
1 tablespoon lemon juice

1/2 to 3/4 cup yogurt
1 tablespoon nutritional yeast
salt and pepper to taste

Blend everything in the blender until velvet smooth. Serves 4.

AVOCADO AND TOMATO SOUP

1 pound (about 3) avocados
juice of 1 lemon
3 1/2 cups broth, divided
1 tablespoon butter
2 green onions, cut up

1 cup peeled, seeded tomatoes
1 tablespoon flour
salt and pepper to taste
1 cup sour cream

Peel avocados and cut into cubes. Put in blender. Add the lemon juice and 1/2 cup of the broth and process several seconds.

Melt the butter in a large pan and sauté the onion. Add it to the blender with the tomatoes, and blend until smooth. Measure the flour into the pan, mix with the butter and 1 cup broth. Stir rapidly until smooth. Stir in the remaining broth plus mixture in the blender, salt and pepper, and the sour cream. Heat, stirring, until hot but not boiling. Serve hot or chilled. Serves 6.

GUACAMOLE

This is an avocado spread with Mexican origins. Do try to eat it all at one meal, as it will discolor.

1 avocado, peeled and cubed
1 small green pepper, seeded and
   cut up
1/2 small tomato, peeled, cut up
1 sprig parsley
2 green onions, in pieces

1 tablespoon oil
1/2 tablespoon lemon juice
1 tablespoon cottage cheese *or*
   ricotta
spices (ground cumin, coriander,
   paprika)
salt to taste

Blend everything in the blender until smooth. If you want to use this as a dip, you can thin it more.

AVOCADO AND GRAPEFRUIT SALAD

2 large grapefruit
1 large (or 2 small) avocado
1/2 cup sugar
1 teaspoon salt
1 teaspoon dry mustard

1 teaspoon grated onion
1/4 cup red wine vinegar
3/4 cup salad oil
pinch paprika

Peel and cut the grapefruit in sections, drain the juice. Peel the avocado and cut it in sections. Prepare the dressing by mixing all ingredients except the oil until the sugar dissolves. Then with an electric mixer *slowly* add the oil so the dressing stays thick.

Arrange the grapefruit and avocado sections on beds of lettuce and drizzle the dressing over (the recipe makes more than you will need, probably; just refrigerate the remainder for later use). Serves 4.

◆

Note: Inside every avocado there's a free tree. Simply wash the pit in tepid water. Drive three toothpicks into it and suspend (broad end down) over a jar, covering only half an inch of seed with tepid water. Place in a warm, preferably dim spot (the upper shelf of a kitchen cupboard is ideal). The seed will take anywhere from two to six weeks to root. When the stem reaches seven inches, cut it in half so it branches. Once the roots are thick and the stem has leafed out, carefully plant it in potting soil. Use a large pot with good drainage and leave the pit half exposed. Then watch it grow.

Other recipes using avocados: Stuffed Eggplant.

Bananas

You can make such marvelous things from overripe bananas. I really have a hard time going by a bunch of them marked down at the supermarket.

☆☆☆ BANANA NUT BREAD

You can spread this marvelous bread with butter and/or honey and serve it for tea. It is also a popular, nutritional snack for the after-school hunger or a lovely sandwich in the school lunch when spread with cream cheese. This bread contains no shortening. The recipe makes one bread loaf or two small 7 1/2 x 3 1/2 loaves.

3 ripe bananas	1/2 teaspoon salt
2 eggs	1 teaspoon baking soda
1 1/2 cups flour	1/2 cup nuts, coarsely chopped
1/2 cup wheat germ or oatmeal	2/3 cup sugar

Mash the bananas well with a fork. In the mixer, beat the eggs until light. Then add the mashed bananas and mix thoroughly. Sift the dry ingredients, except the wheat germ, and add all of them to the first mixture. Stir well. Then add the nuts. Walnuts are very good, but I almost always use toasted chopped almonds, which are superb. Bake at 350° for 1 hour for the large pans, about 50 minutes for the smaller ones. This bread should be cooled before slicing. It freezes very well.

BANANA BREAD

This is a richer, sweeter, moister bread. If you have only a few bananas, you can easily cut this recipe in half.

6 bananas	2 2/3 cups flour
2/3 cup shortening	4 teaspoons baking powder
1 1/2 cups sugar	1 teaspoon baking soda
4 eggs	

Mash the bananas well. Cream the shortening and sugar until light. Add the eggs, one at a time, beating well. Stir in the mashed bananas. Sift together the dry ingredients, and add to the liquid mixture, stirring lightly and quickly, and mixing only until blended. Pour into two bread loaf pans (9 x 5) and bake at 350° for 45 minutes to 1 hour.

BANANA-CARROT TEA BREAD

An interesting combination of the carrot and banana bread. And it has a nice color, too.

2 eggs	1 teaspoon baking soda
1 cup mashed banana (2 or 3 bananas)	1/2 teaspoon salt
	1/2 teaspoon cinnamon
2/3 cup sugar	1 cup finely grated carrots
1/2 cup salad oil	1/2 cup chopped pecans
2 cups flour	1/2 cup raisins (optional)

Beat the eggs well in a large bowl; add the banana, sugar, and oil; beat again. Sift the dry ingredients. Fold into the banana mixture. Stir in the carrots and pecans. Pour into a 9 x 5 pan. Bake at 350° for 55 to 60 minutes. Cool before slicing. Freezes well.

☆☆☆ BANANA ORANGE MUFFINS

These are wonderful with honey or orange marmalade. Do watch them when they are baking, as they have a tendency to burn.

1 cup wheat germ	2 eggs
1 1/2 cups flour	1 cup (about 3) mashed banana
1/2 cup sugar	1/2 cup orange juice
3 teaspoons baking powder	1/4 cup oil
1/2 teaspoon salt	

Measure the wheat germ into a large bowl. Sift the other dry ingredients into it, and stir well to blend. Beat the eggs well and add the banana, orange juice, and oil. Pour the liquid ingredients over the dry. Stir just until all ingredients are moistened. Fill muffin tins (greased) about 2/3 full. Bake at 400° for 20 minutes. Makes 12 to 16 large muffins.

BANANA BRAN MUFFINS

1 1/2 cups bran flakes *or*	3 tablespoons brown or white sugar
1 cup All-Bran	1 beaten egg
1 1/2 cups flour	1 1/3 tablespoons orange juice *or*
3 teaspoons baking powder	milk
1/4 teaspoon salt	1/4 cup melted butter *or* oil
	1 1/2 cups mashed bananas

Measure the bran flakes or All-Bran into a large bowl. Sift the dry ingredients on top and mix together. Combine the liquid ingredients and add all at once. Stir just to moisten the dry ingredients; the batter should be lumpy and rough. Fill greased muffin tins 2/3 full. Bake at 400° for about 20 minutes. Serve hot with butter. Makes 12 to 16 muffins.

BUTTERSCOTCH BUNS

1/2 cup brown sugar	2/3 cup mashed ripe banana
1/2 cup soft butter/margarine	2 tablespoons soft butter/margarine
36 pecan halves or pieces	1/4 cup brown sugar
2 cups biscuit mix (see Appendix)	

Preheat oven to 450°.

Place 2 teaspoons brown sugar, 2 teaspoons butter/margarine, and 3 pecan halves in each of 12 medium muffin cups. Place in the oven to melt the sugar and butter. Watch them carefully, and when all is melted, remove the pans from the oven.

Stir the baking mix and banana together to make a soft dough. Gather the dough together and knead gently a few times. Roll the dough into a rectangle, 15 x 9 inches. Spread with the remaining butter, and sprinkle with the 1/4 cup brown sugar. Roll up tightly, beginning at the wide side. Seal well by pinching the edge of the dough into a roll. Cut into 12 slices, and place slices, cut side down, into the prepared muffin cups. Bake 10 minutes. Immediately invert the pan onto a tray or baking sheet. Leave the pan over the rolls for a minute or so, then remove. Serve the buns warm.

BANANA PANCAKES

You can eat these for breakfast with honey, maple syrup, or Cider Sauce—or for dessert with Rum Syrup (see the Appendix).

2 cups flour	2 eggs, slightly beaten
1 teaspoon baking soda	2 cups buttermilk
1/2 teaspoon salt	2 tablespoons melted butter/mar-
2 tablespoons sugar	garine
	2/3 cup diced or mashed bananas

Sift the flour, soda, salt, and sugar into a mixing bowl. Combine the eggs, buttermilk, melted butter/margarine, and bananas. Stir into the flour mixture just to moisten the flour. Do *not* overmix.

Cook on a hot, lightly greased griddle, turning once.

◆

BANANA CAKE JAMAICA

This is an authentic Jamaican recipe, given to me by a friend who is a native of the island.

1/2 pound butter/margarine	1 cup sour cream
1 cup sugar	1 tablespoon vanilla
3 eggs, beaten well	1 tablespoon rum
2 1/2 cups flour	1 teaspoon cinnamon *or* mixed
1 1/4 teaspoons baking powder	spices
1 1/4 teaspoons baking soda	1 cup lightly mashed ripe bananas

Cream the butter and sugar until light. Add the eggs. Add the flour (sifted twice, then resifted with the baking powder and soda) alternately with the sour cream. Then stir in the vanilla, rum, cinnamon, and bananas with a spoon.

Pour into a 13 x 9 rectangular pan and bake at 350° about 45 minutes, or until done. When the cake is cooled, brush with 3 tablespoons wine or rum. Frost when dry with Light Butter Frosting (see the Appendix).

BANANA-APPLESAUCE CAKE

A very easily made cake, and the combination of bananas and applesauce is delicious.

2 1/2 cups flour	1/2 cup water
1 1/2 cups sugar	1/2 cup butter/margarine (very soft)
1 teaspoon baking powder	1 cup applesauce
1 teaspoon baking soda	1 cup mashed ripe banana
1 teaspoon cinnamon	2 eggs
1/2 teaspoon cloves	1/2 cup chopped nuts
1/2 teaspoon allspice	3/4 cup raisins
1/2 teaspoon salt	confectioners' sugar

Sift all the dry ingredients into the large bowl of your electric mixer. Add the water, butter/margarine, applesauce, and banana. Blend well, then beat at medium speed until creamy. Then add the eggs and beat 2 minutes at medium speed. Stir in the nuts and raisins and pour into a well-greased 13 x 9 pan.

Bake at 350° about 45 minutes. Turn out on a cake rack, and while still warm, sift confectioners' sugar lightly over the top.

BANANA-CAROB CAKE

This is like a sponge cake. You can cut it in squares and serve it plain, or with whipped topping.

4 eggs, separated	1/3 cup sugar
1/3 cup instant dry milk	4 ripe bananas, cut in pieces
3 tablespoons carob powder	4 slices dry whole wheat, cracked
2 teaspoons almond extract	wheat, or white bread

Place the egg yolks, milk, carob, almond, and sugar in the blender. Whirl at medium speed to combine. Gradually add the banana pieces, and continue to blend until very smooth. Transfer the mixture to a large bowl. Make the bread slices into crumbs (about 3/4 cup); mix them in.until well combined. Beat the egg whites until stiff and fold into the batter. Pour into a greased 9-inch square pan. Bake at 350° for 45 to 50 minutes.

PASSOVER CAKE

This takes some time, but it is always a huge success.

7 eggs, separated
1 cup sugar
1/4 teaspoon salt
1 tablespoon grated orange rind

1 cup mashed ripe banana
1 tablespoon thawed orange juice
   concentrate
3/4 cup sifted potato starch

In a large mixing bowl beat the egg yolks until thick and lemon-colored; gradually beat in the sugar. Then add the salt, orange rind, banana, orange-juice concentrate and mix well. Stir in the potato starch.

In another large bowl beat the egg whites until stiff; fold gently into the banana mixture. Grease the bottom (but not the sides) of a 9-inch tube pan; pour in the batter and bake in a 325° oven until the cake pulls away from the pan. This takes 50 to 60 minutes. Invert the pan on a rack until the cake is cool. Remove from pan and serve with warm orange sauce.

ORANGE SAUCE

2 cups orange juice
3/4 cup sugar

1 tablespoon potato starch
2 oranges

Heat the orange juice and sugar over moderate heat, stirring until the sugar dissolves. Bring to a boil, then remove from heat. Stir a little of the hot mixture into the potato starch, and then blend this into the remaining hot mixture. Cook over moderate heat, stirring constantly until thickened. Peel, remove seeds and pith, and section the oranges. Add them to the sauce and reheat gently.

◆

BANANA OATMEAL COOKIES

There are many recipes for banana cookies, but this one is a favorite in my household.

1 1/4 cups flour	1 egg
1/2 teaspoon salt	1 cup mashed ripe bananas
1/2 teaspoon baking soda	1 teaspoon vanilla
1/2 teaspoon nutmeg	1 1/2 cups rolled oats
3/4 teaspoon cinnamon	1/4 cup wheat germ
1/2 cup butter/margarine	1/2 cup chopped walnuts
1 cup sugar	

Sift the flour, salt, soda, nutmeg, and cinnamon. Set aside.

Cream the butter/margarine with the sugar until fluffy; beat in the egg. Then beat in the bananas and vanilla until smooth.

Gradually stir in the sifted flour mixture, oats, and wheat germ. Combine thoroughly. Stir in the nuts. Refrigerate 30 minutes.

Drop batter on cookie sheets, and bake at 400° 12 to 15 minutes, or until golden. Cool. Frost with Orange Glaze (see the Appendix).

LUSH SLUSH

Children love this on a really hot summer day.

1 cup crushed pineapple	1 cup frozen orange juice concentrate
2 cups mashed bananas	2 cups ginger ale *or* lemon soda
1/2 cup sugar	*or* grapefruit drink

Mix and freeze. Stir once during freezing. Serve slushy.

BANANA COCKTAIL

1 1/2 cups orange juice	1 cup crushed ice
2 teaspoons lemon juice	dash of salt
1 or 2 ripe bananas, cut in pieces	

Whirl everything in the blender until smooth. Serve immediately.

Other recipes using bananas: Fruit salads, or mixed fruit bowls, can always have bananas in them; Cantaloupe Fruit Cups (Melons); Molasses Brown Bread (Cereals) has a variation with bananas.

Beans (Green and Wax)

There is nothing better than fresh green or wax beans, picked young, cooked until just tender, and served with a dash of butter and lemon juice. Or chilled on a bed of lettuce with Vinaigrette Dressing (see the Appendix).

BEANS-CELERY-BULGUR CASSEROLE WITH CHEESE

2 cups cut-up green beans
2 cups chopped celery
1/4 cup chopped green onions
1/2 teaspoon celery seed
1/2 teaspoon salt
1 cup raw bulgur
2 tablespoons oil

1 1/2 cups milk
1 1/2 cups water
1 cup grated cheese (sharp cheddar, parmesan, or gruyère)
1/2 cup bread crumbs, *or* crumbled wheat cereal, *or* cracker crumbs
butter/margarine

Cook the beans in boiling salted water (a small amount) about 8 minutes. Drain and reserve the liquid.

In a stove-top casserole, sauté the celery, green onions, celery seed, salt, and bulgur in the oil until the celery is slightly soft.

Stir the milk and water (include any leftover bean stock) together and add them to the casserole. Cover and simmer for about 15 minutes, or until most of the liquid has been absorbed.

Then add the cooked beans along with 3/4 cup of the cheese. Mix well. Sprinkle the remaining cheese over the top, then sprinkle the crumbs over that. Dot with butter/margarine, if you like.

Bake at 375° for about 15 minutes, until the casserole is bubbly. Serves 6 to 8.

GREEN BEAN CASSEROLE

This makes an elegant side dish for a dinner party and is excellent with ham or chicken.

2 pounds beans	1/2 pound cheddar, grated
1 pound mushrooms, sliced	2 teaspoons soy sauce
1 medium onion, sliced	salt and pepper to taste
4 tablespoons butter	1 5-ounce can water chestnuts,
1/4 cup flour	drained and sliced
2 cups milk	3/4 cup slivered almonds, toasted
1 cup light cream	

Prepare the beans French-style, and cook in a very little salted water about 5 minutes. Drain.

Sauté the mushrooms and onion in the butter. Add the flour and cook, stirring, for a minute or so. Add warm milk and cream to the mixture and cook, stirring constantly, until smooth and thickened. Add the cheese, soy sauce, and seasonings. Cook, stirring often, until the cheese melts.

Preheat the oven to 375°. Mix the beans into the mushroom sauce, and stir in the water chestnuts. Pour into a large casserole and sprinkle the almonds over the top. Bake 20 minutes. Serves 12.

THREE-BEAN LOAF

There are some people who won't know this isn't a meat loaf!

2 cups cooked garbanzos	1/2 cup pecans, very finely chopped
2 cups cooked red kidney beans	1 tablespoon paprika
1 cup green beans, cooked and	1/4 teaspoon salt
chopped	1 egg
1/2 cup mushrooms, chopped	1 tablespoon oil
1 cup chopped celery	3 tablespoons flour
1 medium onion, chopped	1 cup tomato sauce
1 tablespoon soy sauce	

Mash the garbanzos and kidney beans in a large bowl with a potato masher. Add the remaining ingredients, except use only 3 tablespoons of the tomato sauce. Stir well to blend.

Spoon the mixture into a 9 x 5 loaf pan. Bake at 375° for 50 minutes. Allow to cool slightly before slicing. Heat the remaining tomato sauce and serve with the loaf.

GREEN BEANS IN TOMATO SAUCE

This dish freezes very well. If you have equipment for freezing in heat-sealed bags, try this one. It is easily reheated in boiling water.

4 tablespoons butter/margarine	1/4 teaspoon pepper
2 medium onions, chopped	1 teaspoon oregano
2 teaspoons sugar	1 bay leaf
6 medium tomatoes, peeled,	1/2 teaspoon thyme
seeded, and chopped	1 1/2 pounds green beans
1 teaspoon salt	

Heat the butter/margarine in a large saucepan. Add the onion and cook over low heat until soft, but not brown. Add everything except the beans. Bring mixture to a boil, lower heat, and simmer, stirring occasionally, 45 minutes.

While the sauce is cooking, cut the beans to 1-inch lengths. Cook in a small amount of salted water about 8 minutes, or until barely tender; drain.

Cool tomato mixture; purée in the blender until smooth (if you have any fresh basil, add a few leaves to the mixture in the blender). Return to the saucepan; reheat. Check the seasoning and add more if you wish.

Add the drained beans to the sauce. Cook for 2 to 3 minutes longer. Serves 6.

GREEN BEANS WITH DILL

A superb Viennese dish. Please use fresh dill, if possible.

2 tablespoons butter/margarine	2 tablespoons chopped dill
1 tablespoon chopped onion	3 1/2 cups cooked sliced beans
2 tablespoons chopped parsley	1/2 cup sour cream
2 tablespoons flour	1 teaspoon lemon juice
1 cup water from the beans	

Sauté the onion, parsley, and flour in the butter. Add the bean stock and dill and simmer 5 minutes. Then add the beans and remaining ingredients. Simmer 5 minutes longer. Add salt to taste. Serves 6.

ALMOND VEGETABLES MANDARIN

This is a lovely combination of summer garden vegetables. Try to find tiny fresh carrots and beans for this one, and be careful that the vegetables stay crisp-tender.

2 tablespoons oil
1 cup green or wax beans, cut
   in 1-inch pieces
1 cup thinly sliced carrots
1 cup thinly sliced cauliflower
1/2 cup sliced green onions

1 cup water
2 teaspoons chicken stock base
2 teaspoons cornstarch
dash garlic powder
1/2 cup sliced almonds, unblanched

Heat the oil over medium-high heat in a large skillet (or electric frying pan), add the beans and carrots and sauté 2 minutes. Add the cauliflower and onions, and cook 1 minute longer. Mix the water, chicken stock base, cornstarch, and garlic. Add to the skillet and stir everything until thickened. If the vegetables are not done enough, reduce the heat, cover, and steam until just tender. Add the almonds, stir, and serve immediately. Serves 4 to 6.

You can double this recipe, but don't try anything larger.

———————◆———————

☆☆☆ BEAN AND EGG SALAD

My brother's favorite salad. My mother never could make enough of it.

3 cups cooked green beans
2 hard-boiled eggs, chopped
1/4 cup mayonnaise

1/4 cup salad dressing (Miracle Whip)
milk, cream, *or* buttermilk

Combine the beans and eggs in a large salad bowl. Mix the dressings and thin with the milk, cream, or buttermilk. Pour over the bean-egg mixture. Chill and serve on a bed of lettuce, along with tomato wedges.

If you like, you can add some chopped celery (the original recipe has none because my brother detests it and always picks it out of everything) and finely chopped green onion. Also, I usually make it with my own mayonnaise (Mock Mayonnaise, see the Appendix); the result is a less sweet salad, something I prefer.

MARINATED BEAN AND CHESTNUT BOWL

2 cups sliced green beans, cooked
   and drained
1/4 cup sliced water chestnuts
1/2 cup halved cherry tomatoes
1/2 cup Vinaigrette Dressing (see
   the Appendix)

2 teaspoons minced onion
1 teaspoon minced parsley
1/2 teaspoon basil
1 small head Boston lettuce

Combine the green beans, water chestnuts, and tomatoes in a large bowl. Combine the dressing, onion, basil, and parsley in a jar with a tight lid. Cover and shake until well blended. Pour the dressing over the vegetables. Cover and marinate in the refrigerator for three hours.

Separate the lettuce into leaves, wash well, and drain. Arrange in a salad bowl. Spoon the vegetables into the bowl on top of the lettuce. Serves 4.

GREEN BEANS AND MUSHROOM SALAD

1 tablespoon vinegar
3 tablespoons oil
1/2 cup minced green onions
1 teaspoon Dijon mustard
1/2 teaspoon salt

1/8 teaspoon pepper
1/2 pound fresh mushrooms
1 pound green or wax beans
1 cup dairy sour cream
cherry tomatoes for garnish

Combine the vinegar, oil, onions, mustard, salt, and pepper in a jar with a tight lid. Shake well until blended. Slice the mushrooms into a large bowl. Pour the dressing over, toss lightly, and let stand.

Cut up the beans, cook in lightly salted water about 8 minutes, drain well, and cool. Combine them with the sour cream, and then add to the marinated mushrooms. Toss lightly.

Chill the salad thoroughly. Remove from the refrigerator about 20 minutes before serving and garnish with the tomatoes. Serves 6.

☆☆☆ HOT DOG SOUP

This entirely original recipe is the best way I know of to use up the old beans that you let go in the garden or missed when you were picking. It is also the best way I know of to get children who don't like cooked vegetables to eat them. Just slice some cooked hot dogs on top, and young people lap it up. At least all the ones I knew did—and do.

2 cups beans	1/2 cup instant dry milk
some celery tops	1 package vegetable broth
1/2 carrot	3 hot dogs

Cut the stem ends off the beans, you can leave the pointed tips on. Cut the beans in convenient-sized pieces, put in a sauce pan with some water; add, if you like, some celery tops and 1/2 of a carrot, sliced thin. Cook until the vegetables are tender. Cool slightly, then whirl it all in the blender along with the broth powder and dry milk. Add more salt and water if you like. My family prefers this soup thick. Return the purée to the pan and heat well. Garnish with hot dogs. You can also serve it chilled with a dollop of yogurt on top. Increase quantities if you like.

Other recipes using green or wax beans: Add beans to any vegetable soup or minestrone that you are making (see the Index); Beef Pot Pie; Leipziger Allerei (Lima Beans); Potato Ratatouille (Potatoes); Perciatelli alla Napoletana (Tomatoes).

Beef

I often cut leftover roast beef into pieces, put them in a container, dump the leftover sauce or gravy over the top, and freeze everything for a later moment.

If you are confronted with a small amount (a half pound or less), you can shred it into hearty vegetable soups or use in some of the ground beef recipes given later. Or try Chinese beef (just follow the recipe under Pork).

☆☆☆ FLEISCHSALAT

leftover roast or pot roast, in cubes
chopped celery
hard-boiled eggs
chopped green onions

chopped dill pickles
diced cooked potatoes
prepared Dijon mustard
mayonnaise plus yogurt

Quantities may vary to suit your needs. You can leave out some ingredients but not the meat, mustard, and mayonnaise—they are essentials. I usually use Mock Mayonnaise (see the Appendix), with extra mustard stirred in. Mix everything together, and chill well before serving. Garnish with tomato wedges, pickle slices, and capers.

BEEF ENCORE

1 tablespoon butter
1 clove garlic, cut in half
2 onions, thinly sliced
1 tablespoon flour
1/2 cup white wine

1 cup beef consommé or broth
leftover roast beef, in thin slices
1/2 teaspoon paprika
1 teaspoon wine vinegar

Melt the butter and sizzle the cut garlic in it for 2 minutes; remove at once. Add the onions, sprinkle the flour over, and stir until light brown. Blend in the wine and consommé and cook slowly, covered, for 15 minutes. Add meat slices and paprika. Do not let the sauce boil, but simmer gently about 10 minutes. Just before serving, stir in the vinegar. This dish is very good with rice or buttered noodles.

MEAT-FRIED NOODLES

This dish has many ingredients, but is very easily made.

1/4 cup chopped onion
1/4 cup chopped celery
1/4 cup chopped green pepper
2 tablespoons oil
6 ounces fine egg noodles, cooked
1 1/2 cups chopped leftover beef

2 eggs, well beaten
1/3 cup evaporated milk
1/2 teaspoon worcestershire sauce
1/2 teaspoon salt
1/4 teaspoon pepper
soy sauce

Sauté the chopped vegetables lightly in the oil, then stir in the noodles. Mix remaining ingredients, except the soy sauce, and pour over the mixture. Turn heat to low and cook, stirring occasionally, until browned. Serve with soy sauce. Serves 4.

BEEF POT PIE

Here is a hearty casserole with a cornmeal topping that has a crunchy texture. Don't roll out the topping until you are ready to use it as it might become too crumbly to handle.

3 carrots, sliced thin	1/2 teaspoon dried crushed basil
1 medium onion, peeled and chopped	1/2 teaspoon paprika
1 1/2 cups green beans	2 cups beef stock, divided
1/8 teaspoon pepper	4 cups coarsely chopped, cooked beef
1/2 teaspoon salt	1/4 cup flour

Into a large saucepan put the carrots, onion, green beans, pepper, salt, basil, paprika, and 1 1/2 cups stock. Cover and simmer until tender about 15 minutes. Stir in the beef.

Mix together the flour and remaining 1/2 cup stock; quickly stir into the beef mixture and cook until thickened, stirring constantly. Pour into an un-greased shallow baking dish (10 x 10).

Prepare topping (recipe follows) and roll it out to fit the top of the baking dish; cut slashes in top to let steam escape and place over the beef filling.

Bake at 425° about 30 minutes, or until filling bubbles and pastry is browned. Serves 6.

CORNMEAL PASTRY

3/4 cup flour	1/3 cup shortening
1/2 teaspoon salt	3 to 4 tablespoons cold water
1/2 cup cornmeal	

Sift together the flour and salt, stir in the cornmeal. Cut in the shortening until fine. Add the water, a tablespoon at a time, stirring lightly with a fork just until dry ingredients are dampened. Form into a ball.

◆

PARTY MEAT BALLS

2 cups ground leftover beef
1 tablespoon chopped onion
1/2 teaspoon salt
1/2 cup soft bread crumbs
1/3 cup milk
flour

2 tablespoons butter
6 tablespoons molasses
1/2 cup catsup
1/2 teaspoon thyme
6 tablespoons white vinegar

Combine the meat, onion, and salt. Mix the bread crumbs and milk and add to the meat. Toss lightly. Form in 3/4 inch balls (size is crucial for success), roll in flour, and brown in the butter.

Combine the remaining ingredients and blend until smooth. Pour into a large pan, add the meat balls, and simmer, stirring occasionally, until the sauce thickens and the balls are glazed (about 30 minutes).

BARBECUED BEEF BURGERS

1/2 cup catsup
2 tablespoons brown sugar
2 teaspoons prepared mustard
dash worcestershire sauce
2 cups crisp cereal

1 egg
1/2 teaspoon salt
1/8 teaspoon pepper
2 tablespoons chopped onion
2 cups ground leftover beef

First prepare the sauce by combining the catsup, sugar, mustard, and worcestershire sauce in a small bowl. Set aside.

Measure the cereal (try Special K, Rice Krispies, corn flakes, or wheat flakes) and crush to 1 1/2 cups. Beat the egg until foamy; add the crushed cereal, salt, pepper, onion, and 1/3 cup of the barbecue sauce. Blend well. Then add the beef and mix only until combined. If the mixture seems a little dry, add a tablespoon of melted butter or rich milk. Shape into 6 patties, about 3/4-inch thick.

Grill patties 5 inches from source of heat about 5 minutes on each side, basting with remaining sauce. Or, bake on a foil-lined shallow baking pan at 375° about 15 minutes. Serve on toasted buns. Serves 6.

Other recipes using beef: The Chicken Stroganoff recipe can be made with beef (substitute beef for chicken, beef bouillon for the chicken broth, red wine for the white).

Other recipes using ground leftover beef: Beef Casserole (Cottage Cheese); Eggs Foo Yong; Kasha Loaf (Grains); Crepes (Ham); Ground Beef with Lentils (Legumes); Stuffed Peppers, Boeuf Choufleur (Peppers); squash stuffings; Johnny Margetti, meat loaves (Tomatoes); Hash (Turkey).

Beets

Many people don't like to cook beets because the cooking time seems endless. With the modern pressure cooker, however, it is a very simple procedure. Put them in the cooker, add 1/2 cup water, bring the pressure to 15 pounds; reduce the heat and maintain this pressure for 30 minutes (ample for medium to large fresh beets—monsters take longer, but are, I find, equally good). Reduce the pressure, dump the beets in cold water, and slip off the skins. They are ready to eat. Try them sliced with a little butter, salt, and pepper. Try them mashed in your mashed potatoes (a Dutch combination, I understand).

☆☆☆ MIXED VEGETABLE SALAD

My favorite way to eat beets is in salads. In fact, my mother, my late aunt, and I used to save up bits of leftover vegetables to make this salad; sometimes the saving took several days, but the salad was well worth the wait.

Into a salad bowl, put what you have in the way of leftover cooked vegetables, cut up in cubes or pieces: **beets (essential), green beans, wax beans, carrots, peas, potatoes, chick peas, lima beans, raw zucchini, celery, radishes**; you can also add **leftover brown rice or bulgur (cooked, of course)**. I think quantities need not be strictly measured; you should aim for roughly equal amounts of the cooked vegetables, with somewhat less raw vegetables. Add some **chopped hard-boiled egg**, if you like.

Over this you put your favorite dressing (here my mother and I differ, as she likes a sweet dressing—see Boiled Dressing). I prefer a vinaigrette dressing, or my favorite "mayonnaise." (Recipes for these are in the Appendix.)

BEET AND POTATO SALAD

4 medium beets, cooked, peeled,
  and cut in cubes
6 small new potatoes, cooked,
  peeled, and cut in cubes
3 tablespoons minced green onions
1 stalk celery, diced

1/2 cup mayonnaise
1/2 cup plain yogurt
1 teaspoon dry mustard
1 teaspoon vinegar
salt to taste

Place the vegetables in a large bowl. Mix the remaining ingredients and stir until smooth. Thin with some buttermilk, if desired. Pour the dressing over the vegetables in the bowl and stir gently to mix. Chill for several hours. Garnish with two hard-boiled eggs (sliced or in wedges) and some fresh dill. Serves 6.

BEET PERFECTION SALAD

This is a very pretty molded salad, ideal for a picnic or dish-to-pass supper.

2 cups diced beets
1 cup shredded cabbage
1 envelope plain gelatin
1 tablespoon vinegar

1 tablespoon lemon juice
1/4 cup sugar
1 teaspoon salt

Save any liquid you have from cooking the beets. Put the beets and cabbage in a bowl. Add water to the beet liquid to make 2 cups. Into it dissolve the gelatin, then add the remaining ingredients. Heat gently in a saucepan (or in a bowl over boiling water), stirring, until the sugar and gelatin dissolve. Do not boil. Cool slightly, pour over the vegetables, stir well, and place in a mold. Chill thoroughly. Then unmold on a bed of lettuce and garnish with hard-boiled egg wedges and slices of dill pickle.

◆

PRINCETON BEETS

4 tablespoons orange juice
2 teaspoons lemon juice
1 teaspoon salt

2 cups shredded beets
1 tablespoon butter
2 teaspoons cornstarch

Combine the orange and lemon juices with the salt in a saucepan. Bring to a boil and add the beets. If the beets are fresh, cook 10 minutes; if canned, about 4. Add the butter. Mix the cornstarch with 1 tablespoon water or extra orange juice. Stir into the beets and continue stirring until the sauce is thickened and clear. Add, if you wish, 1/2 teaspoon grated orange rind. Serves 4.

BLENDER BORSCHT

2 cups shredded cooked beets	juice of 1/2 lemon
2 cups chicken broth	1 cup yogurt

If you want to use canned beets, use one number 2 can, drained. Use the liquid with instant chicken broth powder to make the broth. Put everything in the blender and whirl until smooth. Sweeten, if desired. Chill. Garnish with chopped chives and a spoonful of yogurt, or sour cream. Serves 6.

DANISH BEET SOUP

6 medium-sized beets	2 tablespoons lemon juice
3 tablespoons butter	1/2 teaspoon salt
1/4 cup flour	pepper to taste
5 cups chicken broth	2 tablespoons snipped fresh dill
1 cup dairy sour cream	or chives

Cook the beets until tender. Skin and cut into pieces. Place in the blender and whirl with some of the broth until smooth. Melt the butter in a large pan, add the flour, stirring, then the remaining broth. Cook, stirring, until the sauce is smooth and boiling. Cook several minutes. Then add the beet purée, and remaining ingredients. Stir well, and heat, but do not boil. Serve either hot or cold. Garnish with the dill or chives. Serves 8.

Other recipes using beets: Winter Borscht (Cabbage).

Berries

Black Raspberries

Raspberries come on at the hottest time of the year, so I pick them, dump them into empty milk cartons, and freeze them until the weather cools (who wants to stir the steaming jam or jelly in July?) and the spirit moves me to make jelly. Also, as good green apples aren't available until autumn, I have to wait anyway. I think black raspberries are one of nature's most wonderful gifts: they are easy to grow; you don't have to put on your armor to pick them; they are sweet, juicy, pretty, and their flavor is unique. I grew up on a farm in Delaware, where the black raspberries grew wild along the fence of the vegetable garden. On hot July days, we all went out and gorged ourselves. You can serve a dessert fit for the gods by pouring black raspberries over black raspberry sherbet and topping the whole thing with whipped cream. They also make delicious pies and the best jelly there is.

☆☆☆ BLACK RASPBERRY JELLY

In a large pan mix 4 quarts black raspberries with about 1/2 cup water. Cook gently, stirring occasionally, until the berries are cooked and mushy and juicy. At the same time, slice green apples (do not peel or core the apples, remove just the stems, the stem ends, and the seeds). You'll need about 3 cups. Cook them in a separate pan with 1/2 cup water. When they are mushy, dump them into the berries, juice and all, and stir. Pour this mixture into a jelly bag (which you have dampened as you don't want it to soak up any juice) and leave it to drip overnight. When you are ready to make the jelly, take the bag down and squeeze all the liquid you can out of it. This is a tiring job, but worth it. If you want beautiful hands for the next week, forget this step (and you might as well forget about shelling chestnuts, cutting up apples, or rhubarb, for that matter). Measure the juice. Don't cook more than 6 cups at a time. Put it in a *huge* saucepan (as it must boil up), put it on high heat, boil rapidly for 5 minutes. Then add the sugar. Allow 2 to 2 1/2 cups for 4 cups of juice; try the lesser amount first, you can always add more. Personally, I like my jelly tart. Stir well, then let the jelly boil rapidly for 5 minutes. At this point test it. I use a wooden spoon, take out about a tablespoon of jelly, blow on it a lot and tip the spoon to cool the jelly, then pour slowly back. If the jelly sheets to form thick, slow drops, then it should be ready. This jelly is usually ready 8 to 10 minutes after the sugar is added. Pour the jelly into sterilized jars and cover immediately with melted paraffin.

Blackberries

Blackberries grow abundantly almost anywhere. They are much tougher than their relatives, the black raspberries, and they are much larger, juicier, and more sour. One of our favorite late summer activities is to collect some large pails and go out after some berries. We wear tough clothes and heavy shoes.

Of course you can put blackberries into a pie. Be sure to use enough thickening as they get quite liquid when they cook. I like to stew them with honey, thicken them with cornstarch, and add some grated orange rind. This mixture can be poured over plain cake or warm over vanilla ice cream.

BLACKBERRY ROLL

• Dough •
1 3/4 cups flour
3 teaspoons baking powder
1/2 teaspoon salt
1 tablespoon sugar
4 tablespoons butter
3/4 cup rich milk or cream

• Filling •
3 cups blackberries
1/2 cup sugar
2 teaspoons cornstarch

• Surroundings •
3 cups blackberries
1/4 cup sugar

Prepare the dough by sifting the flour (you can use part whole wheat flour and/or part wheat germ), baking powder, salt, and sugar into a large bowl. Cut in the butter, then stir in the milk, until it forms a ball. Roll out the dough, brush it with 2 tablespoons melted butter. Sprinkle over it the filling (combine the sugar and the cornstarch before mixing them with the blackberries). Roll it up and put it in a greased pan. Then mix together the remaining blackberries and sugar and put them around the roll. Bake at 425° for about 30 minutes. Cut it in slices and serve the pieces with sauce from the pan.

CANTALOUPE AND BLACKBERRIES

This is one of our favorite summer desserts. Prepare it ahead of time so that it can be served chilled. For two persons, take one ripe cantaloupe, cut it in half, crosswise. Scoop out the seeds. Take a curved knife (if you have one, a citrus fruit knife is excellent), cut the cantaloupe into cubes, mix in as many blackberries as the shell will hold. Pour 1 tablespoon sherry over each half, mix gently.

BLACKBERRY BIRDS NEST

• Bottom Layer •	• Top Layer •
1 quart blackberries	1 cup flour
1/4 cup sugar	1/4 cup sugar
1 tablespoon cornstarch	2 teaspoons baking powder
1 tablespoon orange rind	1/4 teaspoon salt
1 tablespoon butter	3 tablespoons shortening
	1/4 cup milk (about)

Place the berries in the bottom of a 1 1/2-quart casserole. Mix the sugar and cornstarch together; stir them into the berries. Heat the mixture in the oven until steamy. Mix in the orange rind, and dot the top with butter.

Combine the dry ingredients, cut in the shortening, and stir in enough milk to make the dough easy to handle. Roll and shape it with your hands to fit over the top of the berries. Bake about 25 minutes at 400°.

WILD FRUIT PUDDING

You can use whatever fruit, or combinations of fruit, you have around at the time. I like especially blackberries with some cut-up apples added. A delicious dessert that uses up all sorts of things.

4 slices stale cake, cut in cubes	3 eggs
2 cups stewed blackberries, thickened with cornstarch	1/4 cup sugar
	2 cups milk, scalded

Put the cake cubes in a 2-quart casserole. Pour the stewed fruit over (and it should be thick). Beat the eggs, add the sugar, then the scalded milk. Mix well. Pour the custard over the fruit. Place the casserole in a pan of hot water (at least 1 inch), bake at 350° until the custard is set (about 1 hour). Serve warm or, better still, very cold.

Blueberries

One of the many advantages of living in rural upstate New York is the opportunity to pick your own fresh fruit in season. We have both wild and cultivated blueberries here, and for me picking blueberries is pure joy. The day must be dry, and hopefully sunny, and the birds singing. You step into the netting covering the bushes. You don't have to stoop or squat, in fact you don't even have to lean over. A basket attached to your waist leaves both hands free, and you can get a good crop in a short time. I bring the berries home in a large, flat box. Some I freeze immediately (the easiest way is to dump them into clean used milk cartons; fill almost full, tape shut, and freeze. If you want to be a purist, you can spread the berries on a cookie sheet with sides, or a flat tray, and thus freeze each berry separately. If you haven't any clean milk cartons, use heavy, air-tight plastic bags). The rest we eat for about a week—with heavy cream and sugar, on cereal, in mixed fruit salads, or just by the handful. I also bake with them. All the recipes that follow can be made with either fresh or frozen berries. If you are putting the berries in a cake, or in bread, be sure to defrost them first, draining off any excess liquid. You can mix blueberries with apples to make a deliciously different pie (about 1 cup blueberries to 6 apples is about right). They are also very good with apples in any baked apple dessert.

BLUEBERRY ORANGE BREAD

grated peel and juice of 1 orange
2 tablespoons oil
1 egg
3/4 cup sugar
1 cup blueberries

2 cups flour
1 teaspoon baking powder
1/2 teaspoon baking soda
1/4 teaspoon salt

In a measuring cup, combine orange peel, juice, and oil. Add water to measure 1/2 cup; set aside. Stir together the dry ingredients. In the large mixer bowl, beat the egg and sugar until light. Stir in alternately small amounts of liquid and flour mixtures, adding berries with the last addition of the flour. Stir just enough to blend. Pour into a greased tube or 9 x 5 bread pan. Bake at 325° 45 minutes for the tube pan, 1 hour for the bread pan, or until the bread tests done with a toothpick. Cool in the pan for 10 minutes. Turn out on a rack and cool completely before slicing. In fact, the bread will slice better the next day.

BLUEBERRY CAKE

1 egg
2/3 cup sugar
1 1/2 cups sifted cake flour
2 teaspoons baking powder
1/2 teaspoon salt

1/3 cup milk
3 tablespoons butter, melted
1 teaspoon vanilla
1 cup blueberries

Beat the egg, gradually add the sugar, beating well. Sift the dry ingredients together, and add them alternately with the milk to the egg mixture. Stir in the butter and vanilla, and mix until smooth. Fold in the blueberries (lightly floured), and pour into a well-greased 9 x 5 loaf pan. Sprinkle the top with sugar or with cinnamon sugar, and bake at 400° for 30 minutes. Serve warm with vanilla ice cream, or with vanilla sauce.

VANILLA SAUCE

1 cup sugar
2 tablespoons cornstarch
2 cups boiling water

2 tablespoons butter
2 teaspoons vanilla
dash nutmeg

In a small saucepan, combine the sugar and cornstarch. Stir in the boiling water, and cook, stirring, until thickened and clear. Stir in butter, vanilla, and nutmeg. Serve warm. Makes about 2 cups.

☆☆☆ BLUEBERRY BUCKLE

This is one of the best breakfast cakes. If you use frozen berries, be sure they are completely thawed before you add them to the batter.

1/4 cup butter
3/4 cup sugar
1 egg
1/2 cup milk
2 cups blueberries
2 cups flour
1 teaspoon baking powder
1/2 teaspoon salt

Topping
1/4 cup soft butter
1/2 cup sugar
1/3 cup flour
1/2 teaspoon cinnamon

Cream the butter, add sugar, and mix well. Beat in the egg. Sift the dry ingredients and add alternately with the milk. Gently fold in the blueberries. Pour the cake in a greased 9 x 9 pan, mix the topping (this is most easily done with the fingers), and sprinkle it evenly over the top. Bake at 375° about 35 minutes, or until the cake comes away from the edge of the pan.

BLUEBERRY GRUNT

This is a traditional Cape Cod dish. It can be made also with apples, or cherries, or peaches.

2 cups blueberries	2 teaspoons baking powder
1/2 cup water	2 teaspoons grated orange rind
1/2 cup sugar	1/4 teaspoon nutmeg
3/4 cup milk	1/4 teaspoon salt
1 1/2 cups flour	

Put the blueberries and water into a skillet. Stir in the sugar. Cook until the mixture starts to bubble. Lower heat. Mix the flour, baking powder, orange rind, nutmeg, and salt. Stir in milk until just moistened. Drop dough by spoonfuls (making 8 dumplings) on top of the simmering blueberries. Cover the skillet and cook for 15 minutes over moderate heat until dough is puffed. Serve the dumplings with the sauce in the skillet, and with thick cream if desired.

BLUEBERRY SLUMP

• Bottom Layer •	• Middle Layer •
1 quart blueberries	1/2 cup sugar
3/4 cup sugar	1/4 cup butter/margarine
1 1/2 tablespoon cornstarch	1/4 teaspoon salt
juice of one lemon	1 egg
	1/2 cup milk
	1 1/2 cup sifted cake flour
	2 teaspoons baking powder

Wash the berries and drain. Mix sugar and cornstarch and stir into the berries. Place in a greased casserole (2-quart size) and sprinkle with lemon juice.

Cream butter and sugar. Add salt. Beat egg and add with milk. Mix well. Stir in dry ingredients briskly and spoon over the berries. Mix Streusel Topping (see the Appendix) and sprinkle it over the top.

Bake at 425° for 20 to 25 minutes.

BLUEBERRY STREUSEL PUDDING

This is one of the easiest hot desserts you can serve.

4 cups frozen unsweetened
   blueberries
1/2 cup flour

2/3 cup light brown sugar
3 or 4 tablespoons butter

Pour the frozen blueberries into a 1 1/2-quart glass dish. Mix together the other ingredients until crumbly. Sprinkle evenly over blueberries. Bake at 350° about 40 minutes. Serve warm topped with vanilla ice cream.

Red Raspberries

I am not including in this collection any recipes for red raspberries. They are so very special, at least in my house, that we just eat them as is. If I am lucky enough to get a quantity, I freeze them (I put them in containers and pour over a light syrup—2 cups sugar or honey to 4 cups water—or I use a sugar pack—2 cups sugar to 8 cups berries). You can also freeze raspberries and currants together; just combine the fruit about half and half and mix in about 3 cups sugar to 8 cups fruit. Or I make jam with red raspberries. A recipe for Currant and Raspberry Jam is under Currants.

Strawberries

You can freeze strawberries just as you do red raspberries (see above).

STRAWBERRY JAM

Do not alter the measurements, or the jam will not jell.

4 cups mashed strawberries   **6 cups sugar**
juice of 1 lemon   **1/2 bottle commercial pectin**

Use slightly underripe berries and remember that the color of the berries determines the color of the jam. Mix the berries with the lemon juice and sugar in a large enamel pan. Bring to a full boil over high heat, stirring occasionally. Boil 5 minutes, stirring often. Remove from the heat and add the pectin. Stir, skim, stir again for about 5 minutes. Put in sterilized jars and cover at once with paraffin.

Other recipes using strawberries: Cranberry-Strawberry Jam uses frozen strawberries; Rhubarb Strawberry Pie and Rhubarb Ring with Strawberries use fresh.
See also Cranberries.

Bread

If your bread gets a little tired or dried out, be sure to use it up quickly, or bake it in the oven until dry and then store it, tightly covered, either as cubes or as bread crumbs (just break up a few pieces at a time and whirl them in the blender). This way the dry bread will keep a long time and is available when you need it.

There are many uses for stale bread: French toast (try dipping it in eggs and orange juice and add a dash of cinnamon for a change), croutons (easily made and you can season them in many different ways), stuffing, topping for vegetables (crumbled bread and cheese with a little margarine and worcestershire sauce). Or, best of all, make bread pudding. I have found over the years that very dry bread pieces make better pudding; it does not have a glue-like quality.

OLD FASHIONED BREAD PUDDING

Unlike the usual rule, this pudding is prepared in a double boiler. It makes its own sauce.

1 cup brown sugar	3 eggs
3 slices bread	2 cups milk
2 tablespoons butter	dash salt
1 cup raisins	1 teaspoon vanilla

Measure the sugar into the top of a double boiler. Butter the bread slices, dice them, and sprinkle over the sugar. Add the raisins. Beat the eggs, milk, salt, and vanilla. Pour over the bread. Do not stir. Place over simmering water and cook 1 hour. Turn out onto a serving plate. Serve warm or cold.

And now, other bread pudding ideas. In general, these puddings are infinitely more tasty with a good cracked wheat or light whole wheat bread. The puddings are baked in the same way. You put the bread in the bottom of a baking dish, mix the other ingredients, and pour them over the bread. The dish is placed in a shallow pan (filled with hot water) and baked at 350° for 50 to 60 minutes. Serve warm or cold with regular or whipped cream, or a hot dessert sauce.

CHOCOLATE BREAD PUDDING

A favorite dessert when I was growing up.

2 squares unsweetened chocolate	1/4 teaspoon salt
3 cups cold milk	1 teaspoon vanilla
3 eggs, beaten	1 1/2 cup bread cubes
1 cup sugar	

Cut up the chocolate into the milk in a double boiler and heat. When melted, beat with a rotary beater until blended. Combine the eggs, sugar, salt. Slowly add the chocolate mixture, whisking vigorously. Stir in vanilla. Put the bread in a baking dish and pour the mixture over the top. Let it stand for two hours before baking.

APPLE BREAD PUDDING

2 cups milk, scalded
3 eggs, beaten
1/2 cup honey
1 teaspoon vanilla
1/2 teaspoon cinnamon

1/2 teaspoon salt
6 slices stale bread, cut up
1 tablespoon butter, melted
2 cups sliced apples

Combine the milk, eggs, honey, vanilla, cinnamon, and salt. Toss the bread in the butter and put in a 1-quart baking dish. Pour milk mixture over. Arrange apples on top (or you can chop the apples and stir them in, along with 1/2 cup raisins).

☆☆☆ LEMON BREAD PUDDING

2 cups bread cubes
2 eggs
1/3 cup sugar

grated rind and juice of 1 lemon
2 cups milk, scalded
1/2 cup chopped pitted dates

Put the cubes in a 1 1/2-quart baking dish. Beat the eggs, sugar, lemon. Beat in the scalded milk and dates. Pour over the bread cubes, stir well.

STEAMED BREAD PUDDING

2 cups homemade whole wheat
   bread crumbs
1 cup raisins
1/2 cup finely cut citron
1/2 cup brown sugar
1/2 teaspoon soda
1 teaspoon cinnamon

1/2 teaspoon allspice
1/4 teaspoon cloves
1/2 teaspoon salt
1/4 cup butter, melted
1 large or 2 small eggs, beaten
1 cup milk

Mix all the non-liquid ingredients in a large bowl. In another bowl, beat the butter, eggs, and milk together. Combine the two mixtures quickly. Pour into a greased mold or glass baking dish, cover tightly, and place on a rack over boiling water. Steam for about 2 1/2 hours. You can add chopped apple and/or nuts, if you like. Serve with hard sauce made from butter whipped with confectioners' sugar and a little lemon juice and/or sherry.

◆

VEGETABLE NUT ROAST

For a delicious, meatless main dish, try this loaf topped with a mushroom, cheese, or tomato sauce. It is tasty, crunchy, and different.

3 tablespoons butter/margarine
1 cup chopped mushrooms
2 large onions, finely chopped
1/4 cup chopped green pepper
3 cups grated carrots
1 1/2 cups chopped celery

1/2 cup sunflower seeds
3/4 cup coarsely chopped walnuts
5 eggs, beaten
3 cups whole wheat bread crumbs
    (not dry)
dash of basil and oregano
salt and pepper

Melt the butter and sauté the mushrooms, onions, and pepper until tender but not browned. Combine this mixture with the remaining ingredients, adding seasoning as desired. Grease a 9 x 5 loaf pan well. Pour the mixture into it and bake at 325° for 1 hour. Serves 8.

PECAN PATTIES

A good vegetarian luncheon dish. Plan to serve these immediately.

1 cup coarse bread crumbs
2 tablespoons minced onion
1/8 teaspoon salt

4 tablespoons milk
1 egg, slightly beaten
1/2 cup finely chopped pecans

Mix all the ingredients, except the pecans, and let stand 30 minutes. Stir in the pecans and shape into small patties. Fry in hot oil, turning once.

Other recipes using bread: Bread puddings under Pumpkin and Rhubarb; meat and vegetable loaves and stuffings (see the Index); toppings for casseroles; Banana Carob Cake; Swiss Carrot Cake, Carrot Ring; Cherry Custard Pudding; Saturday Night Casserole (Cheese); Chestnut Dressing; Fish Timbales, Icelandic Soufflé (Fish); Baked Liver Pâté (Livers); Raisin Apple Betty (Raisins); Ricotta-Zucchini Stuffing (Ricotta).

Broccoli

Broccoli is a beautiful vegetable of exceptional flavor and nutritional value. Please do not overcook it.

CREAM OF BROCCOLI SOUP

This is a French recipe, and the result is very elegant.

1 small onion, sliced thin	2 tablespoons uncooked rice
1 leek, sliced thin	2 cups chicken broth
1 stalk celery, sliced (without leaves)	2 cups cooked broccoli, cut up,
1 tablespoon butter	with cooking liquid
1 teaspoon salt	1/2 cup cream or milk
pinch cayenne	

Put the onion, leek, celery, butter, and 1/2 cup water in a 2-quart saucepan; simmer for about 2 minutes over medium heat. Add salt, cayenne, rice, and 1 cup broth. Simmer for 15 minutes. Do not boil.

Pour broth-onion mixture into a blender container, whirl at high speed until liquefied. Return to the saucepan.

Put the broccoli and remaining 1 cup of broth into the blender and whirl until blended. Add broccoli cooking liquid (about 1/2 cup) to thin if needed to make a vortex in the blender. Add the broccoli to the onion mixture in the saucepan. Add cream or milk. Heat, but do not boil, and serve. Serves 8 to 10.

BROCCOLI SAUTÉ

Quick, easy, unusually delicious.

1 bunch broccoli (about 2 pounds)   3 tablespoons soy sauce
3 tablespoons peanut or vegetable oil   1/2 teaspoon ground dry ginger
2 cups chopped celery   1/2 cup coarsely chopped walnuts
(optional)

Trim outer leaves and tough ends from broccoli. Cut stems and flowerets crosswise into 1/2-inch-thick slices. (There should be about 6 cups.) Wash and drain.

Heat the oil in a large skillet; stir in the broccoli and celery. Cook, stirring constantly, 4 minutes, or just until wilted. Stir in soy sauce and ginger. Cover and steam 10 to 12 minutes, or until vegetables are crisply tender. If you decide to use the nuts, sauté them with the vegetables.

Variation: Omit the ginger and nuts; sauté 2 tablespoons sesame or sunflower seeds with the broccoli.

☆☆☆ BROCCOLI-NOODLE BAKE

I serve this as a main dish. Add a salad and some good hearty bread. Also, do not feel you have to follow these proportions exactly. I think the noodles and broccoli should be roughly equal in quantity, and the mushrooms can be what you have around. If your mixture seems dry, add more cottage cheese or some buttermilk.

2 cups cooked broccoli, cut up   1/2 to 1 cup cooked sliced mush-
2 cups cooked noodles   rooms
1/2 cup raw cashews, broken in   1 cup (or more) creamed cottage
pieces   cheese
   2 tablespoons soy sauce

Mix together the broccoli, noodles, cashews, and mushrooms. Add in any liquid you have leftover from the broccoli and the mushrooms. Blend together the cottage cheese and soy sauce; add more soy sauce to taste, if you like. Then pour this mixture over the broccoli mixture and stir well. Add more liquid if you think it necessary. The casserole mixture should not be soupy—remember that the broccoli will become more juicy as it bakes. Pour it all in a casserole and put over a topping of toasted wheat germ, or whole wheat bread crumbs, or crushed wheat cereal (Wheaties are good, Wheat Chex are even better). Bake at 350° about 30 minutes, or until bubbly and browned. Serves 4.

ITALIAN BROCCOLI CASSEROLE

2 eggs, beaten
1 cup thick cream sauce (see
   Appendix)
1/2 cup shredded cheddar

1/2 teaspoon oregano, crushed
1 cup stewed tomatoes
2 1/2 cups cooked broccoli, cut up
3 tablespoons grated parmesan

Combine the eggs, cream sauce, cheese, and oregano. Stir in the tomatoes and broccoli. Turn this mixture into a 10 x 6 baking dish, and sprinkle the parmesan cheese over the top. Bake in a 350° oven about 30 minutes or until very hot and bubbly. Serves 6 to 8.

◆

BROCCOLI IN MARINADE

I have a friend whose father was Italian, and whose love of good and unusual food has been an inspiration to me. At his house broccoli is often served cold, as a salad or side dish. You simply cut up the broccoli and steam it until crisp and tender. Then prepare a dressing with oil, lemon juice, garlic, lots of pepper, salt to taste, and whatever herbs you like. You pour this over the broccoli and let it stand for several hours. Stir well, then serve as a salad. You can also make a hot marinade by mixing the following in a saucepan: 1 cup vinegar, 1/2 cup oil, 2 cloves of garlic, mashed, 4 sprigs fresh parsley, minced, some pepper, 1/2 teaspoon salt. Boil this mixture for 5 minutes, and pour over the broccoli. Be sure that it is in a non-metal bowl. You can leave it to blend for 24 hours or so. You can add some oregano and sherry to the marinade, with good results.

Other recipes using broccoli: Chicken and Noodle Divan (Chicken); Leipziger Allerei (Lima Beans); Zucchini Puff is excellent made with broccoli.

Buttermilk

I always have buttermilk in my refrigerator; I make salad dressing, and I am always baking something with it.

☆☆☆ OATMEAL SODA BREAD

I bake this bread more often than any other. It can be mixed and put in the oven in less than 15 minutes. For us, one loaf will last through four breakfasts. I developed this recipe myself and it comes to you after much experimenting. I hope you will enjoy it as much as I do. For some strange reason, this bread is improved by freezing.

1 cup white flour	1/4 teaspoon salt
1 cup whole wheat flour (bread or pastry)	1 cup rolled oats
2 tablespoons sugar	1 tablespoon margarine
1 teaspoon baking powder	1 1/2 cups buttermilk
1 teaspoon baking soda	

Mix the flours, sugar, baking powder, soda, and salt in a large bowl. Stir in the oatmeal. Then cut in the margarine. Stir in the buttermilk and form into a loaf. Turn out on a floured board and knead gently, 2 or 3 minutes, adding more flour as needed.

Shape in a ball, place on a cookie sheet, and flatten to a 9-inch circle (about 1 1/2 inch thick). Press a sharp long knife into center of the loaf almost through to bottom. Repeat at right angle to divide loaf into quarters. Place baking sheet on middle oven rack. Bake at 375° for 40 minutes.

Variations:

Fruited: Add 1/2 to 1 cup plumped raisins or currants to the dough when you are kneading it.

White Soda Bread: Omit the oatmeal and whole wheat flour; use 3 cups white flour; increase baking powder to 2 teaspoons, and margarine to 3 tablespoons. Proceed as above.

Whole Wheat Soda Bread: Increase whole wheat flour to 2 cups, add 1/4 cup wheat germ, substitute 1 tablespoon brown sugar for the white sugar, increase salt to 1/2 teaspoon; you can also omit the shortening. This bread is wonderful with Swiss cheese.

BOSTON BROWN BREAD

Yes, this is the real thing, traditionally served on Saturday night with baked beans. Very easy, very good, perfect spread with cream cheese.

2/3 cup all-purpose flour	3/4 teaspoon baking soda
2/3 cup whole wheat bread flour	1/2 cup molasses
2/3 cup cornmeal	1 cup buttermilk
3/4 teaspoon salt	1/2 cup raisins

Mix all ingredients together and pour into three cans (16-ounce size), well greased. Fill only two-thirds full (no more). If someone in your house doesn't like raisins, fill one can with plain batter; add the raisins to the remainder. Cover tightly and place on a rack in a deep kettle. Pour boiling water to come part way up the sides of the cans. Cover and steam about 2 1/2 hours. You can also pressure cook the bread; 2 cups hot water in the pressure cooker with the cans on the rack. Steam 15 minutes over low heat with the valve open, then cook 30 minutes at 15 pounds pressure. Turn out of the cans by removing the bottom and pushing.

BUTTER BATTER BREAD

One of the best batter breads. This recipe makes two lovely round loaves with a nutty flavor.

3 cups whole wheat bread flour	4 tablespoons butter/margarine
2 packages dry yeast	1 1/2 cups rolled oats
2 1/2 cups buttermilk	2 eggs
1/4 cup molasses	2 1/2 to 3 cups white flour
1/4 cup honey	melted butter
1 tablespoon (scant) salt	

Grease two 1 1/2-quart round deep casseroles. Combine the whole wheat flour and yeast. Heat the buttermilk, molasses, honey, salt and butter until warm. Pour into a large mixing bowl. Add oats, whole wheat yeast mixture, and eggs. Blend at low speed with electric mixer until moistened. Beat 3 minutes at high speed.

Stir in enough flour to make a stiff dough. Brush with melted butter, cover, let rise until doubled, about 1 hour. Punch down; turn out on a floured board and toss a few times. Shape into 2 round loaves and place them in the greased casseroles. Cover, let rise until double, about 45 minutes. Bake at 375° for 25 to 35 minutes, or until loaf sounds hollow when tapped. Brush tops with melted butter, if desired.

GRAHAM-BUTTERMILK BREAD

I have tried many different recipes for whole wheat bread over the years. I like this one about the best. It is easy and always turns out very well.

1 cup buttermilk	3 tablespoons brown sugar
1 cup potato water	2 teaspoons salt
1 tablespoon yeast	3 cups hard whole wheat flour
2 tablespoons margarine	(bread or graham)
	about 3 1/2 cups white flour

Warm the two liquids together to lukewarm and dissolve the yeast in them. Pour over the margarine, brown sugar, and salt in a large mixing bowl and stir well. Stir in the whole wheat flour and beat until blended and smooth. Then stir in enough white flour to make the dough easy to handle. Turn out on a floured board and knead about 8 minutes, adding more white flour if necessary. Cover, let rise until double, about 1 1/2 hours. Punch down, form into two loaves, let rise until double. Bake at 400° about 35 minutes.

☆☆☆ CORN ROLLS

I am very partial to any breads made with cornmeal. Here is one of my favorite recipes for rolls. Serve these with hot soup or your next chicken salad luncheon.

4 1/4 cups flour	1 1/2 cups buttermilk
3 tablespoons sugar	1/4 cup butter/margarine
1 teaspoon salt	2 eggs
1 envelope dry yeast	1 cup cornmeal

In a large bowl mix 1 cup flour, the sugar, salt, and yeast. Heat the buttermilk and butter until warm. The buttermilk will curdle, but just ignore that, as it makes absolutely no difference at all. Gradually beat this mixture into the flour mixture, then beat 2 minutes more at high speed. Add the eggs and 3/4 cup flour and beat 2 minutes more. Stir in the cornmeal and 2 1/4 cups flour. Turn dough out and knead until smooth and elastic (do not knead in too much flour, as the dough should be soft and a little sticky). Let rise in a greased bowl until double, about 1 1/2 hours. Punch down and divide into thirds. Then divide each third into twelve parts. Shape in balls and place in muffin cups, or shape in oblongs and place on cookie sheets. Cover and let rise until double, about 1 hour. Bake at 375° about 20 minutes or until golden brown. Makes 36 rolls.

TOPSY-TURVY COFFEE RING

3 1/4 cups flour	• Filling •
1/3 cup sugar	1/3 cup brown sugar
1/2 teaspoon salt	1 teaspoon cinnamon
1 package dry yeast	3/4 cup raisins
3/4 cup buttermilk	1/3 cup chopped walnuts
2 tablespoons margarine	
2 eggs	

Combine 1 cup of the flour, the sugar, salt and yeast in a large mixing bowl. Warm the buttermilk and margarine, stir into the flour mixture, and mix well. Then add the eggs and beat until smooth. Stir in 2 to 2 1/4 cups flour. Cover and let rise until double.

Punch down dough and roll it out to a rectangle 20 x 12 inches. Combine the filling and sprinkle it over the dough. Roll up starting with the 20-inch side. Cut into 2-inch slices and arrange them in a greased 9-inch tube pan, cut sides down. Let rise until double.

Bake at 350° for 35 to 45 minutes. While still warm, drizzle with Confectioners' Sugar Glaze (see the Appendix). Serve warm.

☆☆☆ WHEAT GERM BUTTERMILK PANCAKES

The card with this recipe on it is positively sticky, I have used it so much. This is my favorite pancake recipe.

1 cup flour	1/2 cup wheat germ
1 tablespoon sugar	2 large eggs, separated
1 teaspoon baking powder	2 cups buttermilk
1/2 teaspoon baking soda	1 1/2 to 2 tablespoons melted
1/2 teaspoon salt	butter/margarine

Stir the dry ingredients together in a large mixing bowl. Beat the egg yolks with 1/2 cup buttermilk. Then add the remaining buttermilk and butter. Stir into the dry ingredients. Fold in the egg whites, beaten to soft peaks. Fry on a greased griddle, turning once.

◆

BUTTERMILK DRESSING

This is very good on mixed salad greens, and has the virtue of being very low in calories. Add seasonings to suit your particular taste.

1 cup buttermilk	1/2 teaspoon dry mustard
1 clove garlic, mashed	1/4 teaspoon salt, seasoned if
1/4 teaspoon sugar	you like
	1/8 teaspoon pepper

Combine all the ingredients in a jar with a tight lid. Shake well to blend. Let stand a few minutes before serving. You can add, for additional flavor, 1 tablespoon vinegar and/or 1 teaspoon worcestershire sauce.

PARSLEY DRESSING

This dressing has a pleasing color and is good with seafood. The entire recipe makes about 2 cups of dressing with a total calorie count of 150. Good news for the dieter and for the rest of us too.

1 tablespoon dairy sour cream	1/2 cup minced dill pickle
3/4 cup buttermilk	1/2 cup minced fresh tomatoes
3 tablespoons minced parsley	1/4 teaspoon salt

Blend the sour cream and buttermilk, and let the mixture stand for a while. Combine the remaining ingredients and fold into the buttermilk misture. Chill thoroughly.

LEMON GARLIC DRESSING

1 cup buttermilk	1/4 teaspoon dry mustard
1 clove garlic, mashed	1 1/2 teaspoons lemon juice
1 tablespoon dairy sour cream	

Beat everything together with a rotary beater. Chill, then shake well before serving. Good with fish or mixed green salad.

◆

BUTTERMILK RAISIN PIE

Serve this warm, in small wedges with hard sauce or stiffly whipped cream.

3 cups raisins
3 egg yolks, beaten
1 cup buttermilk
1 tablespoon vinegar
1/2 cup sugar

2 tablespoons flour
1 tablespoon grated orange rind
1/2 teaspoon salt
pastry for 2-crust pie
1 egg beaten with 1 tablespoon water

Plump raisins by covering with boiling water; let stand. With a fork, beat together the yolks, buttermilk, and vinegar; then add the sugar, flour, orange rind, and salt. Mix well. Drain the raisins and stir them into the egg mixture. Pour into pastry-lined 9-inch piepan, adjust top crust; seal and flute edge. Cut vents in crust and brush with the egg-water mixture. Bake at 375° for 50 minutes.

☆☆☆ GINGERBREAD

Here is one of the best and easiest cakes I know of. You can serve it topped with warm Cider Sauce or Lemon Sauce (see the Appendix) or whipped cream.

2 cups flour
1/2 cup wheat germ
1/2 cup sugar
1 teaspoon baking soda
1/2 teaspoon salt
1 teaspoon cinnamon
1 teaspoon ginger (or more, if you like)

1/4 teaspoon cloves
2 eggs
1 cup buttermilk
3/4 cup molasses
1/3 cup oil *or* melted shortening

Combine the dry ingredients in a bowl (use whole wheat pastry flour, if you wish). Stir well. Beat the eggs well and combine them with the liquid ingredients. Pour the wet into the dry and mix thoroughly. Then pour into a 9-inch square pan. Bake at 350° for 35 to 40 minutes. Cool on a rack for 5 minutes before removing from the pan. You can add up to 1/2 teaspoon more ginger if that is to your taste. Cut in squares.

BUTTERMILK POUND CAKE

This cake is more substantial than the usual butter pound cake.

1/2 cup butter/margarine	1 cup buttermilk
2 cups sugar	2 teaspoons vanilla
4 eggs	1 teaspoon almond extract
3 cups flour	grated rind of 1 orange
1 teaspoon baking soda	grated rind of 1 lemon

Cream the butter, then add the sugar and beat until fluffy. Add the eggs, one at a time, beating well. Sift the flour and soda together. Mix the remaining ingredients and add to the creamed mixture alternately with the flour. Begin and end with the dry ingredients. Pour into a 10-inch tube pan. Bake at 350° for 1 hour.

Note: You can add up to a cup of chopped almonds, walnuts, raisins, dates, currants, mixed candied fruits, or a combination. Reserve a small amount of the flour to mix with the nuts and fruits; fold them in last.

CHOCOLATE CAKE

This recipe comes from one of the best cooks I know. The cake is very easily made, a good one for children to try.

1 egg	1 teaspoon baking soda
1/2 cup cocoa	1/2 cup buttermilk
1/2 cup shortening	1 teaspoon vanilla
1 3/4 cups flour	1 cup sugar
1 teaspoon baking powder	1/2 cup boiling water
1/2 teaspoon salt	

Put the ingredients together in the order given, but do not stir until the last ingredient is in. Beat hard until the batter is smooth. Pour in a greased 15 x 10 pan. Bake at 325° for 30 minutes or more.

Let cool a few minutes. Then you add layers of the following:

FUDGE FROSTING

1 cup sugar	3 tablespoons white corn syrup *or*
1 square bitter chocolate	honey
1/4 teaspoon cream of tartar	1/2 cup milk
pinch of salt	1 teaspoon vanilla

Melt the chocolate and then mix in everything. Cook to a soft ball (about 326° on the candy thermometer), stirring as needed. Remove, add vanilla. Then beat until fairly thick.

Spread a thin layer on the cake; beat some more and spread another layer. Keep beating and spreading layer by layer. Let set.

☆☆☆ ORANGE-DATE-NUT CAKE

This cake is a real creation. Not really a gourmet cake, but one with a delicious combination of flavors. Squeeze the orange juice *before* you grate the rind. Reserve some of the flour and mix it with the dates and nuts. My recipe card says— treat this cake *gently*.

1 1/2 cups sugar, divided	1/2 teaspoon salt
1/2 cup butter/margarine	2/3 cup buttermilk
grated rind of 1 orange	1/2 cup chopped walnuts
3 eggs	1 cup chopped dates
2 cup cake flour	juice of one orange
1 rounded teaspoon baking powder	powdered sugar
1/2 teaspoon baking soda	

Cream 1 cup sugar, butter, and orange rind; beat in the eggs, one at a time. Sift the flour, baking powder, soda, and salt. Add alternately with the buttermilk ending with the flour mixture. Fold in the nuts and dates. Pour into an ungreased 10-inch tube pan. Let stand 15 minutes. Then bake at 350° about 45 minutes.

Mix the remaining 1/2 cup sugar and orange juice and bring to a boil. Remove the cake from the pan and prick holes in the top with a cooking fork or a cake tester. Pour the orange syrup over the hot cake, slowly. Sprinkle with powdered sugar (optional). Makes about 16 pieces.

Other recipes using buttermilk: Banana Pancakes; Buttermilk Cheese Bread (Cheese); Orange Pineapple Salad (Cottage Cheese); Orange-Cranberry Cake (Granola).

Cabbage

Cabbage is very good either raw or cooked. Try it sliced thin with Vinaigrette Dressing (see the Appendix). Here are easy ways to cook it. Take a head of cabbage and slice as much as you need. Cut across the slices to make small pieces. Drop it in some boiling salted water, or steam it over boiling water, for a very short time (no more than 5 minutes), or until it is just tender. Do not overcook. Drain, serve with butter and caraway seed. Or, you can heat some oil in a large skillet and stir-fry the cabbage until tender. Cabbage is very good garnished with chopped nuts.

RED CABBAGE, SWEET-SOUR

This is a popular Austrian dish called *Rotkraut*.

1 head red cabbage (about 3 pounds)	3 tablespoons sugar
2 teaspoons salt	1 small green apple
1/4 cup vinegar	1 teaspoon caraway
1/4 cup bacon fat *or* oil	1 tablespoon flour
1 tablespoon chopped onion	1/2 cup dry red wine

Shred the cabbage and sprinkle it with salt and vinegar. In a large skillet with a lid, lightly brown the onion and sugar in the fat.

Peel, core, and slice the apple. Add it, with the cabbage and caraway, to the skillet. Simmer, covered, about 10 minutes, or until the cabbage is tender. (Add a little water only if needed to keep the cabbage from burning.)

Mix the flour and a little of the cooking liquid to a smooth paste. Blend it into the cabbage, and simmer 5 minutes longer, or until thickened. Stir in the wine. Serve with goose, duck, pork, or ham. Serves 8.

WINTER BORSCHT

Here is a hearty soup for a cold evening.

2 tablespoons oil	stock to cover
3 large onions	2 cups stewed tomatoes
1 carrot	1 sprig dill
5 beets	1 tablespoon flour
1 potato	1 tablespoon nutritional yeast
1 head cabbage	1 teaspoon salt

Heat the oil in a large kettle. Chop the onions and carrot, scrape and grate the beets, cube the potato, shred the cabbage. Lightly sauté the vegetables in the oil. Pour in the stock, cover, and simmer until the vegetables are tender. Stir the flour into the tomatoes, and add with the remaining ingredients, stirring until the flour thickens. Garnish with sour cream or yogurt. Serves 6.

HOT CABBAGE SALAD

This dish, though central European, reminds me of our southern wilted lettuce salad. The method is similar. This salad, however, is really a hot dish. It is often served with poultry, and with venison.

1/2 cup wine vinegar	1 head white cabbage (2 pounds)
1 teaspoon caraway	1 teaspoon salt
1 tablespoon chopped onion	6 slices bacon, diced
1 tablespoon water	

Combine the vinegar, caraway, and onion in a small saucepan and bring to a boil. Reduce heat and simmer, covered, 5 minutes. Add the water and cool.

Slice the cabbage very thin, add the salt, and pour boiling water over to just cover. Let stand, covered, 15 minutes. Drain thoroughly.

Pour the cooled vinegar over the hot cabbage, mix well, and keep warm.

Fry the bacon, drain, and pour it with a little of the fat over the salad. Serve immediately. Serves 6.

ORIENTAL VEGETABLE SALAD

An unusual combination.

1 1/2 cups cottage cheese
1/4 cup dairy sour cream
2 teaspoons soy sauce
2 cups bean sprouts or 1 can (18 ounces) sprouts, rinsed and drained
1/2 cup sliced water chestnuts

3 cups finely shredded cabbage
1/2 cup sliced celery
1/2 cup thinly sliced green peppers
1/2 cup sliced green onions
2 teaspoons seasoned salt
pepper to taste

Blend the cottage cheese, sour cream, and soy sauce thoroughly. Add the remaining ingredients and toss lightly. Chill. Serve on crisp salad greens. Serves 8.

HEALTHY SALAD

This salad is the favorite of a friend of mine, who brings it to picnics, quite sure that no one else will provide such an interesting combination.

2 cups shredded cabbage
1/2 cup shredded carrot
1/4 cup chopped celery
1/2 cup salted peanuts, coarsely chopped
1/4 cup raisins

• Dressing •
1/4 cup mayonnaise
2 tablespoons prepared mustard
1 tablespoon milk
1 tablespoon sugar

Put all the salad ingredients in a large bowl and mix well. Blend together the dressing ingredients. Pour over the salad and toss gently. Serves 6 to 8.

Other recipes using cabbage: Beet Perfection Salad; Super Minestrone, Macaroni and Chicken Salad (Noodles and Pasta).

Cake and Cookies

Here are a few ideas for using the old cake and, if you have them, cookie crumbs.

TRIFLE

This is an English dessert, one that deliciously conceals the age of your cake. Take old cake slices, spread them with jam or jelly and liberally sprinkle them with sherry or sweet wine and a dash of brandy. If you like, cover them with red raspberries, peaches, or other fruit. Be sure to include some juice, the moister the better. Cover all of this with some good vanilla custard or pudding, flavored with almond or more spirits. You may also fold in some whipped cream. Sprinkle toasted slivered almonds or coconut on top. With this dessert you can really use up a lot of things.

If your cake is chocolate, use oranges or cherries as the fruit.

ORANGE LAYER DESSERT

Arrange leftover vanilla or orange cake slices in the bottom of a loaf pan. Spread with orange juice concentrate. Add a layer of orange sherbet. Repeat the layers. Decorate with some dabs of vanilla ice cream and colored sprinkles. Freeze. Slice to serve and top with hot chocolate or carob sauce.

COOKIE CRUMB CAKE

This recipe has been made in our house by my younger daughter. It calls for graham cracker crumbs, but you can use any cookie crumbs instead.

1 3/4 cups crumbs	1/2 cup butter/margarine
1/3 cup flour	2 eggs
2 teaspoons baking powder	1 cup milk
1 cup sugar	1 teaspoon vanilla
1/2 cup chopped almonds *or* walnuts	

Put the crumbs, flour, baking powder, and sugar into a mixing bowl and stir until combined. Add the remaining ingredients and stir the mixture well. Then beat the batter until well blended.

Grease and flour a 8-inch square cake pan. Pour the batter into it and bake at 375° for 45 minutes. Cut in squares and serve warm.

Other recipes using cake and cookies: Wild Fruit Pudding (Berries) uses stale cake; Lemon Bisque (Evaporated Milk) calls for cookie crumbs.

A recipe for graham cracker pie crust is in the Appendix; there are bar cookies using these crumbs under Dates and Pineapple; see also Angel Pecan Pie (Egg Whites); Graham Cracker Cake (Pineapple).

Carrots

I think carrots were invented to save mothers. For the child who doesn't like vegetables in general, and cooked vegetables in particular, the scraped raw carrot is an acceptable—and usually desired—vegetable for dinner, or lunch, or picnics.

If your carrots have become limp, scrub them well in cold water and store in a plastic bag in the coolest part of your refrigerator. If this doesn't help, slice them into your stew, or the vegetable soup, or the soups made with chicken and turkey. Their color and flavor will enhance almost any dish.

BAKED CARROTS AND APPLES

A perfect accompaniment to roast pork or ham.

8 medium carrots	2 tablespoons butter/margarine
4 apples	paprika
1/4 cup brown sugar	

Pare or scrape the carrots, cut in 1-inch pieces, and cook in boiling salted water until just tender. Peel, core, and slice the apples. Combine the carrots and apples, and turn into a 9-inch pie plate. Sprinkle with the sugar, dot with butter. Shake a generous amount of paprika over the top. Bake at 350° for 45 minutes.

☆☆☆ CARROTS AND KASHA

This unusual combination can be served as a vegetable or used as a stuffing for chicken or cornish game hens. It is superb with braised veal, and very good with beef dishes with juice—pot roast, for example.

1/4 cup chopped green onions	1/2 cup kasha (buckwheat groats)
5 carrots	1 1/2 cups chicken broth
4 medium mushrooms	1/2 teaspoon salt
2 tablespoons oil	1/8 teaspoon pepper
1 egg	1 tablespoon chopped parsley

Trim and chop the onions. Scrape the carrots and cut them into 1/2-inch cubes (about 2 cups). Chop the mushrooms. Sauté the onions, carrots, and mushrooms in the oil in a large skillet, about 10 minutes. Beat the egg slightly in a small bowl, add the kasha, and mix well. Pour this mixture into the skillet, and cook, stirring, until the kasha separates. Then stir in the broth (just dissolve some chicken broth granules in boiling water), salt, and pepper. Cover. Simmer about 20 minutes, or until the broth is absorbed and the kasha is tender. Sprinkle with parsley. Serves 4.

CALIFORNIA CARROTS

Here is a very different way of preparing carrots. This dish is wonderful with baked ham, or in the summer with molded chicken or turkey or tuna salad.

1 pound carrots	1/2 cup brown sugar
1 cup golden raisins	4 tablespoons butter/margarine
1 cup water	2 tablespoons lemon juice
1 teaspoon salt	

Pare the carrots, and cut diagonally into thin slices. Combine with the raisins, water, and salt in a heavy saucepan. Cover, heat to boiling, then reduce the heat and simmer about 20 minutes, or until the carrots are tender. Drain (save the water for your soup pot).

Sprinkle with the brown sugar, then add the butter and lemon juice. Heat slowly until the butter melts; then cook, stirring often, for 10 minutes, or until the carrots are glazed. Serves 6 to 8.

CARROT RING

It is difficult to find a good recipe for this excellent dish. Fill the ring with peas (beautiful), green beans (also pretty), mushrooms, or, as a main dish, with creamed chicken, ham, or tuna.

2 cups mashed cooked carrots	1 tablespoon flour
2 teaspoons minced onion	1 cup milk
2 tablespoons melted butter	salt, pepper, paprika to taste
2 eggs, well beaten	2 tablespoons chopped parsley
1 cup bread crumbs	1 cup grated parmesan (optional)

Mix everything together and spoon into a well-greased 1-quart ring mold. Set in a shallow pan of hot water. Bake at 350° until firm (40 to 50 minutes). Serves 6.

SUNBURGERS

Serve these with mushrooms and grated cheese.

1 cup ground sunflower seeds	1 tablespoon chopped parsley
1/2 cup grated carrots	1 egg
2 tablespoons chopped onions *or*	1 tablespoon oil
chives	1 pinch basil
1 tablespoon chopped green pepper	1/2 teaspoon salt
1/2 cup finely chopped celery	1/4 cup tomato juice

Combine all the ingredients with enough tomato juice that the patties hold a good shape. Add a little wheat germ, if you like. Arrange in a shallow baking dish, and bake at 350° until browned. Turn and brown on the other side.

◆

CARROT AND RICE SOUP

4 slices bacon	1/2 teaspoon salt
1 small onion	1/8 teaspoon pepper
6 carrots	1/4 teaspoon thyme, crumbled
2 1/2 cups chicken broth	2 tablespoons cream
3 tablespoons uncooked long-grain	2 tablespoons chopped chives
rice	

Cook the bacon in a medium saucepan until crisp and brown. Remove, drain, crumble, and put aside. Pour off all but a little of the fat. Chop the onion (there should be about 1/4 cup), and cook it in the fat, about 3 minutes. Scrape and slice the carrots, add them to the pan, lower the heat, and simmer 5 minutes.

Stir in the chicken broth, rice, salt, pepper, and thyme. Simmer, covered, for 1 hour, or until the rice is tender. Cool.

Purée the soup in the blender. Return to the saucepan and heat to boiling. Stir in the cream. If it is too thick, add water. Garnish with the reserved bacon and the chives. Serve hot or chilled. Serves 4.

CARROT-ORANGE SOUP

A totally different taste for soup, and truly refreshing on a hot day. Try serving it with hot homemade rolls, corn bread, or bran muffins.

4 carrots	juice of 1 lemon
1 1/2 cups orange juice	1 tablespoon finely chopped
1 cup apricot nectar	fresh dill
	salt to taste

Pare, slice, and cook the carrots until tender. Place them in the blender with the orange juice, and whirl until velvet smooth. Pour into a bowl and stir in the apricot nectar, lemon juice, dill, and salt. Chill until ready to serve. Garnish with a thin carrot slice, and a small sprig of dill. Serves 4.

CARROT SALAD IN LEMON-MUSTARD DRESSING

Use tender young garden carrots, if you can get them. This salad is fine for a picnic and makes a perfect accompaniment to cold meats.

6 carrots	• Dressing •
3 cups water	1/4 cup lemon juice
pinch of salt	2 teaspoons Dijon mustard
1 teaspoon sugar	2 teaspoons sugar
	1/4 cup minced green onions
	6 tablespoons olive or vegetable oil
	1/2 teaspoon salt
	dash pepper
	2 tablespoons chopped fresh dill
	or 1 tablespoon dried dill

Wash the carrots, scrape, and cut in julienne strips. Put them with the water, salt, and sugar in a saucepan. Bring to boiling, lower heat, cover. Simmer 5 minutes or until just tender. DON'T overcook. Drain, saving the liquid, cool under cold running water. Drain well and transfer to a salad bowl.

Combine the dressing ingredients in a screw-top jar. Shake until well blended.

Pour the dressing over the carrots, toss lightly to coat. Chill at least 2 hours, but remove the salad from the refrigerator about 30 minutes before serving. Serves 4.

HEALTH SALAD

I can remember eating a variation of this salad as a child. I think my mother made it with a vinaigrette dressing, which you can also do. But do try the combination here. It is unusual and the children should lap it up.

1 can (8 oz.) crushed pineapple
   with juice
1 tablespoon cornstarch
1/4 teaspoon dry mustard
1/4 teaspoon salt
1 1/2 tablespoons vinegar

2 tablespoons yogurt
2 cups shredded carrots
1/2 cup dried currants *or* raisins
lettuce cups
mint sprigs

Prepare the dressing by combining the pineapple, cornstarch, mustard, and salt in a small saucepan. Bring to a boil, stirring constantly, and cook until the mixture thickens and clears. Remove from heat and stir in the vinegar. Cool thoroughly, then stir in the yogurt.

Just before serving, combine the carrots, currants (or raisins), and dressing, and mix lightly. Serve in crisp lettuce cups, and garnish with a sprig of mint. Serves 4.

◆

There are many recipes for carrot cake, but most of them have an enormous quantity of oil in them. The following have a more reasonable—and healthful—fat content.

CARROT-PINEAPPLE CAKE

2 cups flour
1 teaspoon baking soda
1/2 teaspoon salt
1 cup sugar
2 teaspoons cinnamon
3 eggs
3/4 cup buttermilk
1/2 cup oil
2 teaspoons vanilla
1 cup crushed pineapple (undrained)
   (undrained)

2 cups finely grated carrots
1 cup coarsely chopped nuts
1 cup flaked coconut

• Glaze •
2/3 cup sugar
1/4 teaspoon baking soda
1/3 cup buttermilk
3 tablespoons butter
2 tablespoons light corn syrup
1/2 teaspoon vanilla

Sift the flour, soda, salt, sugar, and cinnamon together in a bowl. Beat the eggs with the buttermilk, oil, and vanilla. Add to the dry ingredients all at once and mix until smooth. Fold in the pineapple, carrots, nuts, and coconut, and pour into a greased and floured 13 x 9 pan. Bake at 350° for 45 minutes or until center springs back when lightly touched.

While the cake is baking, prepare the glaze by combining all the ingredients except the vanilla in a small saucepan. Bring to a boil, stirring, over medium heat, and boil gently for 5 minutes. Remove from heat, cool slightly, and stir in the vanilla. Remove the cake from the oven and immediately prick it all over with a fork. Slowly pour the warm glaze over the top. Cool in the pan.

SWISS CARROT CAKE

This cake is rather like a torte. Like the following cake, it calls for virtually no shortening.

small amount of butter	1 cup sugar
1 heaping cup bread crumbs	1 tablespoon grated lemon rind
1 2/3 cups almonds	2 tablespoons lemon juice
2/3 cup grated carrots	
1/2 teaspoon cinnamon	• Glaze •
1/4 teaspoon cloves	2 cups 10X sugar
6 eggs	juice of 1 lemon

Line the bottom of a 8-inch spring form pan with aluminum foil; butter the bottom and sides of the pan and coat with a small amount of the bread crumbs, leaving about 1 cup.

Grind the almonds very fine in the blender. Mix them with the carrots, bread crumbs, cinnamon, and cloves in a large bowl. Use your hands, it's by far the easiest way.

Beat the eggs and sugar until thick and creamy. Stir in the carrot mixture, lemon rind and juice.

Pour into the prepared pan and bake at 350° for 1 hour, or until the cake tests done. Cool, release the spring form, and turn the cake upside down on a plate. Remove the foil. Cover with plastic wrap and refrigerate until entirely chilled.

Prepare the frosting by combining the sugar and lemon juice. Add enough water (probably about 2 teaspoons) until perfectly smooth. Spread over the top of the cake. Let the cake set before serving.

OLD FASHIONED CARROT CAKE

Here is a moist, dark, spicy cake with fruits and nuts, excellent with afternoon tea.. If you use some mixed candied fruit, it is especially pretty.

1 cup sugar	1/2 teaspoon cloves
1 1/3 cups water	1/2 teaspoon nutmeg
1 cup raisins (or chopped candied fruits)	1 cup chopped walnuts
	2 1/2 cups flour
1 tablespoon butter	1/2 teaspoon salt
2 large carrots, finely grated	1 teaspoon baking soda
1 teaspoon cinnamon	2 teaspoons baking powder

Put the sugar, water, raisins, butter, carrots, and spices in a large saucepan. Bring to a boil, simmer everything together for 5 minutes, then cover the pan and let it rest for 12 hours (this is to nicely blend the flavors.) If the weather is very hot, put the mixture to rest in some cool spot.

Then add the remaining ingredients, stir well, and pour into two well-greased loaf pans (9 x 5) or a tube pan, and bake at 275° for 2 hours. Cool, then wrap in foil. Keeps and freezes well.

Variation: Substitute 2 cups shredded raw sweet potatoes for the carrots.

FROSTED CARROT COOKIES

I often make these as treats for Halloween. They are the right color and surely more healthy than the usual fare.

1 cup diced carrots	1/2 cup shortening
1 cup flour	1/2 cup sugar
2 teaspoon baking powder	1/4 cup peanut butter
1/2 teaspoon salt	1 egg
1 cup oatmeal	1 teaspoon vanilla

Cook the carrots in boiling water to cover until very tender. Drain and mash. Combine the dry ingredients. Cream the shortening and sugar, add the peanut butter and egg, and beat until light. Stir in the carrots and vanilla and finally the dry ingredients. Drop by teaspoonsful on cookie sheets. Bake at 350° for 20 minutes or until golden. Cool.

Frost the tops of the cookies with Orange Glaze (use one-half of the recipe; see the Appendix) and decorate with raisins or currants if desired. Faces are very popular.

CARROT BROWNIES

Dark, healthful, chewy bars, fine for afternoon snacks.

1/2 cup butter/margarine	2 eggs
1 cup brown sugar	2 cups finely grated carrots
2 cups flour	1/2 cup chopped walnuts
2 teaspoons baking powder	Cream Cheese Frosting
1/2 teaspoon salt	

Melt the butter/margarine in a large saucepan. Add the brown sugar and stir until blended. Remove from heat and cool slightly.

Sift together the flour, baking powder, and salt. Set aside.

Beat the eggs, one at a time, into the butter mixture. Stir in the flour mixture, blending well. Add the carrots and walnuts. Pour into two 8 x 8 pans, or one 15 x 10 pan.

Bake at 350° for 30 minutes. Cool 10 minutes in pans, then remove and cool completely. Frost with frosting (under Cream Cheese) and cut in squares.

Other recipes using carrots: many salads and soups (consult the Index); Banana-Carrot Tea Bread (Bananas); Almond Vegetable Mandarin (Beans); Vegetable Nut Loaf (Bread); Demi-Cassoulet (Lamb); Pot au Feu (Leeks); Leipziger Allerei (Lima Beans); Carrot Marmalade; Orange Muffins; Turkey Cantonese; Zucchini and Carrots. In Golden Cookies (under Sweet Potatoes) carrots can be substituted for the sweet potatoes.

Cauliflower

During the summer those of us who benefit from having a home garden can enjoy fresh cauliflower. You can separate the head into flowerets, which make a tasty addition to the mixed salad or to your raw vegetable plate (accompanied by a thick dip). Any small amounts of cooked cauliflower make a lovely soup that can be eaten either hot or cold; use chicken or vegetable stock; season with rosemary, dill, or caraway; garnish with chopped water cress, chives, and/or sour cream.

When you cook cauliflower, be sure that it is *just* tender. Nothing but *nothing* is worse than soggy, overdone cauliflower; and the taste deteriorates immediately.

CHOUFLEUR AUX OEUFS

This is one of the simplest and most delicious ways of serving cauliflower.

1 pound cauliflower	juice of 1 lemon
1 hard-boiled egg	2 tablespoons chopped parsley
	dash nutmeg

Steam the cauliflower head until just tender. Drain.

Sieve the egg, while it is warm, and mix with the lemon juice and parsley. Cover the cauliflower with the mixture and add a dash of nutmeg.

SCALLOPED CAULIFLOWER AND HAM

1 small head cauliflower	1/4 teaspoon salt
1 cup baked ham, cut in cubes	pepper to taste
grated cheese (optional)	1/8 teaspoon paprika
2 tablespoons flour	2 cups milk
2 tablespoons butter	

Separate the cauliflower into flowerets, parboil, and drain. Mix with the ham. Make a cream sauce with the remaining ingredients, adding some grated cheese if you want. It is delicious with or without.

In a 1 1/2-quart casserole, make layers of the ham and cauliflower mixture and the sauce, ending with sauce. Sprinkle bread crumbs or a mixture of crumbs and wheat germ on top. Bake at 350° for 20 to 30 minutes, or until bubbly and brown. Serves 6.

☆☆☆ CRUSTED CAULIFLOWER

3 cups steamed cauliflower	1/2 cup wheat germ
1/2 cup stock	1/4 teaspoon nutmeg
3/4 cup grated cheese, divided	2 cups cooked brown rice, wheat
1/2 cup chopped peanuts	berries, *or* whole oats, *or* a
2 tablespoons nutritional yeast	combination

Blend the cauliflower with the stock in the blender until very smooth. There should be about 2 cups.

Stir 1/2 cup of the grated cheese, peanuts (raw are best, if you have them), yeast, wheat germ, and nutmeg into the cauliflower purée. Pour into a 2-quart casserole.

Fluff up the cooked grain with a fork and carefully sprinkle it over the purée. Top with remaining grated cheese.

Bake at 350° for 25 minutes. Serves 6.

Other recipes using cauliflower: Leipziger Allerei (Lima Beans); Boeuf Choufleur (Peppers).

Celery

Celery has gotten to be, as the English say, quite dear. There is no problem dealing with those lovely inside stalks—crunchy, crisp, tender, tasty. One simply eats them. But to get to the heart of the celery, we have to take off those outside stalks, and they are often tough, stringy, and not so sweet in flavor.

I use *all* the celery. I peel off the strings, cut the stalks fine, add the pieces to omelettes, Chinese pork/chicken/beef, casseroles, soups, stir-fried vegetables. The leaves make a tasty addition to any puréed vegetable soup you want to make, and the inside leaves, of course, are wonderful in salads.

BRAISED CELERY

I serve this dish frequently. It is low in calories. If you have some leftover potatoes, slice them into the skillet toward the end.

8 or 10 outside celery stalks	1/8 teaspoon dried basil
1 tablespoon butter or oil	1 bouillon cube *or* 1 teaspoon beef
salt and pepper (if you like, I	bouillon granules
never use either in this recipe)	1/2 cup boiling water

Trim the celery, and remove some strings, if necessary. Cut the celery into pieces about 4 inches long; the larger sections can be split lengthwise.

Heat the butter in a large skillet with a cover over a low flame (I use my electric frying pan set at about 360°); add the celery and seasonings. Brown lightly.

Dissolve the bouillon in the boiling water. Reduce the heat in the skillet and pour the bouillon over the celery. Cover tightly and simmer gently until the celery is tender but not mushy. This takes about 25 minutes. Serve with the bouillon poured over the top. Serves 4.

☆☆☆ BEEF CASSEROLE WITH ALMONDS

This casserole is ideal to take to a friend in need; you can take it either cooked or not. Try serving it with tender, slightly cooked peas.

1 pound ground chuck	1 small onion, chopped
1 cup uncooked white rice	3 cups water
1/2 envelope chicken noodle soup	1/2 tablespoon soy sauce
mix	1/2 cup sliced almonds
1 cup sliced celery	

Sauté the ground beef in a frying pan, breaking it up in chunks, and cooking it until it is pink. Put it in the bottom of a 2-quart casserole.

Then in a large bowl mix together the remaining ingredients. It helps if you heat a small amount of the water and dissolve the soup mix (and especially the flavor lump) in it. Mix well and pour over the meat.

Cover and bake at 350° for about 1 hour, or until the rice is done. Serves 6.

BULGUR AND CELERY AU GRATIN

3 tablespoons oil
2 cups chopped celery
1/4 cup chopped green onions
2 tablespoons chopped chives
1/2 teaspoon celery seed
1/2 teaspoon salt
1 cup raw bulgur

1 1/2 cups milk
1 1/2 cups water or stock
1 cup grated cheese (extra sharp
 cheddar or strong parmesan)
bread crumbs
1 tablespoon butter

Heat the oil in a ovenproof casserole.

Sauté the celery, green onions, chives, celery seed, salt, and bulgur until the celery is tender.

Mix the milk and water/stock and add to the mixture. Simmer partially covered for about 15 minutes, or until most of the liquid has been absorbed. Stir in 3/4 cup of the cheese. Sprinkle the remaining cheese over the top, along with the bread crumbs (whole wheat, if you have them). Dot with a little butter.

Bake at 325° for about 15 minutes, or until bubbly. Serves 6.

Other recipes using celery: Celery fits into many places that I can only summarize here—chicken and turkey dishes, grain combinations, soup and salad recipes, tomato sauces; and especially in Beans-Celery-Bulgur Casserole (Beans); Vegetable Nut Loaf (Bread); Broccoli Sauté; Boiled Chestnuts; Grapefruit Aspic; Pot au Feu (Leeks); Chinese Pork.

Cereals

I shall give recipes first for the commercial breakfast cereals that you eat right out of the box and follow with the cereals that you cook.

All-Bran, Krispies, Flakes, Chex

All these cereals can be crumbled and used as topping on casseroles, vegetables, puddings; you can add them to sauces as thickening, to bread dough, bread puddings, custards; you can mix them with other ingredients to make fillings and stuffings.

☆☆☆ MOLASSES BROWN BREAD

1 cup sifted flour	1/2 cup raisins
1 teaspoon baking soda	2 tablespoons soft shortening
1/2 teaspoon salt	1/3 cup molasses
1 egg	3/4 cup very hot water
1 cup All-Bran	

Sift together the flour, soda, and salt. Set aside.

Beat the egg until foamy. Blend in the cereal, raisins, shortening, and molasses. Add the water and stir until the shortening is melted. Stir in dry ingredients, mixing only until combined.

Fill two greased small loaf pans (7 1/2 x 3 1/2), or two metal cans (4 1/2 inches deep and 2 3/4 inches across), or one 9 x 5 loaf pan.

Bake at 350° about 45 minutes for the large loaf, about 35 minutes for the smaller pans. Slice and serve hot.

Variation:

Bran Banana Bread: Use melted shortening and substitute 3/4 cup mashed ripe bananas for the hot water.

BRAN MUFFINS

One of life's basic items. Serve these hot with lots of butter and homemade jam.

1 1/4 cups flour	1 1/2 cups All-Bran
3 teaspoons baking powder	1 1/4 cups milk
1/2 teaspoon salt	1 egg, beaten
1/3 cup sugar	1/3 cup melted shortening *or* oil

Stir together the flour, baking powder, salt, and sugar. Set aside. Measure the cereal and milk into a mixing bowl and stir to combine; let stand 2 minutes or until cereal is softened. Add the egg and shortening and beat well.

Add dry ingredients to the cereal mixture, stirring only until combined. Pour into 12 greased muffin-pan cups. Bake at 400° about 25 minutes or until golden brown. Serve warm.

———————◆———————

The following cookie recipes are best when you make them with the cereal indicated in the recipe. However, you can substitute other cereals you happen to have around, provided you realize that you may change the taste or texture slightly. Try to substitute similar kinds.

CRUNCHY JUMBLE COOKIES

A very crisp, all-purpose cookie. You can use almost any crisp cereal (or a combination) that you have around.

1 1/4 cups flour	1 egg
1/4 teaspoon baking soda	1 teaspoon vanilla
1/2 teaspoon baking powder	1 tablespoon buttermilk or milk
1/2 cup butter/margarine	2 cups Rice Krispies
1 cup sugar	1 cup chocolate bits

Sift the dry ingredients. Cream the butter and sugar until light; beat in the egg, vanilla, and buttermilk. Stir in the dry ingredients, then the cereal and chocolate bits.

Drop by teaspoons on a cookie sheet. Bake at 350° about 12 minutes.

Variations:
Forest Ranger: Use 3/4 cup brown sugar instead of the white; substitute Wheaties for the Rice Krispies and 1 cup coconut for the chocolate bits.

Toffee: Use brown sugar instead of white and substitute 1 cup toffee chips for the chocolate bits; stir in 1/2 cup chopped nuts.

RAISIN TOFFEE BARS

1 cup flour	2 eggs
1/2 teaspoon salt	1 cup All-Bran *or*
1/2 cup butter/margarine	2 cups 40% bran flakes
1 cup brown sugar	1 cup raisins
1 teaspoon vanilla	

Sift the flour and salt. Cream the butter and sugar thoroughly. Add the vanilla and eggs and beat well. Stir in bran and raisins. Add flour and stir thoroughly. Spread in a 9-inch square pan, and bake at 350° for 30 minutes. Cool in pan; cut in bars.

Variation:

Coconut-Nut: Use only 1/2 cup raisins; add 1/2 cup coconut and 1/2 cup chopped walnuts.

☆☆☆ BUTTERSCOTCH CHEWY BARS

The most popular bar cookie I know. They are hearty and nourishing and are perfect in the school lunch.

2 cups flour	1/2 cup butter/margarine
1 teaspoon baking soda	1/2 cup peanut butter
dash salt	2 eggs
1 1/2 cups bran flakes	1 teaspoon vanilla
3/4 cup brown sugar	1/3 cup milk
1/4 cup white sugar	1 cup butterscotch bits

Combine the flour, soda, salt, and bran flakes; mix well. Cream the sugars, butter, and peanut butter until light; beat in the eggs and vanilla. Add dry ingredients to creamed mixture alternately with milk. Stir in the butterscotch bits. Spread evenly in a 15 x 10 pan, lightly greased. Bake at 350° for 20 to 25 minutes. Cut into bars while warm. Makes 4 dozen bars.

RICE KRISPIES COOKIES

This is an adaptation of a recipe that called for Grape-Nuts (so obviously you can use them if you prefer). This delicate cookie is very good with mixed fruit or ice cream.

2/3 cup flour	1 egg
1 teaspoon baking powder	1 teaspoon vanilla
1/4 teaspoon salt	1/4 teaspoon almond extract
1/2 cup butter/margarine	1 1/2 cups Rice Krispies
1/2 cup sugar	3/4 cup coconut
1/4 cup brown sugar	

Sift the dry ingredients. Cream butter and sugars; beat in the egg, vanilla, and almond extract. Stir in dry ingredients, then Rice Krispies and coconut. Drop by teaspoonfuls on a cookie sheet and bake at 350° for 8 to 10 minutes. Makes 60.

CEREAL CRUMB CRUST

This is an ideal way to use up small amounts of different dry cereals, not to mention any tired crackers you have around. You can make crumbs by putting the cereal in a plastic bag and running a rolling pin over it. Crumbs can also be made in the blender; don't run it more than a few seconds. Combine 1 1/2 cups crumbs with 1/4 cup melted margarine. Pat into a pie pan. This sufficient for a 9-inch pie, and is excellent for quiches or other vegetable or meat pies.

Variation:
Dessert Crust: Use 1 cup crushed cereal, add 2 tablespoons sugar, and blend in the margarine. You can also add 1/2 cup finely chopped nuts and 1/2 cup flaked coconut (lovely for an ice cream pie or for a layered ice cream dessert).

Cooked Cereals

Whole-grain cereals take a long time to cook. You need a proportion of 1 part cereal to 3 to 4 parts water, with salt to taste. Bring the water to a boil, stir in the cereal; reduce the heat, cover partially, and cook, stirring from time to time, for about 30 minutes. This rule is good for steel-cut oats or cracked wheat; the rolled grains take less time. Cornmeal takes almost no time at all (you should whisk it into *cold* water, then bring mixture to a boil, stirring—otherwise you will have lumps); cook until thickened. If you like a good whole grain combination, make your own "lumberman's mush." Simply combine equal parts of cracked wheat, steel-cut oats, and cornmeal (perhaps a bit less than the others). Stir the cereal into the water *before* you heat it, then cook as above.

Another good combination that cooks faster was developed by a good friend of mine. We had both mourned the disappearance of an excellent mixed cereal from the grocery shelf—so she made it up. It is much cheaper than any commercial variety. Combine 2 1/2 cups cracked wheat, 1/4 cup soy grits, and 1/2 cup flax seeds (or, if you prefer, sesame, sunflower, pumpkin seeds). To cook, use 1 cup cereal, 1/2 teaspoon salt, 3 cups water; bring the water to a boil, stir in the cereal, remove from the heat, stir, cover, and let stand overnight. Then the next morning simmer about 5 minutes, adding more water if necessary and stirring. We like to add chopped dates and brown sugar or honey. Also yogurt is wonderful as a topping.

Now, if by chance you have leftover cooked cereal, add it to soups, casseroles, stuffings. Best of all, stir it into your bread dough. I often cook extra cereal just to make bread.

☆☆☆ HEARTY BREAKFAST BREAD

leftover cooked cereal	2 to 3 teaspoons salt
1 1/2 cups milk	4 tablespoons margarine
1 1/2 tablespoons dry yeast	3 cups whole wheat bread flour
1 1/2 cups warm water	5 to 6 cups all-purpose flour
4 tablespoons honey	

Combine the leftover cereal (up to 1 cup) with the milk and blend well. Scald the mixture and cool slightly. Dissolve the yeast in the warm water. Put the honey, salt, and margarine into a large bowl and pour the hot milk-cereal mixture over. Stir well. When lukewarm, stir in the dissolved yeast and the whole wheat flour. Beat until smooth. Then stir in enough of the remaining flour to make the dough easy to handle. Knead on a floured board adding more flour if necessary until smooth and elastic, about 8 minutes. Turn once in a greased bowl and let rise in a warm place until double, about 1 1/2 hours. Divide in three parts and shape into loaves. Put in well-greased loaf pans (9 x 5) and let rise until double, about 45 minutes. Bake at 375° about 35 minutes.

OATMEAL BREAD

2 cups milk	1 package dry yeast
2 cups rolled oats	1/2 cup warm water
1/4 cup brown sugar	5 cups (about) all-purpose flour
2 teaspoons salt	1 egg white
2 tablespoons margarine	rolled oats (about 1 tablespoon per loaf)

Scald the milk and stir in the oats, brown sugar (or use honey, if you like; it's wonderful in this bread), salt, and margarine. Cool to lukewarm. Dissolve yeast in the warm water. Add the milk mixture and 2 cups flour. Beat about 2 minutes. Add enough remaining flour, a little at a time, to make a soft dough. Turn onto a floured board and knead until smooth and elastic, 8 to 10 minutes. Yes, the dough will be sticky, a fact of life with oatmeal breads. Let rise until doubled, 1 to 1 1/2 hours. Punch down and let rise again, about 30 minutes.

Shape into two loaves and let rise until almost doubled, about 1 1/4 hours. Brush tops with the egg white, beaten with a little water; sprinkle with rolled oats. Bake at 375° about 40 minutes.

PORTABLE BREAKFAST

Try these on the children or the commuter on the run, or for afternoon snack with a glass of milk.

1/2 cup butter/margarine	1/4 teaspoon salt
1/3 cup sugar	1 1/2 cups rolled oats
1 egg	1 cup cheddar cheese
1 teaspoon vanilla	1/2 cup wheat germ *or* finely
3/4 cup flour	chopped nuts
1/2 teaspoon baking soda	6 crisply cooked bacon slices

Beat together the butter, sugar, egg, and vanilla until well blended. Add combined flour, soda, and salt; mix well. Stir in oats, cheese, wheat germ, and bacon, which you have crumbled. Drop by rounded tablespoonfuls onto a greased cookie sheet; bake at 350° for 12 to 14 minutes, or until the edges are golden brown. Cool 1 minute, then remove to a cooling rack. Store loosely covered in a cool place. Makes about 3 dozen.

☆☆☆ SESAME-OATMEAL CRISPS

1/2 cup honey	1 1/4 cups whole wheat pastry flour
1/2 cup oil	1 teaspoon cinnamon
1 egg, beaten	1/4 teaspoon salt
2 tablespoons milk	3/4 cup sesame seeds
1 1/4 cups rolled oats	1/2 cup chopped raisins

Blend honey, oil, and egg. Stir in milk, flour, cinnamon, salt, seeds, and raisins. Blend well. Dough should be stiff. If too thick, add more milk. Drop by teaspoonfuls onto a cookie sheet. Flatten with the bottom of a glass dipped in cold water. Bake at 375° about 10 minutes. Makes 4 dozen.

OATMEAL SPICE SQUARES

My second favorite applesauce bar cookie.

1 3/4 cups flour	3/4 cup brown sugar
1 teaspoon baking soda	2 eggs
3/4 teaspoon cinnamon	1 teaspoon vanilla
1/4 teaspoon cloves	1 cup applesauce
1/4 teaspoon nutmeg	1 1/2 cups rolled oats
1/4 teaspoon salt	1 cup chopped dates
1/2 cup butter/margarine	1/2 cup chopped walnuts

Sift the dry ingredients together. Cream the butter with the sugar; beat in the eggs and vanilla. Stir in the flour mixture alternately with the applesauce (if it is very thick, add 1 tablespoon buttermilk or milk). Blend in the oats, dates, and nuts. Spread in a 15 x 10 pan. Bake at 375° for 35 minutes. Cool completely. Spread with lemon glaze (1/2 cup 10X sugar and 2 teaspoons lemon juice). Cut in bars.

OATMEAL STUFFING

This recipe makes about 8 cups, enough for an 8 to 10 pound turkey.

6 cups rolled oats   **1/4 teaspoon thyme**
2 cups minced celery tops   **salt and pepper to taste**
1 cup finely chopped onion   **1/2 cup butter/margarine, melted**
2 tablespoons minced parsley

Spread the oats in a large roasting pan or cookie sheet. Bake at 350° for 20 minutes or until light golden brown. Place in a large mixing bowl and combine with all the ingredients except the butter. Mix thoroughly. Then stir in the butter and toss to blend.

———————————◆———————————

I have found that oat flour is a wonderful addition to breads of all sorts, and I use it all the time for thickening soups, stews, gravies, sauces, and for dredging and browning. The flavor is so much better than white flour. You can make your own by putting about 2 cups rolled oats in the blender; whirl for 1 minute. This makes about 1 1/2 cups flour, which you can store, tightly covered, in a cool, dry place for up to six months.

You can make a wonderful crunch topping with rolled oats. Use it as you would use croutons or bread crumbs over salads, soups, casseroles, or vegetables. Combine 2 cups rolled oats, 1/2 cup butter/margarine, 1/3 cup grated parmesan cheese, 1/3 cup wheat germ, 1/4 teaspoon seasoned salt; mix well. Bake in a large pan at 350° for 15 to 18 minutes or until light golden brown. Cool; store, tightly covered, in refrigerator. Makes 3 cups. For variation, add 1 teaspoon oregano and 1/2 thyme before baking.

Other recipes using dry cereals: Barbecued Beefburgers (Beef).
All-bran: Golden Fruit Bread (Apricots); Banana Bran Muffins.
Corn Flakes: Corn Flake Macaroons (Egg Whites).
Grape-Nuts: Sweet Potato Puff.
Rice Krispies: Buttery Apple Squares; Cereal-Cheese Mounds; Cereal Date Cookies.

Other recipes using rolled oats: Honey and Spice Cupcakes, Oatmeal Saucers (Applesauce); Banana Oatmeal Cookies; Oatmeal Soda Bread, Butter Batter Bread (Buttermilk); Honey Oatmeal Chews (Coconut); Dill Casserole Bread, Snacking Cake (Cottage Cheese); Oatmeal Date Cookies, Peanut Date Cookies (Dates); Currant Drop Cookies (Egg Yolks); Almond Snowcap Cookies (Egg Whites); Golden Oats (Grains); Apple Oatmeal Muffins (Sour Cream); Spicy Fruit Drops (Sour Milk); Meat Loaf (Tomatoes); Zucchini Patties.
Don't forget Granola, and its recipes.

Cheese

Sometimes cheese gets old and moldy. Do use it anyway; trim off the mold, grate the cheese, and cook something with it.

BEER-CHEESE SPREAD

1 pound cheddar
2 tablespoons finely grated onion
1/2 cup beer
1/2 clove garlic, crushed

2 teaspoons worcestershire sauce
dash hot pepper sauce
2 tablespoons catsup (optional)

Shred the cheese into a large bowl and let it come to room temperature. Then beat it with a mixer until creamy. Beat in the remaining ingredients (you can omit the catsup if you like and add a little more beer in its place) until light and fluffy. Chill in a covered container. The flavor improves with time. Store, refrigerated, up to two weeks. Let come to room temperature before spreading. Wonderful on hearty rye bread. Makes 3 cups.

SHERRY-CHEESE SPREAD

This is a more genteel spread than the previous one, with a delicate flavor. It is good on small neutral crackers or melba-toast rounds.

1 pound sharp cheddar
2 tablespoons butter, softened
1/4 teaspoon sugar

1/2 teaspoon salt
dash cayenne
1/3 cup dry sherry

Grate the cheese and let it stand at room temperature about 10 minutes. Cream the butter, add the cheese, sugar, salt, and cayenne. Blend well. Gradually add the sherry, blending thoroughly. Pack into a mold, pressing down. Refrigerate a day or so before using. Makes about 3 cups.

CHEESE ROUNDS

This recipe and the following one make wonderful cocktail snacks. They are also delicious with hot and cold soups.

1/2 pound cheddar, shredded	dash cayenne
1 cup whole wheat pastry flour	3 to 4 tablespoons milk
3 tablespoons oil	1/2 cup finely chopped walnuts
1/4 teaspoon salt	1/4 cup sesame seeds

Mix the shredded cheese, flour, oil, salt, and cayenne until crumbly. Add the nuts and enough milk to form a large ball. Pinch off small amounts, roll in balls (about 1 inch in diameter), then roll in sesame seeds, pressing with the palm of your hand. Place on a cookie sheet, flatten slightly, and bake at 350° for 20 minutes. Makes about 24.

☆☆☆ CEREAL-CHEESE MOUNDS

1 cup coarsely shredded cheddar	1 cup all-purpose flour
1/4 cup butter/margarine	1/8 teaspoon salt
1 cup Rice Krispies	1/2 teaspoon worcestershire sauce
	milk

Shred the cheese into a large bowl with the butter/margarine. Let them stand until they reach room temperature. Then add the remaining ingredients. Work the dough with your fingers, adding just enough milk for the mixture to hold together (probably no more than a quarter teaspoon). Pinch off small pieces, about 1 inch in diameter, form them in balls, and place on a cookie sheet. Flatten them down somewhat. Bake at 350° about 15 minutes, or until lightly browned. Cool and store airtight. Makes about 3 dozen.

BUTTERMILK CHEESE BREAD

Recipes for cheese bread abound. This one is the best that I have tried.

1 cup buttermilk	1 tablespoon dry yeast
1 cup water	1/2 teaspoon baking soda
2 tablespoons margarine	1 1/2 cups shredded sharp cheddar
2 tablespoons sugar	1/2 cup wheat germ
1 teaspoon salt	about 5 cups flour (part whole wheat)

Heat the buttermilk and water with the margarine until the margarine melts. Stir in the sugar and salt and cool to about 120°. In the large bowl of an electric mixer, combine the yeast, soda, cheese, wheat germ, and about 2 cups of the flour. Add the warmed buttermilk and beat at low speed for 30 seconds, then beat on medium-high speed for about 3 minutes. Stir in enough of the remaining flour to make a soft dough. Turn out on a floured board.

Knead about 8 minutes, adding in flour as needed. Cover and let rise about 1 hour or until doubled. Punch down and shape into two loaves; put in 9 x 5 pans and let rise about 45 minutes. Bake at 400° 30 to 40 minutes. Cool before cutting.

FAST CHEESE BREAD

As the name suggests, this bread can be made in a jiffy. A lifesaver for the quick luncheon or supper.

2 cups biscuit mix (see Appendix)	1 egg, beaten
1/2 cup grated cheddar	1/2 cup plus 2 tablespoons milk
2 tablespoons instant minced onion	grated cheese

Combine the biscuit mix, cheddar, and instant onion in a bowl. Combine the egg and milk and stir into the dry ingredients until just moistened. Spread in an 8-inch square pan. Sprinkle more grated cheese on top. Bake at 400° for 20 minutes. Cut in squares and serve warm.

CHEESE SOUP

This soup served with crisp crackers and a crunchy apple salad makes a fine lunch for a cold autumn day.

1/2 cup diced celery	1 tablespoon corn starch
1/2 cup diced carrots	2 tablespoons flour
1 quart chicken stock	2 cups milk
1/2 cup finely diced onions	salt to taste
2 tablespoons butter	1 cup grated sharp cheddar

Parboil the celery and carrots in the chicken stock until tender. In a large pan, sauté the onions until wilted in the butter. Combine the corn starch and flour, add to the sautéed onions, and stir until smooth. Add the milk slowly, stirring constantly. Keep stirring until thickened and smooth. Then slowly stir in the stock, vegetables, salt, and grated cheese. Simmer 15 minutes. Serves 6 to 8.

◆

CHEESE AND BACON QUICHE

Try the crust in this recipe or use your own favorite pie crust.

1 cup crushed cracker crumbs	3 eggs
3 tablespoons butter/margarine	1 cup rich milk *or* half and half
6 slices bacon, crisp and crumbled	3/4 cup milk
1/2 cup finely chopped onion, lightly sautéed	1/2 teaspoon salt
1 1/2 cups shredded Swiss cheese	tomato wedges

Crush the crackers with a rolling pin or use the blender. Crisp rye or wheat crackers are especially good, but try to use some that are only lightly salted. Combine with the melted butter and press firmly onto the bottom and sides of a 9-inch pie plate. Sprinkle the bacon and onion on the bottom of the shell. Then layer the cheese over the top. Beat the eggs well, mix in the half and half, milk, and salt until well blended. Pour into the pie. Bake at 375° about 30 minutes or until the top is puffy and browned. Garnish with tomato wedges. Serves 6.

Variations:

Liver-Mushroom: Add 1/2 cup finely chopped cooked chicken livers along with some chopped mushrooms, lightly sautéed in butter, to the bacon layer.

Vegetable: Try the following combinations: onions and caraway seeds with cheddar, onions and green peppers with cheddar or parmesan, zucchini and tarragon with cheddar, chopped spinach and mushrooms with Swiss, chopped green beans and onions and dill with Swiss. The vegetables should be steamed slightly or stir-fried before going into the bottom layer.

SATURDAY NIGHT CASSEROLE

Trim the crusts from 11 to 12 slices cracked wheat bread (toast the crusts to make croutons or save them for the next bread pudding). Spread each slice lightly with butter. Arrange 3 to 4 slices buttered side down in a 1 1/2-quart casserole, trimming to fit. Cut 8 slices in half diagonally and put 2 halves together, sandwich fashion. Arrange point side up, spoke fashion, around the edge. If you wish, place a tomato slice between each wedge. Then prepare the custard:

4 eggs	2 tablespoons minced onion
2 cups milk	1/4 teaspoon paprika
1 teaspoon seasoned salt	1 teaspoon worcestershire sauce
1 teaspoon dry mustard	2 cups grated sharp cheddar

Beat the eggs well, then add the milk and beat again. Stir in the remaining ingredients in the order given. Pour the mixture over the bread. Refrigerate for 1 hour.

Bake at 325° for about 1 hour, or until the mixture seems firm when the dish is shaken gently. Serve very hot. Serves 6.

CHEESE AND MACARONI BAKE

This casserole has a lot of nutritious and unusual ingredients. Try to use whole wheat macaroni and raw cashews, which are the very best.

8 ounces macaroni, whole wheat	1 cup chopped raw cashews *or*
salt	raw peanuts *or* almonds
1/4 cup butter/margarine *or*	2 cups shredded Emmenthaler
oil, divided	4 slices Emmenthaler
1/4 cup whole wheat pastry flour	1/2 cup dry whole wheat bread
2 cups milk	crumbs
seasoned salt	1 tablespoon poppy seeds

Cook the macaroni in a large amount of salted water about 10 minutes; drain. Melt the butter/margarine and blend 3 tablespoons with the flour. Gradually add the milk and cook, stirring, until thickened. Season to taste with salt. Alternate layers of macaroni, nuts, and shredded cheese in a shallow 1 1/2-quart baking dish. Pour the sauce over the top. Cut the cheese slices in strips and arrange them over the casserole. Mix the crumbs with the remaining 1 tablespoon melted butter, sprinkle with poppy seeds over the top. Bake at 400° about 20 minutes. Serves 6 generously.

Note: Emmenthaler is real Swiss cheese (you can tell it is genuine if it has Switzerland stamped in red on the rind). You can substitute Finnish or other Scandanavian "Swiss" or a good domestic variety.

SWISS LOAF

Meat loaf by any other name is meat loaf just the same. Try this one as a change from the usual fare.

2 pounds hamburger
1 1/2 cups finely diced Swiss cheese
2 beaten eggs
1/2 cup chopped onion
1/2 cup chopped green pepper

1 teaspoon celery salt
1/2 teaspoon paprika
2 cups milk
1 cup dry whole wheat bread crumbs

Combine everything and press into a *large* loaf pan, or deep rectangular baking dish. Bake at 350° about 1 1/2 hours. Let stand a few minutes before slicing. Serves 8.

Other recipes using cheese: Almost everything, or so it seems! Many baked vegetable dishes, casseroles, loaves, quiches, salads, soufflés, stuffings for squash; celery, eggplant, and tomato recipes; Portable Breakfast (Cereals); Calabacitas (Corn); Ham Kabobs; Dinner Chowder (Potatoes).

See also Cottage Cheese, Cream Cheese, Ricotta.

Cherries

Cherries are one of my favorite fruits. Both sweet and sour cherries are available here in July, and there is nothing better than getting to the top of a cherry tree on a warm day to pick them.

It seems strange to me that there are really very few recipes for sour cherry desserts. But the ones we do have are extraordinarily good (to me, for example, the ideal gourmet dessert is a *Schwarzwälderkirschtorte*, a cake every bit as significant as its name). And what could be better than a cherry pie?

GERMAN CHERRY PIE

A standard recipe for cherry pie can be found in any cookbook. The following is a richer, fancier version. I started making it years ago when I was first married, and I make it still. It's a lovely dessert for a party or a special occasion.

2 1/2 cups pitted sour cherries,
   packed
12 tablespoons sugar, divided
1 1/2 cups sifted all-purpose flour
1 1/2 teaspoons cinnamon
1/8 teaspoon salt

1/2 cup butter/margarine
1 beaten egg
4 teaspoons cornstarch
1/4 teaspoon almond extract

If you are using canned cherries (you will need two 28-ounce cans), drain them, reserving the juice. Put the cherries in a bowl and pour over 6 tablespoons of the sugar; stir once. Let this stand about one hour, stirring from time to time.

In the meantime, sift the flour with the cinnamon, remaining sugar, and salt. Cut the butter into these ingredients until blended, then add the egg. It is easiest to work the dough with your hands but only until it holds together. Chill it. Then pat it into a 9-inch glass pie dish. Press it up the sides of the dish and see that it is spread evenly.

Drain the juice from the cherries and measure it. There should be about 3/4 cup. Taste it; if it seems too sour, add a little more sugar. Reserve 1/4 cup and heat the rest in a pan over low heat. Stir the cornstarch into the reserved juice and stir until smooth. When the rest of the juice is boiling, stir in the cornstarch mixture. Cook over low heat, stirring, for several minutes, until the mixture is thick and clear. Add the almond extract.

Place the cherries in the tart shell, pour the hot sauce over them, bake at 350° for about 50 minutes.

CHERRY CUSTARD PUDDING

4 cups milk, scalded
2 cups bread crumbs
pinch salt
1 tablespoon butter

4 eggs, slightly beaten
1 1/2 cups sugar
4 cups cherries, pitted
1/2 teaspoon almond extract

If the bread crumbs are dry and fine, use only 1 1/2 cups. Pour the milk over the crumbs, and then stir in the other ingredients. Pour into a large baking dish and place the dish in a pan of hot water.

Bake at 350° for about 45 minutes, or until set.

☆☆☆ BAKED CHERRY PUDDING

My mother made this dessert when I was a child. She used large muffin cups, making individual puddings. That is fine, if you want to do it, but I prefer an 8-inch square pan (a glass pan or casserole is very good). Somehow it all seems easier, and certainly cleaning up is facilitated. The original recipe says you can fold the cherries (which you have sweetened) into the batter and bake. If you do that, use only 1 cup, and the result is very good. But it is even better as described below.

2 cups flour	1/2 cup sugar
2 1/2 teaspoon baking powder	1 large egg
1/2 teaspoon salt	1 cup milk
3 tablespoons butter	1 1/2 cups pitted sour cherries
	2 tablespoons honey

Sift the dry ingredients. Cream the butter, gradually add the sugar, then the egg, and beat well. Add the flour mixture alternately with the milk.

Place the cherries in the 8-inch square pan with their juice. Drip the honey over them. Then pour the cake batter over the top.

Bake at 350° for 50 minutes. Serve very warm with vanilla ice cream.

CHERRY TORTE

An elegant dessert and very attractive too.

1 cup sour cherries, drained	1/4 cup cherry juice, hot
3/4 cup zweiback crumbs, divided	1/4 cup chopped almonds
4 eggs, separated	1 teaspoon cinnamon
2 cups sugar	

Mix the cherries with 1/4 cup crumbs. Set aside.

Beat the egg yolks with the sugar until lemon-colored. Add the hot cherry juice and stir well. Then add the remaining crumbs, beating until smooth. Fold in the nuts, cinnamon, and the crumbed cherries.

Beat the egg whites until stiff, and fold them in last.

Grease a 9-inch spring form pan, and sprinkle with more zweiback crumbs. Pour the mixture in gently. Bake at 350° about 45 minutes.

☆☆☆ CHERRY SAUCE

Here is one of the essential dessert sauces. It has many uses, but is really best served hot over vanilla ice cream. If you want to have a really luscious simple dessert, try a brownie or chocolate cake squares (the Economy Cocoa Cake under Sour Milk is an excellent choice) à la mode, topped with hot cherry sauce. It is also superb over cheese cake—or over dessert crepes, especially if you pour some brandy on the top and ignite it. You can also thicken the sauce somewhat and use as a filling for your cherry pie.

1/3 cup sugar	1 tablespoon lemon juice
2 cups canned or fresh pitted	1 tablespoon cornstarch
sour cherries	1/4 teaspoon almond extract

Pour the sugar over the cherries and let stand a few minutes, stirring from time to time. Then drain off all the liquid you can, add the lemon juice (if you use fresh pitted cherries, omit the lemon juice), reserve a small amount, and heat the remainder. Mix the cornstarch with the reserved amount, and when the liquid is boiling, mix in the cornstarch. Cook, stirring well, until thickened and clear. Cool somewhat. Stir in the cherries and the almond extract.

Chestnuts

I love chestnuts so much because they take me back to my student days in Paris. On cool autumn days we used to buy roasted chestnuts from the street vendors, peel them, and throw away the shells as we strolled through the city. Also, on special occasions, I would go and buy a lovely canoe-shaped pastry called *crème de marrons,* something that was—and still is—perfection to me.

If you consider chestnuts special, then carry on. You have to be willing to take some time for preparation and, I am sorry to say, your hands will look somewhat like shriveled prunes afterwards. No matter, it's worth it.

The easiest way to prepare chestnuts is to score them by cutting a cross on the flat side with a sharp knife. Put them in a saucepan and pour boiling water over; boil about 30 minutes. Then peel—patiently—and discard any moldy or dark spots. Keep the unpeeled chestnuts in the hot water, and keep at it.

Chestnuts are a seasonal delight and appear in the markets in the middle of November usually. Do cook them as soon as possible, as they spoil rather quickly. You can freeze the chestnuts until you need them.

☆☆☆ CHESTNUT DRESSING

This recipe is sufficient for a 10-pound turkey. Increase amounts for a larger one. Don't skimp on the chestnuts; I tried that once and was very sorry.

1 pound chestnuts	1 cup dry bread crumbs
1/4 cup butter/margarine, melted	2 tablespoons chopped parsley
1/2 teaspoon salt	1/2 cup chopped celery
1/4 cup milk and turkey stock	2 green onions, minced

Shell and skin the chestnuts. If they are not tender, cook them in boiling water until they are soft. Crumble them. Mix together the remaining ingredients and combine the chestnuts with them.

BOILED CHESTNUTS

1 1/2 pounds chestnuts	2 tablespoons butter
2 cups boiling water or stock	1/4 cup hot cream
2 stalks celery	

Shell and skin the chestnuts. Cover them with boiling water or stock. Remove the strings from the celery, cut in crescents, and add to the chestnuts. Cook 25 minutes. Leave in stock to cool.

To serve as vegetable: Mash with the butter and cream; sprinkle with paprika. Serves 4.

To use as garnish: Chop or cut coarsely; combine with cooked green beans or steamed brussel sprouts.

CHESTNUT MOUSSE

This is a superb gourmet dessert. Serve it with whipped cream.

2 cups chestnut purée	1 teaspoon vanilla
2 cups heated milk	6 eggs, divided
9 tablespoons sugar	2 tablespoons Grand Marnier
2 envelopes plain gelatin	*or* dark rum

You can make purée by whirling boiled chestnuts in the blender, adding enough water to make a smooth mixture. Blend the purée with the milk and stir in the sugar. Beat until smooth. Soften the gelatin in a small amount of cold water, add it to the hot mixture, and heat until almost boiling, stirring constantly. Stir in the vanilla.

Beat the egg yolks in a bowl, stir in some of the hot sauce, then add the egg yolk mixture to the hot sauce, stirring rapidly. Cook, stirring, until the mixture thickens. Do not boil. Stir in the Grand Marnier and pour into a large bowl. Let it cool but do not let it set.

Whip the egg whites until stiff and fold into the chestnut mixture. Pour into a lightly oiled mold and refrigerate several hours. Unmold on a beautiful plate and serve with crisp cookies.

CHESTNUT TORTE

This is another very special dessert. If you don't tell anyone what it is in it, your guests might enjoy trying to guess.

4 eggs, separated	1 1/2 pounds chestnuts, boiled
2 cups 10X sugar	and shelled
1 teaspoon vanilla	3 tablespoons rum
	1 cup heavy cream, whipped

Separate the eggs and beat all but 2 tablespoons of the sugar with the egg yolks and vanilla until very creamy and pale. Rice the chestnuts and add 3/4 of the amount. Fold in the stiffly beaten egg whites. Pour into a buttered, floured 8-inch spring form pan. Bake at 350° about 1 1/4 hours or until done. Cool. Remove from pan.

Mix the reserved chestnuts with the rum. Whip the cream with the reserved sugar and stir the chestnuts and rum into it. Spread this over the cake. If desired, garnish with shaved chocolate. Chill before serving.

☆☆☆ CHESTNUT PUDDING

I make this all the time with any chestnuts I have left over.

1/2 pound chestnuts (in the shell)	**1 tablespoon honey**
1/2 cup milk	**1 tablespoon carob powder**

Cook the chestnuts until tender and then purée them in the blender. Transfer to a saucepan. Add the milk (some can be used in the blender to purée) and cook about 10 minutes. Stir in the honey and carob. These amounts can be varied to suit your taste. Often the pudding is thick, so I just add more milk. Chill. Serves 3.

CHESTNUT SAUCE

I have been served ice cream with chestnut sauce in deluxe New York restaurants. It was not so good as this. Also, this sauce is perfect over dessert crepes.

2 tablespoons melted butter	**dash salt**
2 teaspoons cornstarch	**1/2 cup crumbled chestnuts**
1/2 cup water	**2 tablespoons rum *or* brandy**
1/4 cup honey	

Mix the butter and cornstarch in a small saucepan. Stir in the water and honey and cook, stirring, until thickened and clear. Add the salt, chestnuts, and rum (or brandy). Mix well. Serve warm. This makes about 1 1/4 cups. You can easily double or triple it, if you wish.

Chicken

These recipes deal with cooked chicken. There are surely enough ideas for cooking the bird elsewhere; in fact, there are entire books on cooking chicken. What follows is a group of favorite chicken dishes—how you cook the chicken first is for you to decide!

☆☆☆ CHICKEN CRANBERRY À L'ORIENTALE

This recipe, which is truly original, won first prize in the main dish category of the local newspaper's recipe contest some years ago. Preparation is extremely simple, and the combination of flavors is unusually good.

2 cups cooked chicken, cut in small pieces	1/4 cup orange juice
1/2 cup diagonally sliced celery	1 tablespoon soy sauce
1/2 cup whole cranberry sauce	1 tablespoon white vinegar
sliced water chestnuts (6 or 8)	1 tablespoon instant onion
3/4 cup chicken stock and sauce from deglazing the pan	1/2 teaspoon curry powder
	1/2 cup raisins

Mix together the chicken, celery, cranberry sauce (please make your own, it is so much better), and water chestnuts. You can vary the quantities to suit your taste. Make a sauce in a stove-top casserole, using all the remaining ingredients except the raisins. Add the chicken mixture to the sauce, cover, and simmer for at least 1 hour. About 10 minutes before serving, stir in the raisins. Serve over hot rice and sprinkle the top generously with chow mein noodles. Serves 4 to 6.

Variations: Substitute turkey for the chicken. Or make the dish with uncooked chicken. Cut up a chicken and put it in the pot with the celery, cranberry sauce, and chestnuts. Then mix up the sauce and pour it over the top (or you can use a whole chicken; if so, you'll probably want to use more sauce); cover and cook for at least an hour and a half, or until chicken is done.

WALNUT CHICKEN

Another dish with an oriental flavor, also very easy to make.

2 tablespoons soy sauce
1 tablespoon dry sherry
1/2 teaspoon powdered ginger
2 cups cooked chicken, cut
  in 1-inch pieces

3 tablespoons oil
1/3 cup sliced green onions
1 clove garlic, cut in half
1 cup walnuts, coarsely chopped

Combine the soy sauce, sherry, and ginger in a bowl; add the chicken pieces and let stand 15 minutes.

Heat the oil in a large skillet until very hot; add the onions, garlic, and walnuts. Cook 3 minutes, stirring constantly. Discard the garlic. Spoon the walnut-onion mixture into a small bowl and reserve.

Add the chicken mixture to the skillet and stir-fry until the soy mixture begins to coat the chicken, about 5 minutes. Add the reserved walnut mixture and stir to mix. Serve with hot rice. Serves 4.

CHICKEN STROGANOFF

Here is a delicious and economical variation of the famous beef dish.

1 medium onion, chopped
3 tablespoons butter/margarine
1/2 pound mushrooms, sliced
1 tablespoon flour
2 teaspoons paprika
1/2 teaspoon salt
1/4 teaspoon basil, crumbled

1/4 teaspoon thyme, crumbled
1/2 cup chicken broth
1/2 cup dry white wine
1/2 cup dairy sour cream
2 cups diced cooked chicken
2 teaspoons lemon juice
2 tablespoons chopped fresh dill

Sauté the onion in the butter in a large saucepan or Dutch oven until golden. Add the mushrooms and cook, stirring, for 3 to 5 minutes. Blend in the flour, paprika, salt, and herbs. Gradually stir in the chicken broth and wine. Cook, stirring constantly, until mixture thickens and bubbles for a minute. Cover, simmer 5 minutes, and remove from the heat.

Blend in the sour cream. Add the chicken, lemon juice, and dill. Heat thoroughly over low heat, but do not boil. Serve over hot cooked noodles. Serves 4.

CHICKEN SAUCE FOR SPAGHETTI

Here is a change from the usual ground beef plus tomatoes. And if you want a total change, try it over hot, buttered spinach noodles.

2 tablespoons olive oil	1/2 teaspoon sage
1 medium onion, finely chopped	1/2 teaspoon salt
1/2 cup water	1/2 cup dry white wine
1/2 cup finely chopped cooked chicken	grated parmesan cheese

Heat the oil in a heavy skillet, add the onion and water, and boil until the onion is soft. Stir in chicken, sage, salt, and wine. Bring to a boil, reduce heat, and simmer about 7 minutes. Serve hot over freshly-cooked spaghetti or other pasta and sprinkle generously with parmesan. Makes 1 1/4 cups.

CHICKEN-ZUCCHINI FLIPS

A delicious and wonderful variation on the filled-crepe theme.

• Filling •	• Pancakes •
1/4 cup chopped onion	2 eggs, beaten
1/4 cup chopped celery	1/4 cup flour
1 tablespoon margarine	2 tablespoons grated parmesan
1 cup thick cream sauce	1 teaspoon snipped chives
1/4 teaspoon instant chicken powder	1 teaspoon minced parsley
milk (if needed, to thin sauce)	dash of salt and pepper
2 cups diced cooked chicken	3 medium zucchini, shredded and drained

In a small saucepan, cook the onion and celery in the margarine. Add the cream sauce, powder, and milk (if too thick) and blend well. Stir in the chicken. Keep it warm.

Mix together the ingredients for the pancakes, and fry eight on a hot griddle. Take one-half of the filling and spoon it onto the pancakes; fold them. Spoon the remaining filling over the top. Serve at once. Serves 4.

CHICKEN AND NOODLE DIVAN

8 ounces egg noodles, cooked
1 1/4 cups cooked chopped broccoli
  or 1 package (10 oz.) frozen
2 cups cottage cheese
1 egg
5 cups diced cooked chicken

4 tablespoons butter/margarine
1/3 cup flour
1 teaspoon salt
1 teaspoon basil
1/2 teaspoon pepper
3 cups chicken broth
1/2 cup grated parmesan cheese

Combine the noodles, cooked broccoli, cottage cheese (with the egg mixed into it), and diced chicken in a large bowl. Make a sauce with the remaining ingredients, except the cheese. When it is boiling and thickened, pour over the mixture in the bowl, and stir well. Divide into two 2-quart casseroles. Sprinkle each with 1/4 cup cheese. Bake one at 350° for 45 minutes, or until bubbly hot. Freeze the other; bake it at 350° for 1 1/2 hours, when needed.

◆

☆☆☆ INDIAN MELON SALAD

This is a lovely dish for a luncheon, served with homemade hot rolls.

2 cups coarsely cut cooked
  chicken *or* turkey
1 can (5 ounces) water chestnuts,
  sliced
1/2 pound green seedless grapes
1/2 cup chopped celery
1 cup mayonnaise *or* Mock
  Mayonnaise (see the Appendix)

1/2 teaspoon curry powder
1 tablespoon lemon juice
1/4 teaspoon salt
1/8 teaspoon pepper
1 tablespoon soy sauce
1 cup honeydew melon balls
1 cup cantaloupe balls
Boston lettuce cups

Combine the chicken, chestnuts, grapes and celery. Mix the mayonnaise with the curry, lemon juice, salt, pepper, and soy sauce. Combine with the chicken mixture and blend well. Add the melon balls and toss lightly. Serve in the lettuce cups. Serves 6.

FRUITED CHICKEN SALAD

Another chicken-fruit combination, but quite different.

5 cups cooked chicken chunks
2 tablespoons salad oil
2 tablespoons orange juice
2 tablespoons vinegar
1/2 teaspoon salt
3 cups cooked brown rice
1 1/2 cups sliced green grapes

1 1/2 cups sliced celery
1 can (13 1/2 ounces pineapple
   tidbits, drained
1 can (11 ounces) mandarin
   oranges, drained
1 cup toasted slivered almonds
1 1/2 cups mayonnaise *or* Mock
   Mayonnaise (see the Appendix)

Combine the chicken, oil, orange juice, vinegar, and salt. Let stand while you prepare and mix together the remaining ingredients. Add the chicken mixture and toss gently. Serves 12.

CHICKEN-PINEAPPLE BUFFET SALAD

This, and the following recipe, are molded gelatin salads. Both are very attractive and go well to the potluck picnic or supper.

1 envelope plain gelatin
1/2 cup water
2 cups chicken broth
2 1/2 tablespoons lemon juice
6 cups cooked chicken
1 cup crushed pineapple

3 hard-boiled eggs, chopped
1 cup cubed cheddar cheese
3/4 cup celery
1 cup mayonnaise
1 teaspoon salt

Dissolve the gelatin in the water. Heat gently, stirring, until dissolved. Combine with the chicken broth and lemon juice and blend well. Then add the remaining ingredients and stir gently until well combined. Pour into a 3-quart mold and chill until firm. Unmold on salad greens and serve with cottage cheese sprinkled with paprika.

CHICKEN SALAD WITH YOGURT

This is a healthful and light chicken salad combination.

1 envelope plain gelatin	1/4 cup mayonnaise
1 1/4 cups pineapple juice	1 1/3 cup diced cooked chicken
1/2 teaspoon salt	1/4 cup chopped celery
1 cup lemon yogurt	2 tablespoons slivered toasted almonds

Soften the gelatin in the pineapple juice; add the salt. Heat, stirring, until dissolved. Combine the yogurt and mayonnaise, stir in the gelatin. Chill until partially set; fold in the chicken, celery, and almonds. Pour into one large mold or six individual molds; chill until firm. Garnish with cherry tomatoes or clusters of green grapes. Serves 6.

Other recipes using chicken: Cold Cucumber Soup; Chicken Tetrazzini (Evaporated Milk); Chicken Cacciatore (Wine). The dishes under Turkey can be made with chicken.

Coconut

In my view there is but one thing to do with freshly grated coconut, and that is to make a cake. Use your favorite yellow cake recipe (there is a good one under Currants, which you can bake in two 8-inch round pans to make a layer cake), frost it with Fluffy Frosting (see the Appendix), while sprinkling fresh coconut generously on the frosting between the layers and on the tops and sides. An absolutely divine creation.

Most of us don't have fresh coconut easily available and we must buy ordinary grated coconut (do get it by the pound at a health food store—*much* cheaper). Sometimes there is some left over. It can be stored, tightly covered, in the refrigerator, almost indefinitely.

COCONUT POUND CAKE

This is a plain-looking, absolutely scrumptious cake. It is rich and melts in your mouth. I think it is the only recipe in the entire book that starts off with a pound of butter—a fact pointed out to me, somewhat guiltily, by my friend who gave me the recipe.

1 pound butter	6 eggs
2 cups sugar	1 cup coconut
2 cups flour, divided	1 tablespoon vanilla

Cream the butter and sugar. Stir in 1 cup of the flour. Beat in the eggs, one at a time. Combine the coconut with the other cup of flour and blend into the mixture. Add the vanilla. Bake in a tube pan at 350° for 1 hour and 15 minutes. If you wish, you can glaze the warm cake with Honey Glaze (see the Appendix), to which you have added 1 tablespoon dark rum.

COCONUT CUSTARD PIE

Here is a very simple dessert, one the children can make easily. It's one of those magical mixtures that is one thing when you put it in the oven but comes out in two separate layers.

1/2 cup biscuit mix (see the Appendix)	2 cups milk
1/2 cup sugar	1 teaspoon vanilla
4 eggs	3 tablespoons butter
1 cup coconut	

Put everything into the blender and whirl until smooth. Pour into a well-buttered 10-inch pie plate and bake at 400° until the custard sets, between 25 and 30 minutes.

COCONUT CORN BREAD

1 3/4 cups cornmeal	2 teaspoons baking powder
1/2 cup brown sugar	2 eggs, beaten
1 cup white flour	2 teaspoons melted butter
1 teaspoon ginger	2 cups buttermilk
1/2 teaspoon salt	1 cup coconut

Combine the cornmeal and brown sugar in a mixing bowl. Sift the other dry ingredients on top and mix everything together. Then combine the liquid ingredients and stir them into the dry mixture. Stir in two-thirds of the coconut. Pour into a 9-inch square or an 11 x 8 pan and sprinkle the rest of the coconut over the top. Bake at 400° for 20 to 25 minutes. Serve hot with butter and strawberry or raspberry jam.

☆☆☆ ORANGE-COCONUT COFFEE CAKE

This is fancy, very pretty, and easy to make. It is also a pleasure to eat.

3 3/4 cups flour, divided	2 eggs
3/4 cup sugar, divided	1/2 cup dairy sour cream
1/2 teaspoon salt	1 cup toasted coconut
1 package dry yeast	2 tablespoons grated orange peel
1/4 cup milk	2 tablespoons butter, melted
1/4 cup butter/margarine	

Combine 1 cup of the flour, 1/4 cup of the sugar, and the salt in a large mixer bowl. Soften the yeast in warm water. Heat the milk and butter until warm. Add the eggs, sour cream, and warm milk to flour mixture, then the yeast. Blend at low speed until mixed, then beat 3 minutes at medium speed. Stir in remaining flour to form a stiff dough. Turn several times on a floured board to thoroughly blend everything. Cover, let rise until doubled, about 2 hours.

Combine the remaining sugar, the toasted coconut, and orange peel. Set aside.

Punch down the dough and toss on a floured board until no longer sticky. Divide in two and roll out each half to a 12 x 8-inch rectangle. Brush each with 1 tablespoon of the melted butter and sprinkle with 1/2 cup of the coconut mixture. Roll up, starting with the long side. Cut into sixteen 1-inch slices. Place, cut side down, in a greased 9-inch round baking pan. Let rise until light, 30 to 45 minutes. Sprinkle with the remaining coconut mixture.

Bake at 350° for about 30 minutes. Make Orange Glaze (see the Appendix; make about one-third of the recipe) and drizzle on the cooled coffee cakes. Makes two rings, one of which you can freeze for later use.

Note: In my experience, this recipe makes more than two 9-inch cakes. In the past I have used one extra pan, a small rectangular or round one, and made a small cake with six of the rolls.

COCONUT CRESCENTS

These delectable little rolls, in butter layers with a coconut-butter filling, make a very special treat for afternoon tea or a morning coffee party. They will take about 3 hours to make; they are worth every minute.

4 1/2 to 5 cups flour
1/3 cup sugar
1 teaspoon salt
1/4 teaspoon nutmeg
1 teaspoon grated orange peel
1 package dry yeast
1 1/4 cups milk
1/4 cup margarine

2 eggs (reserve one yolk)
1/2 teaspoon vanilla
1/4 cup softened butter

• Filling •
1/2 cup sugar
3 tablespoons butter
1 cup coconut
reserved egg yolk

In a large mixer bowl, combine 2 cups of the flour, the sugar, salt, nutmeg, orange peel, and dry yeast. Heat the milk and margarine until warm and add with the eggs and vanilla to dry ingredients. Mix until blended, then beat 3 minutes at medium speed. Stir in remaining flour. Cover and let rise until doubled, about 1 1/2 hours.

Punch down the dough. Roll out into a 14-inch square. Spread half of the dough with half of the butter. Fold in half and then in quarters; seal edges. Repeat the process, using the remaining butter. Cover and let rest 15 minutes.

Prepare the filling by blending the sugar with the butter. Stir in the coconut and egg yolk and mix well.

Divide the dough in thirds. Roll out each third to a 9-inch circle and cut each circle into 8 wedges. Place a scant teaspoon of filling in the center of each wedge and roll up, starting from the wide end. Place, point-side down, on cookie sheets. Cover, let rise until doubled, about 30 minutes. Bake at 400° for 10 to 12 minutes. If desired, drizzle with Confectioners' Sugar Glaze (see the Appendix). Makes 24 rolls.

———————◆———————

☆☆☆ HONEY OATMEAL CHEWS

1/2 cup butter/margarine
1/2 cup honey, clover if you have it
1/2 cup sugar
1 egg
1 teaspoon vanilla
3/4 cup flour

1/2 teaspoon baking soda
1/2 teaspoon baking powder
1/4 teaspoon salt
1 cup rolled oats
1 cup flaked coconut
1/2 cup chopped almonds

Cream together the butter, honey, and sugar until light and fluffy. Add the egg and vanilla and beat well. Sift together the flour, soda, baking powder, and salt and add to the creamed mixture. Then stir in the oats, coconut, and nuts (try chopped roasted peanuts instead of almonds for variety; some in my house prefer this variation).

Spread in a greased 13 x 9 pan. Bake at 325° for 25 minutes. When cool, sprinkle with 10X sugar and cut into bars.

THREE LAYER COOKIES

• Layer I •	• Layer II •
6 tablespoons butter/margarine	2 eggs
1 cup flour	1/2 cup brown sugar
2 tablespoons rolled oats	1/4 teaspoon baking powder
1/4 teaspoon salt	2 tablespoons flour
1 tablespoon milk	1/4 teaspoon salt
	1 cup chopped walnuts
	1/2 cup coconut
	1/2 teaspoon vanilla

Mix the ingredients in Layer I like pie crust and pat in a 12 x 9 or 11 x 8 pan. Bake at 350° for 12 to 15 minutes.

In the meanwhile, prepare Layer II by mixing together the eggs and sugar. Sift the baking powder, flour, and salt together and add. Then stir in nuts, coconut, vanilla. Spread on the baked crust, return to the oven, and bake another 20 minutes.

When cool, combine ingredients in Layer III (Light Butter Frosting, see the Appendix) and spread over the top. Cut in bars.

COCONUT LEMON BARS

Here is another bar cookie, based on the same principle, but with two layers. Prepare Layer I as above, adding 2 tablespoons sugar to the crust. Then prepare Layer II as follows:

2 eggs, beaten	1/2 cup chopped pecans
1 cup brown sugar	1 tablespoon lemon juice
1 cup coconut	1 teaspoon grated lemon rind

Mix the eggs and sugar, add the remaining ingredients, and spread over the pastry. Return to the oven and bake 30 minutes longer. Cool. Cut into bars.

COCONUT MACAROONS

No coconut cookie discussion could be complete without macaroons. They are so simple, so good, and an ideal way to use up egg whites.

1 1/3 cups flaked coconut	1/8 teaspoon salt
1/3 cup sugar	2 egg whites
2 tablespoons flour	1/2 teaspoon almond extract

Combine the coconut, sugar, flour, and salt in a bowl. Beat the egg whites until stiff and fold into the dry ingredients with the almond extract. Drop by teaspoonfuls onto a greased cookie sheet. Bake at 325° for 20 minutes or until edges are browned. Remove from the sheets at once. Makes about 18 cookies.

Other recipes using coconut: Carrot-Pineapple Cake (Carrots); Cereal Date Balls (Cereals); Snacking Cake (Cottage Cheese); Twelfth-Day Pancakes (Eggnog); Almond Snowcap Cookies, Corn Flake Macaroons (Egg Whites); Granola; Graham Cracker Cake (Pineapple); Festive Raisin Squares, Energy Fruit Bars (Raisins); Ricotta Bonbons; Tropical Coffee Cake (Yogurt).

Coffee

I am one of those rare individuals who does not drink coffee. Not at all. I like the smell of hot coffee but not the taste. However, I do have a few recipes for leftover coffee, tried out by those around me who love the stuff. Please understand that descriptions will be minimal.

RUM ICED COFFEE

1 cup cold coffee
crushed ice
1 jigger rum

1 slice lemon
powdered sugar

Combine the coffee, ice, and rum in a tall glass. Float the lemon on top. Dust with powdered sugar. Serves 1.

COFFEE JELLY

A wonderful way—and probably the easiest—to use the coffee left over from a dinner party. Serve with whipped cream and crisp wafer cookies.

1 envelope plain gelatin
3 tablespoons sugar

2 cups strong coffee, very hot

Dissolve the gelatin in a small amount of cold water. Mix in the sugar, then stir in the hot coffee until the gelatin dissolves. Mold and chill thoroughly before serving. Serves 4.

Variations:
Sherry: Use only 1 1/2 cups coffee. After gelatin is dissolved, add 1/2 cup sherry.
Brandy: Use slightly less than 2 cups coffee, and after the gelatin is dissolved, stir in 2 tablespoons brandy.

COFFEE CUSTARD

1 cup strong coffee
1 cup rich milk
4 tablespoons sugar

1/8 teaspoon salt
2 eggs, beaten

Combine all the ingredients except the eggs and scald; pour over the eggs and beat until well blended. Pour into individual molds, place them in a pan of hot water, and bake at 325° for about 1 hour, or until the custard is set.

To make a mocha custard, increase the sugar by 1 tablespoon and stir in 1 square bitter chocolate (grated) into the scalded mixture.

MOLASSES COOKIES

These are dark, spicy, soft, and much beloved in my family.

1/2 cup butter/margarine	1/4 teaspoon cloves
1/2 cup brown sugar	1/4 teaspoon salt
1 egg	1 1/2 teaspoons baking powder
1/2 cup molasses	1/4 teaspoon baking soda
1 1/2 cups flour	1/2 teaspoon vinegar
1 teaspoon ginger	1/4 cup strong coffee
1 teaspoon cinnamon	

Cream the shortening and sugar until light and fluffy. Beat in the egg and molasses. Sift the dry ingredients and add alternately with the combination of vinegar and coffee. Beat the batter after each addition. Drop by teaspoonsful onto a cookie sheet. Flatten the dough with a spatula dipped in cold water. Bake at 350° about 10 minutes. Makes about 30 medium cookies.

COFFEE FUDGE

2 cups sugar	1/4 teaspoon cream of tartar
1 cup strong coffee	1/8 teaspoon salt
1 tablespoon cream	1/2 teaspoon cinnamon
1 tablespoon butter	1 cup broken nuts

Combine all the ingredients except the cinnamon and nuts in a sauce pan. Stir over low heat until the sugar is dissolved. Then boil quickly, stirring constantly, to the soft ball stage (236°). Remove from the fire and cool slightly. Stir in the cinnamon and beat until the fudge begins to harden. Add the nuts (walnuts or pecans are good, hickory nuts are the best). Pour the candy into a well-oiled 8-inch square pan. Permit it to cool and then cut it into squares or bars. Makes about 1 1/2 pounds.

Other recipes using coffee: The Honey Cake (under Tea) can be made with coffee.

Corn

There are two essential rules for cooking fresh corn. The first is to cook it as soon as possible after it has been picked. The second is to cook it very little. Heat a large pot of water, until it reaches a rolling boil. Drop in the ears of corn, partly cover the pot, keep it boiling, and cook no more than five minutes from the time you add the corn. If the corn is young, four minutes is plenty. Leftover corn can be cut off the cob and combined with other vegetables; you may want to add a little rich milk and butter.

CURRIED CREAM OF CORN SOUP

Serve this with hot buttered muffins and a fruit dessert for a light Sunday supper or luncheon.

6 large ears of corn	1/2 teaspoon salt
1 medium onion, chopped	1/4 teaspoon pepper
2 tablespoons butter	3 1/2 cups chicken stock or broth
1/2 teaspoon curry	1/4 cup cream
1 1/2 tablespoons flour	

Scrape the corn from the cobs; there should be about 3 cups. Set aside.

Sauté the onion in the butter in a large saucepan until tender. Stir in the curry, flour, salt, and pepper; cook, stirring constantly, for 1 minute. Add the chicken stock, bring to a boil, and stir until smooth and slightly thickened.

Add the corn, lower the heat, and cook, covered, about 5 minutes. Cool slightly and purée in the blender. Return the soup to the saucepan, bring to a boil, and stir in the cream. Serves 6.

Variation: Omit the curry (if you want) and the cream. Add 3/4 cups chopped celery (sauté with the onion) and stir in just before serving 6 slices bacon, fried crisp and crumbled.

CORN-CHEESE CASSEROLE

This is an excellent side dish especially good with ham and chicken.

3 tablespoons margarine, divided   1/4 teaspoon pepper
2 tablespoons finely chopped onion   1 cup shredded Swiss cheese,
3 cups fresh-cut corn   divided
1/2 teaspoon salt   1/2 cup evaporated milk *or*
                                            light cream

Dot the bottom of a shallow 1 1/2-quart baking dish with 1 1/2 tablespoons margarine. Combine the corn, onion, salt, and pepper with 1/2 cup cheese and pour into the baking dish. Top with the remaining cheese, then dot with 1 1/2 tablespoons margarine. Drizzle with the evaporated milk. Bake at 350° for 25 minutes. Serves 6.

CORN PUDDING

A light, delicate version of a very popular Southern dish.

6 large ears of corn   1 teaspoon salt
1 1/2 cups light cream   1/4 teaspoon pepper
3 eggs

Scrape the corn from the cobs (there should be about 3 cups). Place 2 cups of corn in the blender, add 1/4 cup cream. Cover and whirl until smooth. Add the eggs, one at a time, the remaining cream, salt, and pepper. Continue to blend until the mixture is smooth.

Pour into a 1 1/2-quart shallow baking dish. Stir in the remaining corn. Place the dish in a pan of boiling water and bake at 350° for about 50 minutes, or until set. Serves 6.

☆☆☆ CALABACITAS

I do not know what the name means. This is a Southwest American Indian dish and an exceptionally good one. I know people who have tried to add herbs to it. My advice is don't do it. It is splendid as is.

3 ears of cooked corn
1 onion, sliced
1 clove garlic, minced

1 medium zucchini, in 1/4-inch slices
2 tomatoes, peeled and cut fine
1/2 cup grated or cubed cheese

Cut the corn off the cob. Combine with the onion, garlic, and a little water in a saucepan, cover, and cook 5 minutes. Add the zucchini (or summer squash, if you like) and cook another 10 minutes. Then stir in the tomatoes and cook until they are warm but not mushy. Fold in the cheese (cheddar is excellent). Toss lightly and serve. Serves 4 to 6. You can vary the amounts of the vegetables according to your taste and what you have handy.

CORN FRITTERS

And, finally, one of the great treats to make with leftover corn. Serve these hot with lots of butter and maple syrup, or as a side dish with a mushroom, cheese, or tomato sauce.

1 cup mashed cooked corn
2 eggs
6 tablespoons flour

1/2 teaspoon baking powder
1/8 teaspoon nutmeg
dash of salt

Make sure the corn is well drained before you measure it. Beat the eggs well and add the remaining ingredients. Fold in the corn last. Cook in a heated skillet as you would pancakes. Makes about 16 fritters. If you like, you can beat the egg whites separately and fold them in last. This makes a lighter fritter.

Other recipes using corn: Ham and Corn Quiche (Ham); Leipziger Allerei (Lima Beans); Stuffed Zucchini.

Cottage Cheese

You can cook with cottage cheese when it gets old, just so long as it is not bitter. Treat it as you would any cheese—that is, scrape off the edges, and carry on.

WHOLE WHEAT AND COTTAGE CHEESE ROLLS

These rolls are dark and moist, ideal with Swiss cheese.

3 cups whole wheat flour, divided	1/4 cup honey
1 tablespoon yeast	2 tablespoons margarine
1/2 teaspoon baking soda	2 teaspoons salt
1 1/2 cups cottage cheese	2 eggs
1/3 cup water	3/4 to 1 cup all-purpose flour

Stir together 1 1/2 cups of the whole wheat flour, the yeast, and soda. Heat together the cottage cheese, water, honey, margarine, and salt (just enough to melt the margarine). Add to the dry mixture, stir well; then add the eggs. Beat at low speed 1/2 minute, scraping the bowl. Beat 3 minutes at high speed. Then stir in the remaining whole wheat flour and most of the all-purpose flour to make a stiff dough. Knead, adding more flour if necessary, until smooth. Let rise until double. Shape into 24 rolls, and place in greased muffin tins. Let rise. Bake at 375° for 12 to 15 minutes.

DILL CASSEROLE BREAD

I am not overly fond of batter breads; the dough is usually too sticky to handle with ease and the baked bread dries out rather quickly. But this bread, which is a classic, is crusty and tasty; slice off wedges from the warm loaf at your next luncheon or supper, and everyone will be pleased.

2 1/2 to 3 cups flour, divided	1 package dry yeast
1 tablespoon sugar	1 cup creamed cottage cheese
1/4 finely chopped onion	1/4 cup water
or 1 tablespoon instant minced	1 tablespoon margarine
2 teaspoons dill	1 egg
1 teaspoon salt	butter, softened
1/4 teaspoon baking soda	

In a large bowl, combine 1 cup of the flour, the sugar, onion, dill seed, salt, soda, and yeast. Heat the cottage cheese, water, and margarine until the mixture is warm. Add to the flour mixture, stir well; then add the egg. Beat three minutes at medium speed. By hand, stir in the remaining flour to form a stiff dough. Cover; let rise in a warm place until doubled in size, about 1 hour.

Stir down the dough. Turn into a well-greased 8-inch round (1 1/2 or 2-quart) casserole. Let rise until light, 30 to 45 minutes. Bake at 350° for 35 to 40 minutes until golden brown. Brush with butter and sprinkle with coarse salt, if desired.

Variation: You can make a quick breakfast bread with this recipe, by omitting the onion and dill, increasing the sugar to 2 tablespoons. You can also substitute 1 cup rolled oats for 1 cup of the flour.

SUNFLOWER COTTAGE CHEESE CRISPS

Try passing these at your next cocktail party or with the soup.

1 cup flour	1 cup cottage cheese (small curd)
1/4 teaspoon salt	1/4 cup sunflower seeds
1/4 cup margarine	

Stir together the flour and salt in a mixer bowl. Cut in the margarine until fine. Beat in the cottage cheese until smooth, then stir in the sunflower seeds. Divide dough in half and roll each half in a 16 x 12 rectangle. Cut in 2-inch squares. Prick each with a fork. Bake at 350° for 12 to 15 minutes, or until lightly browned.

HOLIDAY LATKES

A traditional Jewish pancake. If you don't have matzo meal, use dry bread crumbs and reduce the salt to 1/4 teaspoon.

3 eggs
1 cup milk
1 cup cottage cheese
1 cup matzo meal

1 tablespoon sugar
1/2 teaspoon salt
1/2 teaspoon cinnamon

Beat the eggs with the milk and stir in the cottage cheese. Mix the matzo meal with the sugar, salt, and cinnamon; add to the egg mixture and beat.

Drop by tablespoons on a greased griddle. Brown, turning once. Serve hot with sour cream, applesauce, or sugar. Makes about 24.

TUNA ROMANOFF

This casserole is elegant enough for party fare. Try serving it with lightly cooked green peas.

1 cup cottage cheese
1 cup dairy sour cream
1/4 teaspoon salt
1 can tuna (6 1/2 ounces)
8 ounces egg noodles, cooked and
   drained

1/4 ounce can mushrooms,
   undrained
1/2 cup bread crumbs
2 tablespoons wheat germ
3 tablespoons minced onion
2 teaspoons worcestershire sauce
1/2 cup sliced ripe olives
butter

Mix all ingredients together except the bread crumbs, wheat germ, and butter. Turn into a greased 13 x 9 baking pan. Combine the crumbs and wheat germ and sprinkle over the top. Dot with butter. Bake at 350° about 30 minutes. Serves 6 to 8.

BEEF CASSEROLE

Unlike other beef-pasta dishes in this book (see Johnny Margetti under Tomatoes and the beef casserole under Ricotta), this contains no tomatoes. It has somewhat of a stroganoff effect, and is best with ground leftover roast beef.

2 cups egg noodles *or*
   spinach noodles
1 cup ground beef
1 1/2 cups cottage cheese
1 cup dairy sour cream

1/4 cup chopped onion
1/4 cup chopped parsley
1/2 teaspoon worcestershire sauce
1/3 cup corn flake crumbs
1/2 cup grated cheddar

Cook the noodles about 5 minutes, drain. Combine all ingredients except the crumbs and cheese and toss lightly to blend. Turn into a 1 1/2-quart casserole. Combine the crumbs and cheese and sprinkle over the top. Bake 30 minutes at 350°. Let stand 10 minutes before serving. Serves 4 to 6.

COTTAGE CHEESE POTATOES

You can serve this as a side dish (excellent with baked ham) or as a main dish for luncheon or supper with a mixed green salad.

2 cups diced cooked potatoes
1 1/2 cups cottage cheese

6 slices bacon, crisp and crumbled
buttered bread crumbs

In a greased casserole, place alternate layers of potatoes, cottage cheese, and crumbled bacon. Cover with lots of bread crumbs mixed with melted butter. Bake at 350° about 30 minutes or until brown and bubbly. Serves 4.

◆

HONEY CREAM DRESSING

Just lovely on fruit salads of all kinds. This is so easy that it takes more time to describe than to make.

1 cup cottage cheese
1/4 cup finely chopped pecans
4 tablespoons light cream *or* milk

1 tablespoon honey
1/4 teaspoon allspice

Press the cottage cheese through a sieve into a small bowl; stir in the remaining ingredients. Cover; chill. Stir again just before serving. You can also combine everything (except the nuts) in the blender, which makes a smoother dressing. But remember you have to get it out of the blender. Makes 1 1/4 cups.

ORANGE-PINEAPPLE SALAD

The possibilities of fruit, gelatin, and cottage cheese blended in a molded salad are almost infinite. The following is a model, from which you can fashion your own special version.

1 6-ounce package orange gelatin	1 cup water
1 can (11 ounces) mandarin oranges	1 cup buttermilk
1 can (13 1/4 ounces) pineapple	2 cups small curd cottage cheese
tidbits	walnut or pecan halves

Put gelatin in a mixing bowl (if you use plain gelatin, use two packages and orange juice instead of water). Drain the syrup from the two fruits and measure 1 cup. Combine it with 1 cup water in a saucepan and bring to a boil. Pour over the gelatin and stir until dissolved. Then stir in the buttermilk and cottage cheese. Chill until partially set; fold in the drained fruit. Pour into a mold and chill until completely set. Unmold on a bed of salad greens and serve with your favorite dressing (or mine; see Boiled Dressing in the Appendix). Or try the Honey Cream Dressing above. As I said, you can vary this recipe to suit your taste. It is very good with canned bing cherries, for example. Or try cranberry sauce and canned pineapple. Have fun.

◆

☆☆☆ SNACKING CAKE

I am happy to make this cake very often. It is nutritious and uncomplicated; it goes very well on a picnic, or neatly into the lunch bag. Try serving it with ice cream or yogurt and a hot cherry sauce. By the way, I always make it with carob and coconut.

1/2 cup butter/margarine	1/2 cup cocoa *or* carob powder
1 cup honey	1 teaspoon baking soda
1 cup cottage cheese	1 teaspoon baking powder
2 eggs	1 cup rolled oats
1 teaspoon almond extract	1/2 cup coconut *or* chopped nuts
1 1/2 cups flour	*or* chopped seeds

Cream the butter/margarine with the honey, using an electric mixer. Beat in the cottage cheese. Add the eggs, one at a time, beating well. Stir in the almond extract.

Combine the dry ingredients and gradually add them to the creamed mixture, blending well. Stir in the coconut, nuts, or seeds.

Bake in a greased 11 x 9 (or 13 x 9) pan at 350° for 35 to 40 minutes. Cool and cut into squares.

SKINNY CHEESE CAKE

This is an authentic dieters' dessert. If you dare, add a cookie or graham cracker crumb crust.

1 tablespoon plain gelatin	2 1/2 cups cottage cheese
2 tablespoons lemon juice	2 eggs, separated
1/2 cup hot skim milk	1 cup crushed ice
2 tablespoons sugar	1 teaspoon grated lemon peel

Dissolve the gelatin in the lemon juice; then add the hot milk. Put in the blender with the sugar, cottage cheese, and egg yolks. Blend at high speed for 2 minutes. Add the crushed ice and continue running at high speed until completely blended. Beat the egg whites until stiff, then fold them into the cheese mixture. Add the peel. Pour into an 8-inch mold. Chill until firm, about 24 hours. Serve with any kind of fresh or puréed fruit.

Other recipes using cottage cheese: Broccoli-Noodle Bake (Broccoli); Chicken and Noodle Divan (Chicken); Peaches and Cream Cheesecake (Cream Cheese); Eggplant Bake; Yogurt-Cottage Cheese Spread (Parsley); Hungarian Noodles and Peas, P and P Casserole (Peas); Ham and Potato Salad (Potatoes); summer squash recipes; squash stuffing 4; Tuna-Noodle Casserole and its variation (Tuna); Rice Casserole Italiano, Zucchini and Cottage Cheese Bread (Zucchini).

Cranberries

I *never* have enough cranberries. After the holiday season, watch for cranberries that have been marked down because they are a bit old. Freeze them right away, then pick them over when you want to cook them. They are easier to sort when they are still frozen.

I keep a steady supply of homemade cranberry sauce in my refrigerator. I enjoy mixing the cranberries with other fruits.

My cranberry sauce is tart, simple to make, and not very saucy. Take 2 cups of cranberries, fresh or frozen, put them in a saucepan with 2 tablespoons water and 2/3 cup sugar. Stir everything together, and cook over medium heat for about 5 minutes, or until the sauce bubbles and the berries pop open. At this point you can stir in a little Cointreau or Grand Marnier, and serve the sauce over vanilla ice cream. Or just cool it and store in the refrigerator where it will keep at least a week.

☆☆☆ ALMOND CRANBERRY SAUCE

This recipe is superb. The finished product is beautiful to look at and has a wonderfully tart flavor. It has one disadvantage: it does not mold well. But no matter, just serve it in a pretty glass dish with a pretty spoon and watch it disappear.

1/3 cup blanched whole almonds	1 pound (4 cups) raw cranberries
2 cups sugar	1/2 cup apricot jam
1/2 cup water	1/4 cup lemon juice

Place the almonds in a 350° oven for 5 minutes, then slice into halves, or smaller slices, with a paring knife. Put aside.

Combine the sugar and water in a large saucepan; bring to a boil without stirring and cook 5 minutes. Wash and sort the cranberries (if you use frozen berries, make sure they are defrosted, otherwise they congeal the syrup); add to the syrup and cook 5 minutes more.

Remove from the heat and stir in the spricot jam (or, if you haven't got any, use orange marmalade—apricot jam, however, is better) and the lemon juice. Chill partly, then fold in the almonds. Chill thoroughly. Serves 8 to 10. You can double this recipe (be sure your pan is big enough) or cut it in half, with no problem.

CRANBERRY RELISH

Extremely simple and a wonderful activity for those energetic and excited children who are always in the kitchen at holiday time. If you happen to have some of this left over, you can make it into a very unusual and delicious cake (see Orange-Cranberry Cake, under Granola).

1 pound (4 cups) raw cranberries	1 large orange
2 apples	2 cups (or less) sugar

Wash and sort the cranberries. Do not peel the apples or orange; just remove the core and seeds. Grind the fruit together in a meat grinder, using a medium to coarse blade. Stir in the sugar, but start with only 1 1/2 cups; if the apples are sweet, that may be plenty. Just taste and see. Fill into a quart jar and store in your refrigerator. This will keep for several months.

☆☆☆ CRANBERRY-STRAWBERRY JAM

I make this jam every year. It is unusually simple. And it is, as far as I know, fool-proof. Try it on some warm cornbread. This rule calls for commercial frozen strawberries. If you have some of your own, do use them for the result will taste much better. You may want to change the amount of sugar, however.

2 cups fresh ground cranberries	5 cups sugar
2 10-ounce packages frozen sliced	1/2 bottle pectin *or*
strawberries, thawed	1 box Sure-Jell

Prepare the cranberries, mix with the strawberries, and add the sugar. Heat to boiling. Boil 1 minute, stirring constantly. Remove and stir in the pectin. Stir occasionally until cooled slightly. Put in sterilized jars and seal with paraffin.

CRANBERRY BUTTER

4 cups fresh or frozen cranberries	1/2 cup packed light brown sugar
1 1/2 cups water	grated rind and juice of 1 orange
2 cups sugar	

Pick over the berries, rinse, bring to a boil with the water in a heavy 3-quart saucepan, and cook until the berries burst (about 10 minutes). Whirl in a blender until smooth, or put through a food mill. Return to the pan and stir in the sugars, orange rind and juice. Bring to a boil and simmer, stirring frequently, about 40 minutes, or until the mixture is of spreading consistency. Be sure to stir often enough, as it will stick and burn if you don't. Pour at once into hot sterilized jars. You can seal at once and process the jars in a boiling-water bath for 10 minutes. Or seal at once with paraffin. Serve as a spread for toast, bread, or waffles, or as accompaniment to meat or poultry.

———————◆———————

MOLDED FRUIT SALAD

1 ounce unflavored gelatin   1/2 cup diced chopped apples
1/4 cup boiling water   (don't peel)
3/4 cup pineapple juice   1/3 cup coarsely chopped walnuts
1 cup whole cranberry sauce (*or*   1/2 cup diced celery (optional)
   1 8-ounce can whole berry sauce)

Dissolve the gelatin in the water. Add the pineapple juice and the cranberry sauce and mix well. Chill until slightly thickened. Stir in the remaining ingredients and pour into a 4-cup mold. Chill until firm. This recipe makes 3 1/2 cups or 10 relish servings.

☆☆☆ MY FAVORITE FRUIT SALAD

I have put this recipe under cranberries, because I feel that the homemade cranberry sauce is an essential ingredient. Everything else you can vary. I am a great salad eater, and next to mixed green salad, I eat this salad the most often. Arrange on a bed of lettuce any combination of the following: sliced tart apple, red emperor grapes (cut in half and seeds removed), sliced strawberries, peach wedges, orange wedges, pear slices, blueberries, raspberries, bananas. My favorite combination is half a pear sliced, red emperor grapes, and, of course, the cranberry sauce. Over this you pour a dressing made with equal amounts of Boiled Dressing (see the Appendis), and plain yogurt, mixed with lots of poppy seeds. Over this you sprinkle some homemade granola. A veritable feast.

---◆---

CRANBERRY MUFFINS

The cornmeal makes these muffins different in texture. Although the recipe doesn't say so, I feel it is a good idea to chop the cranberries coarsely. Measure them first.

1 3/4 cups flour   3 eggs, slightly beaten
1 1/2 cups cornmeal   1 1/2 cups milk
3 tablespoons sugar   1/3 cup oil
6 teaspoons baking powder   1 1/2 cups cranberries
1/2 teaspoon salt

Combine the dry ingredients in a large bowl. Mix the eggs, milk, and oil in another bowl, then pour them over the dry ingredients. Combine with a few, quick strokes. Do not overmix. Stir in the cranberries.

Fill well-greased muffin cups 2/3 full. Bake at 425° for 15 to 20 minutes, or until nicely browned. Remove from pans and serve warm. Makes about 20 large muffins.

CRANBERRY ORANGE NUT BREAD

This recipe is a classic. Be sure your loaves are very well cooled before you slice them.

2 cups flour	1 orange
1 cup sugar	2 tablespoons melted margarine
1 1/2 teaspoons baking powder	1 beaten egg
1/2 teaspoon salt	1 cup chopped walnuts
1/2 teaspoon baking soda	2 cups cranberries, halved

Mix together the dry ingredients in a large bowl; set aside. Take the seeds and some of the pulp out of the orange, then grind it in a grinder. Combine this with the margarine and enough water (or orange juice) to make 3/4 cup; stir in the egg. Pour the liquid into the dry ingredients. Stir to mix; add the nuts and cranberries. Spoon into one 9 x 5 loaf pan, or two 7 1/2 x 3 1/2 pans. Run a groove down the middle of the loaf with a spoon. Bake at 350° 50 to 60 minutes for the large loaf, 45 minutes for the smaller loaves.

Variation:

Whole Wheat: Substitute 1 cup whole wheat flour and 1/2 cup wheat germ for 1 1/2 cups of the all-purpose flour. Use 3/4 cup brown sugar instead of the white.

———————◆———————

You can add cranberries to your fruit pies, they are especially good with apples, pears, and strawberries. Because they are sour, however, you may want to add more sugar.

☆☆☆ CRANBERRY APPLE CRISP

• Bottom •	• Topping •
1 1/2 cups cranberries	1 cup rolled oats
2 cups sliced apples	1/4 cup brown sugar
1/4 to 1/2 cup brown sugar	1/3 cup flour
1 teaspoon cinnamon	1/4 teaspoon salt
	3 tablespoons melted shortening

Combine the bottom layer in a 9-inch square pan, or a 1-quart round baking dish. If the apples are bland, use less sugar and sprinkle generously with lemon juice. Combine the topping and mix until crumbly. Sprinkle over the top of the fruit mixture. Bake at 350° for 45 minutes. Serve warm with yogurt, cream, or vanilla ice cream.

CRANBERRY UPSIDE-DOWN CAKE

• Bottom Layer •	• Top Layer •
3 tablespoons butter, melted	4 tablespoons butter/margarine
3/4 cup packed brown sugar	1/2 cup sugar
2 cups cranberries	1 egg, beaten
	1 1/2 cups flour
	2 teaspoons baking powder
	1/2 teaspoon salt
	1/2 cup milk
	1 teaspoon vanilla

In an 8-inch square baking dish mix the bottom layer and spread it evenly. Cream the butter/margarine, add the sugar and egg, and blend well. Sift the dry ingredients; add to the butter mixture, alternately with the milk and vanilla. Pour over the top of the cranberry mixture. Bake at 350° 40 to 50 minutes. Turn upside down immediately, and cut in squares. Serve warm.

Other recipes using cranberries: Paradise Jelly (Apples); Chicken Cranberry à l'Orientale; Marmalade Tea Loaf (Jams, Jellies, Marmalades).

Cream Cheese

I keep very little cream cheese around. When I do buy it though, somehow (like many luxuries) I save it for some special occasion, which doesn't come, and so it gets somewhat tired. Here are a few special treats using the tired cream cheese.

☆☆☆ GERMAN CREAM CHEESE BROWNIES

We might as well start with the best. You can substitute farmers cheese for cream cheese in the following recipes. The result is lower in calories, almost the same in taste, slightly less smooth in texture.

4 ounces German sweet chocolate
   or 1/2 cup semi-sweet chocolate
   bits
	3 eggs, divided
	1/2 cup plus 1 tablespoon flour
	1 1/2 teaspoons vanilla, divided

5 tablespoons butter/margarine, divided	1/2 teaspoon baking powder 1/4 teaspoon salt
1 package (3 ounces) cream cheese	1/2 cup chopped pecans
1 cup sugar, divided	1/4 teaspoon almond extract

Melt the chocolate and 3 tablespoons butter over very low heat, stirring constantly. Cool and set aside.

Cream the remaining butter with the cream cheese until softened. Gradually add 1/4 cup sugar, creaming until light and fluffy. Beat in 1 egg, 1 tablespoon flour, and 1/2 teaspoon vanilla until blended. Set aside.

Beat remaining eggs until light in color. Gradually add remaining 3/4 cup sugar, beating until thickened. Fold in the baking powder, salt, and remaining 1/2 cup flour. Then blend in the cooled chocolate mixture. Stir in the nuts, almond extract, and remaining teaspoon vanilla.

Measure 1 cup of this batter and set aside. Spread the remaining in a greased 9-inch square pan. Pour the cream cheese mixture over the top. Drop reserved chocolate mixture by tablespoonsful onto the cheese mixture, and swirl the two together with a spatula to marbelize.

Bake at 350° for 35 to 40 minutes. Cool. Cut in bars or squares. Cover and store in the refrigerator.

Note: You can use walnuts or almonds instead of the pecans, but personally I prefer the pecans.

CHEESECAKE SQUARES

If you don't want to make an entire cheesecake, here is an alternative, and a simple and delicious one at that. These layered squares are perfect for a fancy tea party or for a special dessert.

• Crust •	• Filling •
1/4 cup (1/2 stick) butter	8 ounces cream cheese
1/3 cup brown sugar	1/4 cup sugar
1 cup flour	1 egg
1/2 cup finely chopped pecans	2 tablespoons milk
	2 tablespoons lemon juice
1/4 cup currant jelly	1/2 teaspoon vanilla
	grated lemon peel (optional)

Cream the butter, add the brown sugar and flour. Blend until crumbly, then stir in the nuts. Reserve 3/4 cup for topping. Press the remainder in the bottom of an 8-inch square pan. Bake at 350° for 15 minutes. Cool slightly and spread the currant jelly over crust.

To make the filling, beat together the cream cheese and sugar. Then beat in the remaining ingredients. Pour this over the crust and sprinkle with the reserved crumb mixture. Bake at 350° for 30 minutes. Cool, then cut into squares.

☆☆☆ PEACHES AND CREAM CAKE

This is not one of your velvet-smooth cheesecakes, but actually I like the texture better. This takes a while to make, but when fresh peaches are in season, I don't know of a better dessert.

• Crust •	• Glaze •
1/4 cup butter/margarine	1 cup orange juice
2 cups rolled oats	1 teaspoon lemon juice
2/3 cup brown sugar	1 tablespoon cornstarch
	1/4 cup sugar
• Filling •	
11 ounces cream *or* farmers cheese	2 cups sliced peaches
3/4 cup creamed cottage cheese	grated nutmeg
3/4 cup sugar	
3 eggs	
1 teaspoon vanilla	
1 teaspoon lemon juice	

To make the crust combine the ingredients until crumbly. Press firmly in a 9-inch spring form pan or a 10 x 8 rectangular pan (if you like a somewhat flatter cake); press the crust up the sides of the pan. Bake at 350° about 10 minutes. Cool while preparing the filling.

Beat the cream cheese and cottage cheese at high speed until smooth. Add the sugar gradually, then the eggs, one at a time. Add vanilla and lemon juice. Pour into the prepared crust. Bake at 350° for 35 to 40 minutes, or until firm.

In the meanwhile make the glaze by combining everything in a small saucepan. Bring to a boil, stirring, and cook until thick and clear. Cool. Arrange the sliced peaches over the cooled cheesecake and pour the glaze over the peaches. Sprinkle lightly with nutmeg, freshly grated if possible. Chill thoroughly before serving.

CREAM CHEESE PIE

This makes a mild, smooth pie, which you can serve with a cherry or blueberry topping, or with fresh or stewed fruit.

9-inch graham cracker crust	**1 teaspoon vanilla, divided**
8 ounces cream cheese	**1 pint dairy sour cream**
2 eggs	**1/8 teaspoon cinnamon (optional)**
3/4 cup sugar, divided	

Prepare and bake the crust (see the Appendix).

Have the cheese and eggs at room temperature. Cream the cheese well, gradually beat in 1/2 cup sugar. Beat the eggs and add them with 1/2 teaspoon vanilla; beat well.

Pour into the prepared crust and bake at 325° for 20 minutes or until firm. Mix the sour cream with 1/2 teaspoon vanilla and 1/4 cup sugar, spread it on the pie, and return to the oven for 5 minutes. Sprinkle with cinnamon, if desired. Cool and chill thoroughly before serving.

CREAM CHEESE FROSTING

This is the standard frosting for carrot cakes, banana cakes, or any bar cookies for which you want a special topping.

3 ounces cream cheese	**2 teaspoons honey, molasses, or**
1 1/2 cups sifted 10X sugar	**maple syrup**

Beat the cream cheese until fluffy. Add the sugar alternately with the honey. If you prefer, use all honey, beating it in a little at a time until you have the right spreading consistency.

Other recipes using cream cheese: Pumpkin Cheese Cake; Mushroom-Stuffed Tomatoes (Tomatoes).

Cucumbers

It is perfectly amazing what one small cucumber plant will produce in the growing season. Many of us end up, almost without realizing it, with tons of cucumbers. My father, who was a Southerner, loved them served very cold with vinegar and a bit of oil. Nothing could be simpler. Of course, cucumbers make a tasty, colorful, and crisp addition to any tossed green salad, and they are an essential ingredient in gazpacho.

CUCUMBERS IN YOGURT

This is a traditional way of serving cucumbers, of Middle-Eastern origin. After all, it is in the Middle East that one gets the best yogurt.

1 clove garlic	2 cups yogurt
1/2 teaspoon salt	3 cucumbers
	pinch of dried mint

Mash the garlic with the salt in the bottom of a bowl. Mix in the yogurt. Peel the cucumbers, slice them thinly, and fold them into the yogurt. Transfer to a clean bowl and chill thoroughly. Just before serving, crumble the dried mint and sprinkle on top. (You can dry your own mint by spreading the leaves on a plate and leaving them several days in a dry place. When they are crisp, store in an airtight jar.)

HUNGARIAN CUCUMBER SALAD

A more elaborate (and more colorful) version of the above. Both recipes are pleasantly low in calories.

3 small cucumbers	1 cup yogurt
2 green peppers	1 teaspoon poppy or sesame seeds
2 medium tomatoes	1/2 teaspoon salt
	1/2 teaspoon paprika

Peel the cucumbers only if the skin is tough or waxed. Slice them and the peppers. Cut the tomatoes into wedges. Place all the vegetables in a salad bowl. Blend the yogurt with the seeds and seasonings and mix into the vegetables. Chill thoroughly before serving. Serves 6.

CUCUMBER-LEMON MOLDED SALAD

1 package unflavored gelatin	1 cup cubed cucumbers
juice of 2 lemons	1/2 cup cashews
1 cup unsweetened fruit juice	
(pineapple, grapefruit)	

Soften the gelatin in the lemon juice. Heat the fruit juice and stir in the gelatin mixture until dissolved. Cool to lukewarm. Add the remaining ingredients, mold, and chill until completely set. Unmold on fresh salad greens, the darker the prettier. Serves 4 to 6.

CUCUMBER-BEAN SALAD

This is a much more robust salad than the previous one. It is wonderfully colorful on a bed of greens.

1 cup dry kidney beans	1/4 teaspoon salt
1 green pepper	1 teaspoon honey
1/2 cup chopped green onions	1 teaspoon worcestershire sauce
1 teaspoon crushed garlic	1 tablespoon catsup
1/2 cup olive oil	2 tablespoons chopped fresh parsley
1/4 cup wine vinegar	1 cup yogurt
1/8 teaspoon paprika	1/4 cup instant dried milk

Cook and drain the kidney beans. Chop the green pepper (you should have about 3/4 cup); add it to the onions and garlic, and mix it all with the beans.

Make a dressing of the oil, vinegar, and all the remaining ingredients except the yogurt and dried milk. Pour this over the bean mixture and toss gently. Refrigerate for at least one hour.

Just before serving, whisk the dried milk into the yogurt and stir into the salad. Serves 6.

◆

CREAM OF CUCUMBER SOUP

This soup is smooth as velvet. It can be served either hot or cold. If served hot, try a garnish of chopped dill. If served cold, garnish with a small amount of grated lemon rind.

3 tablespoons butter	3 sprigs of parsley
2 tablespoons flour	1/4 cup chopped celery leaves
1 cup evaporated milk *or* light cream	1/4 cup chopped chives
1 cup chicken broth	2 cups peeled and coarsely chopped cucumbers

Make a cream sauce of the butter, flour, and milk. Stir constantly until smooth; boil 2 minutes. Stir in the chicken broth and cool somewhat.

Put the sauce in the blender with the remaining ingredients. Blend until smooth, at least 2 minutes. Season to taste with salt and pepper. Serves 4 to 6.

COLD CUCUMBER SOUP

1 cucumber	1 cup diced cooked chicken
1/2 cup sweet cider	1/2 teaspoon salt
1/2 cup sour cream	2 sprigs fresh dill, chopped finely
1/2 cup evaporated milk *or* cream	chopped chives

Peel the cucumber, remove the seeds, and dice. Purée the cucumber with the cider in the blender.

Mix all ingredients together (except the chives). Chill.

Serve in chilled soup cups and garnish with the chives. Serves 4 to 6.

————————◆————————

Although we generally think of cucumbers for salads and soups, they can be served as a hot vegetable. Here are two quick and easy ideas.

(1) Peel and slice cucumbers into a pan of boiling salted water. Reduce the heat and simmer about 5 minutes. Drain and garnish with sour cream and some herbs. Try chervil, dill, basil, or tarragon. Serve at once.

(2) Try cucumbers in a stir-fry. You can combine them with other vegetables, such as broccoli, cauliflower, celery. Or follow the rule under Cauliflower, using 2 medium-sized unpeeled cucumbers, 2 chopped green onions, and 1 minced garlic clove. Instead of stock, add 2 tablespoons soy sauce. Stir-fry about 5 minutes.

BAKED CUCUMBERS MORNAY

6 medium cucumbers	1/2 teaspoon dill or basil
2 tablespoons wine vinegar	3 tablespoons minced green onions
1 teaspoon salt	1/8 teaspoon pepper
1/4 teaspoon sugar	1 1/2 cups medium white sauce
3 tablespoons melted butter	3/4 cup shredded Swiss or parmesan cheese

Peel the cucumbers and halve them lengthwise. Scoop out the seeds with a small teaspoon and cut them in 1/4-inch strips. Toss in a bowl with the vinegar, salt, and sugar; chill about 1 hour to marinate. Drain.

Preheat oven to 375°. Put the cucumbers in a baking dish with butter, herbs, onions, and pepper. Be sure the dish is big enough to accommodate the cream sauce to be added later. Bake uncovered about 1 hour, turning two or three times. Color will remain green, and the texture crisp. Make the cream sauce and blend in the cheese (reserving 3 tablespoons for the top). Fold the sauce into the baked cucumbers, sprinkle with the reserved grated cheese, dot with butter. Return to the oven for about 10 minutes, then broil about 2 minutes until delicately browned. Serves 6.

————————◆————————

Here are three extremely simple ways to make dill pickles. They are the dieter's dream as the calories are negligible.

DILL PICKLES I

1 teaspoon garlic powder	2 quarts cider vinegar
1 teaspoon whole peppercorns	1 quart water
6 whole cloves	1 cup salt
1/2 cup whole dill seed	cucumbers (3 to 4 inches) for 4 quarts

Sterilize 4 quart jars. Combine all the ingredients except the cucumbers. Bring to a boil. Scrub the cucumbers, but do not peel. Fit them into the quart jars and cover with the boiling liquid. Seal.

DILL PICKLES II

Quantities on this are flexible; increase or decrease to suit your needs. Just keep the proportions correct.

cucumbers		4 quarts water
1/4 teaspoon alum	per	1 quart vinegar
3 dill heads	quart	3/4 cup salt
2 cloves garlic	jar	

Try to find cucumbers that are the length of the jar, and cut them in strips. Or use smaller cucumbers whole. Sterilize the jars. Put the alum, dill, and garlic into each jar. Mix the water, vinegar, and salt; boil 1 minute. Stuff the cucumbers into the jars, add the hot liquid, and seal.

Shake well to blend the ingredients. From time to time during the next day or so, shake the jars vigorously.

OVERNIGHT FRESH PICKLES

6 medium cucumbers (about 2 pounds)	1 1/2 cups sugar
	4 tablespoons mixed pickling spices
1 Bermuda onion	1 tablespoon salt
1 1/2 cups white vinegar	1/4 teaspoon cream of tartar

Cut each cucumber in half lengthwise; cut each half into 4 lengthwise strips. Slice the onion and separate into rings. Alternate layers of cucumbers and onion rings in a large glass or ceramic bowl.

Combine the vinegar, sugar, pickling spices, salt, and cream of tartar in a medium-size enamel saucepan. Heat, but do not boil, stirring with a wooden spoon, until the sugar is completely dissolved.

Pour this solution over the cucumber mixture; toss to coat. Cover with plastic wrap; refrigerate for 24 hours, tossing occasionally.

☆☆☆ DILL PICKLE BREAD

The recipe says you can use olive juice instead of pickle juice. Feel free, I have never tried it that way, but then I don't like olives. If you don't have any leftover pickle juice, use all stock or potato water.

2 tablespoons dry yeast	1 scant tablespoon salt
2 cups warm stock	3 cups rye flour
2 cups juice from pickles	3 cups whole wheat flour
3 tablespoons oil	1 cup wheat germ
1/3 cup honey	4 1/2 to 5 cups white flour

Dissolve the yeast in the warm stock; stir in the pickle juice, oil, honey, salt (use less salt if the juice is very salty, sometimes it is), rye flour, whole wheat flour, wheat germ. Add enough white flour to work the dough (you can use all whole wheat with no problems at all). Knead, adding more flour if necessary, until smooth and elastic. Let rise until double (about 2 hours); punch down, knead a minute or two.

Let the dough rest a few minutes, then shape it into 3 loaves. Place the loaves in loaf pans, let rise until double. Bake at 350° for about 45 minutes.

Note: You can also use dill pickle juice (about 1/4 cup) in your next pot roast.

Other recipes using cucumbers: Many salads; Middle East Beans in Pita (Legumes); Macaroni and Chicken Salad (Noodles); Gazpacho (Tomatoes).

Currants

Fresh

If you are so lucky to find large, ripe currants you can serve them plain. In Germany washed currants are served in a dish with a silver fork; you are also given another dish and a sugar bowl. You strip the currants from the stems with the fork, sugar them, and enjoy. After I have stemmed them, I prefer to add honey, let them stand for a while, and then serve them with whipped cream and sponge cake. Currants are also wonderful mixed with red (or black) raspberries (I froze some this year and used 2 cups sugar mixed with 7 to 8 cups combined fruit). Another dessert idea is *Rote Gruetze* (use 3 tablespoons cornstarch to 2 cups sweetened currant juice and follow the method described under Apricot Kisel).

CURRANT AND RASPBERRY JAM

I like many kinds of jam, but I like Currant and Raspberry the best of all. Please be careful and make sure it does not scorch on the bottom. I find that if the mixture gets too hot while cooking, just move it off the burner for a minute or two, stirring now and then. The general rule is stir and watch.

Combine 3 cups red raspberries and 2 cups stemmed currants—or half and half, if you like—in a large kettle. Crush some of the fruit and stir in between 3 and 4 cups sugar. Start with three, cook it up, taste, add more sugar if the jam is too tart. Stir and cook over low heat until the sugar is dissolved. Then boil the fruit rapidly, stirring frequently. Boil until a small amount of jam dropped on a plate will stay in place. With this mixture, it should take between 5 and 8 minutes. Pour into sterilized jars and seal with paraffin.

CURRANT JELLY

Of course you can make currant and raspberry jelly too, but somehow currant jelly is very aristocratic. Take the large stems off the currants, wash them, and place them in a kettle. Add a little water, 1 part water to 5 parts currants. Cook over low heat until the currants are soft and colorless. Drain them through a jelly bag. Then follow the directions under Black Raspberry Jelly, using about 3/4 cup sugar for each cupful of juice. Do not use more than 4 cups of juice at a time.

Consult also the section Jams, Jellies, Marmalades.

Dried Currants

For some strange reason dried currants are not nearly so popular for baking as are raisins. They are wonderful, though, and I suggest you try them in place of raisins in your next cookie batch. It is a good idea to plump them a little (just measure them in a cup, pour boiling water over, and let them stand a few minutes; then drain and add to the recipe). Also you can add currants to your Christmas breads or to white soda bread with delicious results. Here are three special recipes, where currants are essential.

HOT CROSS BUNS

1 package dry yeast	3 1/2 to 4 cups flour
1/3 cup warm water	1/2 teaspoon cinnamon
1/2 cup milk, scalded	3 beaten eggs
1/3 cup oil	2/3 cup currants
1/3 cup sugar	1 slightly beaten egg white
1/2 teaspoon salt	confectioners' sugar

Soften the yeast in the water. Combine the milk, oil, sugar, and salt; cool to lukewarm. Sift 1 cup of the flour with the cinnamon and stir into the milk mixture. Add the eggs and beat well. Stir in the yeast and currants. Add remaining flour and knead gently for several minutes. Cover and let rise until double (about 1 1/2 hours).

Punch down the dough. Roll or pat it out to 1/2-inch thickness on a lightly floured surface. Cut in rounds with a donut cutter, if you have one, or a glass about 3 inches in diameter. Shape into buns with your hands, and put them in muffin cups. Let rise until almost double (about 45 minutes). Brush tops with egg white. Bake at 375° about 12 minutes. Add confectioners' sugar (about 3/4 cup) to remaining egg white and use this as a frosting for piping crosses on the warm buns. Makes 3 dozen or more.

CURRANT SCONES

If you like oatmeal scones, substitute 1 cup rolled oats for 1 cup of the flour. Scones are the Scottish form of our biscuits.

2 cups flour	1 cup plumped currants
3 teaspoons baking powder	2 eggs, beaten (but reserve 1 table-
2 tablespoons sugar	spoon egg white for brushing
1/2 teaspoon salt	on top)
4 tablespoons butter	1/3 cup heavy cream
	sugar

In a bowl combine the flour, baking powder, 2 tablespoons sugar, and salt. Cut in the butter until the mixture resembles fine crumbs. Stir in the currants. Stir in the eggs and cream to make a stiff dough.

Turn out onto a lightly floured board and knead gently until dough sticks together. Divide into two parts. Roll each part out to make a circle about 6 inches in diameter and 1 inch thick. With a knife, cut each circle into sixths, making even wedges. Arrange on a baking sheet about 1 inch apart. Brush tops with reserved egg white and sprinkle with sugar.

Bake at 400° for 15 minutes or until golden brown. Serve immediately. Makes 1 dozen.

CURRANT CAKE

An English tradition with afternoon tea.

1 3/4 cups flour	1/2 teaspoon vanilla
1/2 teaspoon salt	1 cup sugar
2 teaspoons baking powder	2 eggs
1/3 cup butter/margarine	1/2 cup milk
	1 cup plumped currants

Sift the dry ingredients together. Cream the butter, add the vanilla, and beat the sugar in gradually. Beat in the eggs. Add the flour mixture alternately with the milk, starting and ending with the flour. Stir in the currants (if you want to make your cake very special, soak them in a little rum or brandy before you add them to the batter). Pour the cake into a 9-inch square baking pan. Bake at 350° for 30 to 35 minutes. Cool thoroughly before slicing.

Other recipes using currants: Any pound cake recipe is greatly enhanced by the addition of 1 cup dried currants; try Currant Drop Cookies (Egg Yolks).

Dates

You can cut dates fine and add them to fruit cakes, tea breads, bar and drop cookies. Try some in your hot cereal at breakfast. Also, a wonderful confection can be made by stuffing pitted dates with whole peanuts, or walnuts or pecan quarters, or crunchy peanut butter.

DATE-NUT BREAD

Here is a classic tea bread. This particular recipe has the advantages of being extremely easy to make and of containing almost no shortening. The batter is *very* liquid. Do not be bothered by this, the bread turns out dark and delicious. Give the school lunch a boost; make a date-nut bread sandwich spread with cream cheese or with peanut butter.

2 cups cut-up dates	2 1/2 cups white flour
2 cups water	1/2 cup whole wheat flour
2 eggs	2 teaspoons baking soda
1 tablespoon butter	pinch salt
1 teaspoon vanilla	1 cup broken nut meats
2 cups sugar	

Put the dates and water in a saucepan, bring to a boil. Remove from the heat and let cool some.

Beat the eggs, butter, vanilla, and sugar. Stir in the flours, soda, salt, and the date-water mixture, and the nuts (walnuts are best, I think). Pour the batter into two 9 x 5 loaf pans or four smaller loaf pans (7 1/2 x 3 1/2). Bake at 350° one hour for the larger loaves, about 50 minutes for the smaller. If you want, you can add more dates and nuts.

DATE PUDDING CAKE

This cake makes its own sauce. It is moist and very tasty. Serve with lots of whipped cream.

1 tablespoon butter	1 cup flour
2 cups brown sugar, divided	2 teaspoon baking powder
1 cup milk, divided	1 cup cut-up dates
1 egg	1 cup chopped nuts

Mix together the butter, 1 cup brown sugar, and 1/2 cup milk. Spread in the bottom of a 9-inch square pan. Place in an oven at 350° until the sugar melts and forms a sauce.

Beat the egg, add remaining milk and sugar; beat well. Stir in the flour and baking powder. Fold in the dates and nuts. Pour batter over sauce in the pan. Return to the oven and bake for 45 minutes. Invert on a plate; cut in squares and spoon the sauce over.

◆

PEANUT DATE COOKIES

1/2 cup butter/margarine	1 teaspoon vanilla
1/2 cup chunky peanut butter	1 cup flour
1/2 cup sugar	1/4 teaspoon salt
1 cup brown sugar	1/2 teaspoon baking soda
3 eggs	3 cups rolled oats
1/2 cup water	1 cup chopped dates

Cream the butter, peanut butter, and sugars. Add eggs, water, and vanilla and beat until creamy. Sift flour, salt, and soda together; add to creamed mixture and blend well. Mix in oats and dates. Drop by teaspoonsful onto a cookie sheet. Bake at 350° for 10 to 12 minutes. Makes 5 dozen.

☆☆☆ CEREAL DATE COOKIES

These cookies are fun to make, but let me warn you that the procedure is *very* sticky. Try these on a hot summer day when you don't want the oven going.

2 tablespoons butter	2 1/2 cups Rice Krispies *or*
1 1/2 cups chopped dates	cereal flakes
1/2 cup sugar	1/2 cup chopped nuts
2 beaten eggs	1/2 teaspoon vanilla
1/4 teaspoon salt	coconut

Melt butter in a heavy frying pan. Add the dates, sugar, eggs, and salt. Cook about 10 minutes over low heat, stirring constantly, until the mixture gets very bubbly. Remove from heat and cool somewhat.

Add cereal (if you use flakes, crush them), nuts, and vanilla. Use spoons dipped in cold water to shape into balls. Roll in flaked coconut. Or you can drop teaspoonsful into the coconut and roll the balls with your fingers. Store refrigerated.

Variation: Add 2 tablespoons orange marmalade when cooking, and increase the cereal to 3 cups.

☆☆☆ OATMEAL DATE BARS

Filling	Crust
4 cups cut-up dates	1 1/2 cups flour
1/2 cup sugar	1/2 teaspoon baking soda
1 cup water	1/4 teaspoon salt
1/4 cup lemon juice	3/4 cup butter/margarine
1/2 cup walnuts	1 cup brown sugar
	1 1/2 cups rolled oats

Combine the dates, sugar, and water in a saucepan. Stir over medium heat until thickened (about 5 minutes). Remove from heat and stir in the lemon juice and walnuts. Set aside.

Sift together the flour, soda, and salt. Cream the butter and sugar. Stir in the flour mixture and oats. Mix well with your hands.

Press half of the mixture into a greased 9-inch square pan. Spread with the filling. Cover with remaining crust. Press lightly with your hands. Bake at 375° for 30 minutes. Cut in bars while warm.

DATE BROWNIES

This is an unusual brownie recipe, but do try it. Dates and orange juice are a wonderful combination.

2 eggs
3/4 cup brown sugar
1/2 cup flour
1 2/3 cups graham cracker crumbs

1/4 cup oil
1/2 teaspoon vanilla
1 1/2 cups chopped dates
1/2 cup chopped walnuts
1/4 cup orange juice

Beat the eggs until light. Combine the sugar, flour, and crumbs. Add to the eggs, mixing well. Stir in the oil, vanilla, dates, walnuts, and orange juice. Spread mixture evenly in a greased 8-inch square pan. Bake at 350° for 25 to 30 minutes. Cut while warm into 20 bars.

SNOWBALLS

A healthful confection and very popular for children's parties.

1 pound pitted dates
1/2 pound raisins
1/2 pound dried figs

1/2 pound moist dried apricots
3 tablespoons honey
coconut

Grind the fruits in a grinder and mix in the honey. Sprinkle coconut over the bottom and sides of a shallow, oblong cake pan. Pat the candy at a thickness of one inch. Sprinkle heavily with coconut and allow to stand for 24 to 36 hours.

Roll into balls the size of large marbles. Cover with more coconut.

Note: The original recipe says to use powdered sugar everywhere I have said coconut. If *you* want to, do by all means follow the recipe. I find the confection quite sweet enough—and more interesting—with coconut.

Other recipes using dates: Orange-Date Nut Cake (Buttermilk); Oatmeal Spice Squares (Cereals); Fruited Date Sauce (Jams, Jellies, Marmalades); Honey Date Rice Pudding (Rice); Spicy Fruit Drops (Sour Milk); Zucchini Bread.

Eggnog

Part of our traditional Christmas celebration is a tree with real candles; we sit and look at it, and the children drink eggnog. With the usual extravagance that goes with the holidays, I always get too much eggnog and have it left over. This year it turned somewhat "funny" and gelatinous so I put some in a cake and the rest went into bread (I just used the eggnog instead of milk and cut out some sweetening; see Hearty Breakfast Bread under Cereals). Both were unqualified successes. If the eggnog is somewhat sour, don't worry; just add baking soda to your recipe (about 1/2 teaspoon for a cup of eggnog); after all, we use sour milk and cream all the time.

EGGNOG KUCHEN

1/2 cup butter/margarine
1 cup firmly packed brown sugar
2 eggs
2 1/2 cups flour
4 teaspoons baking powder
1 teaspoon cinnamon
1 teaspoon allspice
1/2 teaspoon salt
1/4 teaspoon ground cloves

1 cup eggnog
1 tablespoon rum
1 cup seedless raisins

Topping
1/3 cup brown sugar
1/3 cup finely chopped pecans

Cream butter; gradually add brown sugar and beat until light and fluffy. Beat in eggs one at a time. Sift together the dry ingredients and add them to the creamed mixture alternately with eggnog; begin and end with dry ingredients. Stir in rum and raisins. Spread evenly in a 13 x 9 (or 15 x 10) pan. Combine the brown sugar and nuts for the topping and sprinkle evenly over the top of the batter. Bake at 350° for 35 minutes. Cool on a wire rack.

HOLIDAY EGGNOG PIE

This pie is light and especially pretty if you garnish it with red and green candied cherries or colored decorations.

1 9-inch graham cracker shell	3 eggs, separated
1 envelope unflavored gelatin	1/2 teaspoon grated lemon peel
6 tablespoons sugar, divided	1 tablespoon lemon juice
1/4 cup water	1/4 cup rum
1 1/2 cups eggnog	

Make the graham cracker crust (add 1/2 teaspoon cinnamon to the recipe in the Appendix). Bake and let it cool.

In the top of a double boiler combine the gelatin with 2 tablespoons of the sugar. Stir in the water, eggnog, and egg yolks, beaten slightly. Place over simmering water and cook, stirring now and then, until the custard thickly coats spoon. This will take some time. Remove from heat and stir in the lemon peel, lemon juice, and rum. Cool slightly. Beat the egg whites with the remaining sugar until fairly stiff peaks form. Fold half into the custard, blending well; then fold the remaining egg whites in, blending slightly. Cool a few minutes, then mound into the crust. Decorate as desired.

◆

SPICY RAISIN CORN BREAD

You can always substitute eggnog for the milk in your favorite cornbread recipe, or try this one, which makes a superb coffee cake.

1 1/4 cups flour	1 cup eggnog
3/4 cup cornmeal	2 tablespoons margarine, melted
2 tablespoons sugar	1 egg
3 teaspoons baking powder	1 cup raisins
1/2 teaspoon salt	
1 teaspoon cinnamon	• Topping •
1/4 teaspoon ginger	1/2 cup sugar (brown, if you like)
1/4 teaspoon allspice	1 teaspoon cinnamon
	1 tablespoon margarine

In a large mixing bowl, combine all the dry ingredients. Beat the egg, and the eggnog and margarine to it, then pour over the dry ingredients and mix quickly. Fold in the raisins. Pour into a 9 x 9 pan. Sprinkle the topping (just combine the sugar and cinnamon, then mix in the margarine with your fingers) over the top. Bake at 400° for 20 to 25 minutes. Cut into squares and serve warm.

☆☆☆ HOLIDAY BREAD

I often bake this bread for gifts. Of course, you can use light cream for the eggnog, especially if you are baking it before the holidays.

1 1/2 cups apricot nectar	1/3 cup eggnog *or* light cream
1 1/2 cups raisins	2 3/4 cups flour
1/3 cup (about 12) cut-up dried apricots	3/4 cup sugar
	2 teaspoons baking soda
1 tablespoon grated orange peel	1/2 teaspoon salt
1 egg	1/2 cup chopped walnuts
1 tablespoon margarine, melted	

In a large saucepan, combine the apricot nectar, raisins, apricots, and orange peel. Simmer for 5 minutes; cool. In a large mixer bowl, beat the egg and margarine, then add the remaining ingredients along with the fruit mixture. Mix at low speed about 3 minutes, or until well blended. Pour into 4 well-greased No. 2 cans (or 4 small bread pans). Bake at 350° for 50 minutes or until bread tests done. Remove from cans (pans). Cool before slicing.

TWELFTH-DAY PANCAKES

An unusual breakfast treat, created locally.

1 egg	2 cups whole wheat flour
1 tablespoon vegetable oil	1 cup rolled oats
1 tablespoon honey or sorghum	1 cup wheat germ
1 cup yogurt	1/2 cup grated coconut
1 cup eggnog	1 teaspoon salt
2 cups milk	1 tablespoon baking powder

Mix all the liquid ingredients in a large bowl; stir in the dry ingredients. Add more milk if necessary. Fry, turning once, and serve with syrup, honey, fruit syrup, or jam.

Eggplant

An eggplant is indeed a beautiful vegetable and there are many ways of preparing it. It seems particularly adaptable to vegetable combinations and baked dishes.

☆☆☆ RATATOUILLE NIÇOISE

Here is one of the basic eggplant dishes, provençal in origin. It can be served either hot or cold. I prefer it hot, and I have found that it is one of those marvelous dishes that gets better each time you heat it up. Allow yourself some time to make this. Actual preparation is simple, but ingredients are added in stages.

2 tablespoons olive oil	2 zucchini ‑
2 cloves garlic	2 green peppers
1 large onion	5 ripe tomatoes
1 small eggplant	salt and pepper
flour	1 tablespoon capers, optional

Heat the oil in a large skillet over medium heat, add the garlic, peeled and chopped, and the onion, sliced. Sauté until the onion is golden. While this is cooking, peel the eggplant, and cut it into small cubes. Shake some flour over them and add to the skillet. Cover and cook gently about 30 minutes. Then cut up the zucchini in fairly small wedges, flour them, and add to the skillet along with the peppers, which you have seeded and cut into strips. Cover and cook gently about 1 hour. Then peel the tomatoes and cut them into small pieces, add them to the rest, and simmer, uncovered, until the mixture thickens somewhat. Season with salt and pepper. Serves 5 to 6.

EGGPLANT DIP

Dips are an Arab speciality (this recipe is authentic), and an ideal accompaniment for pieces of pita bread, which make very good scoops.

1 large round eggplant	4 tablespoons lemon juice
2 cloves garlic	olive oil
salt	chopped parsley
4 tablespoons tahini	

Put the eggplant on a baking dish and place it in an oven preheated to 425°. When the skin is blackened, douse it in cold water, and peel it. Mash the garlic to a paste with about the same amount of salt. Mix the tahini (which is sesame seed paste; if you cannot get it, use vegetable oil), lemon juice, and garlic paste. Mash the eggplant pulp to a smooth consistency and blend in the garlic sauce. Serve in a bowl with a small amount of olive oil on top and garnish with parsley. If you prefer, you can put everything in the blender and whirl until smooth.

EGGPLANT WITH CHEESE

Here is the simplest, fastest way to bake eggplant.

Take one eggplant, peel it, and slice it thin. Place the slices on a greased cookie cookie sheet. Sprinkle with salt, pepper, flour, and a generous amount of grated cheese. Bake at 350° for 20 minutes. Turn up the heat briefly to brown. The number of servings depends on the size of the eggplant (not to mention appetites).

EGGPLANT BAKE

5 cups cooked rice, preferably brown	1/2 teaspoon oregano
1 eggplant, peeled and sliced	1/2 teaspoon onion powder
1 can (6 ounces) tomato paste	1/2 teaspoon garlic powder
1 cup cottage cheese	1 cup grated cheese
1 cup yogurt	1 cup whole grain bread crumbs
2 teaspoons fresh chopped basil (or 1 teaspoon dried)	

Oil a shallow baking dish (a lasagna type rectangular dish is good) and spread the cooked rice over the bottom. Lay the eggplant slices over the rice.

Combine the tomato paste, cottage cheese, yogurt, herbs, and seasonings; add enough water, or vegetable stock, to make the sauce easy to pour.

Cover the eggplant slices with the sauce, sprinkle the grated cheese over, then top with the bread crumbs. Dot with some butter.

Bake at 350° for about 30 minutes, until the eggplant is tender, and the top is crispy. Serves 4.

EGGPLANT OMELETTE

• Filling •	• Sauce •
1 small eggplant	3 small tomatoes
salt	1 tablespoon butter
2 tablespoons olive oil	1 small white onion, chopped fine
	1 teaspoon chopped garlic
• Omelette •	1 teaspoon chopped fresh basil
3 eggs	salt and pepper
1 teaspoon cold water	
salt and pepper	
butter	

Remove the stem from the eggplant, but do not peel. Dice, sprinkle well with salt, and allow to stand for about 10 minutes. Wash thoroughly in cold water, drain, and dry well on paper towels. Heat the oil in a pan, add the eggplant, and shake over a fairly hot fire until golden brown all over. Set aside.

Skin the tomatoes and cut into 1/2-inch slices. Heat the butter in a small, heavy skillet, add the onion and garlic. Stir, then add the tomatoes, basil, and salt and pepper to taste. Cook over medium high heat for 2 minutes.

Make the omelette by beating the eggs, water, salt and pepper with a whisk until frothy. Heat the pan over a medium flame, add a dollop of butter, heat until sizzling but not browning. Pour the egg mixture quickly into the pan. Stir with a fork, drawing the mixture toward the center. Tip the pan to fill the holes. Do this until the eggs begin to set, cook another 30 seconds, then remove from heat.

Drain the eggplant and put it on the omelette as filling. Fold the omelette over, turn it out on a plate, pour the tomato sauce over it. Serve at once. Serves 2.

STUFFED EGGPLANT

1 medium eggplant	1 avocado, sliced
1/4 cup grated cheddar	bread crumbs for topping
1/4 cup bread crumbs	grated cheese
2 hard-boiled egg yolks	1/4 cup tomato sauce
1 teaspoon salt	

Cook the eggplant in boiling salted water until tender. Cut in half and scoop out the pulp.

Combine the pulp with the cheese, bread crumbs, egg yolks (which you have mashed fine), and salt.

Fill the eggplant halves, alternate the mixture with avocado slices.

Cover with bread crumbs and grated cheese. Then pour the tomato sauce over the top. Bake at 375° until brown, about 35 minutes. Serves 6.

Other recipes using eggplant: Eggplant and Macaroni (Noodles & Pasta).

Eggs

Cracked eggs can be poured out into a bowl or jar and kept, tightly covered, until needed. Separated egg yolks and whites can be stored airtight in the refrigerator; the egg yolks should be covered with cold water. Egg whites can be frozen; be sure to allow for expansion. They take about an hour to defrost and can be used as fresh ones. Egg yolks also can be frozen; add a little salt to them or they will coagulate.

EGGS FOO YONG

My adaptation of a Chinese dish, in which you can palatably rehash your leftovers. Try chopped ham, beef, lamb, poultry, sea food, or potatoes, grains, or that small amount of rice.

2 tablespoons oil	1 teaspoon herbs: parsley, savory
3 stalks celery and tops	marjoram, oregano, rosemary,
2 green onions, chopped	thyme
6 eggs, beaten	1/2 cup leftovers
1 tablespoon nutritional yeast	salt and pepper to taste
	1 cup sprouts

Heat the oil. Chop the celery tops and slice the stalks thin, diagonally. Sauté the celery and green onions (and, if you like, the leftover meat or fish). Remove from the pan and reserve.

Blend the eggs, yeast, herbs (and select an herb or herbs that compliment your other ingredients) and pour the mixture into the pan. Cover. Cook over low heat for a minute. While eggs are still partly liquid, add meat or fish, salt and pepper to taste, and the sautéed vegetables. Let cook over low heat until firm; turn and cook the other side briefly. Garnish with sprouts. Serves 4.

Egg Yolks

I would guess that there are many more recipes in our world using egg whites than yolks. Hence the need for some ideas to use up the leftover yolks. One simple solution is to drop egg yolks in boiling water and simmer until done; cool and sieve into your salad or use as garnish on top. Egg yolks can be whisked into sauces; be sure that the sauce does not boil after you have added the yolks. You can always add an extra yolk or two to your custard (two yolks are about the equivalent of one whole egg).

SPONGE CAKE

I always like to have some egg yolks around because I love this cake. It is quickly made and lovely with fruit or a fruit sauce topping.

3 egg yolks	3/4 cup cake flour
1/2 cup sugar	2 teaspoons baking powder
1/8 teaspoon salt	1 teaspoon vanilla
1/4 cup boiling water	1/2 teaspoon grated lemon rind

Beat the yolks until light, then beat in the sugar and salt gradually. Add the boiling water. Sift the flour and baking powder and add them to the sugar mixture. Beat the batter until it is smooth. Then stir in the vanilla and lemon rind. Bake the cake in an 8-inch round or square pan or a small tube pan at 350° for about 30 minutes.

CURRANT DROP COOKIES

1 cup sugar	2 cups flour
1/2 cup butter/margarine	1/4 cup rolled oats
3 egg yolks	1 teaspoon baking powder
1 teaspoon vanilla	1/2 cup milk
1/2 teaspoon grated lemon rind	1 cup currants, plumped

Cream the sugar and butter until light. Beat in the egg yolks, vanilla, and lemon rind. Sift the flour and baking powder and mix with the oats (you can use all flour, if you prefer, 2 1/4 cups in all). Add dry ingredients to the butter mixture alternately with the milk; beat the batter until smooth after each addition. Stir in the currants (plump them by pouring boiling water over; let stand a minute or so, drain thoroughly). Drop the batter by teaspoons onto a baking sheet. Bake at 350° about 10 minutes. Makes about 60.

BUTTER COOKIES

This is a lovely cookie, light, easy to make. If you chill the dough, you can put it through a cookie press.

1/2 cup butter	1/2 teaspoon grated lemon rind
1/3 cup sugar	1 1/2 cups flour
3 egg yolks	1/2 teaspoon salt
1/2 teaspoon vanilla *or*	cinnamon sugar
almond extract	nutmeats or candied cherries

Cream the butter and sugar; beat in the yolks, flavoring, rind, flour, and salt. If the weather is warm, chill the dough for several hours. Roll it into 1-inch balls. Flatten them on a lightly greased cookie sheet. Decorate with colored sugar or cinnamon-sugar and a half nutmeat or a candied cherry. Bake at 375° from 10 to 12 minutes, until the edges are light brown.

Egg Whites

If you have one egg white floating around (and I often do because I frequently make Mock Mayonnaise), you can always make an easy fruit whip for one person. Let the egg white come to room temperature, then beat it stiff, adding a little brown sugar; then add some small pieces of fresh fruit (peaches, strawberries, raspberries) or some whole cranberry sauce and a dollop of orange juice concentrate (my favorite combination). Whip until blended. Serve at once.

ANGEL PECAN PIE

3 egg whites	1 cup chopped pecans
1 cup sugar	1 teaspoon baking powder
1 cup graham cracker crumbs	

Beat the egg whites until stiff; slowly mix in the sugar. Combine the dry ingredients and fold the egg whites into the mixture. Pour into a 9-inch greased pie pan. Bake at 325° for 25 to 30 minutes, until lightly browned. Cool. Serve with whipped cream.

Variation:

Soda Cracker Pie: Substitute 1/2 teaspoon cream of tartar for the baking powder and 8 crushed soda crackers (or 14 Ritz crackers) for the graham cracker crumbs; add 1 teaspoon vanilla. Bake at 300° for 30 minutes. Or use other cookie or cracker crumbs or 1 cup finely crushed leftover cereal in either version.

PINEAPPLE SNOW PUDDING

This light dessert tastes very refreshing on a warm summer evening. Try it at strawberry time and garnish it with the strawberries. The result is very pretty.

1 envelope unflavored gelatin	1 can (8 ounces) crushed pineapple
1/4 cup cold water	(in syrup)
1 cup pineapple juice	2 egg whites
	pinch of salt
	1 tablespoon sugar

Soften the gelatin in the cold water in a small saucepan. Add the pineapple juice and cook over low heat, stirring, until mixture is steaming and the gelatin is dissolved. Pour into a bowl and refrigerate until partially set (the consistency of unbeaten egg whites). Stir in the crushed pineapple with the syrup.

Beat the egg whites with a pinch of salt until stiff, beat in the sugar. Fold into the gelatin mixture. Pour into a 1-quart mold that has been rinsed in cold water. Refrigerate until firm. Unmold on a serving plate. Serves 8.

MERINGUES

A fast, simple way to make a really posh dessert out of egg whites.

3 egg whites	1/4 teaspoon vanilla
1/4 teaspoon cream of tartar	3/4 cup superfine granulated sugar
1/8 teaspoon salt	

Combine egg whites, cream of tartar, salt, and vanilla in a large bowl. Beat with an electric mixer at high speed until stiff but not dry. Turn mixer to slow; add sugar gradually and continue beating until mixture is smooth. Butter a 9-inch pie plate, or use buttered waxed paper on a cookie sheet. Spread the meringue mixture to form a shell somewhat higher than the edge (for the pie plate) or shape 6 large meringues with circular motion of the spoon on the cookie sheet sheet. Bake at 250° about 1 hour, until firm but not brown. Cool.

Fillings: Vanilla or peppermint ice cream and bitter chocolate sauce; vanilla or fruit ice cream with fruit topping; lemon sherbet with blueberries.

◆

☆☆☆ CORN FLAKE MACAROONS

I don't know of a quicker or easier way to make up something delicious.

2 egg whites	2 cups corn flakes, slightly crushed
3/4 cup sugar	1/2 cup finely chopped walnuts
1 cup coconut	1/2 teaspoon vanilla

Beat the egg whites until stiff; gradually add the sugar while beating all the time. Then by hand fold in the remaining ingredients. Drop by teaspoonsful on a greased cookie sheet. Bake at 350° until delicately browned, about 12 minutes. Makes about 3 dozen.

Variations:

Almond Macaroons: I make these after Christmas as I usually have almond paste leftover from the Stollen. Substitute confectioners' sugar for the other; omit coconut, corn flakes, and nuts. Add instead 1 cup almond paste, broken up. Decorate tops with almonds and candied cherries, if desired. Makes about 3 dozen.

Other recipes for macaroons can be found under Coconut and Nuts.

ALMOND SNOWCAP COOKIES

This is a delicious combination of layers. These are perfect at a fancy afternoon tea.

1/4 cup butter/margarine	3 egg whites
2 cups rolled oats	1/2 cup sugar
2/3 cup brown sugar	1/2 cup coconut
3/4 cup raspberry jam	1/2 cup sliced almonds

Cream the butter, oats, and sugar together. Press firmly in a 13 x 9 pan. Bake at 350° for 12 minutes. Spread the jam over the hot layer. Beat egg whites until foamy; beat in the sugar, one tablespoon at a time, and continue beating until the mixture is stiff and glossy. Fold in the coconut and spread over the jam. Sprinkle the almonds over the top.

Return to the oven and bake 20 minutes longer. Cool, cut in squares. Store airtight.

HONEY DIVINITY

I eat very little candy, but I have always been a divinity freak. The honey gives it a special flavor and adds to the keeping quality. Add some finely chopped nuts, if you like.

1/4 cup honey	1/4 teaspoon salt
2 1/2 cups sugar	2 egg whites
2/3 cup water	1 teaspoon vanilla

In a 2-quart saucepan combine the honey, sugar, water, and salt. Stir over low heat until the sugar is dissolved. Continue cooking slowly without stirring to 265° on the candy thermometer, or until a small amount of the mixture forms an almost brittle ball in cold water. Meanwhile in a large mixer bowl, beat the egg whites at high speed until very stiff. Slowly pour in the hot syrup, beating constantly at high speed until the mixture loses its gloss and a small amount dropped from a spoon holds its shape. Add the vanilla. Drop by teaspoonsful onto a buttered shallow pan. Makes about 3 1/2 dozen pieces.

Other recipes using eggs: Omelettes, quiches, soufflés, timbales depend on eggs. Most cakes and cookies, many breads, casseroles, puddings call for them. The following recipes use 4 or more eggs: Banana Carob Cake, Passover Cake (Bananas); Cherry Custard Pudding, Cherry Torte; Coconut Pound Cake, Coconut Custard Pie; Chestnut Mousse, Chestnut Torte; Ham Squares; Eggs in Onion Sauce (Onions); Raisin Peanut Butter Tea Cake (Raisins); Poppyseed Cake, Wine Sponge Cake, Weinschaum (Wine).

Other recipes using egg yolks: Buttermilk Raisin Pie (Buttermilk); Concord Grape Kuchen; Mock Goose-Liver Pâté (Livers); Fettucine with Egg Sauce (Noodles & Pasta); Chicken Dijon, Austrian Wine Cream (Wine); Mock Mayonnaise (see the Appendix).

Other recipes using egg whites: Hexenschnee (Apples); Orange-Buttermilk Sponge (Buttermilk); Coconut Macaroons; Grapefruit Sherbet; Jelly Frosting (Jams, Jellies, Marmalades); Spiced Nuts, Nut Macaroons; Fluffy Frosting (see the Appendix).

Evaporated Milk

I have this recipe for Butterscotch Sauce, which calls for part of a can of evaporated milk, so I frequently have some left to dispose of. Most meat dishes with a sauce or that involve grilling and deglazing the pan are improved by a little evaporated milk. You get a creamy sauce without the cream.

VEAL FRICASSEE

By using evaporated milk instead of cream in this recipe, you get the effect of cream with about one-half the calories.

2 pounds lean veal shoulder, boned	2 cups water
3 bay leaves	1 1/2 pounds small white onions
2 teaspoons celery salt	1/2 pound mushrooms
1 teaspoon rosemary, crumbled	1/4 cup evaporated milk
1/2 teaspoon pepper	3 tablespoons chopped parsley
1 envelope instant chicken broth	

Cut the veal in 1-inch cubes and sauté in a small amount of fat until brown in a Dutch oven. Combine bay leaves, celery salt, rosemary, pepper, broth, and water; pour over the veal. Cover and simmer 1 hour.

Peel the onions, place on top of meat. Cover and simmer 45 minutes more, or until veal and onions are tender. Wash and slice the mushrooms. Stir them into the stew with the evaporated milk. Cover and simmer 10 minutes more. Remove the bay leaves.

Sprinkle with parsley. Serve with steamed bulgur wheat, or brown rice. Serves 6.

CHICKEN TETRAZZINI

6 ounces fine spaghetti, cooked	1 small green pepper, slivered
1/4 pound mushrooms *or* 1 can	2 teaspoons salt
(4 ounces) sliced mushrooms	dash white pepper
3 tablespoons flour	1 teaspoon worcestershire sauce
1 cup skim milk	4 cups cooked chicken, diced
1 cup evaporated milk	2 tablespoons grated parmesan
2 tablespoons sherry	

Arrange the spaghetti in a shallow 1 1/2 or 2-quart broiler-proof baking dish. Steam the mushrooms in a little water and blend in the flour with the liquid (or if using canned mushrooms, use the liquid from the can). Combine the two milks and bring to a boil in a 3-quart saucepan. Stir in the flour mixture and cook, stirring, until thickened. Add the sherry, green pepper, salt, white pepper, and worcestershire and mix well. Fold in the chicken. Pour over the spaghetti and sprinkle with the cheese. Bake at 300° about 45 minutes. Put under the broiler several minutes to brown lightly. Serves 6.

☆☆☆ BUTTERSCOTCH SAUCE

Serve this sauce with vanilla ice cream or butter crunch or butter pecan. Top with chopped toasted nuts—almonds, pecans, walnuts. Do not substitute anything in this recipe, the results will be disastrous.

1 1/2 cups brown sugar	2/3 cup white corn syrup
4 tablespoons butter	2/3 cup evaporated milk

Combine the sugar, butter, and corn syrup. Stir constantly over low heat until mixture boils. Then boil without stirring until it forms a soft ball in cold water (236° on the candy thermometer). Cool slightly. Then stir in the evaporated milk. Serve warm.

RICH CHOCOLATE SAUCE

2 squares bitter chocolate	1/2 cup evaporated milk
2 tablespoons butter	1 teaspoon vanilla
2/3 cup sugar	1/4 cup sherry

Melt the chocolate with the butter. Stir in the sugar and evaporated milk. Cook, stirring, over low heat, until sugar dissolves and sauce has thickened. Cool slightly and add the vanilla and sherry. Try this over peppermint ice cream or, better still, orange sherbet.

The following recipes are different versions of the same principle—whipped, flavored evaporated milk (called by one friend "abominable froth"). If it turns out that you have less evaporated milk than the recipe calls for, just whip it up and use the lesser amount. When beating these deserts, cover the bowl with waxed paper; punch a hole in the center and stick the beater stems up through it. You will be glad you did.

CHOCOLATE BAVARIAN

This dessert makes a light finish to a ladies' luncheon. With very little effort you have something quite elegant.

1 envelope plain gelatin	1/8 teaspoon salt
1/2 cup cold water	1 2/3 cups evaporated milk,
1/2 cup sugar	divided
1/4 cup cocoa	1 tablespoon rum

In a small saucepan, soften the gelatin in the cold water. Stir in the sugar, cocoa, and salt. Cook over medium heat, stirring, until the gelatin and sugar dissolve completely, about 5 minutes. Do *not* boil.

Stir in 1 cup evaporated milk. Chill in the small electric mixer bowl until slightly set, but not firm. With the mixer at low speed beat in the remaining 2/3 cup (or less) evaporated milk (which you have chilled) and the rum.

Beat at high speed until the mixture fills the bowl (and it will). Let stand a few minutes, then heap into dessert dishes.

☆☆☆ LEMON BISQUE

1 cup (or more) evaporated milk	1 tablespoon lemon juice
1 package lemon jello	2 teaspoons grated lemon rind
1 1/4 cups boiling water	1 cup crushed vanilla wafer *or*
1/3 cup honey	graham cracker crumbs

Chill the evaporated milk overnight. Dissolve the jello in the boiling water; stir in the honey, lemon juice, and grated rind. Blend thoroughly and set in the refrigerator to cool. Allow it to cool to the consistency of unbeaten egg white.

Spread about 3/4 cup crumbs in the bottom of a 13 x 9 pan, or two smaller dishes (I like to use glass bowls, the result is prettier).

Whip the evaporated milk with an electric mixer until stiff, and then whip the gelatin mixture into it. Pour this over the crumbs and smooth the surface. Sprinkle the remaining crumbs over the top. Chill for 3 hours.

PEANUT MOUSSE

1 1/3 cups evaporated milk
1/2 cup sugar
1/2 cup water

1/4 cup peanut butter
1 teaspoon vanilla

Chill the milk in freezer until ice crystals form around the edges. Meanwhile, combine the sugar and water in a large pan, and bring to a boil, stirring; simmer 5 minutes. Remove from heat and blend in the peanut butter; cool. Whip the milk until stiff peaks form. Fold into the peanut butter mixture along with the vanilla. Pour into a chilled freezing tray or loaf pan and chill until firm.

BUTTER PECAN CHIFFON PIE

1 10-inch pie crust
1 1/2 teaspoons plain gelatin
3 tablespoons cold water
1/3 cup sugar

1 cup evaporated milk
3 tablespoons maple syrup
1/2 cup chopped pecans
1 tablespoon butter

Prepare the crust (crushed cookie or graham cracker crumb crust—see the Appendix) and set aside. Sprinkle the gelatin over cold water in a small sauce-pan; cook and stir constantly over low heat about 3 minutes, or until gelatin is dissolved. Mix together the sugar, evaporated milk, and maple syrup; briskly beat in the dissolved gelatin until thoroughly blended and chill in refrigerator until it begins to set. In the meantime, sauté the pecans in the butter until golden brown; cool. Beat the gelatin mixture with electric beater on high speed until light and fluffy. Fold the nuts gently into the whipped mixture and spoon into the crust. Chill in refrigerator until set.

Other recipes using evaporated milk: Meat-Fried Noodles (Beef); Corn-Cheese Casserole (Corn); cucumber soups; Hermits (Granola); Ham Mousse, Ham and Corn Quiche (Ham).

Fish

Fresh fish, really fresh, is one of the great delicacies on earth. Be very careful not to overcook it. If you can get a whole salmon, do bake and serve it whole, and eat the leftovers cold as salad—sheer perfection. A good way to use up a small amount of leftover fish is to put it in a seasoned cream sauce with some boiled potatoes, or make a fish salad.

FISH SOUP

This is like a fish chowder, but a bit more pure. If you like, add some cut-up boiled potatoes, carrots, celery, peas and thin accordingly.

1/2 yellow onion, minced	3 tablespoons flour
4 tablespoons butter/margarine, divided	2 cups chicken broth, fish stock, or vegetable stock
1 cup milk	salt and pepper
1 cup cooked fish	dash nutmeg

Melt 1 tablespoon butter in a heavy saucepan; sauté the onion but do not brown it. Combine the onion and milk and simmer 10 to 15 minutes.

Flake the fish and purée it in the blender with the onion-milk mixture. Put aside.

Make a velouté sauce by melting the remaining 3 tablespoons butter in the same saucepan, stir in flour until smooth. Cook slowly, stirring constantly until the mixture froths, about 2 minutes. Do not brown. Remove from heat and whisk in the heated broth until well combined. Cook over medium heat, whisking constantly, until the sauce boils 1 minute. Remove from heat and season with salt and pepper to taste.

Combine the fish and milk mixture with the velouté sauce in the saucepan, bring to a boil. Add the nutmeg, and more salt if desired. If too thick, add more milk or broth. Serves 4.

FISH TIMBALES

A delicious way to use any type of leftover fish. Serve the timbales with a cream, mushroom, cheese, or tomato sauce.

3 tablespoons butter
1/4 cup minced celery or green
    pepper, *or* a combination
2 tablespoons minced green onion
1/3 cup soft bread crumbs
1 cup milk
1 1/4 cups flaked fish

1/2 cup finely chopped almonds
2 beaten eggs
1/2 teaspoon salt
1/8 teaspoon paprika
1 teaspoon worcestershire sauce
    or lemon juice

Melt the butter and stir in the celery, green pepper, and onion. Stir for a minute, then add the crumbs, milk, fish, and nuts. Remove the pan from the fire and stir in the remaining ingredients. Pour the mixture into 4 greased individual molds. Place in a pan of hot water and bake at 350° about 30 minutes or until firm. Unmold and serve with sauce. Serves 4.

ICELANDIC SOUFFLÉ

A really rich and delicious main dish. I am told that in Iceland you serve the leftover soufflé, cut in 1-inch slices and sautéed in butter, for breakfast the next morning

1/2 cup butter
1 cup flour
1 1/4 cups milk
1 teaspoon salt
pepper

6 eggs separated
2 cups cooked flaked fish: cod,
    haddock, red snapper
1/2 cup dry bread crumbs

Make a thick cream sauce with the butter, flour, and milk; cook until very thick. Season with the salt and pepper and cool. Then beat in the egg yolks and combine with the fish. Beat the egg whites stiff and fold them in. Pour into a buttered 2-quart casserole coated with crumbs and sprinkle remaining crumbs over the top. Bake at 375° for 55 minutes. Serve at once with melted butter. Serves 6 to 8.

BAKED FISH AND NUTS

2 cups cream sauce (see the
    Appendix)
salt and pepper to taste
cayenne
1 cup flaked fish

1 cup finely chopped peanuts
3 hard-boiled eggs, chopped fine
1 teaspoon worcestershire sauce
cracker crumbs

Make the cream sauce and season to taste with salt, pepper, and cayenne. Then stir in the remaining ingredients, except for the crumbs. Pour into a baking dish and cover the top with crumbs. Bake at 375° for 20 minutes. Serves 4.

BAKED FISH CREOLE

2 cups stewed tomatoes
4 tablespoons chopped onions
4 tablespoons chopped green
  peppers
4 tablespoons chopped mushrooms
1 tablespoon lemon juice

2 teaspoons sugar
pinch oregano
1/2 teaspoon dry mustard
2 pounds fish fillets or steaks
  or 4 cups cooked flaked fish

Put all the ingredients, except the fish, in a saucepan and simmer, stirring occasionally, until the vegetables are tender. Season the fish with salt and pepper and put it in a shallow baking dish. Pour the sauce over. Bake at 350° about 30 minutes, if fish is uncooked. If you use leftover cooked fish, then bake 15 to 20 minutes. Serves 4.

Other recipes using fish: See also Fish Florentine (under Spinach) and the section on Tuna.

Grains

Many grains can be purchased in a grocery store, all boxed. If you have a store in your area which sells whole grains and flour in bulk, you would do well to purchase them there. Not only are the prices much lower and the product fresher, but you can purchase just the amount you need. The one disadvantage is that you must find containers to store the grains. For me this is no problem as I save jars anyway and like having a pantry shelf of different grains, seeds, legumes, and flours.

In many foreign cuisines, grains are used routinely as the main or side dish. We all eat rice, of course, but if you haven't tried bulgur or kasha, I urge you to do so. Bulgur is cracked wheat that has been roasted (in the Middle East this was—and still is, I am told—done on open braziers). Kasha is made with buckwheat groats.

BASIC PILAF

Pilaf is ordinarily made with rice, but you can use other grains, or a combination of grains, with equal success. The procedure is simple: Melt 2 tablespoons butter and/or margarine (or heat 2 tablespoons oil) in a large skillet or stove-top casserole with a lid. Sauté 1 medium onion, chopped, and 1 cup of grain (rice, bulgur, millet), until both are browned (if you use white rice, until it is golden). Stir in 2 cups liquid (water, bouillon, meat or vegetable stock), salt and pepper, herbs of your choice; reduce the heat. Cover tightly and simmer covered until the liquid is absorbed and the grain is tender. Depending on what grain you use, and how long you sauté it, this will take from 20 to 50 minutes. If you use brown rice, you may have to add more liquid. Top with grated parmesan cheese, if desired.

Variations: Variations are almost infinite. Here is where you can add in bits and pieces—sauté any leftover meat you want out of the way and season accordingly. If you prefer, you can add the cooked meat (and vegetables) near the end of the cooking time and steam with the grain. To sauté the meat is preferable, I think; the flavor is richer, and the extra cooking time makes it more tender.

Beef-Tomato: Sauté some ground beef and garlic with the grain; use tomato juice for all or part of the stock.

Sausage-Herb: Brown 1/2 pound of mild sausage with the onion and rice; add 1/2 teaspoon summer savory.

Meat-Vegetable: Sauté 1 to 1 1/2 pounds pork sausage, *or* meat loaf mix, *or* leftover ground roast, *or* leftover meat loaf, 1 chopped green pepper, 2 minced green onions, 3 chopped celery stalks; flavor with 1 tablespoon worcestershire sauce and some salt.

Vegetable: Sauté celery, finely chopped; add vegetable broth, stir in leftover vegetables, and season with lots of parsley.

KASHA

Use medium or coarse buckwheat groats. My experience is that the fine groats make fairly gummy kasha (they are excellent, however, in breads or soups). Kasha is perfect with a rich beef or veal stew.

1 cup buckwheat groats	2 cups boiling water
1 egg	1 teaspoon salt
2 tablespoons margarine or oil	

Beat the egg in a small bowl; stir in the groats and mix well. Heat the oil or margarine in a skillet. Pour in the egg-groats mixture and cook over medium heat, stirring constantly, for 3 to 5 minutes or until the kernels separate and are lightly browned (do not worry; you won't end up with scrambled eggs and groats)! Add the boiling water and whisk until smooth; stir in the salt. Reduce the heat, cover, and cook, stirring from time to time, until the liquid is absorbed. This takes about 20 minutes. This is perfect with a beef or veal stew.

KASHA LOAF

Here is a way to use up the leftover kasha or other cooked grains, not to mention the leftover beef.

1/4 pound chopped lean beef	1/2 cup celery, minced
1 egg, slightly beaten	1/2 pound mushrooms, chopped
1 1/2 cups kasha	salt and pepper to taste
1 tablespoon wheat germ	several drops worcestershire sauce
1 large onion, chopped fine	1/4 cup pine nuts *or* sunflower seeds *or* chopped walnuts

Combine all the ingredients. If the mixture seems a little dry, add a small amount of skim milk. Mix lightly with a fork. Turn into a well-oiled little baking dish or 9 x 5 loaf pan. Bake at 325° for 1 hour, or until done.

GOLDEN OATS

1 1/2 cups rolled oats	3/4 cup broth or water
1 egg, beaten	1/4 teaspoon salt
3 tablespoons butter/margarine, melted	

Proceed in exactly the same way as with kasha. After you have added the water and salt, reduce the heat. Add some herbs, if you like. Do not cover. Cook, stirring from time to time, for about 5 minutes. Serves 4.

BARLEY CASSEROLE

I have made this casserole for many years, especially the version with livers. It is very easy, and a very good accompaniment to lamb stew, or any stew for that matter. Or, you can serve it as a main dish with a fresh green salad.

3 tablespoons butter/margarine	1 cup barley
1 large onion, chopped	2 cups broth, meat or chicken
1/2 pound mushrooms, sliced	

Melt the butter and sauté the onions and mushrooms until soft. Add the barley and brown it lightly. Pour into a buttered casserole. Prepare the broth and taste it for seasoning (use meat or chicken stock, or vegetable stock, or make broth with cubes—2 cubes for 2 cups water). Pour 1 cup broth over the barley and cover. Bake at 350° for 25 to 30 minutes; then uncover and add the second cup of broth. Continue cooking until the liquid is absorbed and the barley is done.

Variations:
Amandine: Sprinkle the top of the casserole with toasted sliced almonds when you add the second cup of broth.
Chicken Livers: Sauté 1/2 pound chicken livers (chopped) for a minute or so, then add to the casserole before baking.
Herbed: Sauté 1/4 cup minced green onions and 1/2 cup chopped celery. Add these and 1/2 cup minced parsley and 1/2 cup toasted almonds to the casserole in place of the onion and mushrooms.
Brown Rice: Substitute for the barley in equal amount.

BULGUR AND GARBANZOS

An unusual grain and legume combination. It is very good with steamed zucchini and herbed quick bread.

1 1/4 cups raw bulgur	1/2 teaspoon dill
3 tablespoons oil	1 tablespoon soy sauce
2 1/2 cups stock	3/4 cup garbanzo beans, cooked
1 bay leaf	1 cup yogurt

Sauté the bulgur in the oil for about 5 minutes until it is slightly brown. Add the stock, bay leaf, dill, and soy sauce. Bring to a boil, lower the heat, cover, and simmer until all the stock is absorbed (about 25 minutes). While the bulgur is cooking, sauté the garbanzos in an oiled skillet for about 10 minutes; they should be browned slightly. When the bulgur is cooked, remove the bay leaf; stir in the garbanzos and the yogurt. Add salt and pepper, if desired. Serves 6.

☆☆☆ GRAIN BREAD

Here is one recipe that I developed myself.

1/4 cup honey	4 cups whole wheat flour
1 1/2 tablespoons dry yeast	1 cup mashed potatoes (unseasoned)
4 cups water, divided	*or* 1/2 cup dry instant potatoes
4 tablespoons margarine	1/2 cup instant dry milk
1 cup grain (cracked wheat, millet,	1 tablespoon (scant) salt
rolled oats), uncooked	5 1/2 to 7 cups all-purpose flour

Measure the honey and pour it into a large mixing bowl. Use the same cup and dissolve the yeast in 1 cup very warm water; stir it well and let stand until foamy. Boil 2 cups water, melt the margarine in it, stir in the grain, and cook, stirring, for about 5 minutes. Pour into the bowl with the honey and mix well. Add the remaining 1 cup water, and when the mixture is lukewarm, stir in the yeast, whole wheat flour, potatoes, dry milk, and salt. Blend well. Let stand in a warm place for 1/2 hour; the bread will be lighter. Then stir in the all-purpose flour, 1 cup at a time, until the dough forms a ball and can be handled. Turn out on a floured board and knead until smooth, about 8 minutes, working in more flour, if necessary. Cover, let rise until doubled, about 1 1/2 hours.

Punch down the dough, divide into thirds. Shape into three loaves and place in greased 9 x 5 loaf pans. Cover and let rise until doubled, about 1 hour. Bake at 375° about 45 minutes, or until the bread tests done. Remove from pans and cool on wire racks. This recipe makes 3 large loaves.

Other recipes using:

Barley: Lentil Loaf (Legumes); Yogurt-Barley Soup.

Bulgur: Beans-Celery-Bulgur Casserole (Beans); Bulgur and Celery au Gratin; Tabouli (Parsley); Yogurt-Spinach Soup (Yogurt).

Kasha: Carrots and Kasha.

Wheat Berries: Crusted Cauliflower; Super Pie (Legumes); Curried Rice Salad. See also: Cereals, Grains, Rice.

Granola

Granola is one of those wonderful inventions that came along with health food and serious thoughts about better nutrition in this country. A number of commercial granolas are sold in the grocery stores. They are good, expensive, and sweet. It is easy to make your own, and then you can bake with it. Be sure to store your granola in a cool place, preferably the refrigerator, and in airtight containers. It can be frozen.

BASIC GRANOLA

6 cups rolled oats
1 cup wheat germ
3/4 cup chopped nuts
1/2 cup sunflower seeds
1 cup coconut

1/2 cup honey
1/2 cup oil
1/3 cup water
1/2 teaspoon salt
1 1/2 teaspoons vanilla

Proceed as in Crunchy Granola, p. 167. Bake at 275° one hour or more, stirring from time to time. You can substitute 1/2 cup brown sugar for the honey, if you prefer. Also there is a branch of my family which adds 1 teaspoon cinnamon. Feel free to do so, if you like that flavor.

GOLDEN GRANOLA

The simplest of all, and the most quickly made. Be sure to watch it, though, as it browns rapidly.

3 cups rolled oats
1 cup coconut
1 cup chopped nuts
1/4 cup honey

1/4 cup oil *or* melted butter/
  margarine
1 teaspoon cinnamon (optional)
1/2 teaspoon salt
2/3 cup raisins

Combine everything except the raisins in a 13 x 9 baking pan and mix well. Bake at 350° for 25 to 30 minutes, stirring occasionally. Stir in the raisins. Cool thoroughly and store airtight. Makes about 6 cups.

☆☆☆ CRUNCHY GRANOLA

I make this the most often. The recipe is written in my mother's hand; she got it from a Swiss friend of hers. I have changed it considerably. You can change it too. This granola is dry and has a wonderful texture. It makes a wonderful topping for mixed fruit salads. It is not so good for baking. The other two recipes are better for that purpose.

4 cups rolled oats	1/3 cup oil
1 cup wheat germ	1/3 cup honey
1/2 cup bran flakes	dash of salt
1 cup sunflower seeds	1/2 teaspoon vanilla
1/2 cup sesame seeds	1 1/2 cups shredded coconut
1/2 cup roasted soy nuts	

Put all the dry ingredients into a large roasting pan; stir to blend well. Measure the oil into a small saucepan; then measure the honey. Heat until warm, add the salt and vanilla. Then pour over the grains and mix thoroughly. Bake at 300° for about 1/2 hour, stirring from time to time. As the granola begins to brown, stir in the coconut; continue baking until crunchy and brown. If you like, add raisins, cut up dates, or other dried fruit, but only after the granola has baked. You can also substitute other nuts, such as chopped almonds, for the soy nuts.

◆

ORANGE-CRANBERRY CAKE

Here is what you do with your leftover relish (see under Cranberries) from the holiday feast. I once used a friend's relish—she had made it with grapefruit (instead of oranges); the cake was delicious.

1/2 cup butter/margarine	2 1/2 cups flour
1 cup brown sugar	1 teaspoon baking soda
2 eggs	1/2 teaspoon salt
1 cup cranberry relish	1 teaspoon cinnamon
1 cup granola	1 teaspoon nutmeg
1 cup raisins	1 cup buttermilk *or* sour milk

Cream the butter, sugar, and eggs until light and fluffy. Stir in the relish, granola, and raisins. Sift the dry ingredients and add alternately with the buttermilk to the creamed mixture. Pour into a greased 9-inch tube pan. Bake at 350° about 1 hour, or until the cake tests done. Cool 5 minutes on a rack, then remove from the pan. When cool, frost with Lemon Glaze (see the Appendix) or dredge with 10X sugar. The cake freezes well. You can also bake it in three small loaf pans, baking about 45 minutes.

GRANOLA BARS

2 cups granola	1 teaspoon vanilla
1/4 cup honey *or* brown sugar	dash of salt
1 egg, beaten	

Combine all ingredients in a medium bowl and mix well. Press mixture firmly and evenly into a well-greased 8-inch square pan. Bake at 350° for 15 to 18 minutes. Cool on a rack for 5 minutes, then cut into bars. Remove from the pan while warm. Wrap in foil or plastic wrap, if desired. Store at room temperature, or in the freezer.

Variations:

Peanut: Add 1/4 cup peanut butter and 1/4 cup finely chopped peanuts.
Sunflower: Add 1/4 cup sunflower seeds and 1/4 cup raisins.
Nut: Add 1/4 cup chopped almonds, pecans, hazelnuts, walnuts.
Apricot: Add 1/4 cup finely snipped dried apricots, 1/4 cup chopped almonds, and 1/8 teaspoon nutmeg.
Coconut: Add 1/4 cup flaked coconut and 1/4 cup chopped nuts.

☆☆☆ SAUCEPAN BROWNIES

Another very easy bar cookie and you make it all in one pan.

3/4 cup flour	1 cup chocolate chips
1/4 teaspoon baking soda	1 teaspoon vanilla
1/4 teaspoon salt	2 eggs
1/3 cup butter/margarine	1/2 cup granola
1/2 cup sugar	1/2 cup chopped walnuts
2 tablespoons water	

Sift together the flour, soda, and salt. Set aside. Combine the butter/margarine, sugar, and water in a saucepan and bring to a boil over moderate heat, stirring constantly. Remove from the heat at once. Stir in the chocolate chips and vanilla and blend until chocolate is melted. Add the eggs and beat well. Stir in dry ingredients, granola, and nuts. Spread in a greased 9-inch square pan. Bake at 325° for about 25 minutes. Cut into squares while warm.

Variation:

Anti-chocolate (dedicated to all of us for whom chocolate is a menace): Increase soda to 1/2 teaspoon, butter/margarine to 1/2 cup; substitute 1/2 cup honey for the sugar and 1/3 cup carob powder for the chocolate bits. Of course, if you can get carob chips, then just substitute them for the chocolate.

HERMITS

This is an old-fashioned cookie—dark, spicy, and easy to make.

1 cup butter/margarine	1 teaspoon nutmeg
1 cup brown sugar	1/2 cup evaporated milk
2 eggs	1 teaspoon vinegar
2 cups flour	2 cups granola
1/2 teaspoon salt	1/2 cup walnuts
1 teaspoon baking soda	1 cup raisins *or* chopped dates
1 teaspoon cinnamon	

Beat the butter, sugar, and eggs until fluffy. Stir together the flour, salt, soda, and spices. Combine the milk and vinegar (or use buttermilk or sour milk). Add flour mixture alternately with evaporated milk mixture, stirring well after each addition. Mix in granola, nuts, and raisins.

Drop by teaspoonsful on a cookie sheet. Bake at 375° for 8 to 10 minutes. While slightly warm, frost with Orange Glaze or Light Butter Frosting (see the Appendix). Sprinkle with non-pareils for a festive touch. Makes 5 1/2 dozen. These make great Christmas gifts and freeze well.

CRUNCHY GRANOLA COOKIES

These are delicious and perfect with mixed fruit. Just follow the recipe for Crunchy Jumbles (under Cereals); omit the chocolate bits and substitute granola for the Rice Krispies.

◆

MOON BALLS

Fun for the kiddies. A good nutritional snack for little hands to make. And delightfully sticky.

1 cup dry milk	1/2 cup peanut butter
1/2 cup honey	1/2 cup granola, crushed

Mix dry milk, honey, and peanut butter together until well blended. Chill. Form into small balls and roll in the cereal. Or you can blend in the cereal, form into balls, and roll them in coconut. Makes 3 dozen.

☆☆☆ GRANOLA-YOGURT BREAD

If your granola has fruits and nuts in it, use it anyway; the bread can only be more interesting.

1 1/2 tablespoons dry yeast	5 to 5 1/2 cups flour
1 1/2 cups very warm water, divided	2 teaspoons salt
1 teaspoon honey	2 cups granola
1 cup plain yogurt	

Sprinkle the yeast into 1/2 cup of the water; stir in the honey and dissolve the yeast. Let stand to proof about 10 minutes; it will bubble very nicely.

Combine the remaining water (1 cup), yogurt, and salt in a large bowl. Stir in the yeast mixture. Beat in 4 cups of the flour with an electric mixer at medium speed about 2 minutes. Stir in the cereal. Gradually stir in remaining flour to make a stiff dough.

Turn out on a floured board and knead until smooth, about 10 minutes. Place in buttered large bowl, turn to grease top. Cover with a towel or plate. Let rise until double, about 1 hour.

Punch down, knead a minute or so; cover with the bowl and let rest for 10 minutes. Then shape into two loaves (you can make braids, or round loaves, or place in 9 x 5 loaf pans). If you make round loaves, cut a deep cross in the top of each. Brush with egg if you like (I never do).

Bake at 375° for 35 minutes or until golden brown.

GRANOLA MUFFINS

2 cups granola	1/4 teaspoon salt
1 cup flour	2 eggs
2 tablespoons sugar	1 cup milk
3 teaspoons baking powder	4 tablespoons butter/margarine, melted

In a medium bowl, stir together the cereal, flour, sugar, baking powder, and salt. In a separate bowl, beat together the remaining ingredients. Pour them all at once into the flour mixture and stir only 8 to 10 times, just to moisten the flour. The batter will be lumpy and thin.

Pour into 12 well-greased muffin cups. Bake at 375° for 25 minutes, or until lightly browned. Serve warm with butter and jelly. Makes 12 large muffins. You can freeze these. You can cut the recipe in half.

Grapefruit

I always associate grapefruit with the Christmas season—the time the really delicious citrus fruit comes in. Generally I eat the grapefruit plain, cut in half, for breakfast. For a dessert you can fancy up the grapefruit by putting a tablespoon of sherry on each half and running this under the broiler for about 5 minutes. Of course grapefruit can be mixed with other fruits in a compote; it is especially good with orange sections.

GRAPEFRUIT JELLY WITH SHERRY

This and the following are delightful aspic salads, especially good with ham or poultry dishes.

2 1/2 tablespoons plain gelatin	1/2 cup sherry
1 cup water, divided	1/4 teaspoon salt
1 cup sugar	cream cheese and chopped nuts
2 1/2 cups fresh grapefruit juice	grapefruit sections
3 tablespoons lemon juice	avocado slices

Soak the gelatin in 1/2 cup cold water. Combine the sugar with 1/2 cup water and cook until it is dissolved. Stir the gelatin into the hot syrup until dissolved. Cool. Then add the grapefruit and lemon juices, sherry, and salt. Pour these ingredients into a well-oiled 9-inch ring mold. Chill the jelly until it is firm. Turn it out on a bed of lettuce and fill the center with cream cheese balls rolled in chopped nuts. Garnish the outer edge with grapefruit sections and avocado slices. Serve with a vinaigrette dressing, or fruit salad dressing (see Avocado and Grapefruit Salad). Serves 10.

GRAPEFRUIT ASPIC

1 1/2 tablespoons gelatin	3 large grapefruit
1 cup cold water	3/4 cup chopped celery
1 cup boiling water	1/2 cup blanched shredded almonds
3 tablespoons lemon juice	lettuce
3/4 cup sugar	

Soften the gelatin in the cold water. Then dissolve this mixture in the boiling water. Stir in the lemon juice and sugar, blending well. Chill until it is about to set. Peel the grapefruit, separate the inner skin from the sections. Reserve the juice and add it with the grapefruit sections to the gelatin mixture. Stir in the celery and almonds. Place in a well-oiled ring mold and chill until firm. Unmold on lettuce and serve with mayonnaise. Serves 8.

GRAPEFRUIT SHERBET

Light as air and wonderfully refreshing.

2 teaspoons gelatin	2 cups fresh grapefruit juice
1/2 cup cold water	1/3 cup orange juice
1 cup boiling water	1/4 teaspoon salt
1 cup sugar	2 stiffly beaten egg whites
1/4 cup lemon juice	dash salt

Soak the gelatin in the cold water. Combine the boiling water and sugar and boil for 10 minutes. Then dissolve the gelatin in the hot syrup. Chill, then add in the fruit juices and salt. Beat the egg whites with the dash of salt and fold them in. Pour into trays in the freezer. Every half hour or so, stir it from the back to the front. Freeze for 4 hours or more. Beat with a wire whisk or electric beater before serving.

CANDIED GRAPEFRUIT

This is fun to make and an excellent way to use all the grapefruit. Take the skins of 4 grapefruit. Cover with cold water and bring to a boil. Pour off the liquid, cover again with water, and boil again. Repeat for 5 times.

Weigh the peel and add an equal weight of sugar plus 1/2 cup water for each pound of sugar added.

Cook over medium heat until the liquid is absorbed, about 20 to 25 minutes. Drain on paper toweling. Roll in granulated sugar and let dry. Store airtight.

Other recipes using grapefruit: Avocado-Grapefruit Salad (Avocado); Chicken Livers and Grapefruit (Livers); Cantaloupe Fruit Cups (Melons).

Grapes

Firm grapes are wonderful in salads; slice them in half, and remove the seeds, if any.

☆☆☆ GRAPE PIE

This pie is so good, I can't begin to think of an adjective for it.

4 cups Concord grapes	1 1/2 tablespoons lemon juice
3/4 cup sugar	1 tablespoon grated orange rind
3 tablespoons flour	9 or 10-inch pie shell

Stem the grapes. If they are seedless, life is very simple. If not, you must slip the pulp from the skins, reserve the skins, cook the pulp until the seeds loosen (about 8 minutes), and press it through a sieve or food mill to remove the seeds. Then combine the pulp and the skins and carry on.

Mix together the sugar and flour. Stir the lemon juice and the orange rind into the grapes, then stir in the flour and sugar mixture. Allow these ingredients to stand for about 15 minutes.

Meanwhile, prepare your favorite pie crust, and line the pie plate. Fill the shell with the grape mixture. Place a lattice over the top (if you want to, I never do). Bake the pie at 450° for 10 minutes, then at 350° for 20 minutes longer. If you are using a 9-inch plate, it is a good idea to put a tray under the pie as it is juicy and apt to boil over. Serve it warm and watch it vanish. Serves not very many very quickly.

CONCORD GRAPE KUCHEN

A cakelike variation of the pie. Serve with whipped cream and finely sliced toasted almonds sprinkled on top.

•Pastry•	•Filling•
2 cups flour	2 pounds (about 4 cups) grapes
1/2 teaspoon salt	3 tablespoons flour
1/4 teaspoon baking powder	3/4 cup sugar
2 tablespoons sugar	1 tablespoon lemon juice
1/2 cup butter/margarine	2 egg yolks
	1 cup sour cream

Pastry: Sift the dry ingredients into a bowl. Cut in the butter/margarine until the mixture resembles crumbs. Press an even layer over the bottom of a 9-inch square pan, and about two-thirds up the sides. Chill.

Filling: If your grapes have seeds, follow the procedure above for removing them. Combine the grapes, flour, sugar, and lemon juice. Pour into the prepared pastry and bake at 400° for 15 minutes.

Beat the egg yolks and sour cream together, pour over the surface of the cake, and return to the oven. Continue baking 25 to 30 minutes longer. Cut in squares and serve.

GRAPE JELLY

You can make jelly from almost any grapes that you like the flavor of, providing they are firm and undamaged. It is fun to try different flavors and colors. My favorite grapes for jelly are Delaware grapes; they are small and firm, and the jelly comes out the marvelous color of a deep-pink *vin rosé*. The flavor too is extraordinary.

Select underripe grapes. Wash them and remove the stems. Put them in a kettle with a small amount of water (about 2 tablespoons to 4 cups of grapes is plenty). Cut up a green apple or two in fine slices and add to the grapes. Cook gently until the fruit is soft. Strain through a jelly bag.

For an explanation of jelly making, see under Black Raspberries in the section on Berries. Boil the grape juice 5 minutes before adding the sugar. Use between 1/2 and 3/4 cup sugar to each cup of grape juice. The amount varies according to the sweetness of the grapes and your taste. Be sure to taste before you add the greater amount of sugar. You can always add more, but you can't take away what is already in. You can, however, always add some lemon juice. Do not cook more than 4 cups of juice at a time.

HEAVENLY JAM

A jam as good as its name and a wonderful way to use up lots of grapes. Use Concord grapes, or another purple sweet grape.

6 pounds grapes	2 pounds raisins
4 oranges	2 cups chopped nutmeats
8 cups sugar	

See above for removing seeds from grapes. Place the grape juice, pulp, and skins in a large kettle. Remove the seeds and pith from the oranges and grind them, peels and all; add with the sugar and raisins. Stir well, taste, and add more sugar if too tart. Cook over high heat, stirring often, until the mixture jells. Add the nutmeats and pour into sterilized jars. Cover immediately with paraffin.

GRAPE JUICE

Wash the grapes you have, pick them over, remove the stems. Cover with boiling water and heat slowly to simmering. Do not boil them. Cook slowly until the fruit is very soft, then strain it through a strainer or bag. Add 1/2 cup sugar to each quart of juice. You can preserve the juice by canning, or you can put it in the refrigerator and drink it.

RAW GRAPE JUICE

A really easy, healthful, deliciously different kind of grape juice can be made by taking several bunches of grapes; take off the stems and put the grapes in the blender, seeds and all. Blend at high speed until the skins are torn up, about 30 seconds. Strain, chill if you like, and drink it up. If you don't have a blender, you can use a food mill (Foley mill). If you are fortunate enough to have a juice extractor, then use that.

Other recipes using green grapes: Indian Melon Salad, Fruited Chicken Salad (Chicken); Turkey Curry.

Ham

Leftover ham disappears all too quickly in our house. We make ham spread, omelettes, potato salad, potato cakes, and scalloped potatoes with ground ham. Many noodle casseroles, hash (see under Turkey), and Saturday Night Casserole (under Bread) are excellent with the addition of ground ham.

HAM SQUARES

This elegant and unusual hot canapé comes from Austria, where the baked mixture is cut in doughnut shapes.

3 tablespoons butter	1 cup sour cream
5 eggs, separated	1/4 cup grated parmesan
	3 1/2 cups finely chopped ham

Cream the butter with the egg yolks and half the sour cream until fluffy. Add all but 1 tablespoon of the cheese, and 2 1/2 cups ham. Fold in stiffly beaten egg whites. Pour this mixture, about 1/4 inch high, into a buttered baking dish (about 14 x 10 inches) and bake at 375° about 15 minutes or until it begins to get firm. Spread with remaining sour cream; sprinkle with remaining ham and cheese. Continue baking 15 minutes longer or until golden brown. While still hot, cut in 2-inch squares. Serve on toast squares or crackers. Makes about 20 canapés.

HAM TARTINES

3/4 cup finely ground ham
1/4 cup mayonnaise

1/4 cup drained and chopped
chutney
1/2 teaspoon curry powder

Mix everything together and spread on small squares or triangles of toast. Chill 1 hour. Then toast at 450° for about 5 minutes.

HAM MOUSSE

1 package plain gelatin
1/4 cup cold water
1/2 cup boiling water

2 cups chopped ham
dash of cayenne
1 teaspoon Dijon mustard
1/2 cup evaporated milk, chilled

Dissolve the gelatin in the cold water; then add the boiling water and mix well; cool somewhat. Stir in the chopped ham, cayenne, mustard. Beat the milk until stiff and fold it in. Chill in a wet mold until set. Unmold on a bed of greens (spinach is wonderful and pretty), garnish with hard-boiled egg wedges and cherry tomatoes.

PARSLEYED HAM

This is a French dish, speciality of Burgundy. If your thoughts turn to the perfect, gourmet picnic, include this one.

3 cups broth or bouillon
1 1/2 tablespoons plain gelatin

3 cups diced cooked ham
1 cup chopped parsley

If you have some clear vegetable or meat stock, use it for the aspic. Or dissolve 2 bouillon cubes in the water. Make sure the bouillon is very hot, and dissolve the gelatin in it. Cool slightly. Combine the ham and parsley and press firmly into a mold or bowl. Pour the cooled gelatin mixture over the ham until it just reaches the top. Cover with a plate and top with a weight. Chill thoroughly.

Unmold on a platter, slice, and serve with Mustard Sauce (combine 1/2 cup Dijon mustard with 1/2 cup very finely chopped sweet and sour pickles mixed— this sauce is delicious with many cold meats). Serves 6.

HAM MUFFINS

Try serving these at your next summer buffet with a large mixed green salad.

1 cup flour	1/4 teaspoon salt
1 cup cornmeal	3/4 cup milk
3/4 cup ground ham	1/3 cup margarine, melted
2 teaspoons baking powder	2 eggs

Stir together the flour, cornmeal, ham, baking powder, and salt in a mixing bowl. Combine the wet ingredients and pour all at once into the dry. Stir just until combined. Spoon into 16 well-greased muffin cups. Bake at 400° for 12 minutes. Serve hot. Wonderful with slices of Swiss cheese or sharp cheddar.

◆

CREPES WITH HAM

• Crepes •	• Filling and Sauce •
2 eggs	2 tablespoons butter/margarine
1/3 cup flour	2 tablespoons flour
1 cup milk	dash salt
1/4 teaspoon sugar	1/8 teaspoon pepper
1/4 teaspoon salt	1/2 teaspoon dry mustard
oil	2 cups milk, divided
	1 1/4 cups shredded gruyère or Swiss cheese
	2 1/2 cups diced ham

To make the crepes, beat the eggs in a medium bowl; beat in the flour, milk, sugar, and salt. Heat a small skillet and brush with oil; pour 2 tablespoons batter into pan, quickly tilt to spread. Cook until edges brown, turn, heat 1 minute longer. Make 12. Remove to a plate, keep warm.

Make a cream sauce with the butter, flour, salt, pepper, and mustard, stirring in 1 1/2 cups milk. Cook, stirring constantly, until the sauce thickens and bubbles; then cook 3 minutes longer. Add 1 cup of the cheese and blend until it melts.

Combine 1 cup of the sauce with the ham; blend remaining 1/2 cup milk into the cheese sauce. Place about 3 tablespoons filling on each crepe. Roll to enclose, fold ends under, and arrange in one layer in a shallow baking dish. Pour remaining sauce over crepes and sprinkle with remaining cheese. Broil, about 5 inches from the heat, until the cheese is melted and browned and the sauce is bubbly, about 5 minutes. Serves 6.

Variation: Substitute finely chopped chicken or turkey for the ham, increase salt to 1/4 teaspoon in the sauce, add 1/4 teaspoon paprika, some chopped parsley, and a little tarragon.

HAM KABOBS WITH SWISS

This recipe makes a great cook-out treat for a children's party. The children assemble their own kabobs, you broil them on the outside grill; everyone is entertained, deliciously fed, and there's no cleaning up. Also fun for grownups.

ham, cut in 1 inch cubes	dill pickle slices
green pepper squares	frankfurter buns *or* Italian rolls,
cocktail onions	split, buttered, toasted
cherry tomatoes	slices of Swiss cheese

Thread ham, peppers, onions, tomatoes, pickles on skewers. Broil several minutes on each side or until lightly browned; brush with mustard, if desired. Cover each half bun with a slice of cheese; broil until cheese is melted. Serve each kabob with cheese-toasted bun.

HAM ROLL-UPS

Here is an easy and very elegant dish. This particular version is a favorite dish of a dear French friend. Ingredients can vary, so can quantities. Use your imagination.

4 slices bacon, cooked, crumbled	chopped shallots
1 small onion, chopped fine	4 to 6 thin slices of ham
1 hard-boiled egg, chopped fine	grated gruyère
2 tablespoons rich milk	butter
thin cream sauce (see the Appendix)	bread crumbs

Fry the bacon and pour off most of the fat. Drain on paper towel and crumble. Sauté the onions. Then combine the crumbled bacon, chopped egg, and some bread crumbs with a small amount of rich milk, just so it holds together. Make the cream sauce and blend in some chopped shallots.

Place the filling on the ham slices, roll up, and place, seam side down, in a flat baking dish. Pour the cream sauce over the top, cover with the cheese, dot with butter, and sprinkle with bread crumbs. Bake at 375° until the cheese is melted and the sauce is browned. Serves 2 to 3.

Variation: Use 6 slices ham and make a filling of 1 cup cracker crumbs, 1 cup brown sugar, 1 tablespoon mustard, moistened with a little milk. Pack the rolls in a buttered baking dish. Pour cream or evaporated milk or thin cream sauce over just to cover. Bake at 350° for 45 minutes. Serves 6.

HAM-CORN BREAD RING WITH PEAS

3/4 cup cornmeal
1 cup flour
1/4 cup sugar
2 teaspoons baking powder
1/2 teaspoon baking soda
1/4 teaspoon salt

1 cup dairy sour cream
1/4 cup milk
1 egg, beaten
2 tablespoons margarine, melted
1 cup ground cooked ham
cooked peas

Combine the dry ingredients in a large bowl. Mix together the wet ingredients, except the peas, and blend into the dry, stirring just to blend. Pour into a well-greased 6-cup ring mold, patting the mixture down and leveling off the top. Bake at 425° about 20 minutes. Let stand 2 or 3 minutes, then turn out on a hot serving plate. Fill the center with peas, creamed or not, as you like. Serves 6.

Variation: Substitute other vegetables for the peas.

☆☆☆ SCHINKEN MAKKARONI

This casserole is very easy to make. I have made this casserole many times and in different quantities; what I give here makes a large casserole; you can easily cut it in half. This is the German version of a very popular and wide-spread central European dish. There are Czech, Polish, and Austrian versions that I know of; the last has egg in it and is called *Schinkenfleckerl.*

3 to 4 cups ground ham
1 pound macaroni

2 cups dairy sour cream
2 cups beef bouillon
parmesan cheese

The ham can be ground with a coarse blade; run a cracker through the grinder to get all the ham and dump that in too. If you possibly can, use *perciatelli,* that is, macaroni in long pieces. Cook it about 6 minutes, then drain well. In a large baking dish arrange layers: macaroni, ham, spoonfuls of sour cream; repeat. Top with a thick layer of macaroni. Sprinkle generously with parmesan cheese. Dissolve 2 bouillon cubes (or a little less, as ham is salty) in 2 cups boiling water, and pour over the top. Bake at 375° for 45 minutes or until the macaroni is brown and crunchy (my children fight over that part of the casserole). Serves 8.

HAM AND CORN QUICHE

1 9-inch unbaked pastry shell
2 eggs, slightly beaten
1 cup cubed ham
1 cup shredded Swiss cheese
2 tablespoons minced green onion

1 cup cooked cut corn
1/2 cup evaporated milk *or*
   light cream

Prepare the pie shell. Combine all the ingredients, except the parsley. Pour into the shell and spread evenly. Sprinkle parsley flakes on top. Bake at 350° 40 to 50 minutes, until filling is set and crust is golden brown. Cool 5 minutes before serving. Serves 6 to 8.

Other recipes using ham: Scalloped Cauliflower and Ham; Basic Soup (Legumes); Macaroni and Chicken Salad; Fettucine with Egg Sauce (Noodles and Pasta); Curried Pear Salad; Stuffed Peppers; Ham and Potato Salad (Potatoes); squash stuffings; Turkey Ham Bake.

Jams, Jellies, Marmalades

We usually don't have much leftover preserves to use up, but I find that occasionally there is that jar of some jam or jelly that no one really wants to eat, or that has gotten a little tired with time. You can melt jelly and use it for a glaze on a fresh fruit tart or a custard pudding.

PINEAPPLE RING

This is a lovely breakfast cake and easy to make. This recipe and the following call for pineapple jam, but you can easily substitute some other flavor.

Dough	2 cups flour
1/3 cup milk, scalded	1/4 cup rolled oats
1/4 cup sugar	3 tablespoons melted butter, divided
1/2 teaspoon salt	
2 tablespoons soft butter	Filling
1 package yeast	1/2 cup raisins
1/4 cup warm water	1/4 cup pineapple jam
1 egg	dash of cinnamon

Stir the milk into a large bowl in which you have put the sugar, salt, and butter. Cool to lukewarm. Dissolve the yeast in the warm water and add it to the milk mixture. Beat in the egg, then stir in the flour and oats. Let rest about 10 minutes.

Toss the dough on a floured board several times, then roll it to a 15 x 8 rectangle. Brush with 1 tablespoon melted butter.

Combine the raisins, pineapple jam, and cinnamon; spread over the dough. Cut the rectangle lengthwise into two strips. Roll each from the long side, seal, pinch edges. Then twist the two rolls together and form them into a ring. Seal the ends carefully. Brush top with remaining melted butter.

Place on a cookie sheet and let rise until double. Bake at 350° for 30 minutes. Cool 10 minutes. Mix together Confectioners Sugar Glaze (use one-half of the recipe in the Appendix) and spread it over the top. Sprinkle with chopped pecans.

GATOS

I got this recipe from the Girl Scouts at some international festival. The origin is South American. The squares are easy to make.

2 eggs	2 cups flour
3/4 cup sugar	2 teaspoons baking powder
2/3 cup oil	1/2 teaspoon salt
2 teaspoons vanilla	1 cup pineapple jam

Beat the eggs, gradually add the sugar, oil, and vanilla. Stir in the dry ingredients. Pour half the batter into a greased 8-inch square pan and spread the pineapple preserve over the top. Then spoon the rest of the batter on top of the jam and spread gently with a knife. Bake at 375° for 30 minutes or until browned. Cool and cut into squares.

FRUITED DATE SAUCE

This is very good over rice pudding, custards, plain layer or sponge cake. It is also splendid over gingerbread.

1 1/2 cups orange juice
3/4 cup apricot preserves
2 tablespoons cornstarch

1/3 cup lemon juice
3/4 cup chopped dates

Combine the orange juice and preserves in a saucepan and simmer, covered, about 5 minutes, stirring occasionally. Blend the cornstarch with the lemon juice until smooth. Add it to the hot mixture and boil, stirring constantly. Cook until thickened and clear. Stir in the dates. Makes 2 1/2 cups.

THREE FRUIT TOPPING

2 small apples
1 can (11 ounces) mandarin
   oranges

1/2 cup strawberry preserves
2 tablespoons kirsch or sherry

Peel, core, and chop the apples fine. Combine with the orange wedges, which you have drained. Heat the jam gently with the kirsch or sherry. Pour this over the fruit mixture and toss to blend. Makes about 3 cups.

JELLY FROSTING

1/2 cup jelly
1 unbeaten egg white

dash of salt

So quick that it is hard to believe. In the top of the double boiler, over boiling water, combine the ingredients. Beat about 5 minutes until the jelly has disappeared. Take off the heat and keep beating until the frosting stands in stiff peaks.

BARBECUE HOT DOGS

Try this for the child's birthday luncheon, or for an informal cocktail party in the back yard.

raw hot dogs, cut up   **2 teaspoons prepared mustard**
old jelly (about 1/4 cup)

Make a sauce from the jelly and mustard. Simmer the cut-up hot dogs in the sauce about 15 minutes. Serve on toast or with toothpicks.

———————◆———————

CARROT MARMALADE

This marmalade has a beautiful color and an excellent flavor. It was popular years ago and certainly deserves a revival.

4 cups cooked, sliced carrots   **2 oranges**
2 lemons   **6 cups sugar**

Put the carrots along with the lemons and oranges (seeded) through a food grinder, using a coarse blade. Be sure to save all the juice. Put in a large heavy saucepan, add the sugar, and cook *very* slowly until thick—this will take some time. You should stir the marmalade frequently. Pour while hot into hot sterilized jars and seal at once with paraffin. Makes about 3 pints.

☆☆☆ PEACH MARMALADE

Peel and slice firm peaches. Allow 1/2 cup sugar for every cupful of sliced peaches. For every 5 cups of peaches, allow 1 seeded orange and 1/2 lemon, cut very fine, rind and all. Let everything stand for 2 hours. Then boil the mixture, stirring frequently, until the syrup is heavy. The marmalade will not be stiff, but it is wonderful. Pour into sterilized jars and seal with paraffin.

ORANGE MARMALADE

4 oranges (2 cups)	sugar
3 lemons (1 1/2 cups)	6 cups water

Slice the fruit very thin, remove the seeds and some pith, and cut in small wedges. Add the water to the prepared fruit and let stand overnight. On the next day cook the mixture until the fruit is tender (about 30 minutes). Let stand overnight again.

On the third day (this begins to sound like the creation story), add 2 cups of sugar for each pint (2 cups) of fruit and liquid. Cook to a jelly stage (about 10 minutes). Pour into sterilized jars and seal while hot with paraffin.

◆

☆☆☆ MARMALADE TEA LOAF

I make this tea bread very often. It helps use up the yogurt (the recipe calls for plain, but if you have some in a compatible flavor—lemon, orange, apple, for example—do use it instead; you might like to reduce the sugar to 2 tablespoons). This bread has a rich orange color.

3 cups flour	2 eggs
1/4 cup sugar	1 1/2 cups orange marmalade
2 teaspoons baking powder	1 cup plain yogurt
1/2 teaspoon salt	1 tablespoon grated orange rind
1 teaspoon baking soda	1/2 cup toasted slivered almonds
	1/2 to 1 cup chopped cranberries

Sift the dry ingredients into a large bowl. Beat the eggs well, stir in the marmalade, yogurt, orange rind, nuts, and cranberries (which are optional. I always add them because I like the taste, not to mention the color).

Fold the egg mixture into the dry ingredients; mix until just blended and no dry flour appears.

Pour into three 7 1/2 x 3 1/2 loaf pans, well-greased. Bake at 350° for about 1 hour. Let cool for 5 minutes and then turn out of the pan.

ORANGE STREUSEL MUFFINS

2 cups flour	1 tablespoon orange rind
1/3 cup sugar	1/2 cup orange juice
3 teaspoons baking powder	1/2 cup orange marmalade *or*
1/2 teaspoon salt	pineapple preserves
1/2 cup chopped pecans	1/4 cup milk
1 egg	1/4 cup oil

Sift the dry ingredients into a large bowl. Stir in the nuts.

Beat the egg well, add the remaining ingredients, and blend thoroughly.

Fold the wet mixture into the dry, stirring only until just blended. Fill greased muffin cups two-thirds full. Sprinkle with a topping made from 1/4 cup sugar, 1 tablespoon flour, 1 tablespoon butter, 1/2 teaspoon cinnamon, and 1/4 teaspoon nutmeg.

Bake at 400° about 20 minutes. Makes 12 large muffins, 16 smaller ones.

☆☆☆ FRUIT NUT SQUARES

Like the Marmalade Tea Loaf, this recipe calls for no shortening. Even so, this makes a sweet, substantial bar cookie, one that everyone likes. I often double the recipe and bake it in a 15 x 10 pan.

1 egg	1/2 cup chopped raisins
1/4 cup sugar	1/2 cup chopped nuts
1/3 cup flour	1/2 teaspoon vanilla
1/3 teaspoon baking powder	1/2 cup orange marmalade
pinch salt	

Beat the egg; blend in the sugar and beat again. Take out 2 tablespoons from the flour and mix with the raisins and nuts. Sift the remaining flour with the baking powder and salt. Add to the egg and sugar.

Stir in the floured raisins and nuts, vanilla, and marmalade, and blend well. Pour into a well-greased 8 x 8 pan.

Bake for 30 minutes at 350°. Remove from oven, and while still warm, glaze with a mixture of 1 tablespoon orange juice, 1 tablespoon lemon juice, and 1 cup 10X sugar. In fact, I use this amount to glaze the double recipe, and it seems like plenty to me. Cool thoroughly and cut into squares.

Other recipes using marmalade: Cream Cheese Cookies; Almond Snowcap Cookies (Egg Whites); Linzertorte, Viennese Rounds (Nuts); Quick Breakfast Cake (Sour Milk); Baked Apples with Wine (Wine).

Lamb

The perfect roast is a leg of spring lamb, laced with garlic slivers, roasted slowly with a generous sprinkling of rosemary, oregano, or thyme over the top. And, for heaven's sake, cooked just until it is pale pink. No more. Then you slice it, cover it with pan juices, and serve with the potatoes you have roasted in the same pan.

Cold roast lamb is almost as good as the warm. Slice it thin and serve with dill pickles or chutney. I look forward to having a roast of lamb because there are such wonderful dishes to make with the remains.

LAMB TERRAPIN

This is a favorite luncheon or supper dish; it has a very unique flavor. Serve it on hot toast, on steaming grain of some sort, or on noodles.

2 cups diced cooked lamb	3 tablespoons flour
2 hard-boiled eggs, chopped fine	1 teaspoon dry mustard
2 tablespoons olive oil	2 cups lamb *or* vegetable stock
1 tablespoon lemon juice	1 teaspoon worcestershire sauce
2 tablespoons butter	salt and pepper

Combine the lamb, eggs, olive oil, and lemon juice; set aside. Make a cream sauce with the butter, flour, mustard, and stock. Stir until boiling and thickened, adding the worcestershire sauce, salt and pepper to taste. Add the lamb and egg mixture and heat thoroughly. Serves 4.

☆☆☆ DEMI-CASSOULET

This recipe is my own invention, because I love the French *cassoulet toulou-sain,* but only about half of it. If I were to eat the whole thing (complete with homemade pork sausage, goose breast, and roast pork slices, not to mention the accompanying fat), I know I should suffer from indigestion for several days. So here is a modest, cut-down version. All the ingredients are readily available, and the result is a very special dish.

1/2 pound navy beans	2 cups chopped tomatoes *or*
4 slices bacon	1 16-ounce can whole tomatoes
2 1/2 cups cut-up roast lamb	pinch of thyme, basil, pepper
1/2 pound Italian sweet sausage	1 bay leaf
1 large onion, chopped	salt to taste
1 clove garlic, minced	

Soak the beans overnight; drain. Put to cook in fresh water to cover and simmer about 1 hour. Drain, reserving the liquid, and put in a large stove-top casserole.

Fry the bacon, drain, and crumble. Drain off most of the fat and sauté the lamb to brown. Add to the beans in the casserole, along with the bacon. Then sauté the sausage, onion, and garlic. Add the tomatoes and herbs. Season with salt and pepper, if desired, and cook about an hour, adding more bean liquid, if necessary.

Dump the tomato mixture into the casserole. Chill overnight. Then cook slowly 3 to 4 hours the next day, adding the remainder of the bean liquid. If you have any left, add reserved lamb juices from the roast, with the fat removed. Good with boiled or mashed potatoes, or rice. Serves 4.

CURRIED LAMB

3 tablespoons butter/margarine	2 cups diced cooked lamb
1 teaspoon curry powder	2 teaspoon flour
1 medium onion, peeled and sliced	1 cup chicken broth *or* stock
1 large stalk celery, sliced	1 tablespoon lemon juice
2 medium apples, peeled and sliced	rice

Melt the butter in a heavy frying pan, add the curry powder (and do feel free to add more if you like it), and sizzle for a minute or so. Then add the onion, celery, and apples and cook until the onion is tender. With a slotted spoon, re-move the vegetables and apple, add the lamb to the pan, and brown it. Remove it as well. Blend the flour into the pan, then stir in the broth. Bring to boiling and cook two minutes, stirring constantly. Return the vegetables, apple, and lamb to the pan, stir in the lemon juice. Add salt if needed. Serve over hot boiled rice with chutney and cold beer. Serves 4.

If you are really doing up the curry properly, serve it with five or six of the following condiments: flaked coconut, crisp bacon pieces, chopped peanuts, chopped chives, chopped green onions, raisins soaked in brandy (or sherry, or wine), chopped fresh green peppers, cherry tomatoes, sliced radishes, sliced hardcooked eggs, finely chopped celery, fresh orange sections, seedless grapes, pineapple chunks, marinated mushrooms.

This curry can be expanded in this way to serve many more people.

LAMB PROVENÇAL STYLE

4 cups cubed cooked lamb	1 1/2 teaspoon crumbled basil,
2 tablespoons olive oil	divided
2 large onions, sliced	1 teaspoon salt, divided
2 cloves garlic, minced	1/4 teaspoon pepper
	3 small zucchini, sliced thin

Make sure the fat is trimmed from the lamb. Heat the oil over medium-high heat and sauté the lamb on all sides until very brown. Reduce the heat somewhat and add the onions; sauté until soft. Add the garlic, 1 teaspoon basil, 1/2 teaspoon salt, and the pepper. Cover the skillet and cook 10 minutes.

Thinly slice the zucchini and add to the skillet with the remaining basil and salt. Cook, stirring gently, until the zucchini are translucent and have rendered their juices. Very good with potatoes or brown rice. Serves 6.

Variation: Add 2 cups peeled, chopped tomatoes with the zucchini.

All the recipes for using slices or pieces of leftover beef can be made with lamb. A delicious hearty soup can be made with the lamb bones, sauce, leftover bits and pieces; be sure it has lots of carrots, celery, and barley in it. My mother always made a casserole from lamb and noodles; I don't remember it with very much joy, but if you like the idea, make Noodle Surprise, and add some finely diced cooked lamb to it. Yogurt Spinach Soup (Yogurt) is excellent with lamb.

Leeks

What a delicate and distinctive flavor leeks have! Be sure to wash them carefully; many layers can hide much dirt. You can slice them thin and add them to your green salad. You can substitute them in any of the recipes under onions, just remember that their flavor is much less pronounced.

POT AU FEU

3 pounds shin bone, cut in two
   or three pieces
salt
6 leeks, sliced
2 onions, cut fine
3 ribs celery with tops

3 carrots
2 to 3 large potatoes, diced
1 bay leaf
thyme
salt and pepper to taste

Put the meat in a large soup pot, sprinkle some salt over it, and add 2 quarts of water. Let it stand for an hour or so. Bring it to a boil, skim off the scum (the dog will love it), reduce the heat, and simmer covered for about 3 hours.

Then add the leeks and onions, the celery cut in 3-inch lengths and the tops chopped, the carrots quartered and cut in 3-inch lengths, the potatoes (leave the skins on), and the seasonings. Simmer until the vegetables are cooked.

To serve, remove the meat, cut in serving pieces, give the marrow to the most deserving, arrange the vegetables around, pour lots of stock over it all, and serve with coarse salt and Dijon mustard. If there is stock left over, add some beef bouillon powder for more flavor, more vegetables, including diced tomatoes, some barley, seasonings to your taste, and you have a wonderful vegetable soup.

☆☆☆ LEEK AND POTATO SOUP

One of the truly superb soups.

3 medium-sized leeks	4 medium potatoes
2 green onions	2 cups chicken broth
1 tablespoon butter	chopped chives

Mince the white part of the leeks and onions. Sauté them, stirring, for about 3 minutes in the butter. Peel the potatoes, and slice them very fine. Add them with the broth; simmer the vegetables until tender.

Now comes your choice between the hearty peasant soup and the elegant gourmet fare. You can season the soup and serve it as is, adding more stock or water if you like. Or you can whirl the soup in the blender for several minutes at high speed, so that it is satin smooth. Thin it with cream, add salt and pepper to taste. Garnish with chopped chives. Serve hot or cold. In this form it is called *Vichyssoise* (please pronounce the s at the end as in Oz). Serves 4 to 6.

Variation: Add 1 1/2 cups chopped sorrel leaves to the soup pot.

LEEKS VINAIGRETTE

This is a common appetizer in good French restaurants. It can also be served as a side dish.

Take a bunch of leeks, small ones if possible, trim them and cut lengthwise almost to the root end. Wash thoroughly to make sure the dirt is all gone. Tie them together neatly, drop into boiling salted water, and simmer until just tender, about 15 minutes. Drain (save the stock for your soup pot) and cool. Mix together 1 teaspoon prepared mustard, salt and pepper, 1 tablespoon lemon juice; slowly add 4 tablespoons olive or salad oil, mixing well. Pour over the leeks and marinate in the refrigerator several hours. Serve well chilled.

LEEKS AU GRATIN

This makes a marvelous side dish with roast beef, for example, or you can serve it for lunch with a green salad. Cook some leeks, using the same method of preparation as above. Drain them, and arrange in a shallow oven-proof dish. Cover with a light cream sauce, sprinkle a generous amount of grated cheddar, or gruyère, or parmesan cheese. Bake at 375° until the sauce is bubbly and the cheese is browned.

You can also purée leeks and garnish them with buttered toasted bread crumbs and chopped parsley.

Other recipes using leeks: Cream of Broccoli Soup.

Legumes

For lack of a better term, I have borrowed this category from *The Joy of Cooking*. Into it go the various highly nutritious dried beans, lentils, split peas.

☆☆☆ BASIC SOUP

Before you start on this soup, though, you must have one essential ingredient —the ham bone. After we've demolished the ham, I put the bone, along with some chopped bits (take off all the fat you can—there is nothing more unappetizing than ham fat swimming in the soup) in the freezer until needed. And when we are ready for a hearty soup, I put the bone and bits into the pot with the following:

2 cups green split peas, lentils,
   navy beans, black beans, garbanzos, *or* any combination
2 quarts cold water
1 chopped onion

2 stalks celery with tops, chopped
3 sprigs parsley, minced
1 carrot, diced
1 bay leaf
salt and pepper

Wash and pick over the split peas (or lentils, or whatever you decide to use), cover with cold water, bring to a boil, turn off the heat, and let stand, covered, for several hours. Dump them into the soup pot with the ham bone and bits and add the remaining ingredients. Cover, bring to a boil slowly. Simmer for 3 to 3 1/2 hours, or until everything is tender. For a smooth soup, put through a food mill or whirl in the blender. Personally I prefer the legumes and vegetables whole. Skim off any excess fat or scum. If necessary, dilute with water or milk. Season to taste with salt and pepper. Remove the bay leaf. Serves 8 to 10.

Variations: Add any or all of the following—1 cup diced cooked or raw potato, 1 cup or so chopped tomatoes, some tomato juice, 1 crushed clove garlic, 1/4 cup raw brown rice, 1/2 teaspoon thyme, 1/2 teaspoon dry mustard, leftover cooked vegetables. These additions can go into the pot when you start the slow cooking.

THREE BEAN SALAD

One of the classic dishes. Here is a tangy, creamy version, one that uses three different dried beans. Serve it very cold.

1/2 cup dry garbanzos
1/2 cup dry kidney beans
1/2 cup dry black beans
1 cup yogurt
4 tablespoons lemon juice
1/2 cup dry milk powder

2 tablespoons honey
1/2 teaspoon salt
1/4 teaspoon curry
1/2 teaspoon crushed basil
3 tablespoons chopped chives
3 tablespoons minced parsley

Cook the beans separately. This way they will keep their individual colors. Cook them until tender, but still firm. Drain well.

Whisk the yogurt until smooth. Stir the lemon juice and milk powder together to make a paste; whisk this into the yogurt. Blend in the honey, salt, and herbs. Pour the dressing over the beans. Toss gently, cover, and refrigerate several hours before serving. Serves 8.

Note: Cooked garbanzos (chick peas) are wonderful in salads, especially mixed green and tuna fish salads.

MIDDLE EAST BEANS IN PITA

Here is a wonderful luncheon idea. Make your own pita bread, or get some at the grocery store. Use whole wheat pita, if you can get it.

4 cups cooked garbanzos, drained	pita breads
2 cloves garlic, minced	shredded lettuce
3/4 teaspoon ground coriander	tomatoes, chopped
1/2 teaspoon cumin	cucumber, chopped
1 tablespoon chopped parsley	onion, chopped
1/4 teaspoon cayenne	plain yogurt
2 tablespoons lemon juice	

Mix the first seven ingredients. Cut the pita breads open at one end with scissors, fill with the mixture, then top with remaining ingredients. Eat as a sandwich. Makes enough for 10 to 12.

GARBANZO AND PINEAPPLE LOAF

I have a child who loves garbanzos; she calls them "French peas," because they frequently appear on the hors d'oeuvre platter in France. I have made this loaf often for her. The leftovers make a great sandwich spread. The texture is light and nicely crunchy.

1/2 cup garbanzos	3 tablespoons oil
1 cup whole grain bread crumbs	1 egg, beaten
1 cup pineapple juice	1 tablespoon yogurt
1 cup chopped onion	1/2 teaspoon salt
1/2 cup chopped celery	2 pinches cayenne
1/4 cup minced parsley	1 cup shredded Swiss *or* aged cheddar

Cook the garbanzos until tender; drain. Combine the crumbs and pineapple juice and let them soak. Prepare the vegetables. Chop the garbanzos coarsely or grind them in a grinder with a coarse blade. Don't purée them; you want them to crunch.

Combine the garbanzos, crumb mixture, and all the remaining ingredients in the order given. Turn into a loaf pan. Bake at 350° about 40 minutes, or until the edges are browned. Serves 6.

BEAN AND PEANUT CURRY

Another well-seasoned luncheon dish. Serve with rice or corn.

1 1/2 cups pinto or other beans	4 tomatoes, chopped
2 tablespoons curry powder	2 onions, chopped
6 tablespoons oil	1/2 cup finely chopped raw peanuts
	salt and pepper to taste

Soak the beans 12 to 24 hours, then boil until tender; drain and reserve the stock. Heat the curry in the oil until it sizzles, then add the tomatoes, onions, and drained beans. Put everything in a pot with the reserved bean stock. Add the peanuts and boil for 1 hour. Season with salt and pepper. Serves 4.

☆☆☆ GROUND BEEF WITH LENTILS

Here is a basic meat-with-legumes combination that you can vary in any number of ways. This dish is particularly good with eggplant and yogurt.

1 1/2 cups lentils	2 tablespoons raw brown rice
1 quart water	1 teaspoon sugar
2 tablespoons butter/margarine	1 teaspoon ground cumin
2 medium onions, chopped	1/2 teaspoon pepper
1 clove garlic, minced	1 tablespoon cider vinegar
1 1/2 pounds ground beef *or* 3	salt to taste
cups ground cooked beef	
2 beef bouillon cubes	

Rinse and pick over the lentils. Bring 1 quart of water to boil in a saucepan, add the lentils, and cook 20 minutes. Drain and reserve lentils and liquid.

Heat the butter in a deep skillet, sauté the onions and garlic until tender, stirring occasionally. Stir in beef and brown well. Dissolve the bouillon cubes in 2 1/3 cups reserved liquid and add to meat mixture; cover and simmer 10 minutes. Stir in reserved lentils, rice, sugar, cumin, and pepper. Bring to a boil, reduce heat, cover, and simmer about 45 minutes, or until lentils and rice are tender and liquid is absorbed. Stir in vinegar and season to taste with salt. Serves 6.

Variations:

Use other legumes, such as kidney beans, pinto beans, small navy beans. You may have to cook them somewhat longer.

Add 1 cup sliced carrots with the rice.

Add 1 cup chopped tomatoes toward the end of the cooking time.

LENTIL LOAF

1 cup lentils	1 clove garlic, minced
1/2 cup barley	1 medium onion, minced
4 cups water	1 stalk celery, sliced thin
1/2 teaspoon salt	2 eggs, beaten
1 cup bread crumbs *or* cracker crumbs	1/8 teaspoon nutmeg

Add the lentils and barley to the boiling salted water. Reduce heat and simmer with lid ajar for about 40 minutes or until most of the water is absorbed. Remove from the heat. Add the crumbs and remaining ingredients and mix well. Place in a loaf pan and bake at 350° for 35 minutes. Allow to cool for 15 to 20 minutes before inverting over a platter to serve. Good with a mushroom, tomato, or cheese sauce. Serves 6 to 8.

Variations: Use other legumes—split peas, soybeans, garbanzos, kidney beans. Substitute brown rice for the barley.

LIMA BEANS IN CASSEROLE

A classic dish that my mother used to make. I have a friend who used this dish as a staple while she and her husband struggled through graduate school on a tight budget. If the budget relaxed a little, she would add the bacon slices.

1 pound dried lima beans	salt and pepper
3 tablespoons brown sugar	bacon slices
1 tablespoon butter	2 tablespoons chili sauce *or* catsup (optional)

Soak the beans overnight; cover with water and cook 30 minutes. Drain off most of the stock. Put in a casserole with the remaining ingredients and put bacon slices over the top. Bake at 350° for 30 minutes.

SOYBEAN CASSEROLE

3 cups cooked soybeans	1/2 teaspoon salt
4 tablespoons butter, divided	1/4 teaspoon pepper
1 medium onion, chopped	1/2 cup tomato sauce
1 cup chopped celery	1/2 cup bread crumbs
2 tablespoons chopped green pepper	1/2 cup shredded cheddar cheese
1 clove garlic, minced	

Let the soybeans soak over night in water to cover. Then boil gently until soft, about 3 hours. Add more water, if necessary, to keep the beans covered.

Heat 3 tablespoons butter in a large skillet; sauté the onion, celery, green pepper, and garlic until lightly browned. Stir in the soybeans (drained), salt, pepper, tomato sauce, and crumbs. Spoon the mixture into a 2-quart casserole. Sprinkle with the cheese and dot with remaining butter. Cover. Bake at 375° for 20 minutes, or until cheese is melted and the casserole is bubbly. Serves 4.

Variations:

Colorful: Add 1 carrot, sliced thin, and 1 tablespoon soy sauce.

Vegetable Rice: Combine with the soybean mixture 2 cups cooked corn and 2 cups chopped tomatoes; stir in 1/2 teaspoon thyme and 1/2 teaspoon summer savory; moisten well with stock and alternate with layers of cooked brown rice; sprinkle wheat germ on top with the cheese. Serves 8.

☆☆☆ SUPER PIE

Creamy and rich tasting, this is a wonderful main dish which you can serve with a tossed salad. It has a delightful combination of textures and tastes.

1 cup cooked wheat berries	2 eggs, beaten
1 cup cooked brown rice	1 cup milk
1/2 cup cooked bulgur	1 cup grated cheddar
1 cup cooked lentils	1 teaspoon salt
1 cup cooked kidney beans	1 teaspoon tarragon, crushed
2 cups chopped onions	1/2 teaspoon worcestershire sauce
1 tablespoon butter	

Prepare the grains and legumes. You can easily use other combinations if you so wish. Sauté the onions in the butter until soft and golden. Set aside.

Beat the milk into the eggs; stir in the grated cheese, salt, tarragon, and worcestershire sauce. Then fold in the onions, beans, and grains.

Turn into an oiled 10-inch pie plate or a rectangular pyrex dish (11 1/2 x 7 1/2). Bake at 325° for 25 to 30 minutes. Let stand 10 minutes, then slice. Serves 8.

Other recipes using:

Navy or pea beans: Demi-Cassoulet (Lamb).

Garbanzos: Bulgur and Garbanzos (Grains).

Kidney beans: Super Minestrone (Noodles & Pasta).

Lentils: Walnut Lentil Loaf (Nuts).

Soybeans: Curried Rice Salad; Soybeans and Rice Boats (Zucchini).

Lemons

Many recipes in this collection use lemon juice and/or grated lemon rind. I can think of no single ingredient that enhances different foods more than lemon. It is my favorite seasoning for fresh green vegetables (in fact it is the only thing I add to green beans, asparagus, broccoli—the combination of tastes is perfect for me). Salad dressing made with lemon is delicious, and lemon sauce on vegetables or sweetened lemon sauce on desserts are often the ideal accompaniment. I love the taste of lemon but it has to be real lemon juice and real lemon flavor. Commercially made (or as some say "store boughten") lemon cookies and cakes are the world's worst.

☆☆☆ LEMON SPONGE DESSERT

This delicious pudding, in some mysterious way, separates while baking, leaving a spongelike top and a saucelike bottom. There is never enough of it.

1 cup sugar	juice and grated rind of 2 lemons
1 tablespoon butter	2 eggs, separated
2 tablespoons flour	1 cup milk

Cream the butter and sugar together. Add the flour, lemon juice and rind, egg yolks, and milk. Beat well until smooth.

Fold in the stiffly beaten egg whites. Pour into greased custard cups and set them in a pan of hot water.

Bake at 350° about 30 minutes.

LEMON REVEL PIE

9-inch baked pie shell (not sweet)	1 teaspoon lemon rind
3 ounces semi-sweet chocolate	1/4 cup unstrained lemon juice
3 large eggs, separated	4 tablespoons lemon jello
12 tablespoons sugar, divided	1/2 cup boiling water
1/4 teaspoon salt	1/4 teaspoon cream of tartar

Melt the chocolate and brush the inside of the cooled pie shell with a thin coating of the chocolate. Reserve the rest for later.

Prepare the filling by mixing together in a saucepan the egg yolks, 6 tablespoons sugar, salt, lemon rind and juice. Cook over low heat, stirring constantly until the mixture boils. Remove from heat. Stir the boiling water into the lemon jello, and then with a beater, beat into the hot custard. Cool until partially set. Beat again until smooth.

Prepare a meringue by beating the egg whites with the cream of tartar until frothy. Add the remaining 6 tablespoons sugar, 1 tablespoon at a time, beating between each addition, until the meringue is glossy and stands in peaks. Fold it into the lemon custard, gently please.

Now, back to that pie shell. Pile one-half of the filling into the shell. Dribble 2 tablespoons chocolate over the top. Then add the remaining filling, smooth the top, and dribble the remaining chocolate in a spiral over the top. Put in the refrigerator to cool and set.

◆

LEMON BREAD

One of my best friends serves this bread as a dessert at luncheon parties. And she is absolutely right because it is the perfect sweet to finish a good meal. The bread is light, cakelike, and has lovely pale yellow color.

6 tablespoons butter/margarine	1 1/2 cup flour
1 cup sugar	1/8 teaspoon salt
2 eggs	1 teaspoon baking powder
grated rind of 1 lemon	3 tablespoons sugar ⎰ for topping
1/2 cup milk	juice of 1 lemon ⎱

Cream the butter and sugar, beat in the eggs and lemon rind. Sift the dry ingredients and add alternately with the milk. Pour into a 9 x 5 loaf pan, and let the mixture stand 20 minutes before baking.

Bake at 325°-350° for 1 hour. Mix the sugar and lemon juice and pour over the loaf while it is still hot. Cool completely, and store for one day if possible before slicing.

Other recipes using lemons: conserves (see the Index); Avocado and Tomato Soup; Lemon Bread Pudding (Bread); Lemon Bisque (Evaporated Milk); Rhubarb Bread Pudding (Rhubarb); Melon in Chablis, Orange and Lemon Jelly (Wine).

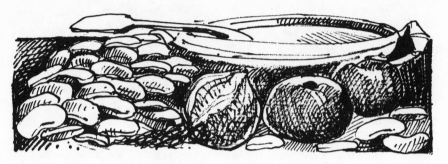

Lima Beans

I grew up in the country, and although we did not have a farm, we did have a wonderful vegetable garden. I can remember the pole lima beans, which we picked young and tender; my mother boiled them just a few minutes, and we ate them by the ton.

One fine way to eat lima beans is in succotash (a good combination of roughly equal quantities of cooked corn and lima beans, seasoned, and served with a sauce of milk and butter). Of course they can be added to vegetable soups, or if you have a quantity left over, just follow the recipe for Hot Dog Soup (under Beans).

QUICK LIMA BEAN SOUP

4 slices bacon, cut in 1/2-inch pieces	3 cups hot water
1/3 cup finely chopped onion	1 1/2 cups cooked lima beans
1 large tomato, chopped	1 tablespoon flour (optional)
2 envelopes instant vegetable broth	1/4 cup grated parmesan

Fry the bacon until crisp. Remove from the pan, drain on a paper towel. Pour off all but a small amount of the drippings. Add the onions and cook until tender. Add the tomato, broth powder, water, lima beans, and half of the bacon. Bring to a boil. Reduce heat and cook gently 15 minutes. If you wish, mix the flour with a little water, and add to the soup. Cook, stirring until thickened slightly. Add salt and pepper to taste.

Serve topped with remaining bacon, crumbled, and the grated cheese. Serves 4.

LIMA BEANS WITH TARRAGON

Several of the savory herbs make a pleasant accompaniment to lima beans. If you like, you can substitute thyme, parsley, marjoram, or savory for the tarragon.

1 1/2 cups fresh lima beans	3/4 cup water
1/2 teaspoon dried tarragon	1 tablespoon butter
1/2 teaspoon salt	

Bring the water to a boil with the salt and add the beans and tarragon to it. Cook until tender, about 20 minutes. Do not drain. Add the butter and serve. You can also serve the lima beans in a cream sauce, to which you have added the tarragon and butter. Serves 3 to 4.

LEIPZIGER ALLERLEI

A traditional German dish, *Allerlei* means medley. I suppose our mixed vegetables is a rough equivalent. The idea is that you can use a combination of vegetables in equal amounts. Lima beans seem to be an essential ingredient in the combination.

3 cups cooked vegetables:	1 cup Mornay sauce:
lima beans, corn, green beans,	1 cup medium cream sauce (see
carrots, peas, cauliflower,	Appendix)
broccoli, zucchini, mushrooms	1 egg yolk
	1/2 cup grated cheese
	dash of dry mustard

Combine the vegetables. Whisk the egg yolk into the hot sauce, then stir in the cheese and mustard; stir until all is well blended. Stir the sauce into the vegetables, and pour into a 1 1/2-quart casserole. Top with bread crumbs, crumbled wheat cereal, toasted wheat germ, or combination. Bake at 400° for 15 to 20 minutes. Serves 6.

Other recipes using lima beans: Perciatelli alla Napoletana (Tomatoes); Veal Casserole. Under Legumes there is a dried lima bean casserole.

Livers

Every good chicken has its liver, and that goes for every good turkey, too, and the best thing to do with them is to collect them in a container in the freezer. When you have enough for a meal or for pâté, defrost them and make any of the following recipes.

◆

Liver pâté is one of the best things you can make from leftover livers (beef and pork as well as chicken). Pâtés are very versatile—you can use them as spreads for sandwiches, or on toast or crackers for lunch. Served with melba toast or attractive crackers, a good pâté is the perfect cocktail accompaniment. Ideally, of course, we should all be able to eat *pâté de foie gras,* but most of us find it an unaffordable luxury. Here is an Austrian imitation—economical, delicious.

MOCK GOOSE-LIVER PÂTÉ

1/2 pound calf or chicken livers	dash nutmeg
1/4 cup rendered bacon fat	1/2 teaspoon salt
3 hard-boiled egg yolks	1/8 teaspoon pepper
1/2 teaspoon dried marjoram	

Remove fat and tendons from the liver and dice it. Fry in bacon fat (you do save your bacon fat, don't you?) until just cooked but still soft. With a mallet, pound it until it is puréed. Sieve the egg yolks and mix in the spices. Combine the yolks with the liver mash and with wet hands, roll into a sausage shape. Wrap in foil and chill overnight. Slice and spread on crackers or toast.

SKINNY PÂTÉ

A boon for the dieter. Very few calories and much food value. Serve this
pâté on zucchini or cucumber slices, or carrot rounds.

1/2 onion, minced	celery salt
2 tablespoons bacon fat	pepper to taste
1/2 pound chicken livers	1/2 teaspoon rosemary

In a non-stick skillet, over medium heat, sauté the minced onion in the fat
until brown; add a little powdered garlic, if desired. Add the livers and cook
about 5 minutes longer. Mash the onion and livers together, add the celery salt
and pepper to taste, and blend well. Pack into a mold and chill thoroughly before serving.

BAKED LIVER PÂTÉ

This resembles what the French call a *pâté de campagne.* It is an excellent
appetizer, served with hot toast.

1 pound chicken livers	1 teaspoon salt
4 slices bacon, thick if possible	1/2 teaspoon pepper
1 clove garlic	good dash each nutmeg and mace
1 cup soft bread crumbs	1 large egg, beaten
	1/2 cup red wine

Soak the liver in cold water for about an hour. Drain and put it, along with
2 slices of the bacon, through a meat grinder twice. Crush the garlic, add it with
the bread crumbs, seasonings, and spices to the liver and bacon, and mix well.
Add the egg, and finally the wine. Pack the mixture into a well-greased casserole,
or loaf pan, arrange the remaining bacon slices over the top. Cover and place in
a tray of boiling water.

Bake at 325° for 1 1/2 hours. Chill thoroughly and slice from the casserole.
The pâté will keep well in the refrigerator, but remove it a while before serving
to restore the flavor.

BLENDER PÂTÉ

1 pound chicken livers	5 tablespoons butter
1 large onion, cut up	salt and pepper to taste
1 large can mushrooms, drained,	1 cup sherry
or 2 cups fresh sliced mushrooms	

Sauté the liver, onions, and mushrooms in the butter until all are golden brown. Remove from the fat with a slotted spoon and place in the blender. Purée until smooth, adding about a quarter of the butter fat, salt, and pepper. Place the sherry in the blender and whirl until smooth. Pour into jars, cover with remaining butter, which forms a protective coat. Keep in the refrigerator until ready to serve.

CHICKEN LIVERS IN WINE SAUCE

1 pound chicken livers	2 tablespoons chopped onions
1 teaspoon salt	2 cups sliced mushrooms
1/8 teaspoon pepper	1 teaspoon cornstarch
1/4 cup flour	1/4 cup water
3 tablespoons butter	1/2 cup dry vermouth
1 tablespoon oil	1 cup chicken broth

Remove fat and membranes from the livers. Place the flour, salt, and pepper in a bag. Shake the livers, a few at a time, in the bag to coat well. Sauté in the butter and oil until brown. Remove and set aside. Then sauté the mushrooms and onions and add them to the livers. Dissolve the cornstarch in the water and make a gravy in the pan by thickening the liquid with the cornstarch mixture. Add the vermouth and broth and heat well; stir in the livers, mushrooms, and onions and bring to a boil. Serve on hot rice. Serves 6.

If you like, add some herbs to the broth: 1 tablespoon parsley, 1/2 teaspoon tarragon. And 1/4 cup toasted slivered almonds to the rice.

CHICKEN LIVERS MARSALA

An easy combination of those lovely tastes of liver and bacon.

4 strips bacon	1/4 pound mushrooms, sliced
1 pound chicken livers	3 tablespoons dry Marsala
1 teaspoon sage	2/3 cup dairy sour cream
1/4 teaspoon marjoram	salt and pepper to taste

Cut the bacon in small pieces and fry until just crisp. Remove from the pan, drain on paper towels, set aside. Pour off the excess grease and brown the livers in the remainder over fairly high heat. Add the sage, marjoram, and mushrooms and sauté for an additional 4 minutes. Stir in the Marsala and the bacon and simmer for about 3 minutes. Reduce the heat, add the sour cream, and heat thoroughly without boiling. Add salt and pepper, if desired. Serve with rice or noodles. Serves 4.

CHICKEN LIVERS, SWEET-SOUR

1 pound chicken livers	1/2 cup vinegar
1 tablespoon oil	1/4 cup sugar
3 green peppers	2 tablespoons cornstarch
4 slices pineapple	1 tablespoon soy sauce
1 cup chicken stock	

Cut the livers in 2 or 3 pieces and sauté in the oil until lightly browned. Set aside and keep warm. Cut the peppers in 1-inch strips. Cut each pineapple slice in 6 pieces. Simmer the peppers and pineapple in the stock (which you have poured into the skillet) for 3 minutes. Mix the vinegar, sugar, cornstarch, and soy sauce. Add to the skillet and stir until thickened. Pour over the livers and serve with steamed rice. Serves 6.

◆

☆☆☆ FRESH SPINACH SALAD WITH GIBLETS

1/4 cup salad oil	6 cups torn-up fresh spinach
2 tablespoons red wine vinegar	(about 8 ounces)
1 tablespoon minced green onion	1/2 cup finely chopped cooked
1/2 teaspoon instant chicken	neck meat and giblets
bouillon	2 hard-boiled eggs, chopped
dash cayenne	
1 clove garlic, crushed	

Combine the first six ingredients in a jar with a tight lid; shake well to blend and let stand while you prepare the salad. Put the spinach, giblets, and eggs in a large bowl and gently toss with the dressing. Serves 2 as main dish (generously) or 4 as side dish.

Other recipes using livers: Cheese and Bacon Quiche (Cheese) and Barley Casserole (Grains) have versions with chicken livers. You can always fold lightly steamed or sautéed chopped livers into fried eggs or omelettes.

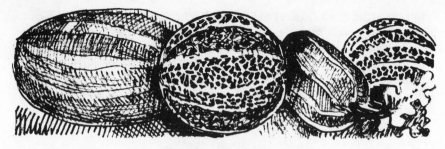

Melons

Nothing is better than a ripe, juicy, chilled melon. A canteloupe or honeydew melon half can appear plain, sprinkled with lemon juice, or try it filled with cottage cheese, sprinkled with paprika, and garnished with fresh grape halves. Or serve it with a thin slice of smoked ham. The melon half can appear also as a dessert, filled with fresh hulled strawberries, or red raspberries, or blueberries, or blackberries.

CANTALOUPE FRUIT CUPS

4 cantaloupes	1 cup grapefruit sections
2 cups peeled sliced oranges	1 cup sugar *or* 3/4 cup honey
2 cups sliced fresh peaches	4 tablespoons sherry *or* rum
2 cups diced pineapple	orange or lemon sherbet
1 cup sliced bananas	

Cut the cantaloupes in halves, remove the seeds, and scallop the edges. Chill. Combine the other fruits, stir the sugar or honey in. Chill thoroughly. Just before serving fill the cantaloupe cups with the fruit. Pour 1 tablespoon sherry or rum over each cup and top with a scoop of sherbet.

MELON SUPREME

Cut melons in balls with a ball cutter. A combination of cantaloupe and honeydew is lovely. Sprinkle with some sugar and rum. Chill thoroughly and serve in chilled sherbet glasses.

FROSTY MELON BALLS

Wonderful on a hot summer evening. Pour 2 cups ginger ale into the freezing tray of the refrigerator and set up the control. Freeze to mush, stirring once. Remove from freezer, fold in 2 cups melon balls.

CANTALOUPE COCKTAIL

1 1/3 cups orange juice	2 cups diced cantaloupe
2 teaspoons lemon juice	1 cup finely cracked ice
	dash of salt

Place all the ingredients in the blender container in the order given. Cover and whirl at high speed until smooth, about 15 seconds. Serve immediately. Serves 3 to 4.

WATERMELON JUICE

There is very little one can do to improve on the watermelon slice eaten in the back yard, where you can drip all over the place and spit the seeds out on the grass. For a change, however, you can try drinking your watermelon. Take a small slice, remove the seeds, peel, dump it in the blender with some of the white rind. Blend on high speed until smooth. Strain and drink at once.

WATERMELON PICKLE

I can remember saving the rind for my mother who made this delicious pickle every summer. What a wonderful way to use it all!

Remove the green peel and red meat from watermelon rind. Cut rind in pieces about 3/4 inch wide or in any shape you like. Weigh it. Cover it well with salted water (1/4 cup coarse salt to 1 quart water). Soak for 12 hours; drain it well. Boil rapidly in boiling water to cover until it is just tender, about 10 minutes. Drain.

For every pound of rind allow the following:

1 cup water	3 inches stick cinnamon
1 cup cider vinegar	8 cloves without heads
2 cups sugar	

Place the water, vinegar, and sugar in a kettle. Tie the spices in a bag and add it to the kettle. Boil for 5 minutes. Add the drained rind and boil it for 30 minutes, or until it is clear. Remove the spice bag. Place the rind in jars, cover it with the boiling vinegar mixture, and seal.

Other recipes using melons: Cantaloupe and Blackberries (Berries); Indian Melon Salad (Chicken); Melon in Chablis (Wine).

Mushrooms

When buying mushrooms, be sure to get fresh ones: check that the caps are plump and firm, smooth, white or creamy colored, *not* grey or yellowish; fresh mushrooms have closed caps. Size is no reliable indication of the mushrooms' quality or flavor, so choose the size you need. One pound of mushrooms will make about 5 cups sliced raw and 2 cups cooked and should feed three or four people.

I have given very few recipes here for mushrooms; they are a part of so many other dishes. Remember that you can serve mushrooms in a cream sauce, seasoned with cheese, curry, herbs (marjoram, rosemary, dill); combined with vegetables or meats; raw in mixed salads or marinated as canapés. Small leftover amounts can be added to your soup pot.

DUXELLES

A classic mixture that you can keep in the refrigerator or freezer to be used in many ways. Try this in omelettes, sauces, gravies, or creamed dishes. Spread it on toast for a canapé. Use to fill sautéed mushroom caps or to stuff fish, poultry, or vegetables.

1 pound mushrooms	1 clove garlic, minced
1/4 cup butter	salt, pepper to taste
2 tablespoons oil	1 tablespoon chopped fresh parsley
6 tablespoons minced shallots *or* green onions	

Chop the mushrooms very fine. Place in a clean cloth and wring out until all the moisture is removed. Heat the butter and oil in a heavy skillet. Add shallots and garlic; sauté until all moisture has evaporated and the mixture is very dark. Season to taste with salt and pepper. Stir in parsley. Makes 2 cups. Can be frozen.

MUSHROOM SOUP

2 quarts beef stock
1/2 cup dry white wine
1 pound mushrooms, sliced
   thinly
4 tablespoons butter/margarine

1 cup chopped onion
4 teaspoons worcestershire sauce
1/4 cup corn starch mixed with
   1/2 cup cold water
salt to taste

Bring the stock to a boil, add the wine and mushrooms. Cover and simmer
for 1 hour. In another saucepan, heat the butter and sauté the onions until soft;
add to the stock pot. Simmer, covered, 15 minutes. Add the worcestershire
sauce and simmer 5 minutes more.

Bring the soup to a rolling boil. Using a whisk, slowly add the corn starch
paste. Cook until thickened slightly. Taste for salt. Serve warm, garnished with
a dollop of sour cream or plain yogurt. This soup can be frozen.

MUSHROOM-STUFFED OMELETTE

This omelette starts on the stove and ends in the oven. Serve it with cheese
sauce, broiled tomatoes, and hot muffins.

1 1/2 cups sliced mushrooms
4 tablespoons minced green onions
2 teaspoons butter
1/2 teaspoon salt, divided
1/4 teaspoon thyme

5 eggs, separated
1/4 cup water
1/4 teaspoon dry mustard
1/8 teaspoon pepper
4 teaspoons oil

In a small skillet, sauté the mushrooms and onions in the butter along with
1/4 teaspoon salt and the thyme until tender. Set aside, but keep warm. Separate the eggs; beat the whites until stiff. Set aside.

Beat the yolks until thick, stir in the water, remaining salt and seasonings;
fold into the whites, very carefully. Heat the oil in a 10-inch oven-proof frying
or omelette pan, making sure the sides and bottom are greased. When the pan
is hot, pour in the egg mixture and cook over a low heat until browned on the
bottom, about 5 minutes. Lift the sides gently to check. Place the pan in a 325°
oven for 10 minutes, or until the omelette has risen and the center is set. Loosen
the omelette with a spatula and spread the warm mushroom mixture gently over
one side. Fold over and slide out onto a serving platter. Serve immediately.
Serves 4.

STUFFED MUSHROOMS

A delicious canapé, or garnish for steak or roast beef. Or serve on hot rice. The unused stems can go into soups, casseroles, creamed dishes.

15 large white mushrooms	1 1/2 cups water
1 tablespoon butter	1/2 onion, sliced
2 cups bread crumbs	1 tablespoon oil
1 clove garlic, chopped	1 bay leaf
3 tablespoons grated romano	pinch of oregano
1 tablespoon minced parsley	salt and pepper
4 mushroom stems, chopped fine	

Carefully remove the stems from the mushrooms. Melt the butter in a skillet; add the bread crumbs, garlic, romano, parsley, and mushroom stems. Add water to the pan to make a paste. Cook for several minutes. Fill the mushroom caps with this mixture. Using a shallow baking pan, place the sliced onion, oil, bay leaf, oregano, salt and pepper on the bottom. Put the filled caps over. Bake at 350° for 35 minutes, basting from time to time.

MUSHROOMS BAKED IN FOIL

Also good on hot rice, or as a side-dish for beef. And what a lovely change, nothing to wash up afterward!

1 pound mushrooms	1 tablespoon dry sherry
1/4 cup chopped parsley	1/2 teaspoon salt
2 tablespoons minced onion	1/8 teaspoon pepper

Place trimmed whole mushrooms in the center of a sheet of heavy-duty foil. Sprinkle the remaining ingredients over them. Bring the edges of foil up over the mixture and crimp to seal. Set in a baking pan and bake at 350° for 45 minutes, or until mushrooms are cooked. Serves 6.

MUSHROOMS AND CREAM

One of my favorite quick luncheon dishes. Serve these on hot buttered toast or rice.

Heat a little butter or oil in a skillet. Slice mushrooms and sauté in the butter, stirring with a wooden spoon. When they are done, add dairy sour cream to make a sauce. Stir until very warm, then stir in a spoonful or so of good sherry. Blend well. Delicious.

Other recipes using mushrooms: Green Bean Casserole, Three Bean Loaf, Skillet Vegetable Medley (Beans); Vegetable Nut Roast (Bread); Broccoli-Noodle Bake (Broccoli); Carrots and Kasha (Carrots); Chicken Stroganoff; Chicken Tetrazzini, Veal Fricassee (Evaporated Milk); Kasha Loaf, Barley Casserole (Grains); chicken liver recipes; Noodle Surprise, Fettucine with Egg Sauce (Noodles & Pasta); Mushroom-Stuffed Tomatoes; Turkey Ham Bake, Mushroom Turkey Salad, Turkey Soup (Turkey); Veal Casserole; Hamburger and Noodle Stroganoff (Wine); Zucchini Boats.

Noodles and Pasta

So many recipes for noodles and pasta appear elsewhere in this collection that I shall include only a few here. One word of warning: don't cook these too long; if you are using the pasta in a casserole that will be baked, cook even less than that.

SUPER MINESTRONE

If you have other vegetables to use up, just add them; surely there will be no harm done.

1 clove garlic, minced
2 tablespoons olive oil
1 cup sliced zucchini
1/2 cup kidney beans, cooked
2 small onions, chopped
2 carrots, sliced
2 stalks celery with leaves, chopped
1 potato, sliced
small bunch of parsley, chopped
   or 2 tablespoons dry parsley

8 cups beef (and/or vegetable) stock
4 tomatoes, peeled and chopped
1/2 cabbage, cored and shredded
1 bay leaf
3/4 cup macaroni
3 tablespoons parmesan cheese
1/2 teaspoon basil
salt and pepper to taste

Sauté the garlic in the oil for 4 minutes in a large kettle. Add zucchini, kidney beans, onions, carrots, celery, potato, and parsley; cook over *low* heat, stirring frequently, until soft. Add the stock, tomatoes, cabbage, and bay leaf and cook over very low heat for 2 hours. Then add macaroni and simmer until it is cooked. Stir in the cheese, more chopped parsley, basil, salt and pepper. Serve with more parmesan and a good red wine. Serves 8 to 12.

☆☆☆ TUNA AND SPINACH-NOODLE SALAD

This wonderful salad is a delicious combination of colors, textures, and tastes. If you have some left over, just store it, covered, in the refrigerator. It is equally good the next day.

4 cups cooked spinach noodles
1 can tuna, flaked
1 cup chopped celery
1 large carrot, coarsely grated
1 zucchini, coarsely grated

3/4 cup chopped green onions
1 cup bean sprouts
1 teaspoon oregano
salt and pepper
Pasta Salad Dressing (see the
   Appendix)

Make sure the noodles are well drained and cooled. Mix them with the vegetables and seasonings and toss lightly with dressing. Add salt and pepper to taste and chill for one hour or so. Add more dressing if desired. Serves 6.

MACARONI AND CHICKEN SALAD

This salad has all raw vegetables in it; the dressing is very good indeed.

4 cups cooked, drained macaroni
2 to 2 1/2 cups diced cooked
  chicken
1 1/2 cups shredded cabbage
1 cup chopped celery
1/2 cup sliced radishes

1 cup diced cucumber
3/4 cup chopped green onions
1/2 cup grated Swiss cheese
1 teaspoon dill weed
salt and pepper, if desired

Mix all the ingredients and toss lightly with Pasta Salad Dressing (recipe in Appendix). Chill and marinate for 1 hour or more. Serves 4 to 5.

◆

☆☆☆ NOODLE SURPRISE

You can eat this casserole all by itself, with a hearty mixed vegetable or green salad. If you like, you can add to it any of the following: chopped cooked meat, poultry, tuna fish; cooked vegetables, chopped hard-boiled eggs. The surprise, by the way, is sunflower seeds that not only taste good but go crunch when you eat the casserole.

2 cups noodles or macaroni
1 medium onion, chopped
6 large mushrooms, chopped
2/3 cup sunflower seeds
3 tablespoons oil
1 cup grated cheese

2 eggs, beaten
2/3 cup plain yogurt
pinch of cayenne
1/2 teaspoon salt
1/2 teaspoon worcestershire sauce
1/4 cup whole wheat bread crumbs

Cook the noodles (and use whole grain noodles if you can) until tender; rinse and drain well. Sauté the onion, mushrooms, and sunflower seeds in the oil until the vegetables are soft and the seeds are crisp.

Combine the noodles and the sautéed vegetables and seeds. Combine three-quarters of the cheese with the eggs, yogurt, and seasonings; blend well. Stir this mixture into the noodle mixture. Turn into a 2-quart casserole, top with bread crumbs and the remaining cheese. Bake at 350° for 30 minutes, or until the casserole is firm.

Note: If you decide to add something more, you will probably want to increase the liquid. Add more yogurt, or some buttermilk, regular milk, or stock.

EGGPLANT AND MACARONI

Here is another scrumptious Italian dish, this one using the delicious combination of eggplant and tomato.

4 large eggplants, peeled and	1 teaspoon basil
sliced	1 pound macaroni
olive oil	1/2 cup cooked peas
1 medium onion, sliced	1/2 pound mozzarella, diced
2 cups tomato purée or sauce	parmesan

Fry the eggplant in very hot oil; drain and set aside. Brown the sliced onion, add the tomato purée and basil. Lower heat and simmer about 20 minutes, or until fairly thick. Cook the macaroni and drain well. Fold the tomato sauce into the macaroni, adding some of the fried eggplant, the peas, mozzarella, and parmesan to taste. Line the bottom and sides of a casserole with eggplant slices. Fill with the macaroni mixture. Cover with more sliced eggplant. Cover loosely with foil and place the casserole in a larger pan of boiling water (with water up to one inch below the top of the dish), cover, and simmer about 30 minutes. Serves 8.

FETTUCINE WITH EGG SAUCE

I remember when I was a student in Europe, I had a birthday dinner in Rome at the famous Alfredo's. And yes, I ate *fettucine.* Unforgettable. This recipe calls for something more complicated than Alfredo's version.

4 tablespoons butter/margarine,	1/4 cup grated parmesan
divided	8 ounces wide egg noodles,
2 cups sliced mushrooms	cooked and drained
2 cups cooked ham strips	2 tablespoons chopped parsley
1/2 cup finely chopped onion	
4 egg yolks	

Melt 2 tablespoons butter/margarine in a large skillet; sauté the mushrooms, ham, and onion for 5 minutes, or until onion and mushrooms are tender and ham is lightly browned. Keep warm.

Beat the egg yolks in the top of a double boiler. Stir in the grated cheese. Cut remaining butter/margarine into small pieces and stir into the egg yolks. Place this mixture over hot, but not boiling, water; stir constantly until the butter melts and the sauce is slightly thickened.

Place the drained noodles in a hot serving bowl (and make sure they are very hot). Pour the egg mixture over; toss well. Spoon the ham mixture over the top. Sprinkle with more parmesan cheese and the parsley. Toss. Serve immediately. Serves 4.

Turkey Variation: Substitute 2 cups shredded cooked turkey for the ham and fold 6 tablespoons diced mozzarella into the sauce.

Other recipes using:

Macaroni: Cheese and Macaroni Bake; Schinken Makkroni (Ham).

Noodles: Meat-Fried Noodles (Beef); Broccoli-Noodle Bake; Chicken and Noodle Divan; Hungarian Noodles (Peas); Tuna-Noodle Casserole; Hamburger and Noodle Stroganoff (Wine).

Spaghetti: Chicken Tetrazzini (Evaporated Milk); Johnny Margetti (Tomatoes); spaghetti sauces (see the Index).

See also casseroles under Cottage Cheese and Ricotta.

Nuts

Nuts are such a delicious and nourishing food and enhance any dish. Most cookies and many cakes contain nuts and throughout this book there are many recipes that use them. I shall give a few here in which nuts are an essential ingredient.

One note first: Nuts are perishable and should be stored cool and used reasonably quickly. Their flavor is also much better when they are fresh. I buy most nuts in the shell; then I crack and shell them and store in jars in the refrigerator, or in plastic bags in the freezer (that way they will keep a very long time).

DRY ROASTED NUTS

The nut treats are very easy. To dry roast, put nuts in a bowl. For each cup add 1 teaspoon soy sauce. Mix well and spread on a cookie sheet. Bake at 350° about 10 minutes. Of course you can also roast nuts in a little oil, at 300° about 20 minutes; then drain and salt (almonds are wonderful this way).

SUGARED PECANS

1/4 cup butter/margarine	1/4 teaspoon ginger
1/4 cup sugar	1/4 teaspoon nutmeg
1/2 teaspoon cinnamon	1 pound pecan halves

Melt the butter in a small saucepan; then stir in the sugar and spices and mix well. Pour over the pecans in a large roasting pan and coat well. Bake at 275° about 30 minutes. Cool and store airtight.

SPICED NUTS

Here is a delicious, less caloric version of the above.

1/2 cup sugar	1/4 teaspoon nutmeg
1/4 cup cornstarch	1/4 teaspoon ginger
dash salt	1 egg white
1 1/2 teaspoons cinnamon	2 tablespoons cold water
1/2 teaspoon allspice	1/4 pound nut meats

Sift the dry ingredients into a shallow pan. Combine the egg white and water and beat slightly. Dip the nuts into this mixture and drop them one at a time into the mixed dry ingredients. Roll them around lightly, and keep them separated. Place on a cookie sheet and bake at 250° for about 1 1/2 hours. Remove from the oven and shake off excess sugar. When they are cold they will be crisp and spicy.

KROKANT

A German confection that is close to our peanut brittle.

1/2 pound almonds or peanuts or walnuts	1 teaspoon vanilla sugar
	1 2/3 cups sugar

If you don't have vanilla sugar, just add 1/2 teaspoon vanilla to the mixture. Chop the nuts coarsely and mix with vanilla sugar. Melt the sugar in a large skillet over low heat, add the nuts, and fry to a golden brown. Grease a baking sheet and rolling pin. Spread the mixture on the sheet, roll out. Cut in squares while still hot. Store airtight.

◆

WALNUT LENTIL LOAF

A delicious vegetarian loaf. Serve it with cheese sauce.

2 cups walnut halves or pieces
2 cups soft bread crumbs
2 cups cooked lentils (2/3 cup
    uncooked)
2 cups stewed tomatoes

2 eggs, lightly beaten
2 tablespoons grated onion
1 teaspoon salt
1/4 teaspoon pepper

Drop the walnuts into rapidly boiling water and boil 3 minutes. Drain well and spread in a shallow pan. Turn the bread crumbs (whole wheat, if possible) into a second pan. Toast both at 350° for 10 to 15 minutes, until lightly browned. Chop the walnuts fine or whirl in blender. Pour lentils, tomatoes, and bread crumbs into the blender and whirl about 2 seconds to chop lightly. Combine with nuts and remaining ingredients. Mix well. Turn into a 9 x 5 loaf pan. Bake at 375° for about 30 minutes, or until set. Serves 8.

VEGETABLE NUT LOAF

Here is another very different vegetarian loaf.

1 cup diced carrots
1 cup chopped celery
1/2 cup chopped onion
3 tablespoons butter/margarine
1/4 cup flour
1 teaspoon salt

dash pepper
1 1/2 cups milk
1 cup grated cheese
1 cup chopped pecans
3/4 cup wheat germ
3 eggs, slightly beaten

Sauté the carrots, celery, and onion in the butter until onion is tender. Stir in the flour, salt, and pepper. Add the milk all at once. Cook over medium heat until thickened, stirring constantly. Add cheese and stir until melted. Then blend in remaining ingredients. Pour into a greased, foil-lined 9 x 5 loaf pan. Bake at 350° for 50 minutes, or until firm. Let stand for 10 minutes before turning out on a serving plate. Slice and serve with cheese sauce. Serves 6 to 8.

PEANUT BROWN RICE

This rice dish makes a perfect accompaniment to chicken or turkey. Or serve it as a main dish with some hearty bread and a green salad. It has an interesting combination of colors, flavors, and textures and has a decided oriental character.

1 1/2 cups brown rice	1/2 cup sliced green onions
1 can (11 ounces) mandarin oranges	1 cup roasted salted peanuts
1/4 cup soy sauce	2 tablespoons honey
3 1/4 cups water	1 tablespoon lemon juice
1 1/2 tablespoons butter	1 can (16 ounces) bean sprouts,
1 large clove garlic, crushed	drained
1 cup thinly sliced celery	3 tablespoons chopped parsley

Put the rice in a large stove-top casserole. Drain the oranges, reserving 1/2 cup of the liquid; set them aside. Add the reserved liquid to the rice in the skillet; add the soy sauce and water. Cover and simmer about 45 minutes, or until rice is tender and liquid is absorbed. In the meanwhile, sauté the garlic, celery, and onion in the butter for about 5 minutes. When the rice is done, stir them in with the peanuts, honey and lemon juice (mixed together), bean sprouts, oranges, and parsley. Heat thoroughly. Serves 8.

◆

CHOCOLATE PECAN PIE

As if pecan pie (see under Pumpkin) weren't rich enough, here is an extra-rich version. I like it better as it is more pudding-like and less sweet. It is also perfectly chocolate.

2 squares unsweetened chocolate	3 eggs, beaten
3 tablespoons butter	1 teaspoon vanilla
3/4 cup sugar	1 cup pecans, coarsely chopped
1 cup light corn syrup	unbaked 9-inch pie shell

Melt the chocolate and butter in a medium saucepan and cool. Combine the sugar and syrup and place on high heat, stirring until sugar dissolves. Then boil 2 minutes. Add in the chocolate mixture and stir. Cool slightly. Beat in the eggs and vanilla. Stir in the nuts. Pour into the prepared pie shell and bake at 325° for 45 minutes.

☆☆☆ LINZERTORTE

This is one of the great Austrian desserts. There are several versions of it. Mine, given to me by an Austrian friend, is absolutely authentic. Use homemade raspberry jam, if you possibly can.

1 1/4 cups shelled hazelnuts
2 sticks (less 1 tablespoon) sweet
   butter
1 1/4 cups flour

3/4 cup sugar
cinnamon (generous dash)
raspberry jam

Grind the nuts in a Mouli mill or whirl in the blender until fine. You can substitute some walnuts for hazelnuts if you like. Combine the nuts, butter, flour, sugar, and cinnamon. Wade in with your hands and blend thoroughly. Chill for several hours. Press a bit more than three-quarters of the dough on the bottom and sides of a large baking pan (preferably one with a removable center) or in several smaller tart tins. Cover generously with jam, which you can stretch some, if you like, with good tart currant jelly. Roll out remaining dough, cut in strips and arrange them in a lattice over the pie. Make them thin (about 1/2 inch) and fairly far apart. Bake at 350° about 45 minutes for a large tart, 30 minutes for small ones. The crust will be medium brown and the jam a bit bubbly when the tart is done. Enjoy.

GÂTEAU AUX NOISETTES

This cake-pie comes from the French part of Switzerland. A close friend of an uncle of mine used to eat it there as a child. It is very easily made.

1 cup chopped nuts
1/2 cup brown sugar
1 cup white sugar

1 cup heavy cream
unbaked 8 or 9-inch pie shell

Mix all ingredients together with a fork and put into the prepared shell. Bake at 350° about 40 minutes, or until knife inserted in the baked mixture comes out clean.

☆☆☆ VANILLA-NUT ICEBOX COOKIES

Here is a basic recipe in which you can use any kind of nuts. If you are lucky enough to get some hickory nuts, and if you are lucky enough to survive removing them from the shells, make these cookies with them. Also good are brazil nuts, pecans, walnuts, hazelnuts. Whirl them in the blender to grind.

2 cups flour	1/2 cup white sugar
1 1/2 teaspoons baking powder	1 egg
1/4 teaspoon salt	1 teaspoon vanilla
1/2 cup butter/margarine	1 cup ground nuts
1/2 cup brown sugar	

Sift together the flour, baking powder, and salt and set aside. Cream the butter, then gradually add in the sugars, beating all the time. Add egg and vanilla and continue beating until very light and fluffy.

At low speed beat in half the flour mixture, then stir in the rest, along with the nuts, and mix with your hands until well combined. Divide the dough in half and shape each half into a roll about 7 inches long. Wrap in plastic wrap and refrigerate until firm (about 8 hours or overnight). You can store the dough about 10 days in the refrigerator and months in the freezer. Slice and bake as desired. If you prefer, you can pack the dough firmly in 6-ounce orange juice concentrate tins and cover well with aluminum foil or plastic. When you are ready to slice, cut out the bottom of the tin, and use it to push the dough out. Slicing is very easy that way. Cookies are best about 1/8 inch thick.

Bake at 375° for 8 to 10 minutes, or until lightly browned. Makes about 9 dozen.

☆☆☆ VIENNESE ROUNDS

One of my favorite Christmas cookies. If you don't feel up to making a Linzertorte, here is a similar taste, although the texture is quite different.

3/4 cup butter	1 teaspoon vanilla
1/2 cup 10X sugar	1 cup ground hazelnuts
2 cups flour	raspberry jam

Cream the butter and sugar until well blended. Stir in flour, vanilla, and nuts. Roll the dough, a level teaspoon at a time, into balls. Place 2 inches apart on a cookie sheet. Lightly grease the bottom of a measuring cup and dip in 10X sugar; press over each ball and flatten to a 1-inch round. Bake at 350° about 10 minutes, or until golden brown around the edges. Cool completely.

Spread the bottoms of half the cookies with raspberry jam; top, sandwich style, with remaining cookies, flat side down. Store in a cool place and allow them to age a few days.

NUT CRESCENTS

A traditional Christmas cookie from Northern Europe. Usually these are made with almonds or hazelnuts. The nuts should be ground, or chopped *very* fine.

1/2 cup butter	2 teaspoons water
1/2 cup margarine	1 cup ground almonds *or*
1/2 cup 10X sugar	hazelnuts
1 tablespoon brandy	2 cups flour

Cream the butter, margarine, and sugar until very light. Mix in the brandy and water. Stir in the nuts and flour. Chill. Shape small pieces of dough into crescents and put on an ungreased cookie sheet. Bake at 350° for 12 to 15 minutes. While still warm, roll in 10X sugar. Makes about 4 dozen.

Variation:

Vanilla Crescents: Reduce nuts to 1/2 cup; use 2 1/2 cups flour, 1/4 cup granulated sugar; in place of the brandy and water, stir in 1 teaspoon vanilla. Proceed as above.

NUT MACAROONS

This recipe calls for salted peanuts, but you can use almonds, pecans, walnuts, filberts, or a mixture. If the nuts are not salted, reduce the sugar to 1/2 cup.

1 pound roasted salted Spanish	3 tablespoons flour
peanuts	3/4 cup sugar
3 egg whites, beaten very stiff	

Grind the nuts in a food mill. Add other ingredients and stir to mix well. Drop by teaspoonfuls onto a greased and floured cookie sheet. Bake at 300° for 15 minutes. Let cool and store in cardboard boxes, where they will keep for ages. Makes 5 dozen.

NORWEGIAN ALMOND COOKIES

This and the following rule make delicious and unusual bar cookies. Both are easy to make.

1 cup butter/margarine
1 cup white sugar

2 1/2 cups sifted flour
1 cup unblanched almonds
1 egg, beaten

Cream the butter and sugar, add flour and almonds, coarsely chopped. Spread over a greased cookie sheet (13 x 9 inches). Spread the beaten egg (or 2 eggs if necessary) to glaze over the top. Bake at 350° for 20 to 30 minutes. Cut into bars while hot. These keep very well.

CASHEW-CARAMEL BARS

3/4 cup flour
1/2 teaspoon baking powder
1/4 teaspoon salt
2 eggs, slightly beaten
1/4 cup white sugar

1 cup chopped, roasted, salted
  cashews, divided
3/4 cup brown sugar, divided
2 tablespoons butter, melted
1 1/2 tablespoons light cream

Sift flour, baking powder, and salt. Into the beaten eggs, stir white sugar and 1/2 cup brown sugar. Blend in 1/2 cup nuts and the flour mixture. Spread in a well-greased 9-inch square pan. Bake 20 to 25 minutes, or until crust springs back when lightly touched with a finger.

Make the topping by stirring together the butter, 1/4 cup brown sugar, cream, and 1/2 cup nuts. Spread immediately on baked layer, covering top completely. Place under the broiler about 1 minute, or until topping bubbles and is light brown. Cut into 36 bars while still warm; cool thoroughly in the pan.

Other recipes using nuts:

Nuts are a basic ingredient in many quick breads and cookies; in baked apple desserts, conserves, candies, chicken dishes; Energy Fruit Bars (Raisins).

Almonds: Green Bean Casserole, Almond Vegetable Mandarin (Beans); Swiss Carrot Cake; Beef Casserole with Almonds (Celery); Almond Cranberry Sauce; Fish Timbales; Turkey Cantonese.

Peanuts: Crusted Cauliflower; Cheese and Macaroni Bake (Cheese); Baked Fish and Nuts; Bean and Peanut Curry (Legumes).

Pecans: Huguenot Torte, Praline Apple Pie (Apples); Three Bean Loaf (Beans); Pecan Patties (Bread); Butter Pecan Chiffon Pie (Evaporated Milk); Pumpkin Pecan Pie; Sweet Potato Pie, Sweet Potato Muffins.

Walnuts: Vegetable Nut Roast (Bread); Oatmeal Spice Bars (Cereals); Heavenly Jam (Grapes); Winter Pear Walnut Pie.

Onions

I never serve onions as a vegetable dish, and I almost never put raw onions in my salads. I find the flavor too strong. I do consider onions absolutely essential in so many dishes as a flavor ingredient.

ONION PURÉE SOUP

I am sure you can find many recipes for French onion soup. Here is a different onion soup, smooth, flavored with sherry.

1 pound onions, sliced	1/4 cup sherry
2 tablespoons butter	salt and pepper
3 to 4 cups beef stock	1/4 cup grated parmesan

Brown the onions in the butter. Add the stock and simmer, covered, about 30 minutes. Put it in the blender and whirl until very smooth. Thin with more stock, if necessary. Add the sherry and salt and pepper to taste. Ladle into ovenproof soup cups. Top each with a generous sprinkling of parmesan cheese, and brown under the broiler. Serves 4.

SWEET AND SOUR ONIONS

A very unusual way of preparing white onions and a delicious accompaniment to pork roast or baked ham.

1 pound very small white onions	**1/2 cup white vinegar**
1 cup raisins	**1/2 cup water**
1/3 cup white wine	**1 teaspoon salt**
1 tablespoon sugar	

Leave the onions whole. Peel and soak them in cold water for an hour. In the meanwhile plump the raisins in the white wine.

In a saucepan combine the onions, sugar, vinegar, water, and salt. Cover and cook for 40 minutes over low heat. Add the raisins.

Drain and serve hot with melted butter. Serves 4 to 6.

ONIONS IN MADEIRA CREAM

A richer and sweeter way of serving onions, and a dish that is perfect with steak, grilled chops, or sautéed liver.

3 tablespoons butter	**salt and pepper**
4 large mild onions	**1/4 cup cream**
1/2 cup Madeira *or* sweet sherry	**1/4 cup finely chopped parsley**

Melt the butter in a large pan, add the onions (which you have peeled and sliced thickly), and turn so they are coated with butter. Cover the pan and cook for 10 minutes over very low heat. Shake the pan now and then.

Raise the heat somewhat and stir in the Madeira. Cook, stirring carefully until the wine is gone, and the onions are soft and caramelized.

Season with salt and pepper, stir in the cream and parsley. Bring to a boil, then lower the heat and simmer for just 1 minute. Serves 4 to 6.

EGGS IN ONION SAUCE

This is a quick and very delicious luncheon or supper dish.

6 hard-boiled eggs	1/4 teaspoon salt
3 large onions, thinly sliced	dash of nutmeg and pepper
3 tablespoons butter/margarine	3 tablespoons flour
2 tablespoons minced parsley	2 cups light cream *or* rich milk
1 teaspoon thyme	chives *or* toasted sesame seeds
	for garnish

Peel and quarter the eggs and set aside. Sauté the onions in the butter until well softened and transparent but not browned.

As the onions cook, stir in the parsley and seasonings. Reduce the heat to low and sprinkle the flour over the onion mixture, stirring well to blend. Add the cream very slowly, stir and cook until the sauce thickens. Remove from the heat.

Place the egg quarters in a small casserole and pour the sauce over the top. Place, uncovered, in a 350° oven for a few minutes until the sauce bubbles. Serve over toasted whole wheat bread and garnish with chives or sesame seeds. Serves 4 to 6.

———————◆———————

HEARTY ONION BREAD

1 package dry yeast	2 teaspoons salt
1/2 cup warm water	2 cups cooked brown rice
2 medium onions, finely chopped	3 cups rye flour
2 tablespoons oil	3 cups whole wheat flour
2 tablespoons honey	3 cups (about) all-purpose flour
2 1/2 cups hot potato water *or*	poppy seeds
vegetable stock	

Proof the yeast in the warm water. Sauté the onions in the oil until soft. Combine the honey, hot potato water, salt, sautéed onions with the oil, brown rice, rye flour in a large bowl. When the mixture is lukewarm, stir in the proofed yeast and the whole wheat flour. Stir well. Then stir in some of the all-purpose flour and knead, adding the remaining flour as needed, until the bread is smooth and elastic, about 10 minutes. Cover, let rise to double. Punch down, form in two loaves, let rise again. Bake at 400° for 15 minutes, then at 350° for 25 minutes more, or until the bread is done.

GOLDEN ONION ROLLS

2 1/2 to 3 cups flour
1 tablespoon sugar
1/2 teaspoon salt
1 package yeast
3/4 cup milk
2 tablespoons margarine
2 eggs (beat slightly and reserve
   2 tablespoons)

• Onion Topping •
2 tablespoons butter
1 cup chopped onion
1/8 teaspoon salt
1 tablespoon reserved egg
1 tablespoon milk
poppy seeds

In a large bowl, combine 1 cup flour, sugar, salt, and dry yeast. Heat milk and margarine until milk is warm; then add to the flour mixture with the eggs. Blend at low speed until moistened, then beat 2 minutes at medium speed. By hand stir in remaining flour. Knead on a floured surface until smooth and elastic, about 3 minutes. Place in a greased bowl, cover, let rise until double, about 1 1/2 hours.

Prepare topping by heating the butter in a frying pan; sauté the onion until golden. Stir in the salt. Remove from heat, cool, and stir in a mixture of 1 tablespoon reserved egg and milk.

Shape the dough into 2-inch balls; place on greased cookie sheets. Make a large indentation in the center of each with your finger. Spoon about 1 teaspoon of the topping into the center of each. Brush tops with remaining reserved egg. Sprinkle with poppy seeds. Let rise until double, about 45 minutes. Bake at 375° for 12 to 15 minutes, or until golden brown. Serve warm.

Other recipes using onions: Onions go into so many different dishes—most recipes with vegetable combinations, legumes, mushrooms, potatoes, tomatoes, zucchini; many meat and vegetable loaves, salads, soups, stuffings.

Oranges

If you have loads of oranges to use up, you can always make freshly squeezed orange juice, ambrosia in itself. Many cakes and cookies use orange juice and rind; many relishes, preserves, and desserts throughout this collection are made with oranges as an essential ingredient. The Lemon Sponge Dessert (under Lemons) can be made orange; substitute 1 orange for the 2 lemons in the recipe and reduce the sugar to 3/4 cup.

SLICED ORANGES IN WINE

3/4 cup sugar
1 cup water
1 cup dry red wine
1 stick cinnamon

2 cloves
2 slices tangerine
2 slices lemon
6 large oranges

Dissolve the sugar in the water and add the wine. Tie the cinnamon, cloves, tangerine and lemon slices in a cheesecloth. Bring the wine mixture to a boil, add the cheesecloth bag, and boil until the liquid becomes syrupy. Remove the bag and discard.

While the syrup is cooking, peel and seed the oranges and cut off all the white membrane. Cut in segments. Add the fruit to the warm syrup, cool, and refrigerate until very cold.

Serve ice cold, garnished with sliced toasted almonds, and some grated orange peel.

ORANGE MUFFINS

3 cups flour
2 teaspoons baking soda
1 teaspoon salt
1/4 cup wheat germ
1 cup butter/margarine
2 cups sugar

4 eggs
2 seedless oranges
1 cup pecans
1 cup raisins
1 cup grated carrots
1 1/2 cup sour milk

Sift together the flour, soda, and salt. Stir in wheat germ and set aside.

Cream the butter and sugar; beat in the eggs, one at a time. Cut up the oranges and grind them together with the pecans and raisins; add to the creamed mixture along with the grated carrots. Then add alternately the dry ingredients and sour milk (you can sour fresh milk by adding 1 teaspoon vinegar or lemon juice to 1 cup fresh milk).

Fill muffin tins 1/2 full. Bake at 375° for 20 minutes. Makes about 4 dozen. These can be frozen.

Other recipes using oranges: fruit drinks, conserves, jams, marmalades; Passover Cake (Bananas) has a sauce with oranges; Orange Date Cake (Buttermilk); Orange Marmalade and its recipes (Jams, Jellies, Marmalades); Cantaloupe Fruit Cups (Melons); Orange and Lemon Jelly (Wine).

Parsley

Especially in the summer and early fall, I like to have a lot of parsley around. It is an herb that grows well in a pot, and if you are so inclined, keep some with your house plants. That way you can keep it all year around.

Parsley is most commonly used as a garnish. I can remember as a child turning my nose up at the eternal sprig of parsley which accompanied the meat at dinner. But my mother was right, the parsley was pretty and decorative and added color to the meal. Sprinkle chopped parsley on your vegetables, creamed dishes, smooth soups. My favorite stuffing (see under Chestnuts) uses parsley, and in fact you can add it to any dressing you make (about 1/2 cup per 4 cups stuffing). I like it chopped up in salad with brown rice, tomato wedges, chick peas, and torn leaf lettuce, all mixed with a strong tangy Italian dressing. The French herbed omelette by the way, is made most often with parsley. You can add up to 1/2 cup for every two eggs.

The aunt of my closest French friend taught me how to chop parsley. Remove the stems, tear the parsley in pieces, and put it in a small narrow cup (a 1-cup measure or a narrow custard cup, for example). Then take your kitchen scissors and cut away. It is amazing how neat and quick the whole process is. To freeze parsley, chop it raw, stems and all. Put it in small envelopes and seal.

Many recipes throughout this book make use of parsley. I have listed some at the end of this section.

PARSLEY BUTTER SAUCE

This very simple and delicious combination is lovely on asparagus or other vegetables, especially the yellow ones (carrots, squash), or fish. And it is the perfect accompaniment to tiny boiled new potatoes. Melt 1/4 cup butter and add 2 tablespoons finely chopped parsley. If you use the sauce on fish, add 3 teaspoons lemon juice.

YOGURT-COTTAGE CHEESE SPREAD

This delicately flavored and colored spread is very good on wheat or cornmeal crackers, cucumber, zucchini, or carrot slices. It has only 18 calories per tablespoon.

2 cups cottage cheese   1/2 cup shredded parsley
1 cup yogurt   1 hard-boiled egg
1 tablespoon chopped chives

Put everything but the egg in the blender and whirl until very smooth. Shell the egg, cut in pieces, and press through a sieve. Stir it into the spread. Add seasonings, if you like. Cover and chill for at least 30 minutes before using.

TABOULI SALAD

This is one of the marvelous summer salads, with an extraordinary combination of taste and texture.

1 cup bulgur wheat   1 onion, chopped fine
2 cups chicken bouillon   2 fresh tomatoes, chopped fine
    or water *or* a combination   pinch of basil
1/4 cup mint leaves, finely chopped juice and pulp of 2 lemons
1 to 2 cups finely chopped parsley 2 to 4 tablespoons olive oil

Bring the bouillon to a boil and pour it over the bulgur. Let it soak for two hours or until the wheat absorbs all the liquid. Stir in the mint and parsley and let stand a while longer. Then add in the onion, tomatoes, and basil; stir well. Finally, add the lemon juice and pulp, and the quantity of olive oil that suits your taste. Add more salt if you want. Toss and chill thoroughly. Serve cold.

Other recipes using parsley: Parsley Dressing (Buttermilk); Tuna Eggplant Spaghetti (Eggplant); Veal Fricassee (Evaporated Milk); Parsleyed Ham; Super Minestrone (Noodles); Eggs in Onion Sauce, Onions in Madeira Cream (Onions); Evergreen Zucchini.

Peaches

Peaches can be canned, but these days most of us freeze them (I use a light syrup, 2 cups sugar or honey to 5 cups water, prepared in advance and chilled; be sure to add some powdered ascorbic acid fruit preservative to retard discoloration—follow directions on the container). Scrub, peel, and pit the peaches—reserve the peels, brown spots, and pits for jelly (see below). Slice the peaches into the syrup and pack in freezer containers or empty milk cartons, well washed. Seal well and enjoy all winter. I cannot think of any fruit that freezes better.

During the season we eat peaches all the time—on breakfast cereal, or sliced with milk or cream. Try them sliced and mixed with honey and a little lemon juice to serve over vanilla ice cream (add a dash of brandy or a tablespoon or so of Marsala for added pleasure). With sweetened sliced peaches you can make peach shortcake, something that is as good as strawberry shortcake. Top it with whipped cream and toasted almonds.

PEACH BREAD

Here is a lovely tea bread. It will take between 6 and 8 peaches to make the purée. Just scrub and slice them, leaving the skins on. Use the blender; in fact, you can chop the nuts first, then purée the peaches.

1 1/2 cups sugar	1 teaspoon cinnamon
1/2 cup butter/margarine	1 teaspoon baking soda
2 eggs	1 teaspoon baking powder
2 1/4 cups peach purée	1/4 teaspoon salt
2 cups flour	1 teaspoon vanilla
	1 cup finely chopped pecans

Cream the sugar and shortening together. Add the eggs, beating well, then the peach purée and dry ingredients and blend thoroughly. Stir in vanilla and pecans until well blended. Pour into two loaf pans (9 x 5) that have been well greased and floured. Bake at 325° for 55 minutes to 1 hour. Let cool a few minutes before removing from pans and cool completely before slicing. Spread with honey and/or cream cheese. You can instead make three smaller loaves; bake them 50 minutes.

◆

If you do not have fresh peaches, these can be made with canned or frozen peaches. You should keep in mind that you might want to adjust the sweetening. These recipes involve the same principle: peaches on the bottom layer and something interesting on top.

PEACH UPSIDE-DOWN CAKE

This recipe should go under Pineapple, because that is the traditional idea. But this is surely a legitimate version and fits so well with the upper-and lower-layer baked desserts collected here.

3 large peaches	1/2 teaspoon salt
1/2 cup butter/margarine, divided	1/2 cup milk
1/2 cup brown sugar	1 teaspoon vanilla
1 1/2 cups flour	2 eggs
1/2 cup sugar	sliced almonds
2 teaspoons baking powder	

Slice the peaches. Melt the butter in a 9-inch square baking pan in a 350° oven. Sprinkle the brown sugar evenly in the pan. Arrange the peach slices in rows over the sugar.

Sift the flour, sugar, baking powder, and salt into a large bowl. Add the shortening, milk, vanilla, and eggs. Beat at low speed just until mixed. Then beat at high speed for 4 minutes, or until very smooth and fluffy. Spoon the batter over the peaches, covering completely.

Bake at 350° for 45 minutes, or until the center springs back when lightly pressed. Loosen the cake around the edges and invert onto a serving plate. Let the pan sit there a minute, then lift off. Garnish the top with sliced almonds and serve at room temperature.

PEACH MACAROON

This is a simple baked dish and so delicious.

peach halves	1/2 cup flour
2 tablespoons butter	1/4 teaspoon baking powder
1/2 cup sugar	dash salt
1 egg, beaten	1/4 teaspoon almond extract

Arrange peeled peach halves in a shallow 1-quart baking dish. Mix everything else together and spoon on top. Bake 25 minutes at 400°.

PEACH COBBLER

Here is a more extended and heartier version of the preceding rule. With your biscuit mix ready made (see the Appendix), this hearty old-fashioned dessert is quickly made.

3 to 4 large peaches	1/8 teaspoon salt
1/2 cup sugar	1 cup biscuit mix (see the
1 tablespoon cornstarch	Appendix)
1 teaspoon grated lemon rind	1 tablespoon sugar
2 tablespoons lemon juice	1/2 cup light cream

Peel, pit, and slice the peaches (about 4 cups). Combine the sugar and cornstarch; then stir into the peaches along with the lemon rind and juice and salt and put all this in a medium saucepan. Bring to a boil, stirring constantly; pour into a 1 1/2-quart baking dish.

Bake at 375° for 10 minutes. Meanwhile combine the biscuit mix and the 1 tablespoon sugar in a medium bowl. Stir in the cream until a soft dough forms. Remove the peaches from the oven and drop the dough by tablespoonfuls over the peaches so that the fruit is completely covered. Return to the oven and bake 20 minutes more or until the crust is golden. Serve warm with cream or ice cream. You can also add 1/2 teaspoon cinnamon and 1/2 teaspoon nutmeg to the peach mixture if you like.

PEACH SPONGE

This is a three-layer dessert—fruit, custard, and a spongelike topping. It is light and perfectly delicious.

2 cups sliced peaches *or*	1 teaspoon grated lemon rind
1 can (16 ounces), drained	2 tablespoons butter, melted
2/3 cup fine-curd cottage cheese	3 eggs, separated
1 cup sugar	1/4 cup lemon juice
1/4 cup flour	1 cup milk
1/4 teaspoon salt	

Arrange the peach slices in a 1 1/2-quart baking dish; spread with the cheese. Mix the sugar, flour, salt, lemon rind, and butter.

Beat the egg whites until stiff; set aside. Beat yolks until thick and lemon-colored; add lemon juice and milk and stir into the first mixture. Fold in egg whites and pour over the peaches and cottage cheese. Set the dish in a pan of hot water and bake at 325° about 1 1/4 hours. Any leftover pudding can be served cold.

EASY PEACH TOPPING

This recipe comes from a camping cookbook, the idea being that you open a can of peaches, add the ingredients, and put it on the back of your camp stove while preparing the meal. It has been adapted to frozen peaches and is a lifesaver when unexpected guests arrive.

1 quart frozen peaches	generous dash nutmeg
2 tablespoons brown sugar	1 tablespoon margarine
1/2 teaspoon cinnamon	brandy

If you want to use fresh peaches, slice about 4 cups and add 1/4 cup water to them (you may want to add some sugar also). If not, put the lump of frozen peaches in a large saucepan, add the other ingredients, except the brandy, and simmer on a back burner. Stir the mixture from time to time and heat to very warm, but not boiling; this will take from one-half to one hour. Add some brandy just before serving, if desired. Pour over vanilla ice cream or plain cake. The remainder will keep in the refrigerator; just reheat before using.

THE PITS
OR
PEACH JELLY

And now we come to the ultimate of using it all. With peaches so expensive, it really pays to get every ounce of good out of them.

Save the skins and pits from the peaches prepared for freezing (or for desserts or for marmalade). I keep a large plastic container in the refrigerator and add to it. You can also add any brown spots that have not spoiled, and, if you just happen to have any, apple skins and cores too (they will help with the jelling).

When you have a good amount, dump everything in a large kettle, cover completely with water, and let stand overnight. (*Please* don't be upset by the sight of the juice. It will be, quite frankly, a mucky brown; carry on—and you will marvel at the miracles nature hath wrought.)

The next morning, bring the mixture to a boil; stir a few times, boil a minute or two and then remove from the heat. Let it cool and drain off all the juice. Combine 3 1/4 cups juice with 1/4 cup lemon juice in a very large kettle. Stir in one package of Sure-Jell. Bring to a boil and add 4 cups sugar. Then bring to a full, rolling boil that can't be stirred down; boil 1 minute. Turn off the heat, and skim the jelly. Pour into hot, sterilized jelly glasses, and cover immediately with hot paraffin.

If you think you have enough apple skins to forego the Sure-Jell, then boil the peach and lemon juices five minutes, add sugar to desired sweetness (from 1/2 to 3/4 cup sugar to 1 cup juice). Then follow the rule under Black Raspberry Jelly. You can add 2 cups of cut-up peaches when cooking to make jam.

Other recipes using peaches: Cantaloupe Fruit Cups (Melons); Sherry Pork Chops (Wine); Apple coffee cakes, Plum Cake and Pflaumenkuchen (both under Plums) can be made with peaches.

Pears

If you have too many pears, you can start by stewing them. And you can freeze what you stew to eat all winter long. I love pears, but I really do not like canned ones—they are always too sweet and lack flavor. Make a sugar syrup (1/3 cup sugar to 1 cup water) and boil it for about 5 minutes. Then add the pears, cored, peeled, and in halves or quarters. Cook gently for a very short time, usually less than 5 minutes, until just tender. Do watch them, because they turn to mush in no time. If your pears are underripe, or are hard-textured like winter pears, the cooking time will be longer, sometimes as long as 20 minutes.

Variations:
Honey: Use a honey syrup (1/3 cup honey to 1 cup water, or a little less), and cook *very* gently; honey is better if simmered, not boiled.

Wine: Or make a syrup of 1 1/2 cups white wine, 1/2 cup light corn syrup or honey, 1 strip lemon rind; poach the pears in this mixture (about 4 large pears for this quantity of syrup), put them in a bowl, pour the syrup over, and chill. Before serving stir in 1 tablespoon Grand Marnier.

Fruit: You can also stew pears in orange juice, or syrup with lemon juice added.

POIRE À LA BELLE HÉLÈNE

With those lovely pear halves you have stewed, make this popular French dessert. The name, I think, is a reference to Helen of Troy. Take 1 pear half per serving, place in a pretty dessert dish, round side up, on top of a generous dip of vanilla ice cream. Pour a warm, thick chocolate sauce (see Rich Chocolate Sauce under Evaporated Milk) over the pear half and top with whipped cream.

☆☆☆ PEAR PIE

Prepare 4 cups of good, firm winter pears, peeled and cut in half inch cubes. Follow the rule for Grape Pie, using pears in place of the grapes. And please, even if you've never heard of pear pie, try it. It is scrumptious.

WINTER PEAR WALNUT PIE

Another pie with pears, much fancier, much richer.

• Walnut Pastry •
1 cup flour
1/2 teaspoon salt
1/4 cup ground walnuts
1/3 cup shortening
2 to 3 tablespoons water

• Walnut Topping •
1/2 cup brown sugar
1/3 cup flour
1/4 cup butter
1/2 teaspoon cinnamon
1/4 cup chopped walnuts

• Filling •
4 fresh winter pears
2 tablespoons flour
1/2 cup dark corn syrup
1/4 cup brown sugar
dash of salt
2 tablespoons butter
1 tablespoon lemon juice

Make the pastry by combining dry ingredients. Cut in the shortening and add cold water, one tablespoon at a time, stirring lightly with a fork. Combine the topping ingredients and set aside.

Core and slice pears. Reserve 6 slices for garnish. Toss remaining slices with flour. Arrange them in the pie shell. Combine the corn syrup, brown sugar, salt, butter, and lemon juice. Heat to melt butter and sugar. Pour over the pears. Arrange reserved slices in a circle in the center of the pie. Sprinkle with the walnut topping. Bake at 400° for about an hour.

---◆---

☆☆☆ CURRIED PEAR SALAD

2 large pears
leafy salad greens
2 cups cooked rice
3/4 cup diced cooked turkey *or* ham
1/3 cup raisins
1/4 cup chopped salted peanuts

1/4 cup chopped celery
2 tablespoons chopped green onions
1/2 cup mayonnaise
1 tablespoon lemon juice
1 teaspoon curry powder
dash salt

Cut the pears in half, peel, core; arrange around the edges of 4 individual salad bowls lined with greens. Combine the rice, turkey, raisins, peanuts, celery, and green onions. Blend together the mayonnaise (or use Mock Mayonnaise—see the Appendix), lemon juice, curry powder, and salt. Toss with the salad. Spoon into the prepared bowls. Serves 4.

PEAR BREAD

This is one of the simplest ways of using up pears.

1/2 cup butter/margarine	1/2 teaspoon baking soda
1 cup (scant) sugar	1/4 teaspoon nutmeg
2 eggs	1/4 cup yogurt *or* buttermilk
2 cups flour	*or* sour milk
1/2 teaspoon salt	1 cup chopped pears
1 teaspoon baking powder	1 teaspoon vanilla

Cream the butter/margarine and gradually beat in the sugar and the eggs, one at a time. Combine the dry ingredients and add to the egg mixture alternately with the yogurt. Stir in the pears and vanilla. Pour into a greased 9 x 5 loaf pan. Bake at 350° for 1 hour.

◆

PEAR "HONEY"

4 large ripe pears	grated rind and juice from 1 lemon
1 can (8 ounces) unsweetened	*or* lime
crushed pineapple, with juice	2 cups sugar

Peel, quarter, and core the pears. Force through the fine blade of a food chopper. Combine with the pineapple, lemon rind and juice, and sugar in a kettle. Bring to a boil over medium heat and simmer, uncovered, stirring frequently, for 30 minutes, or until thick and translucent. Pour at once into hot sterilized jars, filling to within 1/4 inch of the top. Seal at once, then process in boiling-water bath for 10 minutes. Serve as a spread for toast or bread, or as a dessert topping. Makes about 4 half-pints.

PEAR BUTTER

Wash pears. Do not peel. Slice them and add a small amount of water to start cooking. Cook until very soft and then press through a food mill. To each cup pulp add 1/2 cup sugar, 1/2 teaspoon lemon juice, 1/4 teaspoon cinnamon, and 1/4 teaspoon nutmeg. Cook until thick, stirring frequently to prevent scorching. Or, better still, spread in a rectangular 15 x 10 pan and put in an oven at 300°; bake, stirring from time to time, until thickened. This may take several hours, but at least you don't have to stand over the stove and stir all the time. Pour into hot sterilized jars and seal with paraffin.

RAW PEAR CONSERVE

Very easy indeed and perfectly delicious. It will keep for several weeks in the refrigerator in tightly covered glass jars.

2 cups diced pears	1/2 cup nuts
1/2 cup raisins	1/4 cup crushed pineapple, drained
1/2 cup honey	

Put everything in the blender and whirl until you have a thick jam.

MEATLESS PEAR MINCEMEAT

Use this as a filling for pies or tarts (combine with chopped apples for a great pie) or heated as sauce for ice cream.

7 large ripe pears	1/2 cup white vinegar
1 lemon	1 1/2 teaspoons *each* ground cloves,
1 package (15 ounces) raisins	cinnamon, nutmeg, and allspice
3 1/2 cups sugar	1/2 teaspoon ginger

Peel, quarter, and core the pears. Cut the lemon in quarters, removing the seeds. Grind the pears, lemon, and raisins in a food chopper, using a coarse blade. Combine this mixture with the sugar, vinegar, and spices in a large kettle. Bring to a boil over medium heat, and simmer uncovered, stirring frequently, about 40 minutes, or until thick. Pour into sterilized jars, process in a boiling-water bath for 25 minutes. Makes about 4 pints.

PEAR CHUTNEY

A delicious combination of pears with a subtle blending of spices which goes well with all meats.

1/2 teaspoon whole allspice	4 cups sugar
1/2 teaspoon whole cloves	1/2 cup chopped crystallized ginger
10 cups sliced pears (1/4-inch slices)	3 cups cider vinegar
1 1/2 cups seedless raisins	1/2 teaspoon salt
1/2 cup finely chopped green pepper	2 pieces stick cinnamon (2 inch)

Tie the allspice and cloves in a cheesecloth bag. Combine all ingredients in a large saucepan. Leave uncovered and bring to a boil. Reduce heat, simmer slowly 1 hour or until thick. Stir from time to time. Discard spices. Spoon into hot sterilized jars and seal. Makes 8 half-pints.

Peas

The season for fresh peas is dreadfully short, but when we can have them, we all set to and shell the peas for dinner. They are worth it. The newly developed edible podded peas are wonderful. You can use them cut up in small pieces in any of the following recipes or whole in those for the puréed soups. Just be sure you remove any strings from the pods before putting them in the blender.

One cardinal rule for preparing peas. Don't cook them an instant longer than you have to. In fact, with fresh peas and frozen, I add some water to the pan, turn the heat on high, bring the water to a rapid boil, shake the pan a few times to be sure that all the peas have been hit by the boiling water, cover the pan, turn out the heat, and leave the pan on the stove (my stove is electric, so if you cook with gas, you may want to leave the heat on a little longer) for only a minute or two.

Try some mushrooms with the peas, or fresh corn sliced off the cob, or tiny onions, or chopped green onions, or tender carrot slices. Peas are wonderful creamed with boiled potatoes and topped with parmesan. They are excellent— raw or cooked—in mixed green or vegetable salads.

☆☆☆ VENETIAN RICE

2 green onions, chopped	1/2 teaspoon seasoned salt
1 tablespoon margarine	2 1/2 cups water
1 cup uncooked rice	1 chicken bouillon cube
2 pinches crushed basil	2 cups peas, cooked and drained
	2 tablespoons parmesan cheese

Sauté the onion and rice in the margarine in a large pan. Cook, stirring, until the rice is golden. Stir in the basil, salt, water (in which you have dissolved the bouillon cube). Heat to boiling. Reduce heat and cover.

Simmer 30 minutes until the rice is tender and the liquid absorbed. Stir in the peas. Sprinkle with parmesan, toss lightly to mix and fluff the rice. Serves 4 to 6.

P AND P CASSEROLE

The "P"s stand for Peas and Potatoes. This dish is very good with baked ham.

2 cups thinly sliced potatoes
1 medium onion, finely sliced
1 cup peas
1/2 cup stock

1/2 cup cottage cheese
1/2 teaspoon marjoram
1 tablespoon margarine, melted

Arrange the vegetables in a casserole. Stir the stock into the cottage cheese and mix well, then add the marjoram and melted margarine. Pour over the vegetables and stir the whole thing well. Top with some grated cheese, or bread crumbs. Bake at 350° about 40 minutes.

Variation: Add 1/2 to 1 cup finely chopped ham.

HUNGARIAN NOODLES AND PEAS

If you like a study in green, try spinach noodles in this one.

2 cups uncooked fine egg noodles
1 1/2 cups peas
1/2 cup onion, chopped
1 cup dairy sour cream

1/2 cup cottage cheese
1 tablespoon poppy seeds
1/2 teaspoon salt
2 tablespoons grated parmesan

Cook the noodles until just tender, rinse, and drain. Cook the peas and onion together until just tender; drain. Combine the sour cream, cottage cheese, poppy seeds, and salt. Then mix everything together, gently please, and sprinkle the parmesan over the top. Serve at once. Serves 6.

◆

MINTED PEA SOUP

Really cool and refreshing on a hot summer day.

2 cups cooked peas
1 cup chicken broth

1 cup plain yogurt
1 tablespoon finely chopped mint
salt

In a blender, whirl the peas and chicken broth at high speed for several minutes, until very smooth. Stir in the yogurt, mint, and salt to taste. Chill until ready to serve. Garnish with dollops of plain yogurt and a sprinkling of paprika. Serves 4.

FRESH PEA SOUP

This soup has a beautiful color. You can serve it either hot or cold, garnished with fresh chopped chives.

4 cups peas	2 to 4 tablespoons butter
2 cups vegetable broth	2 to 4 tablespoons flour
1/2 cup white wine	2 cups hot milk
	salt and pepper

Cook the peas in the vegetable broth about 5 minutes. Be sure not to cook them too long, they should be bright green. Purée them in a blender, cool, and stir in 1/2 cup white wine. Make a cream sauce with the butter, flour, and milk, using the smaller amounts of butter and flour if you want a light soup. Season with salt and pepper, and then whisk into the pea purée. Heat the soup through, making sure everything is blended. Serves 6 to 8.

Other recipes using peas: Leipziger Allerei (Lima Beans); Eggplant and Macaroni (Noodles & Pasta); Pork-Peas-Rice (Pork); Crunchy Tuna Salad.

Peppers

Sweet green pepper is a necessary part of Chicken Chow Mein, as well as many tomato dishes. Sliced peppers can be stir-fried, flavored with garlic and oregano. Thin slices of green and/or red sweet peppers are beautiful in a mixed green salad, and they add flavor too. The hot peppers that go with much Spanish and Mexican food are not in my domain. The following are for sweet peppers, usually green; try red ones if you like.

STUFFED PEPPERS

Here is one of those wonderful ways to use up the bits and pieces you have leftover in your refrigerator. A little cooked rice or other grain, some ground ham or leftover roast beef, pork, or lamb, leftover cooked dried beans or other legumes, raw and cooked vegetables, cheese, bread crumbs, all moistened with tomato sauce or juice and seasoned well, can be combined in various ways. Use your imagination, remembering that your combination should complement—and compliment—the flavor and texture of the pepper cases.

To prepare the peppers, cut off the tops, and save for the filling. Cut out the membrane and scoop out the seeds. Turn the peppers upside down on a rack over boiling water (very little), and steam about 10 minutes. You want them to be barely soft. Save the liquid in the pot, and add it to your soup jar. The following is my favorite stuffing. It is ample for 4 peppers.

1 cup ground cooked meat	1/4 teaspoon salt
(beef, ham, pork)	1/8 teaspoon pepper
1 tablespoon chopped onion	1/2 cup tomato juice
1 cup Rice Krispies *or* Special K	grated cheese
or wheat or corn flakes	dry bread crumbs

Mix the ground meat and the onion in a bowl. Crush the cereal slightly and add to the meat, blending well. Stir the seasonings into the tomato juice and then combine it with the other mixture. If it seems too dry, add some more tomato juice. Fill the peppers and arrange upright in a baking dish. Sprinkle the tops with grated cheese and bread crumbs. Bake at 350° about 30 minutes.

PORK SHOULDER WITH PEPPERS

A neighbor who likes to experiment in the kitchen made up this recipe. It is economical and delicious. And it is one of those recipes where you can vary amounts to your taste.

pork shoulder, about 1-pound slice	1 can (small) mushrooms
1 green pepper, sliced	with juice
1 large onion, sliced	salt and pepper

Cut away some of the fat from the pork. Heat a little margarine in a heavy pan with a tight lid, and brown the pork. Then arrange the onion and pepper slices over the pork. Cut the mushrooms in small pieces and spread them on top. Add some salt and freshly-ground pepper. Cover the pan and cook gently about 30 minutes, or until the meat is done. Serves 2.

BOEUF CHOUFLEUR

This is an unusual skillet dish with an oriental accent. Serve it with hot fluffy rice and a mixed green salad with tomatoes.

1 small head cauliflower	1/4 cup soy sauce
1 pound round steak, cut in cubes *or*	1 clove garlic, minced
2 cups leftover roast beef cubes	1 tablespoon cornstarch
1 tablespoon margarine	1/2 cup beef bouillon
1 green pepper, cut in 3/4 inch	1 cup water or stock
pieces	1 cup sliced green onions with tops

Separate the cauliflower into flowerettes (about 4 cups). Brown the meat in the margarine about 5 minutes. Add the cauliflower, pepper, soy sauce, and garlic. Stir lightly to coat the vegetables with the soy sauce. Cover the pan and simmer until the vegetables are barely tender, about 10 minutes. Blend the cornstarch with the bouillon. Add it with the water and green onions to the meat mixture. Cook, stirring constantly, until the sauce is thickened. Serves 6.

PEPPER RELISH

1/4 cup hot red peppers, dried	1 teaspoon salt
5 green peppers	2 tablespoons lemon juice
1/2 cup chopped parsley	

Cut up and measure the red peppers, spread them on a baking sheet, and leave for several hours in a 200° oven, stirring from time to time. Remove the stem and seeds from the green peppers and chop them. Use leaf parsley, if you can get it, and cut it fairly fine. Mix all ingredients together and place in a covered container. Let stand one or two days before using. Good with Falafel.

Other recipes using peppers: Guacamole (Avocado); Swiss Loaf (Cheese); Ratatouille Niçoise (Eggplant); Ham Kabobs; Chicken Livers, Sweet-Sour; Chicken Hawaiian (Pineapple); Mexican Casserole (Ricotta); Piperade, Gazpacho, Easy Tomato Sauce (Tomatoes); Salade Niçoise, Tuna-Dill Spread, Tuna-Noodle Casserole (Tuna); Festive Zucchini; many salads.

Pineapple

I rarely have any pineapple to use up in this house; we often have it baked with the ham, and *if* any is left, someone polishes it off. These recipes call for canned pineapple. Try to use the unsweetened kind, it is better and more health-ful. If you are able to use fresh pineapple, do so, but remember that if you are making a gelatin dessert, you must cook the fresh pineapple juice before mixing it with the gelatin. For some mysterious reason, which I do not understand, fresh pineapple prevents the gelatin from jelling.

PINEAPPLE-GRAHAM SQUARES

1/4 cup butter/margarine	1/2 cup graham cracker crumbs
1/2 cup brown sugar	1 can (8 3/4 ounces) crushed
1 egg	pineapple
1/2 cup flour	1/2 cup chopped walnuts

Cream the butter with the sugar until light and fluffy. Beat in the egg. Stir in flour, crumbs, pineapple (which you have drained well), and walnuts. Pour into a lightly greased 8 x 8 pan.

Bake at 350° for 30 to 35 minutes, or until browned. Cool in pan, and cut into squares.

PINEAPPLE PECAN LOAF

This bread makes a lovely accompaniment to afternoon tea. Slice it thin and serve it with sweet butter, if you like, or just plain.

1/4 cup butter/margarine	1/2 teaspoon salt
3/4 cup brown sugar	1 6-ounce can orange juice
1 egg	concentrate
1 3/4 cups flour	1 can (8 3/4 ounces) crushed
1/4 cup wheat germ	pineapple with juice
1 teaspoon baking soda	1/2 cup chopped pecans

Cream the butter/margarine with the sugar. Add the egg and beat well. Sift the flour, soda, and salt, mix in the wheat germ, and add alternately with the thawed orange juice concentrate. Then stir in the pineapple and nuts.

Pour into a 9 x 5 (or two 7 x 3) pan(s). Bake at 350° for 60 minutes (for the large pan) or about 50 (for the smaller size pans). Cool before slicing.

---◆---

SLIM PINEAPPLE RING

Here is a wonderful refreshing salad for the dieter. If you use plain yogurt with 2 tablespoons lemon juice for the lemon yogurt, the slim ring will be even slimmer.

1 can (20 ounces) crushed	1 package plain gelatin
pineapple with juice	1 cup lemon yogurt
1 18-ounce can unsweetened	
pineapple juice	

Drain the pineapple, reserving all the juice. Soften the gelatin in the reserved juice, then heat over hot water until the gelatin is dissolved. Stir in the pineapple juice. Stir in the yogurt. Chill to the consistency of unbeaten egg white. Fold in the pineapple. Chill until firm, overnight at least. Serve with cottage cheese, a dusting of nutmeg, and a taste of honey.

CHICKEN HAWAIIAN

2 whole chicken legs	2 tablespoons cornstarch
2 whole chicken breasts	1/2 cup cider vinegar
1/4 cup flour	1 tablespoon soy sauce
3 tablespoons oil	1/4 teaspoon ginger
1 teaspoon salt	1 chicken bouillon cube
1/4 teaspoon pepper	1 large green pepper, cut crosswise
1 can (20 ounces) sliced pineapple	in circles (about 1/4-inch thick)
1/2 cup sugar	

Wash the chicken, pat dry with paper towels. Coat with flour.

Heat the oil in a large skillet and add the chicken, browning it on all sides. Remove the pieces to a shallow roasting pan, skin side up. Sprinkle with salt and pepper.

Make the sauce by draining the pineapple, pouring the syrup into a 2-cup measure. Add water to make 1 1/4 cups. In a medium saucepan, combine the sugar, cornstarch, pineapple syrup, vinegar, soy sauce, ginger, and bouillon cube, dissolved in 1/4 cup water. Bring to boiling, stirring constantly. Boil 2 minutes. Pour over the chicken.

Bake at 350°, uncovered, for 30 minutes. Add the pineapple slices and green pepper, and bake 30 minutes longer, or until the chicken is tender. Serve with fluffy brown rice. Serves 4, generously.

PINEAPPLE PRESERVES

1 envelope unflavored gelatin	1 can (20 ounces) crushed pineapple
1 can (6 ounces) unsweetened	5 tablespoons sugar
pineapple juice	

Sprinkle the gelatin over the pineapple juice in a saucepan. Let stand 5 minutes. Add the crushed pineapple and sugar to the gelatin mixture. Heat to boiling over medium heat, stirring constantly. Lower heat, and simmer 2 minutes. Pour into sterilized jars and seal with paraffin, or pour into jars, cool, cover, and store in the refrigerator. Makes 3 cups.

PINEAPPLE-ORANGE SAUCE

1 cup orange juice	1/4 cup raisins
1/2 cup sugar	1 apple, peeled and chopped
1/4 cup crushed pineapple with	
juice	

Combine all the ingredients in a saucepan. Bring to a boil, stirring frequently, then reduce heat and simmer 30 minutes, stirring from time to time. Makes about 2 cups.

MAI TAI MOLD

A beautiful dessert. If you have individual molds, do use them. Serve this with whipped cream.

1 can (20 ounces) pineapple chunks in juice	2 cups cold water
	1/2 cup dark rum
2 packages (6 ounces each) orange gelatin	mint sprigs
	12 maraschino cherries
3 cups boiling water	1 orange, peeled and sectioned

Drain the pineapple, reserving juice. Dissolve the gelatin in the boiling water. Stir in cold water and rum. Arrange the mint sprigs, 3 or 4 cherries, and several pineapple chunks in the bottom of a Bundt pan. Pour in 1/2 of the gelatin mixture. Chill until firm.

Chill the remaining gelatin to the consistency of unbeaten egg white. Fold in remaining pineapple, cherries, and the orange sections. Pour over the firm gelatin. Chill firm overnight.

GRAHAM CRACKER CAKE

This cake is not for dieters.

2 sticks butter/margarine	2 teaspoons baking powder
1 1/2 cups sugar	1 cup milk
5 eggs	1 cup chopped nuts (pecans
1 teaspoon vanilla	are splendid)
1 pound graham crackers, crushed	1 cup coconut

Cream the butter and sugar. Add the eggs and vanilla, and beat well. Mix the dry ingredients together and add alternately with the milk. Stir in remaining ingredients. Bake in two 9-inch layers for 25 to 30 minutes at 350°.

And now to the icing, which is the link with pineapple.

1/4 cup butter	1 can (16 ounces) crushed
1 pound (about) 10X sugar	pineapple, drained

Cream the butter and add about three quarters of the sugar, beat until fluffy. Stir in the pineapple, and enough sugar to make spreading consistency.

If you are wondering how to use all that pineapple juice drained from the pineapple in the recipes, you can use it as liquid in gelatin desserts, or mix it half and half with orange juice as a wonderful fruit drink. You can make a sauce by blending about 1 teaspoon lemon juice, 1 cup pineapple juice, 1/4 cup sugar, and 1 tablespoon cornstarch; cook, stirring, until sauce is thick and clear. Or, best of all, make yourself a very cold cocktail with pineapple juice and rum.

Don't forget Pineapple Upside-Down Cake (follow the rule under Peaches and use 9 pineapple slices instead).

Other recipes using pineapple: Apricot Filling and Bars; Lush Slush (Bananas); Health Salad, Carrot-Pineapple Cake (Carrots); Orange-Pineapple Salad (Cottage Cheese); Pineapple Snow Pudding (Egg Whites); Chicken Livers, Sweet-Sour; Cantaloupe Fruit Cups (Melons); Pear "Honey," Raw Pear Conserve; Rhubarb-Pineapple Jam; Baked Hubbard Squash; Turkey Cantonese.

Plums

You can stew plums, of course. And what you stew can be frozen. Make a sugar syrup (or, if you prefer, a honey syrup), 1/3 cup sugar to 1 cup water will be good if the plums are quite ripe and sweet. If they are not, you may want to add more sweetening. Boil the sugar and water together for about 5 minutes, then add the plums, pitted and cut in halves or quarters. Cover the pan and cook them gently for several minutes. Be sure not to overcook them and make mush. Plums can also be frozen raw (mix 1 cup sugar to 5 cups cut-up fruit). When you defrost them, you can stir them and eat them just like that, or use them for fruit compotes or baked puddings. One friend freezes her plums, whole, in plastic bags, then cuts them up on the plum cake (easiest of all).

☆☆☆ APPLE-PLUM COMPOTE

I make this dessert at least once a week during the late summer and early fall. Then I freeze part of it to enjoy during the winter months. Do try to get a real vanilla bean; it makes all the difference in the world.

1 1/2 cups water	4 large tart cooking apples
1/2 cup sugar	9 Italian plums
1 inch vanilla bean	

Combine the water, sugar, and vanilla bean in a large saucepan. Boil gently for 5 minutes. Peel the apples, remove the core, cut into quarters, and then each quarter into thirds. Add to the boiling syrup, stir well, cover the pan, and cook gently 5 to 8 minutes, or until the apples are just tender. Meanwhile remove the pits from the plums, cut in quarters, and add them to the apples. If you have an electric stove, cook everything 1 minute, then turn off the heat, and leave the pan to cool on the burner. If you have a gas stove, cook the mixture about 3 minutes after you have added the plums, stirring once. Remove the vanilla bean, and chill. Wonderful with sponge cake and whipped cream.

PLUM-APRICOT PARTY DESSERT

Here is something you can do with those plums you have frozen, either stewed or raw. Be sure to defrost them, and drain off the syrup, as it will be needed.

2 cups plums, drained	1/2 cup sweet vermouth
2 cups (1 16-ounce can) apricot halves	vanilla ice cream

Drain the apricots and mix in a pyrex casserole with the plums. Pour in 1/2 cup of the juices you have drained, and the vermouth. Bake, uncovered, in a 325° oven. Cook about 1 hour, adding more liquid as needed. Take it out of the oven when you serve your meal, so it will be warm at dessert time. Serve with a dollop of ice cream. Serves 4 to 6. You can use canned plums instead of frozen. Drain them, and remove the pits before proceeding.

PLUM-CRUMB PUDDING

Another hot plum dessert, one of my favorites.

3 pounds fresh plums	**1/4 cup rolled oats**
1 1/4 cups sugar, divided	**1/4 cup butter/margarine**
1 cup flour, divided	

Wash the plums, remove pits, and cut in quarters. Add 3/4 cup sugar and 1/4 cup flour to the plums and mix well. Place in a 2-quart (or larger) baking dish. Mix remaining sugar and flour with the rolled oats, and cut in the butter/margarine until of crumb consistency. Sprinkle over the plums.

Bake at 375° about 1 hour. Serve warm with vanilla ice cream.

Note: Be sure the baking dish is big enough. This dessert does bubble up, and there is no point having a sticky mess in the oven. Also, you may want to mix some cut-up apples with the plums. The combination is very good.

PFLAUMENKUCHEN

This is a traditional German cake. If you can get damson plums, and if you have the patience to pit them and cut them and arrange them on the cake, do so. You'll then have something very close to the prized (and almost unpronounceable) Austrian *Zwetschgenkuchen,* which is superb and *must* be served *mit Schlag,* that is, stiffly whipped cream with *no* sugar. It is worth the effort, I can assure you.

1 cup flour	**1 egg**
2 teaspoons baking powder	**1/2 teaspoon vanilla**
1/4 teaspoon salt	**1 1/2 (about) tablespoons milk**
2 tablespoons sugar	**plums (Italian prune plums)**
1 1/2 tablespoons butter	**more sugar**

Measure the flour and sift it with the baking powder, salt, and sugar into a mixing bowl. Cut in the butter, then beat in the egg, vanilla, and milk. This makes a stiff dough. Press it with floured hands into a greased 10-inch pie plate or oven-proof dish. Cover the top very closely with sliced or quartered plums, which you arrange closely in rows with the skin side down. Sprinkle *generously* with sugar, and some cinnamon, if you wish. You can also dot the fruit with butter. Bake at 425° for about 20 minutes.

The last time I made this cake, I used whole wheat pastry flour. The result was delicious.

PLUM CAKE

1/2 cup butter/margarine
1 cup sugar
2 eggs, separated
1 teaspoon vanilla
1 cup flour

1 teaspoon baking powder
1/2 teaspoon lemon juice *or*
 1 tablespoon rum, brandy, or
 bourbon
plums (dark red)

Cream the shortening, sugar, and egg yolks until fluffy. Add the flavoring (I think plum-rum sounds wonderful, but I really like brandy best), and the dry ingredients. Beat the egg whites until stiff and fold them in.

Pour into a greased 9-inch square or round pan. Place sliced plums closely on top. Dot with butter. Bake at 350° until the cake tests done, 45 to 50 minutes.

Note: This cake, as the previous one, can be made with apples, or peaches, or Italian prune-plums. If you use green apples, extend the cooking time and lower the temperature to 325°. The recipe can be doubled. The cake can be frozen.

PLUM CONSERVE

I confess that my attempts to make plum jam have always been disastrous. The jam always turns fizzy and then becomes inedible. The same is not true for conserve. This one is delicious; serve it as an accompaniment to meat.

2 pounds red firm plums
3 cups sugar
1 orange

1 lemon
1/2 cup seedless raisins
1/2 cup walnuts

Wash plums well, then remove the pits, and chop coarsely. They should measure 4 cups. Combine in a kettle with the sugar and let stand while preparing the other fruits. Wash the orange and lemon, dry, and shred the rind very fine. Peel the fruits, removing all white membrane. Slice, remove seeds and pith, then dice. Pour boiling water over the nuts, boil 2 minutes, then drain and chop. Add all ingredients, except the nuts, to the plum-sugar mixture. Bring to a boil over moderately high heat, stirring until the sugar dissolves. Boil rapidly, uncovered, stirring often to avoid burning, 25 to 30 minutes, or until thickened and clear. Stir in the nuts. Pour at once into hot sterilized jars, filling to within 1/2-inch of top. Seal at once, then process in a boiling-water bath 10 minutes. Makes about 4 half-pints.

Pork

A juicy roast pork can be a true culinary delight. It is so good with browned or baked potatoes and apple sauce. But cold pork, no matter how you serve it, leaves something to be desired.

☆☆☆ CHINESE PORK

This is not only my favorite way of using up that small amount of pork roast or leftover chop or two, it is also one of my favorite meals. It makes very good use of any number of remainders you might have sitting in the refrigerator. The proportions given here are approximate and, quite honestly, arbitrary. Use this as a guide, and just add what you have. It will be good, I guarantee it.

1 tablespoon oil or margarine	sprouts
1 cup diagonally sliced celery	snow peas
3 green onions, minced	water chestnuts (optional)
1/2 to 1 cup cooked pork, in	soy sauce
strips or chunks	stock or bouillon
1 cup cooked rice	

Heat the oil in a large frying pan over medium heat. Stir in the celery and onions, and cook, stirring, for a minute or so. Then add in the pork and rice and continue cooking, stirring from time to time, until somewhat browned. Then add some sprouts, snow peas, and water chestnuts, if you like. Cover the pan, lower the heat, and steam for a minute or so. Stir in enough stock or bouillon or water to make the dish somewhat liquid, but not soupy. Add soy sauce to taste, and serve over chow mein noodles. You may add thinly sliced carrots, strips of green pepper, and/or any compatible leftover vegetable. Sauté these at the beginning. If you like, you can use sliced potatoes instead of the rice.

CHINESE PORK AND VEGETABLES

A more elaborate version of the previous recipe. And, I should add, you can substitute any lean leftover meat in this and the previous recipe—try that small remainder of London broil or roast beef, for example, or chicken or turkey.

6 ounces frozen snow peas	1/2 pound fresh spinach
3 stalks celery	2 tablespoons oil
3 medium onions	1/4 cup chicken broth
1 large carrot	1 1/2 to 2 cups diced leftover
1 medium turnip	cooked pork
10 water chestnuts	2 tablespoons soy sauce

Let snow peas stand at room temperature until ready to use. Or, if the season is right, use fresh (about 1 cup). Cut the celery in thin slices, diagonally. Slice the onions and cut the carrot diagonally in as thin slices as possible. Cut the turnip in thin slices and each slice into "matchstick" slivers. Slice the water chestnuts in slivers. Tear the spinach into small pieces.

Heat the oil over medium heat in a large skillet. Add the celery, onions, carrot, and turnip. Stir to coat vegetables. Cover and let steam briefly. Add stock, stir to blend. Cover and steam for 4 minutes. Then add water chestnuts and pork. Stir again. Cover and cook 4 minutes more. Vegetables should be tender but still crisp. Add the snow peas, spinach, and soy sauce. Blend, cover, and steam for a minute or so more. If you want, thicken the juices with 1 teaspoon cornstarch blended with 1 tablespoon water and stirred into the mixture until it thickens. Serve with hot rice and sprinkle Chinese noodles over the top. Serves 4.

☆☆☆ PORK-PEAS-RICE

I suppose this is simply *risibisi* with pork. In any case, nothing could be easier, and this dish has been certainly popular in my house over many years.

1 cup lean pork, in cubes	2 tablespoons butter
2 cups cooked peas, undrained	salt and pepper to taste
3 cups cooked rice	

Make sure you trim the fat from the leftover pork. Cut the pieces in about 1/2-inch cubes. Heat a little oil in a large frying pan and brown the pork on all sides. The outside should be crusty and brown, while the inside remains tender. Reduce the heat, stir in the peas, rice, and butter. Season to taste. If too dry, add some stock. Serves 3 to 4.

ENGLISH PORK HASH

Be sure when you roast the pork to deglaze the pan. Save the liquid, chill it, remove the fat, and make a thin gravy to use in this recipe.

1 tablespoon margarine	pepper
2 cups cooked pork, in small cubes	3/4 cup gravy or sauce from roast
1 medium onion, coarsely chopped	1 teaspoon vinegar
1 tablespoon flour	1 teaspoon prepared mustard
1/2 teaspoon salt	

Melt the margarine in a heavy skillet. Add the pork and brown lightly on all sides. Remove to a plate and set aside.

Sauté the onion in the same pan until brown; sprinkle with the flour, add seasonings, and stir well. Continue cooking until the flour is brown. Then stir in the gravy, vinegar, and mustard. Bring to a boil; then stir in the pork and mix everything well. Serve over mashed potatoes. Serves 4.

PORK AND RAISINS

1 tablespoon oil	2 tablespoons brown sugar
2 cups cubed cooked pork	1 teaspoon ginger
2 onions, sliced	1/2 teaspoon poultry seasoning
1 cup orange juice	1/2 teaspoon marjoram
1 tablespoon lemon juice	1/2 cup raisins

Heat the oil in a skillet. Brown the pork with the onions. Then pour in the remaining ingredients, along with salt and pepper to taste. Cover, and cook gently, for about 45 minutes. Serves 4. You can substitute 4 pork chops, 1 inch thick, for the cooked pork and proceed in the same way.

Other recipes using pork: Pilaf (Grains), Pork Shoulder with Peppers, Stuffed Peppers; Sherry Pork Chops with Fruit (Wine). Where the recipe calls for chops, you can always substitute leftover cooked roast pork or chops, cut up.

Potatoes

We eat potatoes baked (and fight over the skins), boiled, mashed, fried. Potatoes are essential in stews and many soups and are delicious in omelettes and breads. Save the potato water and add it to the next bread dough you prepare. Do the same with boiled potatoes; sieve them and stir in with the flour.

GERMAN POTATO SOUP

This is an *echt* German recipe, coming from old family friends.

8 potatoes	1 teaspoon basil
4 carrots	2 cups milk
3 small onions	1 tablespoon parsley
salt, pepper	

Peel and cut up the vegetables; boil in salted water with pepper and basil until tender. Put everything through a food mill. Add the milk and heat thoroughly. Taste and adjust seasoning. Float some parboiled wieners on top and sprinkle with parsley. If you are using cooked potatoes, cook the carrots and onions first; then add the potatoes at the end of the cooking time.

DINNER CHOWDER

2 cups diced potatoes	1/4 teaspoon pepper
3/4 cup minced onion	1/2 teaspoon dry mustard
1/2 cup chopped celery	1 1/2 teaspoons catsup
1 teaspoon salt	2 cups (or more) milk
2 1/2 cups boiling water	1/4 pound sharp cheese
4 tablespoons butter	1 tablespoon chopped parsley
4 tablespoons flour	2 cups fresh or canned tomatoes

Combine the potatoes, onion, celery, salt, and water in a large pot. Cover and simmer until tender (about 15 minutes). Melt butter in a double boiler, stir in flour, pepper, mustard, catsup, and milk. Cook, stirring, until thickened. Grate the cheese, add it to the cream sauce, and stir until melted. Stir this into the soup. Finally add the parsley and the tomatoes, cut up. Heat thoroughly and serve. Serves 4 to 6.

POTATO RATATOUILLE

One of those wonderful mixtures that can be varied *ad infinitum.* Feel free to add those leftover vegetables you have around.

3 slices bacon	3 medium zucchini, sliced
2 tablespoons oil	2 large tomatoes, in wedges
1 medium onion, sliced	1 teaspoon salt
1 clove minced garlic	pepper to taste
5 potatoes, peeled and in cubes	1/2 teaspoon basil
1 cup fresh green beans	2 tablespoons minced parsley

Fry the bacon in a large skillet; drain on a paper towel, crumble, and set aside. Drain the fat from the pan and add the oil. Sauté the onion and garlic until soft. Add the vegetables, sprinkle the bacon over, and stir in the remaining ingredients. Cover and simmer 45 minutes, stirring gently from time to time. Or, if you prefer, you can put the whole mixture in a covered baking dish and bake at 350° for 45 minutes. Serves 6 to 8.

Variations:
Omit the bacon for a vegetarian version.
Substitute 1/4 cup chopped green pepper for the green beans, and cook about 30 minutes.
Add 1/2 cup chopped green pepper and 1/2 cup chopped celery to the vegetables.
Use yellow summer squash instead of zucchini. Carry on.

POTATO POLENTA

This is a popular Italian dish and an interesting change from potatoes, rice, or noodles.

3 medium potatoes, diced	3/4 cup cornmeal
1 quart water	2 tablespoons butter
2 teaspoons salt	

Put the potatoes in a deep, heavy kettle with the water and salt. Stir in the cornmeal and bring to a boil. Cook over low heat, covered, about 45 minutes, stirring frequently. Stir in the butter and turn onto a buttered hot platter.

☆☆☆ SCALLOPED POTATOES WITH GRUYÈRE

This dish was served to us by a French friend who comes from the Auvergne, a region known for its hearty meals and nourishing breads. In our household, this dish is traditionally served with the baked ham.

6 to 8 medium potatoes	milk
flour	salt and pepper
gruyère, shredded	

Parboil the potatoes, drain, and reserve the potato water. Peel, slice, and arrange in a 2-quart casserole. Make a layer or two of potatoes, sprinkle generously with flour, add a generous layer of the cheese. Continue making layers, ending with a heavy layer of cheese. Add instant dry milk to the reserved potato water to make milk, and pour enough milk over the casserole until you can see it through the top layer. Bake at 375°, uncovered, until thoroughly done and very brown on top, between 45 minutes and 1 hour.

SWEDISH POTATOES

A way to bake potatoes which does not require "baking" potatoes.

4 medium potatoes	1 tablespoon dry bread crumbs
5 tablespoons melted butter	1 tablespoon grated parmesan
1 teaspoon salt	

Take oblong shaped potatoes, peel them, and then with a sharp knife, slice each crosswise about every 1/4 inch, cutting to within 1/2 inch of the bottom, so that the potato remains whole.

Place the potatoes in a pie plate, drizzle with 2 tablespoons of the butter, sprinkle with salt, and bake at 425° for 30 minutes. Sprinkle the crumbs over the potatoes, drizzle with the remaining butter, and bake 20 minutes longer. Sprinkle with the cheese, baste with the butter in the plate, and bake 10 minutes longer, or until the potatoes are tender (test with a skewer near the bottom). Serves 4.

POTATO PARMESAN SOUFFLÉ

Here is a dandy way to use up those leftover mashed potatoes, providing you can resist making fried potato cakes out of them (I never can).

4 cups mashed potatoes	**1/2 teaspoon salt**
6 eggs, separated	**1/2 teaspoon cream of tartar**
3/4 cup grated parmesan	

Warm the potatoes, and beat in the egg yolks, one at a time; blend in the cheese. Beat egg whites until foamy, add salt and cream of tartar, beat until soft peaks form. Fold the egg whites into the potato mixture and spoon into a buttered 4-quart soufflé dish (or two 2-quart baking dishes with straight sides).

Bake at 375° allowing 1 hour for the large soufflé, 45 minutes for the small. Serves 8 to 10.

☆☆☆ GERMAN POTATO SALAD

Here is a quick and easy main dish that is guaranteed to please all your family.

4 potatoes	**vinegar**
4 slices bacon	**garlic**
chives	**mustard**

Boil the potatoes in their skins, then peel them, and cut into cubes. If you have leftover cooked potatoes, here is an ideal way to use them up. Place the potatoes in an oven-proof bowl in a 250° oven to keep very warm. Fry the bacon until crisp, and if you like, cut up a small onion and fry it along with the bacon. Drain the bacon on a paper towel, and pour off most of the bacon fat from the pan. Stir in some vinegar and blend in the pan scrapings; heat the dressing to which you can add some garlic and prepared mustard, until it is quite hot. Crumble the bacon over the potatoes, add some chopped chives, and pour the hot dressing over. Stir well and serve immediately.

If you don't want to use a dressing made with bacon fat, you can prepare a good vinaigrette, or Italian, or zesty cream dressing and pour it over the potatoes and bacon. Just be sure the dish is served very hot. Serves 2 as a main dish.

HAM AND POTATO SALAD

Classic potato salad is made with diced boiled potatoes, chopped celery, some minced onion, cut-up radishes, hard-boiled egg, and a mayonnaise dressing. Be sure to include celery seeds, lots of them. They are essential. You can also add leftover chicken, turkey, roast beef. Or try this salad.

2 cups cottage cheese	1 teaspoon celery seed
1/4 cup finely chopped onion	2 cups cubed cooked ham
1/2 teaspoon salt	2 cups cubed cooked potatoes
2 tablespoons vinegar	4 hard-boiled eggs, finely chopped
2 teaspoons prepared mustard	

In a large bowl, combine the cottage cheese, onion, salt, vinegar, mustard, and celery seed. Mix well. Add the ham, potatoes, and eggs. Chill several hours to blend flavors. Serve on lettuce. Serves 6 to 8.

◆

POTATO PUFF ROLLS

These are light and perfect for company dinner. Serve them very hot.

1/2 cup mashed potatoes	1 package dry yeast
1 cup milk	1/4 cup warm water
1/4 cup shortening	4 to 4 1/2 cups flour
1/4 cup sugar	1 egg
1 teaspoon salt	

Prepare the potatoes, but do not season. Scald the milk; add the shortening, sugar, salt, and potatoes. Cool to lukewarm.

Dissolve the yeast in the warm water. Combine the milk mixture, yeast, 2 cups flour, and egg. Beat well about 2 minutes. Stir in enough flour to make a soft dough. Turn out onto a lightly floured board and knead until elastic, 5 to 10 minutes. Put in a greased bowl, turning once. Cover and let rise until doubled, about 1 1/2 hours. Punch down.

Turn onto a board. Shape into rolls. Cover and let rise until almost doubled, about 1 hour. Bake at 375° for 10 to 12 minutes. Makes about 36 rolls.

Variation: Substitute honey for the sugar, and reduce the milk to 3/4 cup.

REFRIGERATOR POTATO BREAD

This is a handy dough to have on hand. You can use it as a pizza base when rolled out. Or braid the dough and make one big loaf of bread, glazed with egg white and sprinkled with poppy seeds.

1 large potato	3 large eggs
1 teaspoon salt	2 packages dry yeast
1 cup water	1/4 cup warm water
1/4 cup butter/margarine	1 teaspoon sugar
1/4 cup sugar	5 to 5 1/2 cups flour
1/2 cup dry milk powder	

Peel and dice the potato. Boil in the salted water until tender. Remove from the heat, stir in the butter and sugar. Beat with an electric mixer until the potato is mashed. Add the milk powder and eggs and beat until well blended. Dissolve the yeast in the warm water with the teaspoon of sugar. Add to the potato mixture and stir in the flour, using enough to make a soft dough. Knead until smooth and elastic.

Place in a buttered bowl, cover, and let rise until doubled. Punch down and store in the refrigerator until needed. The dough will keep a week to 10 days. When you are ready to use it, let the dough rise at room temperature for 2 hours. Shape into rolls, loaf bread, braids. Put into pans, cover, and let rise again until doubled. Bake rolls at 400° about 20 minutes. Bake loaves at 425° for 10 minutes, then at 350° for 20 to 35 minutes longer, depending on size.

Variations:

Whole Wheat Healthy: Use honey in place of sugar and 3 cups whole wheat flour in place of the same amount of white flour.

Triple Healthy: Add 1/2 cup soy flour and 1/4 cup wheat germ; reduce white flour accordingly.

Other recipes using potatoes: Cottage Cheese Potatoes; Grain Bread; Pot au Feu, Leek and Potato Soup (Leeks); P and P Casserole (Peas); Salade Niçoise (Tuna); Hash (Turkey); many soups and stews.

Pumpkin

If you have hesitations about preparing a pumpkin, don't. It is easy and what you get is so much better than the canned variety. All the following recipes call for pumpkin purée and can be made with canned pumpkin—remember that canned pumpkin has much less liquid generally, and you may have to adjust accordingly.

The easiest way to prepare pumpkin is to cut it in half, scrape out all the stringy fiber and seeds. (Wash the seeds, dry, sprinkle with a little oil, and bake at 250° about an hour, stirring occasionally; season with your favorite herbs or seasoned salt—delicious cocktail snack or munchies for the children.) Place the halves, cut side down on a flat baking dish, add a little water so that they don't stick, and bake at 325° about 1 hour or until fork tender. Scrape the pumpkin pulp from the shells and mash it. If you want it fairly smooth, then run it through a food mill or purée it in the food processor.

You can also boil pumpkin. Cut it into pieces, remove any pith, and boil it in as little water as possible until tender. Then peel and purée it in the food mill or a blender, using as little liquid as you can. You can also mash it with a fork. You may want to drain off some of the liquid.

Either method works well. From experience I recommend the baking process. It is both quicker and easier.

In many cultures pumpkin is eaten as a vegetable. You can substitute it in winter squash recipes, for the carrots in the carrot ring recipe, or for sweet potatoes in Sweet Potato Pie and Golden Cookies.

For a while it was difficult to find recipes for pumpkin bread. This situation, fortunately, has changed in the past few years.

PUMPKIN BREAD (WITH YEAST)

This bread is a lovely color, mild in flavor, very nourishing, and a perfect accompaniment to fruit salad, or hot or cold vegetable soups. It makes one loaf, but you can double it easily.

1 package dry yeast	3 tablespoons instant dry milk
1 cup warm milk	3 tablespoons bran flakes
2 tablespoons sugar	1/2 teaspoon cinnamon
1 egg, beaten	1/4 teaspoon ginger
1 teaspoon salt	dash nutmeg
2 tablespoons oil	1 1/2 cups white flour
1/2 cup pumpkin	2 to 3 cups whole wheat flour

Dissolve the yeast in the warm milk. Stir in the sugar and let it stand until foamy. In a large mixer bowl, beat the egg, then add the salt, oil, pumpkin, dry milk, bran flakes, spices, and white flour. Mix well and then stir in the yeast. Gradually add enough whole wheat flour to make the dough easy to handle. Knead until smooth, adding more flour if necessary. Let rise in a warm place until doubled. Punch down, put in a 9 x 5 bread pan, or two smaller 7 1/2 x 3 1/2 pans, and let rise until doubled. Bake at 350° for 50 to 60 minutes. The smaller loaves will take less time.

CLASSIC PUMPKIN BREAD

2 1/4 cups sugar	2 teaspoons baking soda
1/2 cup shortening	1/2 teaspoon salt
2 eggs	1 teaspoon cinnamon
1 large can pumpkin (2 cups)	1/2 teaspoon cloves
2/3 cups water	2/3 cup dates or raisins
3 1/3 cups flour	2/3 cup nuts
1/2 teaspoon baking powder	

Cream the shortening and sugar, stir in the eggs, which you have beaten, pumpkin, and water. Sift dry ingredients and add to the mixture. Finally mix in the dates and nuts. Put in two greased and floured bread pans (9 x 5) or four smaller (7 1/2 x 3 1/2) pans. Bake at 350° for 1 hour and 15 minutes for the large loaves, about 55 minutes for the smaller ones.

Variation:
Sherry: Substitute sherry for the water; omit the fruit and use chopped pecans.

☆☆☆ PUMPKIN-MINCEMEAT BREAD

3 1/2 cups flour	4 eggs, beaten
1/2 cup wheat germ	2/3 cup water
1/2 cup sugar	1 cup oil
2 tablespoons pumpkin pie spice	2 cups pumpkin
2 teaspoons baking soda	1 9-ounce package mincemeat,
1/2 teaspoon salt	crumbled
1 1/2 cups brown sugar	1 cup chopped walnuts or pecans

Sift the dry ingredients (except the brown sugar) into a large bowl. Mix in the brown sugar. Make a well in the dry ingredients, and add the eggs, water, oil, and pumpkin. Beat at low speed until well mixed, then at medium-high speed for 3 minutes. Stir in the mincemeat and nuts. Pour into four 7 1/2 x 3 1/2 pans, greased and floured. Bake at 350° for 55 to 60 minutes or until the bread tests done. The top will crack. This bread freezes well and makes a much appreciated Christmas present. Yes, that is the right amount of pumpkin pie spice. A little less is okay too.

FRESH PUMPKIN MUFFINS

2 cups flour	1 egg
1/4 cup sugar	1/2 cup milk
3 teaspoons baking powder	1 cup pumpkin
1/2 teaspoon salt	1/4 cup oil
1 teaspoon cinnamon	

Sift together the dry ingredients into a bowl. Beat the egg, mix in the milk, pumpkin, and oil. Make a well in the center of the flour mixture and add the liquid all at once. Stir quickly until the flour is just moistened. Fill greased muffin cups two-thirds full. Bake at 425° for 25 minutes. Serve immediately. Makes about 15 muffins.

Variations:
Bread: You can use this same rule for one loaf (9 x 5) of bread. Increase the eggs to 2, reduce the baking powder to 2 teaspoons. Bake at 350° for 55 minutes.
Sweet Potato: Substitute 1 cup mashed sweet potatoes for the pumpkin.

PUMPKIN SCONES

This recipe comes from Australia, and if you are partial to scones, you will find these wonderful. They contain no spices at all.

2 cups flour	1 tablespoon melted butter
3 teaspoons baking powder	1 cup pumpkin
1/2 teaspoon salt	1 egg
2 tablespoons sugar	

Sift the dry ingredients together. In a separate bowl, combine the butter, pumpkin, and egg, which you have beaten. Add to the flour mixture and blend lightly. If the dough requires more liquid, add a tablespoon of light cream. Pat to a 3/4-inch thick round on a lightly floured board. Cut into triangles, sprinkle with sugar. Bake at 425° (what the Australians call a "quick" oven), until lightly browned, about 20 minutes. Serve hot with butter, honey, or marmalade. Serve with afternoon tea.

PUMPKIN MOLDS WITH MINCEMEAT SAUCE

1 cup pumpkin	1/4 teaspoon cinnamon
1/2 cup brown sugar	1/8 teaspoon cloves
1/4 teaspoon salt	1 quart vanilla ice cream, softened

Blend everything except the ice cream and mix well. Add the ice cream and stir until smooth. Pour into 6 individual molds or a 1-quart mold and freeze at least 24 hours. Dip molds in warm water and shake out on a plate. Serve with warm sauce.

Mincemeat Sauce:

Prepare 1 package mincemeat as directed on the label for pie filling. Remove from the heat and add 1 tablespoon grated orange rind and 1/2 cup apricot nectar or apple cider. Mix well. Makes 2 cups.

PUMPKIN-RUM PIE

2 cups mashed pumpkin	1 cup milk
3/4 cup sugar	3 eggs
1 teaspoon salt	1/4 cup light rum
1 1/2 teaspoon cinnamon	nutmeg
	piecrust for a 10-inch pie

Mix all ingredients together, and fill the piecrust. Grate nutmeg over the top. Bake at 350° for 1 hour or until a knife comes out clean when tested. Cool. Top with whipped cream, if desired.

PUMPKIN-PECAN PIE

3 eggs
1 1/2 cups pumpkin
3/4 cup dark corn syrup
3/4 cup sugar

1/2 teaspoon cinnamon
1/4 teaspoon salt
1 cup broken pecans
1 unbaked 9-inch pie shell

In a mixing bowl, beat the eggs until frothy. Stir in the remaining ingredients (except nuts), pour into the pie shell. Sprinkle with pecans. Bake at 350° for 50 to 60 minutes. Chill. Serve with whipped cream, if desired.

Variation: If you wish to make a regular pecan pie, use this recipe, reduce the sugar and corn syrup to 2/3 cup, cut the salt down to a pinch, omit the pumpkin and cinnamon, add 1 tablespoon melted butter. Bake at 325° about 45 minutes.

PUMPKIN CHIFFON PIE

Here is a lighter version of pumpkin pie, and perhaps the best thing after all that turkey.

3 eggs, separated
1 cup sugar, divided
1 1/4 cups pumpkin
1/2 cup milk
1/2 teaspoon salt
1/2 teaspoon cinnamon

1/2 teaspoon ginger
1/2 teaspoon nutmeg
1/2 cup cold water
1 envelope unflavored gelatin
1 9-inch baked pie shell, preferably
   graham cracker crust

Beat the egg yolks, and combine with 1/2 cup sugar, pumpkin, milk, and seasonings. Cook over boiling water until of custard consistency.

Pour cold water into a bowl, sprinkle gelatin on top, and stir. Add to the hot pumpkin mixture and stir until dissolved. Cool until thick but not set.

Beat the egg whites until stiff. Add the remaining sugar. Fold into the pumpkin mixture. Pour into the prepared shell. Chill for at least 6 hours.

PUMPKIN CHEESE CAKE

This dessert is satin smooth. You can make it with canned pumpkin, but it is much better with fresh.

• Crust •	• Filling •
5 tablespoons butter/margarine	2 8-ounce packages cream cheese
1/3 cup sugar	1/2 cup sugar
1 egg	2 cups pumpkin
1 cup flour	1 teaspoon cinnamon
1/4 cup quick-cooking oats	1/4 teaspoon ginger
	1/4 teaspoon nutmeg
	dash of salt
	2 eggs

Cream butter and sugar until light and fluffy. Blend in the egg, beaten. Add flour and oats and mix well. Spread dough on bottom and up 2 inches of the sides of a spring-form pan. Bake at 400° for about 10 minutes. Cool.

Combine softened cream cheese and sugar. Beat at medium speed with mixer until smooth. Add eggs, one at a time, and beat well. Blend in pumpkin, spices, and salt. Pour into cooled baked crust. Bake at 350° for 50 minutes. Remove from pan. Chill. Garnish with whipped cream, if desired.

☆☆☆ PUMPKIN CUSTARD

Some people bake this custard in a pie shell.

2 eggs	1/2 teaspoon cinnamon
1/3 cup brown sugar	1/2 teaspoon pumpkin pie spice
1/4 teaspoon salt	3/4 cup light cream, half-and-half,
1 cup pumpkin	or milk
dash ginger	

Beat the eggs with the brown sugar. Blend the spices into the pumpkin and add the mixture. Finally mix in the cream. I have never used cream, I always use skim milk, or if the pumpkin is thin, I simply add 1/3 cup instant milk powder to it instead of milk. In this case, increase the amount of pumpkin to 1 1/2 cups. The recipe says to scald the cream/milk. I never have. Bake (in a pan of hot water) at 325° for at least an hour, or until set.

☆☆☆ PUMPKIN BREAD PUDDING

This is a wonderful bread pudding.

2/3 cup sugar
2 tablespoons margarine, melted
1 1/2 cups milk
6 slices bread, crumbled
1/2 teaspoon vanilla
3 eggs
1 3/4 cups pumpkin

3/4 cup raisins
1 1/2 teaspoons cinnamon
1/2 teaspoon ginger
1/4 teaspoon cloves
1/8 teaspoon nutmeg
1 can (14 1/2 ounces) evaporated
   milk
1/2 cup chopped pecans

Stir together the sugar and margarine. Add the milk, bread (which you have toasted, it's better that way), and vanilla. Beat in the eggs. Stir in pumpkin, raisins, and spices. Gradually stir in the evaporated milk (and if you have less than a full can, just use what you have) until well blended. Pour into a greased 12 x 8 baking dish, and sprinkle the pecans over the top. Place the dish in a pan of hot water, and bake at 350° for 50 minutes (if you use less evaporated milk, the baking time will be shorter). Increase temperature to 425° and bake 10 minutes longer, or until the pudding is a rich, golden color. Cut into squares and serve warm or cold with whipped cream or vanilla ice cream. Serves 12.

———————————◆———————————

For those who wonder where the pumpkin cake and cookie recipes are, I find that the cake recipes are almost identical to those I have called breads (just add glaze and call them cakes); as to cookies with pumpkin, I really have tried, but I have not yet found a recipe that I like. Try the Applesauce Spice Squares (under Apples).

Other recipes using pumpkin: Pumpkin can be substituted for sweet potatoes in Sweet Potato Rice Pudding (Rice) and in Sweet Potato Pie, Golden Cookies (Sweet Potatoes).

Raisins

Adding raisins improves almost any cake or cookies, many salads and puddings. In the following, raisins are essential.

RAISIN APPLE BETTY

The raisin variation on a popular theme.

3 cups bread crumbs	1/2 cup brown sugar *or* honey
2 cups seedless raisins	1/4 teaspoon cinnamon
2 large tart apples, sliced thin	1/4 cup water
3 tablespoons butter	

Place 1 cup bread crumbs (use whole wheat or cracked wheat if you can—they should be somewhat dry) in a baking pan, add half of the apples, raisins, and sugar or honey; dot with 1 tablespoon butter. Repeat these layers. Cover with the remaining crumbs and dot with remaining butter. Sprinkle with cinnamon. Add the water (if you have used honey, use only 2 tablespoons water). Cover the dish and bake about 1 hour at 350°. Serve warm with cream or vanilla ice cream.

Variation: Substitute 2 cups stewed apricots, drained, for the apples. Use apricot juice in place of the water.

SOUR CREAM RAISIN PIE

1 unbaked 8-inch pie shell	1/4 teaspoon salt
2 large eggs	1/4 teaspoon nutmeg
1 cup dairy sour cream	1 cup raisins
3/4 cup sugar	more sour cream for topping
1 teaspoon vanilla	(optional)

Beat the eggs, sour cream, sugar, vanilla, salt, and nutmeg together until well blended. Stir in the raisins. Pour into the pie shell. Bake on a lower oven shelf at 375° for 40 minutes, just until set. Cool. Top with more sour cream, if desired.

BOILED RAISIN CAKE

This recipe comes from my British mother, whose family calls it "wet" cake. It is indeed moist and substantial and delicious. It is also easy to make.

1 pound raisins	3 cups flour
1/2 pound butter/margarine	2 teaspoons baking powder
1 1/2 cups sugar	large pinch pumpkin pie spice
3 eggs	

Simmer the raisins (or mixed dried fruit) in water for about 5 minutes and drain thoroughly. While still very hot, chop in the butter. Add the sugar and mix well. Add the eggs and beat thoroughly. Blend in the flour, baking powder, and spice. Pour into a 9-inch square tin, lined with waxed paper, and bake at 325° for about 2 hours.

RAISIN PEANUT BUTTER TEA CAKE

3 cups flour	1 1/4 cups sugar
2 1/2 teaspoons baking powder	4 eggs
1/4 teaspoon salt	1/2 cup milk
1/2 cup butter/margarine	1 1/2 cups raisins
1/2 cup peanut butter	

Sift the flour, baking powder, and salt together. Beat the butter/margarine, peanut butter, sugar, and eggs in a large bowl at high speed until light and fluffy. Add milk alternately with the flour mixture. Beat until smooth, but do not overbeat. Fold in the raisins. Spoon into a well-greased tube pan.

Bake at 325° for 1 hour and 20 minutes, or until the cake tests done. Cool the pan on a wire rack for 5 minutes, then remove the cake from the pan and cool completely.

DARK ORANGE RAISIN BREAD

This makes a moist rye loaf, flavored with that wonderful combination of raisins and orange.

2 cups rye flour	1/4 cup shortening
2 teaspoons salt	2 cups warm water
2 tablespoons grated orange peel	1 cup raisins
2 tablespoons dry yeast	4 to 4 1/2 cups flour
1/2 cup molasses	

In a large bowl, combine the rye flour, salt, orange peel, and dry yeast. Add the molasses, shortening, and warm water. Blend until moistened, then beat 3 minutes at medium speed. By hand, stir in the raisins and enough flour to make a stiff dough. Knead about 5 minutes, using the flour. Let rise until doubled, about 1 hour.

Punch down, divide dough in half, and shape into 2 loaves. Place them in 9 x 5 loaf pans. Cover, let rise until doubled, about 45 minutes. Bake at 350° for 45 to 50 minutes.

☆☆☆ FESTIVE RAISIN SQUARES

These are superb layered, bar cookies. If you can get them, use seeded raisins; the flavor is richer.

• Layer I •	• Layer II •
1/2 cup butter/margarine	2 eggs
1/4 cup brown sugar	1 cup brown sugar
1/4 teaspoon salt	1 teaspoon vanilla
1 cup flour	pinch salt
	2 tablespoons flour
	1/2 teaspoon baking powder
	1 cup chopped raisins
	3/4 cup chopped pecans
	3/4 cup flaked coconut

Cream together the butter and brown sugar. Blend in the flour and salt. Press into an 8-inch square pan and bake at 325° for 15 minutes.

In the meantime, beat the eggs well; beat in the brown sugar and vanilla. Add the remaining ingredients in the order given. Spoon onto the baked crust and bake 35 minutes longer, or until firm. Cool and cut in squares.

ENERGY FRUIT BARS

Here is one of your healthful kitchen-sink mixtures. You can really add whatever you like, especially in the way of nuts and seeds. I usually make these with only one cup of nuts; the second cup is a mixture of coconut, sesame seeds, and sunflower seeds.

1 cup raisins	1/4 cup bran
1/4 cup chopped dates *or* apricots	2 cups chopped nuts or combination
1/2 cup honey	2 tablespoons oil
1/2 cup instant dry milk	1 teaspoon vanilla
1/2 cup wheat germ	3 tablespoons fruit juice
1/3 cup wheat flour	

Combine everything. The batter will be thick and rather sticky. Spread it in a greased 8-inch square pan and bake at 300° for 30 to 40 minutes until firm. Cool, cut into squares.

RUM RAISIN SAUCE

This sauce will keep a long time, covered, in the refrigerator. Reheat to serve on ice cream, plain cake, or puddings.

1/4 cup honey	1/2 cup sugar
3 tablespoons butter	1 tablespoon cornstarch
grated rind of 1 lemon	dash salt
1 cup golden raisins	2 tablespoons dark rum
2 tablespoons lemon juice	

Combine the first 5 ingredients and 1 cup water in a saucepan. Add the sugar mixed with the cornstarch and salt. Bring to a boil, stirring, and simmer 4 to 5 minutes. Cool slightly and add the rum. Serve warm. Makes 2 cups.

Other recipes using raisins: Many quick breads and cookies; bread and rice puddings; conserves; curry dishes; granola recipes; Buttermilk Raisin Pie; California Carrots, Health Salad, Old Fashioned Carrot Cake (Carrots); Snowballs (Dates); Meatless Pear Mincemeat, Pear Chutney; Pork and Raisins; Wheatena Cupcakes (Ricotta).

Rhubarb

To stew rhubarb, take tender stalks, cut away blemishes and tough strings; cut it in pieces about one inch long. Put it in a saucepan, if you are around to stir it from time to time, and cook over low heat. Otherwise, use a double boiler over boiling water. If the rhubarb is young, it will be done in about 15 minutes. Do *not* add liquid, there is quite enough in the rhubarb. Add sugar to taste, and it will take quite an amount, as rhubarb is very acid. Personally I like it sour; the best way to get the right sweetness for your own wishes is to add and keep tasting. For people who use sugar substitutes, rhubarb can be sweetened with them, without changing the taste. Brown sugar is excellent to sweeten rhubarb; the result is delicious. Honey is also delicious, but the rhubarb will be more liquid. You can also bake it at 325° in a covered casserole.

Stewed rhubarb can be served in any number of ways. Try it with yogurt, or mashed cottage cheese, or ricotta. It is good with a simple boiled or baked custard, or over sponge cake. I also eat it mixed with applesauce, or cut-up raw apple, or pineapple chunks, or—best of all—with cut-up fresh (or frozen) strawberries.

☆☆☆ RHUBARB CAKE

I make this cake many times during the rhubarb season.

1/2 cup butter/margarine	1 cup sour milk *or* buttermilk
1 1/4 cup white sugar	2 cups flour
1/2 teaspoon salt	2 tablespoons wheat germ
1 egg	3 cups finely cut rhubarb
1 teaspoon baking soda	

Cream the shortening and sugar together until fluffy. Then add the salt and egg, and beat well. Stir the soda into the milk and add to the creamed mixture, alternately, with the flour and wheat germ. End with the dry ingredients. Then stir in the rhubarb.

Pour into a greased 13 x 9 pan. Mix Cinnamon Topping (see the Appendix) and sprinkle over the top of the batter.

Bake at 350° for 45 minutes. Cool thoroughly and cut in squares. Because it is very moist, this cake is better if you take it out of the pan as soon as it is cool enough. It freezes well.

☆☆☆ RHUBARB BREAD PUDDING

I save up dried bread cubes all winter, just waiting for the spring and the rhubarb so I can make this pudding. The better the bread, the better the pudding.

2 cups rhubarb, diced	1 1/2 tablespoons lemon juice
1/2 cup sugar	1 cup milk
2 cups dried bread cubes	1 egg
1 tablespoon grated lemon rind	

In a large bowl combine the rhubarb, sugar, bread, lemon rind and juice. Beat the egg well, combine it with the milk, and pour this over the rhubarb mixture. Stir well. Put the pudding in a 1-quart baking dish, set the dish in a pan of hot water. Bake uncovered at 375° for about 1 hour.

RHUBARB STRAWBERRY PIE

In my view a perfect pie.

1 cup sugar	3 cups rhubarb, in 1/2-inch slices
1/4 cup flour	1 cup sliced strawberries
1/4 teaspoon salt	crust for a 9-inch pie
1/4 teaspoon nutmeg	

Combine all the ingredients in a bowl and mix well. Let them stand about 20 minutes.

Make your favorite pie crust and line a 9-inch pie plate. Spoon the fruit into the shell, and dot with butter. Cover with a top crust, or make a lattice covering. Bake at 400° about 45 minutes or until bubbly. Serve slightly warm.

☆☆☆ **RHUBABA**

You should serve this warm, but not hot.

• Bottom •	• Top •
3 tablespoons butter	3 eggs, separated
1/2 cup brown sugar	1 teaspoon lemon juice
2 cups diced rhubarb	1 cup sugar
1/4 cup dry sherry	1/4 cup hot water
	1 cup flour
	1 1/2 teaspoon baking powder
	1/4 teaspoon salt

Melt the butter in a large round (at least 10-inch round) flat baking dish, stir in the brown sugar. Top evenly with the rhubarb and drizzle the sherry over the top.

Beat the egg whites stiff, and set aside. In a large bowl beat the egg yolks and lemon juice until thick, then gradually add the sugar and beat until light. Slowly stir in the hot water. Sift the dry ingredients together and add them to the egg yolk mixture, stirring gently until well combined. Fold in the egg whites; spoon evenly over the rhubarb.

Bake at 325° for 1 hour, or until the cake tests done. Remove from the oven, let stand 5 minutes. Loosen the sides and invert onto a serving plate. Cut in wedges and serve with whipped cream.

RHUBARB CRISP

• Bottom •	• Top •
4 cups rhubarb (1-inch pieces)	1/2 cup brown sugar
1/2 cup white sugar	1/2 cup rolled oats
1 tablespoon grated orange peel	1/2 cup flour
dash salt	4 tablespoons butter/margarine

Combine the ingredients that go on the bottom and place in a greased 8 x 8 baking dish.

Then combine the top ingredients, cutting in the butter until crumbly or wading in with the fingers until crumbly. Sprinkle the mixture over the rhubarb.

Bake at 350° about 40 minutes, or until rhubarb is tender and the top is browned.

Serve warm with whipped cream or ice cream.

RHUBARB RING WITH STRAWBERRIES

In contrast to the preceding, here is a light dessert, one that is especially pretty for a spring ladies' luncheon. It can be made well ahead of time.

1 1/2 pounds rhubarb	2 envelopes unflavored gelatin
1 cup sugar	1/4 cup orange juice
1 1/4 cups water	1 tablespoon lemon juice
2 cups strawberries	10X sugar

Wash the rhubarb, cut off root and leaf ends, but do not peel. Cut in 1-inch pieces and combine in a saucepan with the sugar and 3/4 cup water. Bring to a boil, reduce the heat, and simmer for 5 to 10 minutes, until rhubarb is tender, stirring gently once or twice. Sprinkle the gelatin over the remaining 1/2 cup water, then stir into the hot rhubarb. Keep stirring until the gelatin is dissolved. Add the orange and lemon juice, stir well, and pour into a 5-cup, 8-inch mold. Let cool to room temperature, then chill several hours until firm. Unmold onto a chilled plate. Arrange the berries (which you have washed and hulled) in the center of the ring and sprinkle with 10X sugar.

◆

RHUBARB PINEAPPLE JAM

This jam is easily made and is unusual in flavor. If you object to commercial jello, make your own by mixing together two packages unflavored gelatin, 1/2 cup sugar, a dash of salt, and 4 tablespoons lemon (or whatever flavor you want) juice. Add as you would the jello and stir well. The lemon juice aids with the jelling process, but so does concentrated apple syrup, if you happen to have any (see under Black Raspberry Jelly for indications on how to make it).

8 cups rhubarb, cut fine	1 20-ounce can crushed pineapple
6 cups sugar	1 large package strawberry or raspberry jello

Cook the rhubarb and sugar together (use a very large kettle), and stir until the mixture starts to boil. Cook 12 minutes at a rolling boil.

Drain the pineapple, add it to the rhubarb, turn off the heat, and simmer 3 minutes. Finally add the jello. Stir until it is dissolved. Ladle into sterilized jars and seal immediately with paraffin.

RHUBARB CONSERVE

Another way to use a large quantity of rhubarb. And what a delicious way too!

10 cups rhubarb, in 1-inch pieces	**2 oranges**
8 cups sugar	**1 lemon**
1 pound seeded raisins	**chopped walnut meats**

Wash and cut up the rhubarb. Squeeze the juice from the oranges and lemon, add to the rhubarb. Put the orange and lemon skins through the fine blade of a food chopper, and add them too. Put all this mixture, along with the sugar in a large kettle (stainless steel or enamelware). Mix, cover, and let stand 1/2 hour. Then bring to a boil, stirring several times, reduce the heat, and let *simmer* 45 minutes, stirring often. Add the chopped walnut meats (about 1 cup), if you like them. Fill sterilized jelly glasses with the conserve, seal with paraffin. Makes about 8 pints.

RHUBARB TEA

Lovely and refreshing, and a change from the usual iced tea.

Cook 1/2 pound rhubarb, chopped, in 1 cup water about 10 minutes. Drain and cool. Then combine 1/2 cup black China tea, chilled, 1/4 cup rhubarb liquor, and 1/4 cup sugar syrup (2 cups water plus 3/4 cup sugar, cooked 5 minutes). Serve over ice, garnished with a lemon wedge.

Rice

If you like brown rice, do use it (it is excellent in these dishes; only the Rice Pudding is better with white rice). A recipe in which you can use up your rice (Basic Pilaf) can be found at the beginning of the Grains section.

CURRIED TUNA SQUARES

1 cup chunk-style tuna	1/4 teaspoon pepper
2 cups cooked rice	2 eggs, beaten
1 tablespoon chopped onion	3/4 cup milk
1 tablespoon lemon juice	1 cup corn flake crumbs, divided
1 teaspoon curry powder	1 tablespoon margarine
1/2 teaspoon salt	

Drain and flake the tuna. Combine with rice, onion, lemon juice, seasonings, eggs, milk, and 3/4 cup crumbs. Mix well.

Spread in a greased 10 x 6 baking dish. Mix remaining crumbs with melted margarine; sprinkle over the top.

Bake at 350° about 20 minutes. Cut into squares and serve with lemon wedges. Serves 6.

BACON CHIVE RICE

My children love this dish. It is quick and very economical.

4 slices bacon	1/4 teaspoon salt
2 cups cooked rice	dash pepper
1/4 cup chopped chives *or* chopped onion	1 tablespoon worchestershire sauce

Fry the bacon until crisp. Drain on a paper towel, and pour off most of the fat. Add the rice, chives (*or* onion, which you have fried with the bacon), and seasonings. Crumble the bacon and mix well. Heat thoroughly before serving. Serves 4.

RICE SALAD

Similar to Tabouli (see under Parsley). Middle-Eastern in concept, and a fine salad for a summer buffet.

1 1/2 cups rice	4 tablespoons olive oil
1 cup chopped artichoke hearts	1 firm large tomato, diced
2 hard-boiled eggs, sliced	juice of one lemon
1 tablespoon capers, drained	

Cook rice until just tender. Rinse in cold water. Mix all the remaining ingredients into the rice. Let stand 1 hour before serving. Serve at room temperature. Serves 8.

☆☆☆ CURRIED RICE SALAD

I have made this salad to take to large picnics, and it always arouses curiosity and brings compliments. The recipe makes a huge quantity.

• Salad •	• Dressing •
1 cup whole wheat berries, cooked	1/4 cup oil
1 1/2 cups raw brown rice, cooked	1 tablespoon curry powder
1 cup dry soybeans, cooked	1/3 cup cider vinegar
1 1/2 teaspoons salt, divided	2 tablespoons lemon juice
1 1/3 cups shredded cheddar, divided	2 tablespoons honey
2 onions, chopped	1 cup raisins
4 stalks celery with tops, chopped	

Do not substitute anything for the wheat berries (not only are they delicious, they will arouse the most curiosity). Cook the first three ingredients separately from each other, and be sure to allow enough time.

When the wheat berries are done, stir in 1/2 teaspoon salt and 2/3 cup of the cheese. Stir until the cheese melts, then chill until very cold. Do the same with the rice, using the remaining cheese and salt. Drain and chill the soybeans. You can do all of this the day before, if you like.

Chop the vegetables and set aside.

Prepare the dressing by heating the oil and stirring in the curry powder; sizzle it for about 1 minute. Then add the remaining ingredients and simmer until the raisins puff, about 6 minutes.

Toss the grains gently to separate the kernels. In a very large bowl combine the grains, soybeans, and chopped vegetables. Pour the dressing over and toss again. Chill thoroughly. Serve on a bed of fresh greens. Serves an army.

RICE PIZZA

Here is a variation on a familiar theme that is appreciated by many, but especially by those who are allergic to wheat flour.

•Crust•	•Topping•
3 cups cooked rice	2 cups tomato sauce
2 eggs, beaten	1/2 teaspoon each oregano, basil,
1 cup shredded mozzarella	garlic powder, salt
	1 cup grated mozzarella
	2 tablespoons grated parmesan

To make the crust, combine the rice, eggs, and cheese. Press firmly into a 12-inch greased pizza pan (or use two 9-inch pie pans), spreading evenly with a spatula. Bake at 450° for 20 minutes.

Combine the tomato sauce and seasonings. Spread evenly over the baked crust. Sprinkle the cheeses over the top. Bake 10 minutes longer. Cut in wedges. Serves 6.

RICE BREAD

This is very unusual, as breads go, and easy to make. It should be eaten very fresh; it is wonderful sliced and toasted.

1 envelope dry yeast	3 teaspoons sugar
1/2 teaspoon salt	1 cup cooked rice
1/2 cup lukewarm water	4 1/2 cups flour
1 1/2 cups warm milk	

Put in the blender container the yeast, water, and salt. Let stand for 5 minutes, then cover and blend on high speed for 20 seconds. Add the milk, sugar, and rice; cover and blend for 10 seconds. Put the flour in a large mixing bowl; pour the rice mixture over the top. Stir with a spoon until well mixed. Gather up the dough with floured hands, and toss on a floured board. Shape into a loaf and put in a 9 x 5 pan, well greased. Let rise until double in bulk. Bake at 375° for 50 minutes, or until browned.

☆☆☆ RICE PUDDING

The classic recipe. Do use white rice for this one.

2 cups cooked rice	1/3 cup brown sugar
1/2 cup water	1/3 cup raisins
2 cups milk	1/2 teaspoon vanilla
2 eggs	

Put the rice in a saucepan with the water, cover, and cook gently until the water is absorbed. Then stir in the milk (and if you have one, a 1-inch vanilla bean), and cook, stirring from time to time, for about one-half hour, or until the rice becomes thick and creamy. Beat the eggs with the brown sugar in a 1 1/2-quart casserole, add a dash of salt, and pour the hot rice over, beating vigorously. Stir in the raisins which are plumped (pour boiling water over them, let stand a few minutes, then drain). Add the vanilla.

Put the casserole in a pan of hot water, bake at 325° about 1 hour or until set. Serve with raspberry sauce, or with cream.

Variation: Try this, if you have some orange yogurt to use up. A pretty and delicious change. Reduce the milk to 1 1/2 cups and the sugar to 1/4 cup. Stir in 1/2 cup yogurt (orange, lemon, raspberry, strawberry, peach) with the raisins.

HONEY DATE RICE PUDDING

The second favorite rice pudding. This is more like a custard and, with the brown rice, has also a chewy quality.

2 cups cooked brown rice	2 eggs
1 cup finely cut dates	3 tablespoons honey
2 cups milk	1 teaspoon grated lemon rind

Put the rice in the bottom of a 1 1/2-quart baking dish; sprinkle the dates over, place in a pan of hot water in a 325° oven. Scald the milk. Beat the eggs and honey together; add the milk and mix well. Stir in lemon rind and pour the mixture over the warm rice and dates. Stir a little. Return to the oven and bake for 1 hour.

SWEET POTATO RICE PUDDING

A queen of rice puddings, a lovely color, and a collection of good things and tastes.

3 cups cooked brown rice	2/3 cup dry milk powder
1 cup mashed sweet potatoes	1 teaspoon cinnamon
1 1/2 cups water	1/4 teaspoon salt
2 cups orange juice	2 eggs, beaten
1/3 cup honey	2 apples, chopped
2 teaspoons vanilla	dash salt

Combine the rice, sweet potatoes, water, and orange juice. Stir in the honey and vanilla. Add milk powder, cinnamon, and salt. Blend well, making sure the milk is dissolved. Add the eggs and stir in the apples and salt. Pour into a lightly greased oblong baking dish. Sprinkle sesame seeds or wheat germ on top and bake at 350° for 45 minutes to 1 hour, until firm.

Variation: Substitute 1 cup mashed pumpkin for the sweet potatoes.

Other recipes using rice: Crusted Cauliflower; Fruited Chicken Salad; Eggplant Bake; grain dishes; Peanut Brown Rice (Nuts); Hearty Onion Bread; Venetian Rice (Peas); Pork-Peas-Rice (Pork); Herbed Spinach Bake; Rice Casserole Italiano, Zucchini Deluxe, Soybean and Rice Boats (Zucchini).

Ricotta

Try adding ricotta to your yeast bread recipe in place of some of the milk. If the recipe calls for 2 cups of milk, substitute 1/2 cup ricotta for 1/2 cup milk. It makes a moister, somewhat heavier bread, but the flavor is wonderful. The same substitution can be made in baked custards, bread puddings, or rice pudding.

In recipes that call for cottage cheese, you can substitute ricotta for all or part of that ingredient.

Empty ricotta containers make excellent storage for leftover foods. I often have frozen tomato sauce in them. I even have one that is a lovely pale blue.

RICOTTA ZUCCHINI STUFFING

The following amount is more than enough for a 10-pound turkey.

2 small onions	salt and pepper
6 tablespoons butter/margarine	1 tablespoon marjoram
2 pounds zucchini	2 eggs
6 ounces ricotta	parmesan cheese (about 1/4 cup)
1 1/2 cups toasted bread crumbs	stock

Chop the onions in fine pieces. Melt the butter/margarine in a large pan, stew the onions about 10 minutes, remove from the pan, and put aside. In the same pan, sauté the zucchini, which you have coarsely grated, for a few minutes, then add it, butter and all, to the onions.

Mash the ricotta, stir in the bread crumbs, salt, pepper, and marjoram. Beat the eggs, add them to the mixture, and stir well. Then mix in the onion and zucchini. Add the parmesan. If the stuffing seems too dry, mix in a little stock. Fill the cavities with the stuffing; if there is any left over, bake it in a separate dish, with some butter and stock poured over the top.

MEXICAN CASSEROLE

This dish has a rather muddy appearance, but it is most unusual in taste and extraordinarily delicious.

3/4 cup brown rice	2 tablespoons coriander
3/4 cup black beans	salt and pepper
3/4 cup stock or water	1 clove garlic, minced
2 tablespoons oil	1/2 pound jack cheese, grated
1 cup onion, chopped	1 15-ounce container ricotta
1 minced hot pepper	

Cook the brown rice, black beans, and stock in a large covered pot for 2 hours. Keep adding liquid as the mixture cooks.

In a frying pan, heat a small amount of oil. Sauté together the onion, pepper, coriander, salt, pepper, and garlic (the original recipe calls for 5 cloves of garlic, so add more if you want to).

In a large casserole, make layers of beans, 1/2 of the vegetables, cheese; repeat, ending with beans. Put a sliced tomato on the top, if you want to (or if you have some leftover tomato sauce, pour that over), and bake at 350°, uncovered, about 30 minutes, or until bubbly. Serves 4 to 6.

SPINACH RICOTTA TART

This dish has a lovely color and the custard is creamy and tasty. You can substitute about 2 1/2 cups grated zucchini for the spinach, and 1/2 teaspoon tarragon for the nutmeg.

crust for a 1-crust pie
2 1/2 pounds fresh spinach
or 2 packages (10 ounces each)
frozen chopped spinach
1 small onion, minced (1/4 cup)
3 tablespoons butter/margarine
1/2 teaspoon salt

1/4 teaspoon nutmeg
dash black pepper
1 15-ounce container ricotta
1 cup light cream or half-and-half
1/2 cup grated parmesan
3 eggs, beaten

Prepare the crust and line a 9-inch pie plate; flute edge, making a high rim to hold all the filling. Prick bottom and sides with a fork. Bake at 400° for about 10 minutes.

Trim and cook the spinach. Drain in a large strainer, squeeze out the excess liquid by pressing the spinach against the sides of the strainer. Chop in fine pieces, strain again. Set aside.

Sauté the onion in the butter until transparent. Stir in the spinach, salt, nutmeg, and pepper.

In a large bowl combine the ricotta, cream, parmesan, and eggs; mix thoroughly. Then stir in the spinach mixture.

Pour into baked pastry shell. Bake at 350° about 50 minutes, until the custard is set and top is lightly browned. Garnish with parsley and cherry tomatoes. Serve hot or warm. Serves 6.

Variations:

Herb-Nut: Omit the nutmeg; add 2 teaspoons caraway seed and 1/4 cup chopped nuts; substitute shredded cheddar for the parmesan.

Cheese: Add 1 cup shredded Swiss cheese and 2 teaspoons worcestershire sauce; omit the nutmeg.

BAKED MACARONI WITH RICOTTA

This casserole is a variation of the lasagna dish. It is very economical and easily made.

2 cups raw macaroni, cooked
    and drained
1/2 pound ground beef
1 clove garlic, minced
4 cups tomato sauce
2 tablespoons chopped parsley
1 teaspoon basil

1 teaspoon salt
1/2 teaspoon oregano
1 15-ounce container ricotta
    or 1 pound cottage cheese
1/2 cup shredded mozzarella
grated parmesan

Cook the macaroni, according to package directions. The last time I made this casserole, I used sesame-whole wheat spirals along with some spinach noodles. Attractive and very good.

In a skillet, brown the beef, and drain off any excess fat. Add the garlic and sauté a few minutes, or until tender. Stir in the tomato sauce, parsley, basil, salt, oregano, and simmer uncovered for 15 minutes.

You can combine the sauce, macaroni, and ricotta in one large pan and dump it into a 2-quart baking dish. Or you can put it in layers, starting and ending with the macaroni. Sprinkle the mozzarella evenly over the top, and add some parmesan over the top of that. Cover and bake at 350° for about 20 minutes. Then uncover and bake 10 to 15 minutes more, or until brown and bubbly. Serves 6.

RICOTTA DRESSING

Here is a lovely pale pink dressing, low in calories, and perfect with tuna, shrimp, crab, or lobster. Many similar dressings are based on mayonnaise (at many calories per tablespoon). This is a delicious alternative, and if you use part skim milk ricotta, a real dieters' dressing.

1 cup ricotta
1 hard-cooked egg, shelled
1/4 cup tomato juice

1 teaspoon prepared mustard
2 tablespoons finely chopped onion
2 tablespoons finely chopped parsley

Combine the ricotta, egg, tomato juice, and mustard in a blender, whirl until very smooth. Stir in the onion and parsley. Makes 1 1/3 cups.

◆

WHEATENA CUPCAKES

1/2 cup butter/margarine
1 cup brown sugar
1/2 teaspoon salt
2 eggs
1 teaspoon lemon flavoring
1 cup ricotta

2 cups flour
1 teaspoon baking soda
1/4 cup Wheatena, uncooked
1/2 cup milk
3/4 cup finely chopped raisins

Cream the shortening, sugar, and salt together. Add the eggs and continue to beat until light. Blend in lemon flavoring and ricotta.

Sift the flour (and do use some whole wheat pastry flour, if you want) and soda; combine with the Wheatena. Add to batter alternately with the milk. Stir in the raisins.

Fill muffin pans (which you can line with paper linings) about 2/3 full. Bake at 375° for 25 or 30 minutes, or until they test done. Cool. Makes 24.

If you like, frost with Light Butter Frosting (see the Appendix) or Ricotta Frosting.

RICOTTA FROSTING

Here is a creamy rich frosting you can make with ricotta, or if you prefer, with farmer cheese.

4 tablespoons ricotta
4 tablespoons softened butter

1 teaspoon vanilla
1 1/2 cups 10X sugar

Beat the ricotta and butter in a small bowl until creamy smooth. Stir in the vanilla, and the 10X sugar, then beat until fluffy. Makes about 1 cup.

RICOTTA BONBONS

A lovely confection. Keep it refrigerated.

1 cup ricotta
pinch salt
2 tablespoons honey

1/4 cup nuts, chopped fine
1/2 cup shredded coconut

Mix everything together. Shape into balls. Chill before eating. Makes 2 dozen.

Other recipes using ricotta: Spicy Sweet Potatoes calls for ricotta.

Sour Cream

Yes, we all buy cream from time to time, and yes, it does go sour. We can't throw it out, it would be like pouring gold down the sink. So let's use it. Cultured soured cream (dairy sour cream) is also available in the supermarkets and many recipes call for it (it is made, by the way, by adding lactic acid bacteria culture to light cream). My experience is that you can use dairy sour cream in all all recipes calling for sour cream, but not the reverse. So be sure that you have the right ingredient for the recipes that follow. Sweet cream can be soured by adding 1 teaspoon lemon juice or white vinegar to 1 cup cream.

SOUR CREAM COFFEE CAKE

This is a classic coffee cake recipe. It is rich, tender, and entirely worthy of its popularity.

1 stick butter	2 cups flour
1 cup sugar	1/4 teaspoon salt
3 eggs	1 1/2 teaspoons baking powder
1 cup sour cream	1 teaspoon vanilla
1 teaspoon baking soda	

Cream the butter and sugar. Add the eggs, one at a time, beating well after each addition. Mix the soda with the sour cream and add alternately with the sifted dry ingredients. Stir in the vanilla.

Pour one-half of the mixture into a greased 9-inch tube pan. Double the recipe for Cinnamon Topping (see the Appendix), using 1 cup nuts; sprinkle one-half over the batter. Pour in the rest of the mixture, run a knife through the batter to marbelize, then sprinkle with the remaining topping.

Bake at 350° 45 to 50 minutes. Serve warm.

SOUR CREAM CHOCOLATE DROPS

My mother remembers these from her childhood. They are a soft cookie, wonderful with vanilla or peppermint ice cream, lemon or orange sherbet.

3 cups flour	1/2 cup butter/margarine
1/2 teaspoon baking soda	1 cup sugar
1/2 teaspoon baking powder	2 eggs
1/2 teaspoon salt	1 cup sour cream
2 squares unsweetened chocolate	1 teaspoon vanilla

Sift together the flour, soda, baking powder, and salt. Set aside.

Melt the chocolate over very low heat, or over hot water.

Cream the shortening with the sugar and eggs until light and fluffy, about 3 minutes. Then beat in the sour cream, vanilla, flour mixture, and chocolate. Chill the dough for an hour.

Drop by heaping teaspoonsful, 2 inches apart, onto cookie sheets. Bake at 375° about 10 minutes. Cool on a wire rack. Makes about 6 dozen.

OLD-FASHIONED SOUR CREAM COOKIES

A non-chocolate version of the above. Proceed by the same rule, omit the chocolate, increase the baking powder to 1 teaspoon, and add 2 teaspoons grated lemon peel, if desired. Sprinkle with a topping made from 1/2 cup sugar and 1 teaspoon cinnamon.

☆☆☆ SPICE CAKE

This old family recipe has been a favorite for years and years. It should be; it is one of the best cakes I have ever eaten. It is very easily made.

1/2 cup butter/margarine	2/3 teaspoon baking soda
1 cup sour cream	2 teaspoons cinnamon
1 egg	1 teaspoon nutmeg
1 cup sugar	1/2 teaspoon cloves
1 1/2 cups flour	1/4 teaspoon ginger
1 teaspoon baking powder	

Cream shortening and sugar; blend in the sour cream and egg. Sift the dry ingredients and add them gently.

Pour into a well-greased 8-inch square pan. Bake at 350° for 30 minutes. Frost with Fluffy Frosting (see the Appendix).

Dairy Sour Cream

MAPLE PECAN CAKE

Do make this cake with real maple syrup. The flavor is unusual and a change from the usual tea cakes.

3/4 cup maple syrup	1 1/2 teaspoon baking powder
1/2 cup sugar	1 teaspoon ginger
1/4 cup butter/margarine	1/2 teaspoon baking soda
1 egg	1/2 teaspoon salt
1 cup dairy sour cream	1/2 cup chopped pecans
2 cups flour	

Beat together the syrup, butter, and sugar. Blend in the egg. Sift the dry ingredients and add alternately with the sour cream. Stir in the pecans. Bake in a greased and floured pan, 11 x 8 or in three small bread pans. Bake at 375° for 35 to 40 minutes for large pan, 30 minutes for the bread pans. Cool thoroughly. Frost with Cream Cheese Frosting (under Cream Cheese), using maple syrup in the recipe.

SOUR CREAM CAKE

This recipe uses both a cake mix and instant pudding mix. Please do not be put off. It makes one of the fastest and best cakes. Do try it. I make it frequently in 5 small bread pans (7 1/2 x 3 1/2), baking the small cakes 40 minutes, to give as gifts.

1 yellow cake mix	5 eggs
1 package French vanilla instant pudding	1/3 cup brown sugar
	1/2 cup chopped walnuts
1 cup dairy sour cream	1 teaspoon cinnamon
1/4 cup salad oil	

Beat the first five ingredients together until smooth. Put a layer of batter in the bottom of a 9-inch tube pan. Mix together the remaining ingredients, fold them into the remaining batter, and pour this into the pan. Run a knife through the batter to marbelize. Bake at 350° for 50 minutes, or until golden brown. Let cool on a rack for 15 minutes, then loosen and remove from pan.

APPLE OATMEAL MUFFINS

1 cup flour
1/3 cup sugar
2 teaspoons baking powder
1/2 teaspoon salt
1/2 teaspoon baking soda
1 cup rolled oats

1 egg, well beaten
1/2 cup dairy sour cream
1/2 cup milk
3 tablespoons melted butter/
    margarine
1/2 cup finely chopped tart apple

Sift the dry ingredients and stir in the oats. Combine the liquid ingredients with the apple, and stir into the first mixture, stirring until just moistened. Bake at 425° for 12 to 15 minutes in well-greased muffin tins. Makes 12 medium muffins.

CARAMEL NUT FUDGE

This excellent confection is *very* easy to make, and unlike most chocolate fudge I've encountered, it stays creamy smooth.

1/4 cup butter
1 cup brown sugar
1 cup white sugar
1/4 teaspoon salt

1/2 cup dairy sour cream
1 teaspoon vanilla
3/4 cup coarsely chopped walnuts
    or mixed salted nuts

Melt the butter in a heavy 2-quart saucepan. Add the sugars, salt, and sour cream. Cook over low heat, stirring, until the sugar dissolves. Cover and boil slowly 5 minutes. Uncover, cook rapidly without stirring until the candy tests 236° on a candy thermometer (if you don't have one, that means soft-ball stage, reached when a bit of the candy can be formed into a soft ball when you drop it in some cold water). This happens quickly, usually in 2 to 3 minutes. Remove from the heat and cool to lukewarm. Add the vanilla and beat until the mixture is creamy and begins to hold its shape. Stir in the nuts (if you use salted nuts, omit the salt in the recipe). Drop by teaspoonsful onto waxed paper. Makes about 1 3/4 pounds.

Other recipes using:

Sour Cream: Avocado and Tomato Soup (Avocado); Banana Cake Jamaica; Green Beans with Dill; Grape Kuchen; Ham Squares.

Dairy Sour Cream: Green Bean and Mushroom Salad (Beans); Danish Beet Soup; Chicken Stroganoff; Orange-Coconut Coffee Cake (Coconut); Beef Casserole (Cottage Cheese); Cream Cheese Pie; Cold Cucumber Soup; Ham Corn-Bread Ring, Schinken Makkaroni (Ham); Chicken Livers Marsala; Mushrooms and Cream; Hungarian Noodles and Peas (Peas); Sour Cream Raisin Pie (Raisins); Mushroom-Stuffed Tomatoes (Tomatoes); Tuna-Noodle Casserole (variation); Veal Paprika; Hamburger and Noodles Stroganoff (Wine).

Sour Milk

Milk that is a little funny or even quite sour can be cooked in a number of good dishes that call for sweet milk. Add 1 teaspoon baking soda to each cup of milk you use, and add it to bread pudding, custards, rice pudding, cream sauces and soups, coffee cakes, breads, rolls, biscuits. I am not totally convinced that you can use sour milk and buttermilk interchangeably; certainly in all recipes calling for sour milk, you can substitute buttermilk. I am not sure about the reverse, and for this reason there is a separate section called Buttermilk.

CORN BREAD

There are a few of us in this world who could retire to a desert island and eat corn bread. Of all the quick breads it is far and away the very best. Try it warm with homemade strawberry jam, for example, or slices of sharp cheddar. I often double this recipe and bake it in a 15 x 10 pan; then I freeze half of it for a future treat.

1 cup flour, part whole wheat	3/4 cup cornmeal
1/2 teaspoon baking soda	1 cup sour milk
2 teaspoons baking powder	2 eggs
2 tablespoons sugar	2 tablespoons melted margarine *or*
1/2 teaspoon salt	bacon fat

Grease a 9-inch square baking pan well and put it in the oven, which you are preheating to 425° while you make the bread.

Sift the dry ingredients and stir in the cornmeal. Combine the liquid ingredients and then stir them into the dry with a few swift strokes. Pour into the hot pan and bake at 425° for about 30 minutes. Serve warm.

OATMEAL PANCAKES

These seem richer than they are. The flavor is wonderful. The batter will be thinner than the usual pancake recipe.

1 1/2 cups rolled oats	1 tablespoon sugar
2 cups sour milk	1 teaspoon baking soda
1/4 cup all-purpose flour	1/2 teaspoon salt
1/4 cup whole wheat flour	2 eggs, beaten

Heat the griddle slowly while you are mixing the batter. Pour the sour milk over the oats in a large bowl and let stand a few minutes. Then beat in the remaining ingredients. Cook on a greased griddle, turning once. Makes 12 4-inch pancakes.

APPLE STREUSEL COFFEE CAKE

This is quickly made and the apple-crunchy topping makes this a good choice for an autumn Sunday breakfast.

2 cups biscuit mix (see the Appendix)	1 teaspoon baking soda
	1 egg, slightly beaten
1 cup brown sugar	1 cup diced apples
1/2 teaspoon cinnamon	1/2 cup raisins
1/4 teaspoon nutmeg	1/2 cup coarsely chopped pecans
1/4 cup butter/margarine	*or* walnuts
2/3 cup sour milk	

Combine the mix, sugar, and spices. Cut in the butter, until crumbly. Set aside 2/3 cup. To the remaining mixture, add the sour milk, into which you have dissolved the soda, and the egg. Mix well.

Spread in a greased 8-inch square pan. Combine the apple (which you can peel or not as you choose), raisins, and nuts. Spread them over the batter. Then top with the reserved crumb mixture.

Bake at 350° about 45 minutes. Serve warm.

QUICK BREAKFAST CAKE

The last time I made this cake the jam, for some unknown reason, distributed itself through the batter, instead of remaining on top as it usually does. The cake looked something like those pictures of the moon's surface, pebbly, filled with cracks. My, was the cake good, though! Serve it warm.

1/4 cup butter/margarine	1/2 teaspoon baking soda
1/4 cup sugar	2/3 cup jam (apricot, cherry, mar-
1 egg	malade) *or* apricot-pineapple
1 1/2 cups flour	filling
2 1/2 teaspoons baking powder	1/4 cup brown sugar
3/4 cup sour milk	1/4 cup chopped walnuts

Cream the butter and sugar, beat in the egg. Add the sifted dry ingredients alternately with the milk, in which the soda is dissolved. Spread in an 8-inch square pan. Dot the top with the jam. Combine the sugar and nuts and sprinkle that on top of the jam.

Bake 30 minutes at 375°.

☆☆☆ SPICY FRUIT DROPS

These cookies are wonderful with apple sauce or any stewed fruit, ideal for the school lunch or afternoon snack.

1 1/4 cups flour	1/2 cup shortening
1 cup wheat germ *or* rolled oats	1 cup brown sugar
1/2 teaspoon baking soda	2 eggs
1/4 teaspoon salt	1/4 cup sour milk
1 teaspoon cinnamon	1 cup cut-up dates
1/4 teaspoon cloves	1 cup raisins
1/4 teaspoon nutmeg	1/2 cup chopped walnuts

Measure the dry ingredients onto a plate or into a bowl. Stir well to blend.

Cream the shortening, sugar, and eggs thoroughly. Add blended dry ingredients alternately with sour milk. Stir in the dates, raisins, and nuts. Drop by teaspoonsful onto a baking sheet.

Bake at 350° for 15 to 18 minutes. Makes 4 dozen.

If desired, glaze while warm with Orange Glaze (see the Appendix).

ECONOMY COCOA CAKE

This is an amazing cake. With very little in the way of ingredients, one produces a full-fledged cake, and a very good one too. The last time I made it, I used 4 tablespoons carob powder instead of the cocoa. It was delicious.

2 tablespoons butter	1/2 teaspoon baking powder
1 cup sugar	1/8 teaspoon salt
3 tablespoons cocoa	1 cup sour milk
1 egg	1 teaspoon baking soda
2 cups flour	

Cream the butter and sugar, blend in the cocoa. Beat in the egg. Sift the flour, baking powder, and salt, and add alternately with the sour milk, in which you have dissolved the soda.

Bake in two 8-inch layers, or in one 11 x 8 pan, well greased, for 25 minutes at 350°. Cool. Frost, if desired, with Fluffy Frosting (see the Appendix) or sprinkle with confectioners' sugar. If you omit the frosting, you can put squares in lunchboxes or picnic baskets.

SPICED TORTE

A lovely rich-flavored cake with its own topping baked right on.

3/4 cup shortening	1 teaspoon salt
2 cups brown sugar, divided	1 1/3 cups sour milk
2 eggs, separated	2 1/2 cups flour
1 teaspoon cinnamon	1 tablespoon baking powder
1 teaspoon cloves	2 teaspoons baking soda

Cream the shortening and 1 1/2 cups sugar. Beat in the egg yolks, and then stir in the remaining ingredients. Pour the batter into a big pan, 15 x 10, or a large tube pan.

Whip the egg whites until stiff. Slowly beat in the remaining 1/2 cup brown sugar. Spread this meringue over the top of the cake. Bake at 325° for at least 1 hour.

Other recipes using sour milk: Orange-Cranberry Cake (Granola); Orange Muffins; Rhubarb Cake.

Spinach

I keep spinach in my refrigerator all year. I love it in salads. All of the following call for fresh leaf spinach, but you can substitute frozen spinach in most of them. I personally do not find it nearly so good, and as we can get tasty, well-washed (thank goodness) leaf spinach almost any time, why not use it?

To cook spinach rinse it, remove the stems, and put it in a pan. Don't add any water, as what remains on the leaves is quite enough. Heat to boiling over low heat (keep the pan tightly covered), and after it has reached the boiling point, stir once, turn off the heat (I have an electric stove), and let it stay on the burner until it isn't cooking any more. Drain, if desired, and chop.

SLIM SPINACH SOUP

10 ounces spinach	nutmeg (optional)
1/2 cup minced onion	salt and pepper
1 teaspoon butter	2 cups skim milk
2 teaspoons flour	1/2 hard-boiled egg, sieved

Cook the spinach until just tender. Purée in the blender. Sauté the onion in the butter. Add the flour and combine with the spinach. Stir until smooth. Add seasonings and milk and heat, stirring, until smooth and slightly thickened. Serve with a garnish of sieved egg. Makes 3 cups, or 4 servings.

Variations:

For a very smooth soup, sauté the onion in the butter and purée it along with the spinach.

Substitute 1 1/2 cups chopped asparagus for the spinach.

SPINACH FRITTERS

Even the children will eat these. They are delightful and easy to make.

2 cups cooked spinach, drained	1/4 teaspoon salt
2 eggs, well beaten	3 tablespoons finely minced onions
1/2 cup fine cracker crumbs	oil

Chop the spinach fine and add the eggs. Stir in the crumbs, salt, and onion, and mix well. Heat the oil in a skillet; drop the spinach mixture by rounded spoonfuls into the hot oil, and fry gently, turning once.

CREAMED SPINACH

Of course you can chop the spinach and stir in a cream sauce and top it all with cheese. But you can also try the following.

2 tablespoons oil	1 egg, beaten
3 tablespoons flour	4 cups chopped fresh spinach
1 cup hot milk	3 tablespoons grated parmesan
1/2 teaspoon salt	1/4 cup yogurt
1/2 teaspoon nutmeg	toasted sesame seeds

Heat the oil in a saucepan; stir in the flour and cook over low heat about 2 minutes. Stir in the hot milk, salt, and nutmeg. Cook, stirring, until the sauce thickens.

Add some of the sauce to the beaten egg, stir well, and then return this mixture to the saucepan. Whisk well to avoid curdling. Cook about 1 minute, then stir in all of the spinach.

Cover and simmer for 5 minutes, just until the spinach wilts. Remove from heat. Stir in the parmesan and the yogurt. Serve over dark bread, toasted, and sprinkle the sesame seeds on top. Serves 3.

SPINACH ROULADE

3 shallots, minced
1 tablespoon butter
4 slices cracked wheat bread
3 cups cooked spinach
1 teaspoon chervil
milk

1/4 cup grated Emmenthaler,
   gruyère, or cheddar
1/2 teaspoon salt
5 eggs, separated
2 tablespoons soft bread crumbs

Sauté the shallots in butter (or use 4 chopped green onions); do not brown. Soak the bread in milk to cover, then squeeze dry. In the blender, purée the bread, spinach, shallots. Turn out into a bowl. Add the butter from the pan, chervil, cheese, and salt; stir well. Beat the egg yolks slightly and add to the spinach mixture, blending well. Beat the egg whites stiff and fold into the mixture with the bread crumbs.

Cover a baking sheet with buttered heavy paper and spread the mixture on it. Bake 10 to 15 minutes, or until the roulade can be loosened from the paper. Cover with filling (sautéed mushrooms, or a combination of chopped meat and vegetables, or creamed eggs with or without ham), roll while hot, and serve with hot melted butter. Serves 4.

FISH FLORENTINE

This can be a rather fancy dish. If you use skim milk, it is wonderfully low in calories. Use any fish fillets you like, or leftover fish, flaked and seasoned.

2 10-ounce packages fresh
   or frozen leaf spinach
1 1/2 pounds fillets, or leftover
   fish (about 3 cups)
1/2 cup water
2 tablespoons lemon juice

1 teaspoon salt
1/2 teaspoon pepper
1/4 cup milk
1 1/2 tablespoons flour
1/4 cup grated parmesan

Cook the spinach, drain well. Arrange the fillets in rolls down the center of a shallow, rectangular baking dish. Pour the water and lemon juice over, sprinkle with salt and pepper. Cover the dish with foil. Bake at 350° about 15 minutes. (If you use cooked fish, bake only half that time.) Remove from the oven and drain the cooking liquid into a cup (there should be about 3/4 cup). Heat the liquid to boiling in a saucepan. Combine the milk and flour and mix well. Stir into boiling liquid, and cook, stirring constantly, until the sauce thickens.

Spread the drained spinach around the fish; pour the sauce over everything, and sprinkle the grated cheese on top.

Bake at 425° about 5 minutes, or until the sauce bubbles. Serves 6.

☆☆☆ HERBED SPINACH BAKE

You can vary quantities in this recipe to suit your taste.

1 10-ounce package fresh spinach	2 tablespoons finely chopped onion
1 cup cooked rice, preferably brown	1/2 teaspoon worcestershire sauce
1 cup shredded sharp cheddar	1/2 teaspoon salt
2 slightly beaten eggs	1/4 teaspoon rosemary, crushed,
1/3 cup milk	*or* thyme

Cook and drain the spinach, reserving liquid; then chop it. (You can use instant dry milk with the liquid to make part of the milk measure.) Then mix everything together and pour into a round or rectangular (1 quart) baking dish. Top with crumbs and more cheese, if desired. Bake at 350° for 20 to 25 minutes. Cut in wedges or squares. Serves 6.

◆

FRESH SPINACH SALAD

Here is an elegant version of a classic, always good.

• Dressing •	• Salad •
1/2 cup salad oil	1 pound fresh spinach
1/4 cup wine vinegar	2 hard-boiled eggs
2 tablespoons white wine	1/4 pound fresh mushrooms, sliced
2 teaspoons soy sauce	2 green onions, minced
1 teaspoon sugar	5 slices bacon
1 teaspoon dry mustard	
1/2 teaspoon curry	
1 small clove garlic, crushed	

Combine the dressing ingredients in a jar and shake well. Wash and dry the spinach and tear it into bite size pieces. Place in refrigerator to keep crisp.

Fry the bacon until crisp and drain on paper toweling. Chop or slice the eggs and crumble the bacon for topping.

Arrange the salad in a large bowl. Place the sliced mushrooms over. Remove the garlic clove, shake the dressing well, and pour it over the spinach. Garnish with the crisp, crumbled bacon and chopped or sliced egg.

SPINACH AND MUSHROOM SALAD

You can make this salad with leafy lettuce. In fact, we often had it that way, (without the mushrooms and carrots) when I was growing up.

4 slices bacon	1 pound fresh spinach
2 teaspoons sugar	1/4 pound fresh mushrooms, sliced
2 tablespoons vinegar	2 medium carrots, shredded
2 tablespoons water	2 hard-boiled eggs (optional)
1/2 teaspoon salt	

Cook the bacon in a skillet until crisp. Drain on paper toweling, crumble, and reserve. Measure the bacon fat and return 1 tablespoon to the skillet. Stir in the sugar, vinegar, water, and salt. Keep warm over low heat.

Wash and sort the spinach, break it into pieces in a salad bowl. Pour the warm dressing over and toss until coated and wilted.

Top with mushrooms, carrots, and bacon; then toss. Garnish with egg wedges, if desired. Serves 4.

SPINACH SALAD RING

This is very popular salad, one I have served often. Fill the ring with cherry tomatoes, or tomato wedges for a lovely sight.

1 small package lemon jello	1 package frozen chopped spinach
3/4 cup boiling water	*or* 1 bag fresh, steamed and
1 tablespoon vinegar	chopped
1 cup mayonnaise	1/2 cup finely chopped celery
	1 small onion, chopped fine
	1/4 teaspoon onion salt
	1 cup small curd cottage cheese

Dissolve the jello (or make your own with 1 package plain gelatin, 2 teaspoons lemon juice, 2 teaspoons sugar, *or* use the combination under Tuna Vegetable Mold) in the boiling water. Stir in the vinegar. Place in the refrigerator until somewhat thickened. Then beat in the mayonnaise (I use at least one-half Mock Mayonnaise; see the Appendix).

While the jello is cooling, cook and drain the spinach. Add the remaining ingredients to it and stir well. Then add this mixture to the jello-mayonnaise mixture and blend. Put in a ring mold (6-cup size) or a round bowl. Chill thoroughly. Serves 8 to 10.

Other recipes using spinach: Fresh Spinach Salad with Giblets (Livers); Chinese Pork and Vegetables (Pork); Spinach Ricotta Tart; Yogurt Spinach Soup; Spinach-Stuffed Zucchini.

Squash

Summer Squash

For additional squash recipes, see the section on Zucchini; many of the recipes there could be made with yellow summer squash.

SQUASH SOUFFLÉ

This dish has a delicate flavor; it is light and nutritious, and easily made.

1 1/2 pounds yellow squash *or* part yellow, part zucchini	3/4 cup shredded cheddar or gruyère
1 tablespoon salt	1/2 cup cottage cheese
1/2 onion, minced	1/2 cup whole wheat bread crumbs
1 tablespoon butter *or* oil	2 tablespoons chopped parsley
4 eggs, well beaten	salt and pepper to taste
	2 tablespoons melted butter

Grate the squash and toss with the salt. Let sit for 20 minutes. Meanwhile, sauté the onion in the butter or oil until tender. Combine with the beaten eggs, cheeses, bread crumbs, parsley, salt and pepper.

Squeeze out the excess water from the squash and rinse well. Squeeze in a towel to dry, then stir into the egg cheese mixture. Turn into an oiled casserole or soufflé dish and pour the melted butter over the top. Bake for 45 minutes at 350°. Serve at once. Serves 6 to 8.

CHEESE CUSTARD IN SQUASH SHELLS

Quick, easy, and a pleasant summer luncheon dish or accompaniment to sliced ham, or chicken salad.

4 medium summer squash *or* zucchini 1 cup cottage cheese 1 cup shredded cheddar 2 eggs	1/2 teaspoon dill 1/2 teaspoon salt 1/4 teaspoon pepper 1/2 cup buttered soft bread crumbs

Cut the squash in half lengthwise; parboil about 8 minutes. Drain and carefully scoop out seeds. Mix the remaining ingredients, except the bread crumbs, and spoon into the squash halves. Do not mound.

Bake at 350° for 25 minutes, or until the custard is set. Sprinkle with the bread crumbs and bake 5 minutes longer, or until the crumbs are toasty-brown. Serves 4.

Winter Squash

Winter squash are very popular around here. They keep well, and they can be used in a variety of interesting ways. I have a friend who has the same feeling about butternut squash that I have about chestnuts. She prepares it in the simplest way; peeled, sliced about 1/2 inch thick, seasoned with salt, pepper, honey, sometimes spices, dotted with butter, and baked in a moderate oven until tender. Or you can try winter squash the way it is prepared in central Africa, by combining 2 1/2 to 3 cups steamed, mashed squash with 1 cup coarsely chopped roasted peanuts, 2 tablespoons peanut oil, and salt to taste. Heat this mixture through, add white or brown sugar to taste, if desired, and serve with ham.

BAKED STUFFED SQUASH

Use two small squash (acorn, butternut) or one large one. Cut the squash in half, remove seeds and membrane. Arrange cut side down in a shallow pan and pour in about 1/4 inch water. Bake at 400° about 30 minutes. In the meantime prepare the stuffing, and spoon it in the cavity of the squash. Put the squash back in the pan, this time cut side up, bake at 400° for about 20 minutes, or until lightly browned. Serves 4.

Stuffing 1

1/2 cup whole wheat bread
   crumbs
1/4 cup wheat germ
1/2 cup finely cut celery
1/4 cup ground nuts (or soy grits)

1/2 clove garlic, mashed
1/2 teaspoon salt
2 tablespoons oil
stock (vegetable or chicken) to
   moisten, about 1/4 cup

Stuffing 2

1 cup ground cooked ham
1 egg
1/4 teaspoon pepper
1 teaspoon crumbled basil

1 tablespoon chopped pimento
2 tablespoons chopped green pepper
1/4 cup shredded Swiss or cheddar
1 tablespoon oil

Beat the egg first, then mix in the other ingredients.

Stuffing 3

Unlike the preceding, this stuffing is sweet; it is enough for 3 butternut or
acorn squash, and the recipe will serve 6. After the squash has been baked until
tender, scrape out the pulp (getting about 3 3/4 cups).

squash pulp
4 tablespoons butter/margarine
1/4 teaspoon salt
4 tablespoons brown sugar, divided

2 tablespoons raisins
1/2 cup chopped walnuts
1/4 cup light corn syrup or honey
2 teaspoons sherry or dry vermouth

To the pulp add 3 tablespoons butter/margarine, the salt, and 1 tablespoon
brown sugar. Beat until smooth. Fold in the raisins and walnuts. Put the filling
back into the shells, place in a shallow dish. Combine the remaining brown sugar
and butter, with the corn syrup. Drizzle this mixture over the squash. Bake at
450° about 15 minutes or until the top is crusty.

Stuffing 4

My sister told me about this one; it is ridiculously easy and delicious. Beat an
egg, blend with cottage cheese; season as desired with herbs, chopped green
onions, chives. Fill squash; cover top with grated sharp cheese and bake.

BAKED HUBBARD SQUASH WITH PINEAPPLE

1 medium sized winter squash	1/2 cup crushed pineapple
brown sugar	2 tablespoons sugar
salt	1/2 cup hot orange or pineapple
butter	juice
	1 tablespoon grated orange rind

Steam the squash until nearly tender. Peel it, and cut it into slices about 1/4 inch thick. Place the squash in layers in a greased baking dish, and sprinkle each layer with brown sugar, salt, and crushed pineapple. Dot with butter. Combine the remaining ingredients with a dash of salt and pour this mixture over the squash. Bake at 350° for about 1 hour. Serves 6.

SQUASH SOUP

Mix 1 cup mashed squash with 1 1/2 to 2 cups milk. Stir in 1/4 cup crumbled cooked chestnuts (or if you want to go African, chopped roasted peanuts), basil, and salt to taste. Bring to a boil. This makes a thick soup, so add more milk if you wish. Garnish with chopped parsley. Serves 4.

◆

SPAGHETTI SQUASH

A phenomenon that has appeared in the farm markets fairly recently. It is a fun vegetable and very tasty. What happens is that the inside of the cooked squash comes out in strings or spaghetti-like strands.

The quickest way to prepare this squash is to cut it in half, remove the seeds, place cut side down in 2 inches of water, and boil about 30 minutes. You can also cook it whole; it takes about 45 minutes boiled or steamed, 1 1/2 hours baked at 350°. If you cook it whole, be sure to pierce the shell in several places to relieve the pressure inside.

Serve with butter or margarine and seasonings to taste. Try your favorite spaghetti sauce over the top, or 2 cups shredded cheese with 2 tablespoons butter and seasonings. Another idea is herbs and cheese—a blend of 1/2 cup softened butter/margarine, 3 tablespoons finely chopped parsley, 1/2 tablespoon Italian herb seasoning, 1/4 teaspoon garlic salt, some pepper, and 1/4 cup grated parmesan.

A good way to bake it is au gratin. Use one half of a spaghetti squash, cook, peel, and put the strands in a saucepan. Add 1 1/2 cups dairy sour cream and cook over high heat, stirring constantly, about 2 minutes. Then remove from the heat, stir in 1/2 teaspoon powdered ginger, salt and pepper to your taste. Put in a shallow baking dish, sprinkle with 1/2 cup grated parmesan. Put under the broiler until it turns golden brown. Serves 4 to 6.

Other recipes using squash: Calabacitas (Corn).

Sweet Potatoes

Sweet potatoes can be prepared many of the ways you prepare white potatoes. I can remember that as a child we always had both kinds, and we were given a choice. My mother used to take parboiled sweet potatoes (cooked in boiling water about 10 minutes, then skinned) and slice them into a small amount of hot bacon fat or butter. She fried them until brown, turning once. They were delicious, and still are. You can sprinkle some brown sugar and nutmeg over them, if you like.

Yes, there is a difference between sweet potatoes and yams. The former are oblong in shape and pale yellow in color. Yams are much more round, are very orange in color, and oilier. You may substitute yams for any of the following recipes. The color and texture will be slightly different, that is all.

SPICY SWEET POTATOES

3 eggs
1 cup milk
2 cups cooked and mashed sweet
   potatoes
1/2 cup ricotta
1 cup toasted sunflower seeds

1 1/2 teaspoon cinnamon
3/4 teaspoon nutmeg
1/2 teaspoon allspice
1/4 teaspoon cloves
2 tablespoons honey

Beat the eggs and then add in the milk and beat again. Stir the mixture into the mashed sweet potatoes and blend thoroughly.

Mash up the ricotta (I often use cottage cheese which is equally good) and stir the sunflower seeds and spices into it. Then add to the sweet potatoes with the honey, and mix well.

Put into a casserole (1-quart size). Bake at 350° for about 25 minutes. Serves 6.

SWEET POTATO PUFF

I wouldn't substitute another kind of cereal for the Grape-Nuts. The taste and texture contrasts are unusual in this dish.

3/4 cup Grape-Nuts cereal	2 eggs, well beaten
1/4 cup sugar	2 tablespoons orange juice
2 tablespoons butter/margarine	2 teaspoons baking powder
3 cups mashed cooked sweet potao potatoes	1 teaspoon salt
3 tablespoons butter/margarine	

Mix the cereal with the sugar and the 2 tablespoons of butter/margarine until crumbly. Set aside.

Combine the sweet potatoes with the remaining ingredients and mix well. Place one-half of this mixture into a greased shallow baking dish. Top with one-third of the cereal mixture, then add the remaining potato mixture. Sprinkle the remaining cereal mixture over the top.

Bake at 350° for 30 minutes. Serves 8.

SWEET POTATO PUDDING

Serve this lovely dessert either hot or cold, with whipped cream.

2 cups mashed sweet potatoes	4 eggs
2 tablespoons butter, melted	2 teaspoons vanilla
2/3 cup brown sugar	2/3 cup orange juice
1/2 cup white sugar	1/2 teaspoon cinnamon

Beat the eggs well, then add in the other ingredients, and blend well. Pour into a 2-quart casserole. Bake uncovered at 350° for 30 minutes or until the center is done.

GOLDEN COOKIES

1/2 cup molasses	1/2 cup wheat germ
1/3 cup oil	1 tablespoon nutritional yeast
1 cup mashed sweet potatoes	1 cup powdered milk
2 eggs, beaten	1/2 teaspoon salt
1 cup whole wheat flour	1/4 teaspoon each of cinnamon, nutmeg, allspice, ginger

Beat the eggs first, then blend in the molasses and oil. Add the remaining ingredients. The batter will be stiff, but if it is too thick, add some orange juice. Drop by teaspoonsful onto a cookie sheet. Bake at 350° until lightly browned, about 15 minutes. Makes about 4 dozen.

Variations:
Substitute mashed carrots, pumpkin, or squash for the sweet potatoes.
Add 1/2 cup raisins, or cut dates, or 2 teaspoons grated orange or lemon rind.
Substitute 1/4 cup oatmeal for 1/2 cup wheat germ.

◆

SWEET POTATO PANCAKES

If you'd like a golden breakfast, here is a way to start off your day with sunshine.

2 cups raw, grated sweet potatoes	1/3 cup milk
2 eggs, beaten	1/2 cup powdered milk
1/2 teaspoon salt	1/3 cup whole wheat flour
3 tablespoons orange juice	1 teaspoon wheat germ

Combine all the ingredients. If the mixture is too thin, add more powdered milk; if too thick, add more liquid milk. Brown on each side on a hot, oiled griddle. Serve with hot applesauce, Cider Sauce, or fruit syrup.

Other recipes using sweet potatoes: Sweet Potato Rice Pudding (Rice). Old Fashioned Carrot Cake and Fresh Pumpkin Muffins have variations using sweet potatoes.

Tea

I almost never have any tea left over. I am an inveterate and incurable tea drinker, and so I just drink it all. However, sometimes there is simply too much, or it seems a good idea to extend it or drink it in another form. The simplest way is to add some honey, some lemon juice, and a good slug of rum to a cup of hot tea. Cures all sorts of problems.

TEA WITH MILK

This is an Indian-style beverage, very unusual. You can easily double the milk combination and use as needed. It will keep several days in the refrigerator; reheat to use.

2 cups milk	1/2 teaspoon ground almonds
1/2 cinnamon stick, broken	brown sugar or honey to taste
1/2 teaspoon ground cardamon	2 cups hot strong black tea
1/4 teaspoon saffron	

Combine all ingredients except the sweetening and tea in a heavy sauce pan. Simmer for an hour or so, stirring occasionally. Add the sweetening and remove from the stove. Combine the hot milk with the hot tea, pour back and forth between two containers several times. Strain and serve.

APRICOT-ORANGE TEA

2 cups apricot nectar
1 cup orange juice
1 cup water
1 tablespoon sugar

1 teaspoon cinnamon
4 lemon slices
12 whole cloves
2 cups hot strong tea

Combine the juices, water, sugar, and cinnamon in a saucepan. Insert three cloves in each lemon slice, and add to the saucepan.

Heat just to boiling; reduce heat, cover, and simmer 5 minutes. Stir in the tea. Serve hot. Serves 6.

TEA PUNCH

Here is a way to make tea for thousands—or almost. You can double or quadruple the recipe with no problems.

4 cups tea
3 cups orange juice
1 can frozen lemonade concentrate

2 cups sugar
3 cups grape *or* pineapple juice
4 cups water

Mix everything together. Just before serving add 2 cups ginger ale. Good as it is, or add some gin, if you like. Serves 25.

APPLE FLIP

3 cups strong tea
1 quart apple juice

2 tablespoons lemon juice
sugar or honey

Cool the tea, stir in the apple and lemon juices. Sweeten to taste with sugar or honey. Pour over ice cubes in tall glasses. Garnish with a lemon wedge, if desired. Serves 8.

CRANBERRY TEA

And now a cool drink with a whollop. It reminds me of what certain fashionable places call "tea" in the late afternoon.

1/2 cup orange pekoe tea, cooled
3 ounces cranberry juice (2 jiggers)

1 1/2 ounces (1 jigger) grand marnier
1 1/2 ounces (1 jigger) lime juice

The recipe says simply: stir.

HONEY CAKE

4 eggs	1/2 teaspoon allspice
1 cup sugar	1 teaspoon cloves
1 cup honey	1/2 teaspoon cinnamon
2 tablespoons oil	2 tablespoons brandy
1/2 cup strong tea or coffee	3 2/3 cups flour
1/2 cup raisins	1 teaspoon baking soda
1/2 cup chopped walnuts	1 1/2 teaspoons baking powder
1/2 cup diced candied fruit	

Beat the eggs well, add the sugar gradually and continue beating until light. Beat in the honey in a fine stream; stir in the oil, tea (or coffee), and then the fruit, nuts, and spices. Sift the flour, soda, and baking powder and stir in. Pour into two paper-lined and oiled loaf pans, and sprinkle with a few almond halves. Bake at 350° for 70 minutes. Invert pans and allow the cakes to cool before removing from the pans. Cakes will stay fresh for a month or longer if wrapped air tight and kept cool.

Other recipes using tea: Rhubarb Tea uses black China tea.

Tomatoes

There are always too many tomatoes. One evening a friend arrived at a gathering with a huge basket of tomatoes and a bunch of paper bags. He had twenty-four plants, he told us, and he and his wife had canned umpteen quarts of tomatoes, and had made ketchup, juice, and sauce. Would someone, he asked, *please* take some home? Here are two recipes that will take care of the tomatoes in bulk.

TOMATO JUICE AND SPAGHETTI SAUCE

30 medium tomatoes
some celery tops
2 stalks cerery, cut fine
2 carrots, sliced thin

1 tablespoon salt
1/2 teaspoon celery salt
1 1/2 tablespoons worcestershire
   sauce
2 large onions, minced

Wash the tomatoes, cut them in pieces, and put in a large kettle with all the other ingredients. Bring to a full boil, cook until the vegetables are tender. Cool somewhat. Drain through a food mill, taking what liquid comes off easily. Cool this liquid and use as tomato juice.

To make the sauce, take what is left in the mill, remove some seeds and skin. Put in a blender with the following and blend on high speed, for several minutes:

1/2 teaspoon oregano
1 teaspoon basil
1 tablespoon parsley flakes
2 tablespoons brown sugar

1 clove garlic, peeled
1 tablespoon instant beef bouillon
1/2 tablespoon worcestershire
   sauce

Cool before freezing. This makes a mildly flavored sauce, to which you can add seasonings of your own taste and, of course, chopped mushrooms, ground beef or other leftover meat, Italian sweet sausage, meat balls. At the end of this section are suggestions for using all the tomato sauce.

TOMATO COCKTAIL

8 quarts tomatoes
4 medium onions
4 bay leaves
10 whole cloves

2 tablespoons salt
1/2 cup sugar
1/2 cup vinegar
1/2 cup lemon juice

Cut up the tomatoes and onions; put with the bay leaves and cloves in a large kettle. Boil everything 20 minutes, then strain in a food mill.

To the strained liquid, add the remaining ingredients, and boil 5 minutes.

All of the above preparations are easily canned, but are more easily frozen. Empty milk and cream cartons, washed thoroughly, make excellent containers. Be sure to leave at least an inch head room at the top, and seal very well.

———————◆———————

MUSHROOM-STUFFED TOMATOES

An excellent appetizer, but also a good accompaniment to baked fish or bar-becued chicken or steak.

4 medium ripe tomatoes
1/2 pound mushrooms, finely
   chopped
1 tablespoon butter
1/4 teaspoon salt
3 tablespoons minced green onion

1 package (3 ounces) cream cheese
   or 3 ounces farmer cheese
1/2 cup dairy sour cream
1 tablespoon finely chopped fresh
   dill *or* 1 teaspoon dried dill

Cut a 1/4-inch slice off the top of each tomato. Discard any seeds, chop coarse-ly, and reserve 2 tablespoons. With a knife, make a pocket in each tomato by re-moving about 2 tablespoons of the pulp.

Sauté the mushrooms in the butter in a large skillet, stirring once or twice, about 5 minutes. Add the salt and onion and cook 1 minute. Whip the softened cream cheese and sour cream until smooth. Add the reserved chopped tomato and the mushroom mixture along with the dill. Spoon into tomato shells and chill several hours. Garnish with fresh dill. Serves 4.

GAZPACHO

A wonderfully simple recipe, ideal for the blender. The whole preparation should take about five minutes.

1 clove garlic, peeled and sliced
4 ripe tomatoes, quartered
1/2 green pepper, seeded and sliced
1/2 small onion, peeled and sliced
1 cucumber, sliced

1 teaspoon salt
1/4 teaspoon pepper
2 tablespoons olive oil
3 tablespoons wine vinegar
1/2 cup ice water

Peel the tomatoes and the cucumber, if you want to. Put all the ingredients into the blender, cover, and blend on high speed for about 5 seconds only, or until the vegetables are coarsely chopped. Chill thoroughly before serving. Gar-nish with croutons. Serves 4.

CREAM OF TOMATO SOUP

A dieter's treat. If you use skim milk, each serving is only about 75 calories.

1 medium tomato, quartered	1/4 teaspoon salt
1/2 cup tomato juice	generous pinch dried basil
2 tablespoons instant dry milk	1/4 teaspoon parsley
	1/2 cup milk

Put everything into the blender except the milk, and whirl until blended. Pour into a saucepan, then rinse out the blender jar with the milk. Add this to the soup and heat thoroughly. Do not boil. Serves 2.

FRIED TOMATOES

You can serve these with fried bacon, also for breakfast, if you like them that way. Take medium-sized slightly underripe and firm tomatoes. Remove the core, and slice about 1/4-inch thick. Dip the slices in beaten egg (or, if you like a less substantial crust, you can skip the egg), then in dry bread crumbs (whole wheat are best) or a mixture of bread crumbs and wheat germ. Heat some bacon fat in a skillet, to a medium-hot temperature (if you have an electric frying pan, 360° is about right). Fry the tomatoes just until brown, turning once. Do not over-cook. Serve at once.

OPEN TOMATO-BACON-CHEESE SANDWICH

With a fresh, ripe tomato right out of your garden, nothing could be better. Take slices of whole wheat or cracked wheat bread and toast them lightly. Arrange on each slice some cheddar cheese, sliced thin, thin slices of tomato, and several pieces of bacon (I prefer to fry the bacon in advance; otherwise, everything else is done before *it* is). Put the sandwiches under the broiler until the cheese is bubbly and the tomatoes hot. If you don't want to bother with bacon, try thin strips of ham or corned beef. But let me add that bothering with the bacon is really worth it!

TOMATO OMELETTE WITH HERBS

3 green onions, chopped fine	1/2 teaspoon fresh parsley
1 medium tomato, peeled, cut fine	dash salt
1 tablespoon salad oil	4 eggs
1 medium cooked potato (optional)	1 tablespoon milk
1/2 teaspoon fresh basil	1/4 cup cottage cheese

Heat the salad oil in a large skillet, and sauté the green onions, tomato, and potato, if you have one and want to use it up. Although not essential, it does enhance the taste. Cook slowly until tender, about 5 minutes. Chop the herbs very fine and add them with salt and pepper. Beat the eggs with the milk and pour them into the pan. By small spoonfuls, add the cottage cheese. Cook slowly until firm. You can put this in a 350° oven for a few minutes to set the top. Serves 4.

PIPERADE

This is a Basque dish, almost as easy as scrambled eggs, but infinitely more interesting.

2 tablespoons olive oil	1/2 teaspoon oregano
1 large onion, sliced	1/2 teaspoon marjoram
1 clove garlic, minced	1 teaspoon salt
4 green peppers	pepper to taste
2 red peppers	6 large eggs
2 large tomatoes, peeled and chopped	

In a heavy skillet, sauté the onion and garlic in the oil until tender. Seed and slice the peppers in thin strips, add them to the pan and cook a few more minutes. Then add the tomatoes and seasonings. Stir well; then cook covered, about 15 minutes, until saucy and fragrant. Beat the eggs (if your eggs are small, add 1 or 2 more), pour them into the tomato sauce, and stir well. Taste and adjust seasoning, if necessary. Cook, without stirring, until the eggs are set. Remove from the heat immediately and serve at once. Serves 8.

TOMATOES WITH CHEESE DUMPLINGS

A wonderful and unusual dish, very different from the usual fare. Perfect for a luncheon or supper, served with a crisp green salad.

Sauce	Dumplings
1 tablespoon green pepper	1/2 cup flour
2 tablespoons chopped onion	2 teaspoons baking powder
2 tablespoons oil	1/2 teaspoon salt
2 tablespoons flour	1/2 cup cornmeal
2 teaspoons salt	2 tablespoons shortening
dash pepper	1/2 cup grated cheddar
4 cups chopped tomatoes	1 tablespoon fresh parsley
1 tablespoon chopped celery tops	1/2 cup milk
1 teaspoon sugar	

In a large pan, with a tight-fitting lid, sauté the pepper and onion in the oil until tender. Blend in the flour, stir until smooth. Then add the salt, pepper, tomatoes, celery tops, and sugar. Cook, stirring, until the mixture comes to a boil. Reduce the heat to low, simmer several minutes.

While the tomatoes are simmering, sift together the flour, baking powder, and salt. Stir in the cornmeal. Cut in the shortening until the mixture looks crumbly. Blend in the cheese and parsley. Finally, add the milk all at once, and stir only until the flour is dampened. Please do not overmix. Dip a tablespoon into cold water, drip the batter in mounds onto the hot tomato mixture. Cover tightly. Steam gently for 20 minutes. Do *not* lift the cover and peek. Serve at once. Serves 4.

◆

DILLED CHICKEN-TOMATO SKILLET

1 broiler-fryer, cut up	1 tablespoon minced fresh dill
1 tablespoon margarine	*or* 1 teaspoon dried dill
3 large tomatoes, peeled and chopped	2 tablespoons lemon juice
1 teaspoon sugar	1 clove garlic, crushed

In a large skillet, brown the chicken in the margarine. Add the remaining ingredients, bring to a boil, reduce the heat; cover, and simmer 35 to 40 minutes, or until the chicken is fork-tender.

Reduce the sauce, if desired, by boiling rapidly uncovered. Serve on a bed of brown rice. Serves 4.

CHICKEN CACCIATORE

A wonderful standby for any occasion. The recipe I have always used calls for 1 can (2-pound 3-ounce size) of Italian tomatoes. If you can use fresh tomatoes, the flavor of the dish is extraordinarily improved.

1 3-pound chicken, cut up	1/4 teaspoon pepper
4 cups cut-up tomatoes	1/2 bay leaf
2 tablespoons salad oil	1/4 teaspoon thyme
1/2 cup chopped onions	1/4 teaspoon marjoram
1 teaspoon salt	1/2 cup dry white wine

Sauté the chicken until golden brown in the oil; use a large pot with a lid. Then put the remaining ingredients over the top of the chicken. Cover the pot and simmer for about 1 hour. Remove the cover to permit the sauce to reduce somewhat. Cook until the chicken is tender. Serve it with boiled spaghetti. Serves 4 to 6.

☆☆☆ PERCIATELLI ALLA NAPOLETANA

This is very easy to make and the children love it. The recipe can be doubled, but you will have to use a *large* pot.

1/2 pound ground beef and Italian sweet sausage	1/2 teaspoon garlic *or* onion salt
	dash pepper
1 1/2 cups chopped tomatoes *or* canned tomatoes with juice	1/2 teaspoon chopped parsley
	1/2 teaspoon Italian seasoning
1 cup lima beans, fresh or frozen *or* 1 cup cut green beans	1/2 pound macaroni
	6 ounces mozzarella, diced

Brown the meat, using about three inches of sausage, cut in small pieces. Drain off the fat. Add the tomatoes, beans, salt, and seasonings. Cook briskly about 5 minutes, then lower the heat and simmer 30 minutes. Cook the macaroni (I use elbows, but you could use shells, or ziti, or bows, or cut perciatelli pieces), drain, and add to the skillet. Mix thoroughly, heat through, then add the mozzarella. Stir for a minute and serve immediately. Serves 4.

☆☆☆ BEEFSTEAK PIZZA STYLE

Another Italianated dish, equally simple to prepare, equally popular.

2 pounds chuck steak, at least
   1 inch thick
3 cups cut-up tomatoes
1/2 teaspoon oregano
1 teaspoon snipped parsley
1 clove garlic, minced

2 tablespoons minced onion
1/4 teaspoon salt
dash pepper
2 tablespoons oil
4 slices mozzarella

Place the steak in a baking dish. Put the tomatoes through a food mill and spread evenly over the meat. Sprinkle the remaining ingredients, except the cheese, over the top. Bake covered at 350° for 1 1/2 hours. Top with the cheese and bake 1/2 hour longer, uncovered. Serve with rice or noodles. Serves 4 to 6.

FRESH TOMATOES AND SPAGHETTI

The following method for preparing spaghetti with fresh tomatoes was described by a close friend of mine whose father was Italian. I regret not to be able to include the gestures.

2 pounds tomatoes
6 ounces mozzarella, diced
1 tablespoon fresh basil or oregano
   or 1 teaspoon dried

2 tablespoons butter
pepper, lots
1 tablespoon salt
1 tablespoon olive oil
1 pound spaghetti

Peel and cut up the tomatoes (you will need roughly 8 small, 6 medium, or 4 large); they should be very ripe and, if you can get them, use Italian pear-shaped sauce tomatoes. Put them in a bowl in the oven at lowest possible heat for about 15 minutes. If a good deal of liquid forms, drain it off (it is good to drink but too much for the sauce).

Add the mozzarella, herbs, and butter to the tomatoes and toss well. Put the bowl back in the oven to warm the ingredients, adding a vast (or so it seemed to me) amount of freshly ground pepper.

While this mixture is mellowing, boil 6 quarts of water in a large pot, add the salt and olive oil, and cook the spaghetti in it, "al dente."

Drain the spaghetti (but do not pour cold water over it to stop the cooking), and quickly return it to the pot. Add the tomato mixture. Toss it all together. Serve immediately on heated plates.

EASY TOMATO SAUCE

A delicious, standard recipe, and one that I make all the time during the tomato season. You can make a larger quantity than indicated here, and I have found over the years that you can vary the ingredients to your taste or according to what you happen to have (or not have) in your refrigerator and pantry. For example, I often omit the green pepper, because I often don't have any in the house. Also the original recipe states that you begin by frying the onion, pepper, celery, carrot, and garlic in 3 tablespoons of olive oil. I have *never* done this, but I pass it on for what it is worth.

6 large fresh tomatoes	1/2 bay leaf
1 large onion, chopped	1 tablespoon brown sugar
1/2 green pepper, chopped	2 sprigs parsley *or* 1 tablespoon
2 ribs celery with tops, cut up	dried
1 or 2 carrots, cut fine	1 teaspoon dried basil *or* tarragon
1 clove garlic, minced	1 teaspoon salt

Peel the tomatoes, if you want to (I very often don't, depending on how thick the tomato skins are and/or how tired *I* am), and cut them in small pieces. Put them in a large pot with all the other ingredients. If you can get some fresh basil, do use that, as it will greatly enhance the flavor of the sauce. Cook the sauce gently until the vegetables are tender. This takes about an hour, sometimes longer. Stir it from time to time.

Pour the sauce through a strainer, and save the juice for tomato juice. Remove the bay leaf, if you can find it, and whirl the sauce in the blender until smooth. Add more seasoning, if you like. This sauce will keep for several days, and freezes very well indeed.

An easy recipe for tomato sauce is in the section on Beans.

Tomato Juice

This section seems to have what they call in the television trade spin-offs. I can think of no better pre-dinner beverage for the serious dieter than a tomato juice cocktail. You can chill the juice, and season it with any of the following: seasoned salt, dry vegetable or beef bouillon powder, cayenne pepper; celery, onion, or garlic salt; lemon or onion juice; worcestershire or soy sauce; such savory herbs as basil, chervil, dill, parsley, tarragon, thyme.

☆☆☆ MEAT LOAF

This is the only meat loaf I make regularly. I have been known to make an exception for my older daughter, who does not like this recipe.

2 eggs	1/2 teaspoon seasoned salt
1 cup tomato juice	3/4 cup rolled oats
1 tablespoon minced parsley	1 1/2 pounds ground beef

Beat the eggs well, add the tomato juice and seasonings. Stir in the oatmeal, and then add the ground beef. Mix well with your hands and place in a 9 x 5 loaf pan. Bake at 350° for 55 minutes. Drain off excess fat, and let stand at least 5 minutes before cutting. Serves 8.

This meat loaf is wonderful the next day. I cut 1/2-inch slices and brown them in a frying pan over medium heat. Turn once and place a thin slice of cheddar on top; cook until the cheese is melted.

ITALIAN MEAT LOAF

The exception. I should make it more often. But it is more complicated, and somehow, to me, meat loaf is the epitome of the simple meal.

1 1/2 pounds ground beef	2 eggs, beaten
1/2 pound Italian sweet sausage	3/4 teaspoon oregano *or*
2 cups bread crumbs	Italian seasoning
1/2 cup tomato juice	1 teaspoon salt
1/2 cup grated onion	1/4 cup chopped parsley
	1/4 cup grated parmesan
	2 cups tomato sauce (optional)

Mix well all ingredients except the tomato sauce. Put in a 9 x 5 loaf pan. Bake at 350° about 1 hour and 15 minutes. Let stand 10 minutes before slicing. Serve with hot tomato sauce and spaghetti. Serves 8.

JOHNNY MARGETTI

Get your butcher to grind the pork fresh for you.

1 1/2 pounds lean ground pork	1 cup grated cheese
1 medium onion	tomato juice
12 to 16 ounces egg noodles	

Cook the ground pork lightly in a frying pan, along with the onion, chopped fairly fine. Cook the egg noodles about 5 minutes and drain. Mix in the pork, and add the cheese (cheddar, Swiss, gruyère, hard gouda, provolone). Then mix in enough tomato juice to make the casserole moist, but not too soupy. At this point you can freeze it for baking later. If you bake the whole thing, use a 3-quart casserole, top with more grated cheese (freshly grated parmesan would be wonderful) and some buttered bread crumbs. Bake at 375° until brown and bubbly, about 30 minutes. Serves at least 6.

Variations: Substitute ground beef (either freshly ground or leftover cooked meat) or ground lamb for the pork. You can substitute tomato sauce or spaghetti sauce for the tomato juice. You can use spinach noodles, or macaroni. You can add all sorts of herbs to your taste. Also salt, if you like it.

CHILLED TOMATO SOUP

A light, easy, and refreshing summer soup. Serve with crusty bread, crackers, and some cheddar cheese.

2 cups tomato juice	1/2 teaspoon celery salt
1 cup milk	1/2 teaspoon grated onion
1 teaspoon sugar	1/2 teaspoon worcestershire sauce
1/2 teaspoon salt	

Combine all the ingredients and chill thoroughly. Top each serving with chopped chives and, if you like, a dollop of plain yogurt. Serves 3 to 4.

Other recipes using:
Tomatoes: Many salads; Avocado and Tomato Soup; Italian Broccoli Casserole; Winter Borscht (Cabbage); Calabacitas (Corn); many eggplant recipes; Demi-Cassoulet (Lamb); Bean and Peanut Curry (Legumes); Super Minestrone, Eggplant and Macaroni (Noodles & Pasta); Walnut Lentil Loaf (Nuts); Dinner Chowder, Potato Ratatouille (Potatoes), tuna dishes, zucchini recipes.

Tomato Juice: Sunburgers (Carrots); Stuffed Eggplant; Stuffed Peppers; Salade Niçoise (Tuna); Yogurt and Tomato Dressing.

Tomato Sauce: Eggplant Parmigiana; Soybean Casserole (Legumes); Rice Pizza; Baked Macaroni with Ricotta (Ricotta); Hamburger and Noodles Stroganoff (Wine).

Tuna

TUNA OMELETTE

This is the very best way to use up just a tidbit of tuna; if you have more than that, just add it in anyway.

1 clove garlic	1 1/2 teaspoons milk
1 tablespoon margarine or oil	salt and pepper
2 green onions, minced	leftover tuna
3 large eggs	1/4 cup cottage cheese

Peel the garlic and rub it hard around the bottom and sides of your skillet. Then heat the margarine or oil, and sauté the onions in it until tender. Beat the eggs well, stir in the milk, and pour into the pan. Add salt and pepper, make sure the tuna is in small pieces, and sprinkle it over the eggs. Then distribute the cottage cheese over the top of that and cook, bringing the outsides toward the center with a fork, and rotating the pan. Fold over and serve. Serves 2.

◆

On a hot day a tuna salad makes an excellent meal. The tuna can be stretched by adding any or all of the following: chopped hard-boiled eggs, cooked chick peas (absolutely essential to tuna salad in my view) chopped green onions, cut up celery, grated carrot, diced, boiled or baked potatoes, cooked brown rice or kasha, dill pickle slices, capers, soy nuts, toasted sunflower or sesame seeds. Moisten this with Mock Mayonnaise (see the Appendix), or any mayonnaise mixed half and half with plain yogurt, or a good vinaigrette dressing.

☆☆☆ TUNA VEGETABLE MOLD

This salad is refreshing and very attractive looking on a warm summer evening. Try it with Venetian Rice (under Peas), hot corn bread, and a good dry chilled white wine.

1 package Italian salad gelatin	3/4 cup diced celery
2 tablespoons vinegar	3/4 cup diced raw carrot
2 tablespoons minced onion	1/4 cup sweet or dill pickle, diced
1 can tuna, drained and flaked	1 hard-boiled egg, optional

Dissolve the gelatin in 1 cup hot water, then add 1 cup cold water. (Or make your own gelatin with 1 envelope plain gelatin, sprinkled on 1/2 cup cold water; add 1 cup boiling water, 2 tablespoons sugar, 1/2 teaspoon salt, 1/4 cup lemon juice, 1/4 teaspoon celery salt, 1/2 teaspoon worcestershire sauce.) Stir in the vinegar and onion. Chill until somewhat thickened. Fold in the tuna, celery, carrot, and pickle. Arrange the sliced egg in the bottom of a 1 1/2-quart mold, pour the mixture over, chill until firm. Unmold on salad greens and serve with mayonnaise. Serves 4 to 6.

CRUNCHY TUNA SALAD

My children love this salad. Try to eat up all this salad as it does not stay crunchy, alas.

1 can tuna, drained and flaked	1/4 cup Italian *or* vinaigrette
2 cups cooked green peas	dressing
2 tablespoons finely chopped onion	1 tablespoon lemon juice
or green onion	1 5-ounce can chow mein noodles

Combine all the ingredients, except the noodles. Toss to mix well, cover, and chill thoroughly. Add the noodles just before serving. Arrange on lettuce with tomato and hard-boiled egg wedges. Serves 6.

SALADE NIÇOISE

This is a variation of the traditional French dish. If you want to make the real thing, the essential ingredients are tuna, anchovies, tomato wedges, diced potatoes, cut green beans, hard-boiled eggs, and black olives, all mixed with a vinaigrette dressing. Usually the oil is not drained from the tuna, and you can adjust your dressing accordingly. The following is much less caloric, and I really like it better.

1 can tuna, drained	2 tablespoons vinegar, preferably
1 medium green pepper, cut	tarragon
1 cup cooked green beans	1/2 teaspoon worcestershire sauce
1 small tomato, in wedges	1/2 teaspoon dry mustard
1/2 cup diced boiled potatoes	1 clove garlic, crushed
1/2 cup tomato juice	2 teaspoons chopped chives

Combine the tuna and vegetables in a large bowl. Mix the remaining ingredients and pour over the top. Stir well and marinate several hours, until ready to serve. Arrange on a bed of lettuce, or tear up the lettuce in pieces, and toss the salad with it just before serving. Serves 4 to 6.

TUNA-DILL SPREAD

This is lovely on crackers with cocktails, and makes a deluxe sandwich.

8 ounces cream cheese *or*	1/4 teaspoon seasoned salt
farmer cheese, softened	1/2 teaspoon dill weed
1 can tuna, drained	dash white pepper
1 tablespoon dry sherry	1/4 cup minced green pepper
1 tablespoon lemon juice	(optional)
	1/4 cup minced celery (optional)

In a medium mixing bowl, combine the cheese, tuna, sherry, lemon juice, and seasonings. Beat until light and fluffy; stir in the minced pepper and celery. Cover and refrigerate. Makes about 2 cups.

◆

☆☆☆ TUNA NOODLE CASSEROLE

An old standby in my household, and after the garlic omelette, the most frequently used method of eliminating the tuna from the refrigerator. This recipe is my own, and I love it. It is easy and quick and, with hot green peas, makes a wonderful and nourishing meal.

8 ounces egg noodles	1/2 cup chopped celery *or*
1 cup grated cheese	green pepper
1 can tuna, drained and flaked	1 cup milk
1 cup cottage cheese	crumbled cereal for topping

Cook the noodles about 5 minutes; rinse and drain. Grate the cheese (you can use sharp or mild cheddar, or Monterey Jack, or Swiss, or gruyère, or a combination). Mix everything together and put in a 2-quart casserole. Sprinkle cereal over the top (wheat flakes or corn flakes are the best). Bake at 350° for 35 to 40 minutes. Serves 6.

TUNA CURRY

An easy, economical, quickly prepared dish with a very unusual flavor and texture. Serve it with chutney, if you wish.

1 tablespoon margarine	1 cup uncooked white rice
1/2 cup chopped green onions	2 cans tuna, drained and flaked
(including some green tops)	1/2 cup seedless raisins
2 teaspoons curry powder	1/2 cup chopped roasted cashews
2 1/2 cups chicken broth	*or* peanuts
	additional chopped green onions

In a heavy saucepan with a tight-fitting lid, heat the margarine; sauté the onions until soft. Add the curry powder (more, if you like it hot) and broth and heat to boiling. Stir in the rice, reduce the heat, and cover; simmer for 30 minutes.

Mix in the tuna, raisins, and nuts and heat for 5 minutes. Sprinkle each serving with additional chopped green onion or chopped chives. Serves 6.

TUNA MARENGO

1 tablespoon oil
1 medium onion, chopped
1 clove garlic, minced
2 cans tuna, drained
1/4 teaspoon salt
dash pepper

1/4 teaspoon marjoram, crushed
1/2 cup dry white wine
1 4-ounce can mushrooms, drained
   or 1/2 cup chopped cooked
   mushrooms
2 tomatoes, peeled and seeded
1 tablespoon parsley flakes

Heat the oil in a large skillet. Sauté the onion and garlic until tender. Break the tuna into large chunks, and add to the skillet with remaining ingredients. Cover, bring to boiling; lower heat and simmer 5 to 10 minutes. Stir once or twice. Serve over spaghetti or brown rice. Serves 4.

◆

Don't forget that your dog and/or cat will love the oil or water drained from the cans of tuna. The water-pack tuna has a liquid that can be used in a cream sauce for fish, or in fish soup.

Other recipes using tuna: Tuna Romanoff (Cottage Cheese); Tuna and Spinach-Noodle Salad (Noodles & Pasta); Curried Tuna Squares (Rice); Zucchini-Tuna-Cheese Salad (Zucchini).

Turkey

At certain times of the year there are enormous quantities of turkey to deal with. So here goes with what some call "rehashing the beast."

☆☆☆ TURKEY CANTONESE

Once you have the turkey and vegetables cut, this special dish is very quickly made.

2 tablespoons margarine	1/4 teaspoon ginger
1 cup diagonally sliced celery	1/8 teaspoon nutmeg
1 cup thinly sliced carrots	1 tablespoon soy sauce
1 medium onion, chopped	1 teaspoon lemon juice
1/4 cup slivered almonds	1 cup (or more) cooked turkey,
3/4 cup canned pineapple chunks	in small pieces
1/4 teaspoon salt	1 can (5 ounces) water chestnuts,
1 tablespoon cornstarch	thinly sliced

Melt the margarine (or use butter, if you prefer) in a stove-top casserole pot; sauté the celery, carrots, onion, and almonds until the nuts are lightly browned. Drain the pineapple, measure the chunks. Add enough water to the juice to make 1 1/4 cups. Blend into this the salt, cornstarch, ginger, nutmeg, soy sauce, and lemon juice; blend well. Stir into the casserole and cook, stirring, until thickened. Add the pineapple, turkey, and water chestnuts; heat thoroughly. Serve on hot rice and sprinkle chow mein noodles over the top. Serves 4.

CURRIED TURKEY

The same kind of dish, but an entirely different taste. It is also good with hot rice.

2 tablespoons butter	1/8 teaspoon cumin
1 onion, finely chopped	1/4 teaspoon ginger
1/2 cup chopped celery	2 cups turkey broth
1/2 tart apple, finely chopped	3 cups diced or shredded turkey
1 tablespoon curry powder	1/2 cup green grapes, halved, *or*
2 tablespoons flour	light raisins

Melt the butter; sauté the onion, celery, and apple until tender but not browned. Sprinkle the flour and spices over the top and cook, stirring, for 2 minutes. Then stir in the broth (if you don't have turkey broth, use chicken) and bring to a boil, stirring constantly. Cook until smooth and thickened. Add the turkey and heat thoroughly, but do not boil. Stir in the grapes and serve immediately. Serves 6.

Variations: Add 1/2 cup sliced mushrooms to the sautéed vegetables. Add toppings: grated coconut, finely chopped peanuts, crumbled bacon, minced green onions or chives.

TURKEY HASH

Hash is a very good and basic way to use any leftover meat or poultry. This rule can apply to chicken, beef, ham, pork, veal. The general idea is to heat together leftover turkey and gravy, and add whatever suits your fancy or your refrigerator situation: cooked mushrooms, celery, potatoes, green peppers, parsley. Proportions can be varied. If you haven't got gravy, use milk or cream, or a tomato or cream sauce. If you use cream or milk, you may add some sherry, Madeira or wine. Sprinkle cheese on top, if desired. Have fun.

Here is a general model from which you can create your own dish:

1 1/2 cups diced turkey	1 tablespoon chopped parsley
1 cup cooked diced potatoes	1 tablespoon chopped chives
1/2 cup cooked chopped celery	seasonings
1 cup gravy or sauce	

Combine everything and heat, either in a frying pan or in the top of a double boiler over hot water.

TURKEY HAM BAKE

Here is a good casserole with a lovely flavor.

1/2 cup chopped onion	2 tablespoons dry sherry
2 tablespoons margarine	2 cups cubed turkey
3 tablespoons flour	1 cup cubed ham
1/2 teaspoon salt	1 can (5 ounces) water chestnuts,
1/4 teaspoon pepper	sliced
1 can (3 ounces) sliced mushrooms	1/2 cup shredded Swiss cheese
or 1/4 pound sauteed fresh	1 cup soft bread crumbs
mushrooms	2 tablespoons melted margarine
1 cup light cream	

Sauté the onion in the margarine until tender. Blend in the flour, salt, pepper; add the mushrooms (undrained) and cream and cook, stirring, until thickened. (If you use fresh mushrooms, sauté them with the onion and add about 1/4 cup water.) Stir in the sherry, turkey, ham, and water chestnuts. Pour into a 1 1/2-quart casserole. Top with the cheese and the bread crumbs, which you have combined with the melted margarine. Bake at 400° for 25 minutes. Serves 6.

✩✩✩ HOT TURKEY SALAD

Make a turkey salad, using celery, green onions, and almonds or water chestnuts. Amounts may vary according to what you have on hand. Moisten with mayonnaise or Mock Mayonnaise (see the Appendix). Put the salad in a shallow baking dish, sprinkle some grated cheese on top, and bake until hot and the cheese is browned. You can also spread this on toasted whole wheat or cracked wheat bread slices, sprinkle cheese on top, and broil until browned and bubbly. Serve immediately.

MUSHROOM TURKEY SALAD

A variation from the usual turkey cum mayonnaise salad. You can add some shredded spinach leaves.

1/4 cup sliced mushrooms	2 tablespoons lemon juice
2 3/4 cups diced cooked turkey	1/4 cup olive *or* salad oil
1 cup diced celery	1/2 teaspoon salt
1/4 cup thinly sliced radishes	1/2 teaspoon crumbled savory leaves
2 tablespoons minced green onion	pepper to taste
1 tablespoon chopped parsley	

Toss the mushrooms in a salad bowl with the turkey, celery, radishes, onions, and parsley. Blend the remaining ingredients and pour over the salad. Mix lightly, chill well, and serve on beds of lettuce. Serves 6.

———————◆———————

TURKEY SOUP

The last appearance of the turkey. I prefer to postpone this special treat for
a while, so I put the turkey bones and carcass (broken up into reasonably sized
pieces) in a large plastic bag in my freezer. I also freeze any leftover broth or
gravy. Of course, you can always make the broth from the carcass; pick off the
bones, discard them; then freeze the broth and tidbits for a later use.

turkey carcass	1 medium onion, diced
1 bay leaf	1/2 to 1 cup minced celery (and use
1/2 teaspoon marjoram	the tops too)
1/2 teaspoon thyme	salt and pepper
1/2 teaspoon basil	1/4 cup raw rice
1 tablespoon minced parsley	1 or 2 envelopes chicken broth
1 tablespoon margarine	1/2 pound mushrooms, sliced and
2 tablespoons flour	sautéed
2 carrots, quartered and sliced	3 tablespoons sherry

Break up the carcass and put it in a large pot in which you have melted a dab
of margarine. Brown the bones for a few minutes, add enough water to cover
along with the herbs and bay leaf. Simmer for 3 to 4 hours. Strain through a
sieve, sort out the turkey bits, clean off the bones, add the meat to the broth,
and set aside.

In the pot melt the margarine, add the flour, and cook a minute. Then stir in
the stock gradually. Bring to a boil and add the carrots, onion, celery, rice, and
seasoning to taste. Simmer until the rice and vegetables are done. Add the mushrooms and just before serving stir in the sherry. Serves about 10.

Variations: Substitute 3 medium potatoes, pared and cubed, for the rice. Add
some garlic powder. Add a small can evaporated milk. Add leftover turkey, cut
very fine. Leave out the flour. Add any other compatible vegetables you'd like
to get rid of. Serve this soup with hot buttered corn bread or Italian bread and
a green salad, and you have a complete meal.

TURKEY PITA SANDWICHES

Here are two ideas for stuffed pita sandwiches. In each case you cut the breads in half, open the pocket, fill it, wrap the bread in foil, and heat at 400° for 15 minutes.

• Filling 1 •
1 cup diced cooked turkey
1/3 finely diced celery
1 tablespoon minced onion
1/2 cup grated sharp cheddar
1/3 cup diced bread and butter pickles
1/4 cup mayonnaise
2 6-inch pita breads

Combine all ingredients and fill the bread halves. Serves 4.

• Filling 2 •
sliced turkey breast
4 tomato slices
2 cheese slices
mayonnaise
1 6-inch pita bread

Spread the bread halves with mayonnaise. Fill the pocket with the other ingredients. Serves 2.

Other recipes using turkey: Most chicken recipes, but especially Chicken Cranberry à l'Orientale, Indian Melon Salad (Chicken); Chicken Tetrazzini (Evaporated Milk); Macaroni and Chicken Salad (Noodles & Pasta); crepes with turkey (see under Ham); Curried Pear Salad.

Veal

I wish that veal were as popular here in the States as it is in Europe. It is such a delicious, tender, succulent meat, and yet it is hard to find and expensive besides. Many wonderful dishes can be made with veal cutlets, but as I am dealing here with remainders and/or excesses, the delicate, rare, and expensive cutlet does not fall into either category. My favorite veal recipe can be found in the section on wine, and included there are suggestions for serving the remainders *en gelée*. Here are a few other ideas for using up the veal.

VEAL CASSEROLE

This is a very easy combination of several very good foods.

4 cups veal, cut in 1-inch cubes	1/2 can tomato paste
2 tablespoons butter	1/2 cup finely chopped celery
2 tablespoons flour	1 bay leaf
oregano, chervil, salt, and pepper	1/2 pound small mushrooms
1 large onion, sliced	1 1/2 cups baby lima beans, fresh
1/2 cup white wine	or frozen
1/2 cup stock	5 slices bacon, fried crisp and
	crumbled

Brown the veal in the butter. Sprinkle the flour and seasonings over the meat and mix well. Put in a casserole and add the onions, wine, stock, tomato paste, celery, and bay leaf. Bake uncovered at 300° for about 2 hours. Add more wine and stock if necessary. Stir well, then add the mushrooms (sliced or whole as you wish), lima beans, and bacon. Bake 30 minutes longer. Serves 8.

VEAL CURRY

Serve this light dish with lots of fluffy rice and a mixed green salad.

3 cups cut-up veal	2 teaspoons curry powder
1 tablespoon margarine	1/2 teaspoon ginger
1/2 cup chopped onion	1 teaspoon sugar
1 tart apple, cut in cubes	1 1/2 cups bouillon
1/2 teaspoon salt	

Brown the meat in the margarine, along with the onion. Place this in a pot and sprinkle the other ingredients over the top. Cover, and cook gently about 1 1/2 hours. Serves 4. (You can substitute lamb for the veal.)

VEAL PAPRIKA

An enormously popular and widely consumed European dish. It has many forms and several different names. It is traditionally served with noodles; if you are able to get or make them, *Spätzle* are the very best accompaniment.

2 pounds veal	1/2 cup slivered almonds
flour	1 cup dairy sour cream
2 tablespoons margarine	1 tablespoon paprika
2 cloves garlic, cut fine	poppy seeds
1/2 cup water	

Cut the meat in 1-inch cubes and sprinkle flour over. Brown the veal in the margarine along with the garlic. Add the water, some salt and pepper. Cook, covered, about 1 1/2 hours. Add more water if necessary. Brown the almonds in a little butter. Remove the meat from the pan and mix with the almonds. If the sauce is too thin, add in a little flour. Then stir in the meat, almonds, and some poppy seeds; stir well. Finally blend in the sour cream and paprika. Serves 6.

VEAL LOAF

I like to serve this with mashed potatoes and homemade applesauce. The loaf
has a lovely flavor, and it is good the next day warmed up with cheese. Serve
with a light gravy, preferably containing mushrooms.

1 1/2 pounds (about 3 cups) ground veal	3 tablespoons minced parsley
1 egg, beaten	1 cup minced celery
1 onion, chopped fine	1 teaspoon poultry seasoning
1 teaspoon instant chicken broth powder	

Mix all the ingredients lightly and shape into a loaf. Put on a rack, which you
then put in a baking pan. Bake at 325° for one hour. Serves 4 to 6.

Other recipes using veal: Veal Fricassee (Evaporated Milk); Hash (Turkey);
Braised Veal (Wine).

Wine

There are books, brochures, and leaflets on cooking with wine. There are
cooking specialists and gourmets who are convinced that one should *never* cook
with wine that you wouldn't serve to guests with the meal. I feel if the wine one
cooks with is so good, I'd prefer to drink it; besides I am convinced that it is an
excellent thing to make a tasty dish or cake out of wine that would otherwise be
thrown away. Not only does this puff me up with moral pride, but what I cook
with wine, often very ordinary wine, tastes very good to me. I hope it will to
you too. Somehow, once you've put a little wine in a recipe, the same dish never
tastes quite so good again without it.

Here are a few easy tips for using wine in the kitchen:

1. Add a teaspoon or so of sherry to cream soups—chowders, mushroom,

puréed vegetable. Use a little dry sherry or vermouth to deglaze the pan after you have fried mushrooms, and pour over them.

2. Use red wine to marinade economy cuts of beef, 6 to 8 hours in the refrigerator, turning frequently. This principle is used in the famous German *Sauerbraten,* for example.

3. Add some red wine to your next stew; simmer the stew a long time.

4. Some sherry, Madeira, or port will enhance any fruit compote or mixed fruit salad.

BAKED CHICKEN WITH *FINES HERBES*

This dish is easy and economical, and you can get it all made and cooking before your guests arrive. Then you can enjoy their company. *Fines herbes,* a mixture of finely chopped dried thyme, oregano, sage, rosemary, marjoram, and basil, is available commercially.

1 frying chicken, cut up	1/2 cup white wine
2 tablespoons margarine or oil	1/4 cup water
flour	*fines herbes*

Flour the chicken pieces and sauté them in the margarine in a large oven-proof skillet. Let them cook long enough so that they are nicely brown and crisp. Turn them so that the brown side is up, shake the *fines herbes* over the top, and salt and pepper to your taste. Bake, uncovered, about 1 hour at 350°. Serve with brown rice, and pour the sauce from the pan over the chicken and rice. Serves 4 easily.

CHICKEN DIJON

1 3-pound chicken, cut up	1 bay leaf
2 tablespoons butter/margarine	1/2 teaspoon salt
1/2 cup dry white wine	2 egg yolks
1/4 teaspoon tarragon	2 tablespoons sour cream
pinch of thyme	3 teaspoons Dijon mustard

In a large skillet with a cover (an electric frying pan is excellent), brown the chicken in the butter. Add the wine and seasonings, and bring to a boil. Reduce the heat, cover, and simmer 45 minutes. Discard the bay leaf. Remove the chicken from the pan and keep warm.

Beat the egg yolks with the sour cream and some of the pan juices. Stir into the pan along with the mustard, and heat, stirring constantly. Do not boil. Return the chicken to the sauce and simmer gently for 5 minutes. Serve with hot egg noodles or herbed rice. Serves 4.

☆☆☆ BRAISED VEAL

An excellent company dish, easy and delicious, and again, one that cooks while you enjoy a drink before dinner with your friends.

6 pounds veal leg or rump	pepper to taste
2 tablespoons butter	1/2 teaspoon thyme
3 green onions, cut fine	1 bay leaf
1 clove garlic, crushed	1/2 cup dry white wine
1 teaspoon salt	1/4 cup water

Have the butcher bone and roll the veal for you, and ask him to give you the bones. Shake some flour over the veal, melt the butter in a large Dutch oven, over moderate heat, and brown the veal roll on all sides. This will take a while because it should cook slowly, and you do not want to burn the butter.

Reduce the heat and add the remaining ingredients to the pot. Also add the bones (if there is room in the pot, you can brown them along with the veal). Cover closely and simmer gently for four hours, adding more liquid if necessary (I have never found it necessary). Slice thin, serve with the sauce. Bulgur wheat is especially good with this dish, as is brown rice. Or try Carrots and Kasha (under Carrots). Serves 8.

After you have eaten off this piece of meat and the veal is down to a small amount, cut up what is left in small pieces, slice a hard-boiled egg in the bottom of a small mold, mix the veal pieces with the remaining sauce, season it to taste, add some minced chives and/or green onions, and pour it all over the egg. Chill until firm. *Voilà!* a veritable French *oeuf en gelée*, which makes a lovely summer salad or hors d'oeuvre. If you butcher did not give you your veal bones, you will have to forget this delight, or else use plain gelatin (1 envelope to 2 cups liquid).

BOEUF BOURGIGNON

This traditional French dish appears routinely—and rightly so—on restaurant menus.

2 tablespoons butter or oil	1 1/2 cups young red wine, divided
1 1/2 pounds stewing beef	1 small can mushrooms and juice
2 leeks (optional)	*or* 1/2 cup fresh, sliced and
2 small stalks celery	sautéed
2 medium onions	generous pinch of thyme and parsley
1 clove garlic	1 bay leaf
1 tablespoon flour	salt and pepper to taste

Heat the butter or oil in a pan with a lid. Cut up the meat, leeks, celery, onions, and garlic in small pieces, and sauté in the pan. Remove all of this to a plate. Make a paste with the flour and 1/2 cup wine, add to the pan; stir until thickened. Then blend in the remainder of the wine. Stir well, add the meat and vegetables, mushrooms, and seasonings.

Cover tightly and cook over a *very* low fire until the meat is tender, at least two hours. Serves 4. The dish is excellent with boiled potatoes, hot buttered rice or noodles, and a crisp green salad.

☆☆☆ HAMBURGER AND NOODLES STROGANOFF

This is an elegant way to serve hamburger. A good accompaniment would be a green vegetable—green beans, broccoli, spinach—or a crisp mixed green salad.

6 to 8 ounces egg noodles	1 tablespoon flour
1 tablespoon butter	1 cup tomato sauce
1/2 cup finely chopped onion	1/4 cup dry red wine
1 clove garlic, minced	1 cup beef bouillon
1/2 pound mushrooms, thinly sliced	salt and pepper to taste
or 1 can (5 ounces) sliced	1 cup sour cream
mushrooms	1/2 cup grated parmesan
1 pound ground chuck	

Cook the noodles and drain. Melt the butter and sauté the onions, garlic, and mushrooms about 5 minutes. Add the beef and cook, stirring, until brown Remove from heat, and stir in the flour, tomato sauce, wine, bouillon, salt and pepper. Simmer 10 minutes, stirring occasionally. Blend in the sour cream.

In a 2-quart casserole make three layers with the noodles and the meat mixture. Sprinkle with the cheese. Bake, uncovered, for 25 minutes at 375°. Serves 4 to 6.

SHERRY PORK CHOPS WITH FRUIT

6 large center-cut pork chops
3 medium apples, cored and sliced
1/4 cup brown sugar
1/2 teaspoon cinnamon

2 tablespoons butter
salt and pepper
3 peaches, peeled and sliced
1/2 cup dry sherry

In a heavy skillet, brown the meat on both sides. Arrange the apple slices in a buttered baking dish; sprinkle with brown sugar and cinnamon and dot with butter. Drain pork chops on a paper towel and arrange over apple slices. Top with sliced peaches. Add the sherry, cover, and bake at 350° for 35 minutes, or until tender. Serve on hot rice. Serves 6.

SKILLET LAMB SHANKS

An unusual and very economical main dish. Serve the shanks with lots of bulgur wheat, steamed with some green onions.

2 lamb shanks (about 1/2
   pound apiece)
2 tablespoons shortening
2 tablespoons minced onion
1/2 teaspoon paprika

1/2 teaspoon rosemary
1 bay leaf
1/2 cup dry white wine
1/2 teaspoon grated lemon rind
1 tablespoon lemon juice

Roll the lamb shanks in flour. Brown them well in the shortening. Stir in the remaining ingredients.

Heat slowly to boiling. Cover, reduce the heat, and simmer, turning two or three times, at least 2 hours, or until the meat is very tender. Serves 2, very generously.

◆

BAKED APPLES WITH WINE

Take some tart baking apples, peel, slice thin, and arrange the slices in a buttered pie plate. Dot the top with currant jelly. Pour white wine over all. Bake at 350° about 30 minutes, or until apples are tender. Serve warm.

MELON IN CHABLIS

This, and the following, are light, refreshing wine desserts using fruit and gelatin. Both are ideal for a ladies' luncheon dessert or for the ending of a summer dinner.

1 lemon	6 whole allspice
2 envelopes plain gelatin	2 cups chablis
1 1/4 cups water	1 medium-size ripe honeydew melon
1/2 cup sugar	*or* cantaloupe

Pare the zest from the rind of the lemon and reserve. Squeeze the juice into a cup and sprinkle the gelatin over it to soften.

Combine the water, sugar, lemon rind, and allspice in a saucepan. Heat to boiling; lower heat and simmer 5 minutes. Remove rind and allspice. Stir in softened gelatin until dissolved.

Pour into a medium-size bowl and stir in the wine. Chill 30 minutes, or until gelatin begins to thicken. In the meantime, halve the melon and remove the seeds. Scoop enough melon into balls with a melon scoop, or the 1/2 teaspoon of the measuring set, to get 2 cups.

Fold the melon into the gelatin and spoon into individual serving glasses. Chill 2 hours, at least. Serve with whipped cream and crisp cookies.

ORANGE AND LEMON JELLY

1 cup white wine	3 tablespoons sugar
juice and rind of 2 oranges	1 envelope plain gelatin
juice and rind of 1 lemon	

Grate the rind from the fruit before squeezing the juice. Measure the wine, add the fruit juices. If necessary add water to make 2 cups. Stir in the grated peel and bring to a boil with the sugar. Remove from the heat. Dissolve the gelatin in a small amount of water. Stir this into the hot liquid and mix thoroughly. Chill. Serve with vanilla cream.

AUSTRIAN WINE CREAM

This dessert is a cousin to the Italian *zabaglione,* but with dry white wine instead of Marsala.

2 egg yolks	**1 cup dry white wine**
3 tablespoons sugar	

Over simmering water, whisk together all the ingredients. Use a *large* double boiler or bowl, since the cream will froth up to about 4 times its original volume. When the mixture is very light and frothy, spoon into champagne or sherbet glasses. Serve warm with ladyfingers or sponge cake.

☆☆☆ WEINSCHAUM

The German cousin of the above. It uses whole eggs, and thus is even more frothy. I find this excellent over dry fruit cake or fruit compote.

1 3/4 cups white wine	**4 eggs**
1/4 cup Marsala	**1/4 cup sugar**
1/4 cup water	

Put the wine in the top of a double boiler over boiling water. If you can't get Marsala, use cream sherry or all white wine. Add 1/4 cup water. Beat the eggs well with the sugar and add to the wine. Beat vigorously with a whisk and cook until it thickens, whisking all the time. Serve it hot or cold.

WINE SPONGE CAKE

Lovely and light and the perfect accompaniment to a chilled fruit compote.

3/4 cup whole almonds	**8 eggs, separated**
1 1/4 cup flour	**1 1/4 cups sugar**
1/4 teaspoon salt	**1/3 cup sweet sherry**
1/2 teaspoon cinnamon	**1/3 cup orange juice**

Whirl the almonds in the blender until fine. Sift the dry ingredients and mix with the nuts.

Beat the egg whites until soft, moist peaks hold. Set aside. With the same beaters, beat the yolks until thick, add in the sugar gradually, beating all the while. Stir in wine and orange juice. Fold in the dry ingredients. And last, fold in the egg whites gently.

Pour into a 9-inch tube pan. Bake at 325° about 1 hour. Invert pan until completely cooled. Sprinkle 10X sugar over the top.

☆☆☆ POPPY SEED CAKE

My favorite way to deal with the sticky sweet wine.

1 package yellow cake mix	1/4 cup poppy seeds
4 eggs	1 cup white wine *or* 1/2 cup
1/2 cup oil	sherry and 1/2 cup water
1 package instant pudding	

Put everything in the large bowl of your mixer (I like French vanilla pudding best, but you can use coconut cream or banana or plain vanilla with great success). Beat on low speed until blended, then beat at high speed for 4 minutes.

Pour into a 10-inch tube pan, and bake at 350° for about 50 minutes. Cool, turn out on a plate, and dust the top with 10X sugar. Slice it thin, and it will serve many.

Other recipes using:

Wine: Banana Cake Jamaica; Beef Encore; Chicken Stroganoff, Chicken Sauce for Spaghetti; Chicken liver dishes (Livers); Mushroom Soup; Sweet and Sour Onions; Sliced Oranges in Wine; Fresh Pea Soup; Stewed Pears; Plum-Apricot Party Dessert (Plums); Chicken Cacciatore (Tomatoes).

Sherry: Trifle (Cake & Cookies); Sherry Cheese Spread; Coffee Jelly (variation); Chicken Tetrazzini, Veal Fricassee, Rich Chocolate Sauce (Evaporated Milk); Grapefruit Jelly with Sherry; Three Fruit Topping (Jams, Jellies, Marmalades); Blender Pâté (Livers); several mushroom recipes; Onion Purée Soup; Onions in Madeira Cream; Classic Pumpkin Bread (variation); Rhubaba (Rhubarb); Turkey Ham Bake, Turkey Soup.

Yogurt

The recipes that follow call for plain yogurt, with one exception. The flavored yogurt is very sweet to my taste. If you like flavors, try making up your own: add honey, or molasses, or maple syrup, mashed fresh or canned fruit, and, of course, coffee and vanilla.

The combination of yogurt with vegetables is delicious. Here are two yogurt soups based on this principle. Both are Middle Eastern; the first is from Lebanon, the second from Iraq.

YOGURT-BARLEY SOUP

2 cups water	1 tablespoon flour
1/4 cup barley	1 small onion, chopped
1 cup yogurt	1/2 teaspoon margarine
1 1/2 cups chicken *or* vegetable stock	salt and pepper to taste
	1 teaspoon chopped mint leaves
1 large egg, slightly beaten	1 tablespoon chopped parsley

Bring the water to a rolling boil. Trickle in the barley so the water does not stop boiling. Lower heat and simmer for about 30 minutes, or until done. Drain.

Meanwhile, stir the yogurt into the stock. Add the egg and blend well. Then add the flour, a little at a time. Heat almost to a boil, stirring constantly. Reduce heat and continue to stir for a few minutes until the mixture thickens. Do *not* let it boil.

Sauté the onion in the margarine until golden. Stir into the yogurt mixture with the drained barley, salt, and pepper. Heat thoroughly. Serve in warm soup bowls, with a sprinkling of mint and parsley. The soup can also be chilled and served cold.

Note: You can double the recipe.

YOGURT-SPINACH SOUP

This soup is a meal in itself; serve it with hearty whole wheat or rye bread. Although the recipe calls for uncooked meat, you can add instead a cup or so of coarsely ground leftover roast beef, pork, or—best of all—lamb.

10 ounces fresh spinach
    or 1 package frozen chopped
    spinach
10 ounces very lean chopped
    meat (lamb)
	2 tablespoons bulgur wheat
	2 cloves garlic, minced
	salt and pepper
	4 cups yogurt

Remove the stems and steam the spinach until tender (just a minute or so). Chop fine. If you use frozen spinach, thaw it enough to break it in pieces. Put the spinach in a pot with the meat, bulgur, and garlic; stir in the yogurt. Let the soup simmer until the meat is done, at least half an hour. If you use cooked meat, then the soup needs to simmer until everything is very heated and flavors are blended; this should take at least 20 minutes, maybe longer. Serves 4.

◆

TOMATO-YOGURT DRESSING

This dressing is *very* low in calories and is good on lettuce, cabbage, or mixed-vegetable salads.

1 cup tomato juice 1 cup plain yogurt 2 tablespoons vinegar	1 tablespoon oil 1/2 teaspoon salt 1 clove garlic, crushed

In a covered jar mix all the ingredients. Add some herb blend for salads, if you like. Let stand in the refrigerator several hours before using. Makes about 1 3/4 cups.

YOGURT GARLIC SAUCE

This makes a good dip, or salad dressing, or topping over raw or steamed zucchini slices or eggplant.

1 clove garlic, minced 1/4 teaspoon salt 1 teaspoon vinegar	3 tablespoons oil 1 cup yogurt 1/4 cup grated cucumber

Mix the garlic, salt, vinegar, and oil into the yogurt and stir until well blended. Then add the cucumber (which you have drained) and mix well.

YOGURT-NUT DRESSING

This low-calorie dressing is very good on fresh fruit.

1 cup yogurt
1/4 cup walnuts, chopped fine

2 teaspoons honey
1/2 teaspoon vanilla

Mix all ingredients until well blended. Refrigerate a few hours before serving. Makes 1 1/4 cups.

◆

YOGURT SWIRL

Here is an easy, refreshing, and pretty drink. The recipe calls for apricot nectar, but you can also use peach nectar, or pineapple juice. Or try 3/4 cup orange juice concentrate mixed with 3/4 cup water.

12 ounces apricot nectar
   (about 1 1/2 cups)
1 cup yogurt
1/4 teaspoon vanilla

1 tablespoon (or less) honey
3 to 4 ice cubes
ground nutmeg

Combine the nectar and yogurt in the blender container; add the vanilla and honey. Cover and whirl at high speed until smooth. Add the ice cubes, one at a time, cover; whirl until crushed. Pour into two *tall* glasses. Sprinkle with nutmeg.

◆

HEARTY YOGURT BREAD

1 1/2 tablespoons dry yeast
2 cups warm water
2 tablespoons honey
1 cup yogurt

2 teaspoons salt
1 1/2 cups rye flour
7 to 9 cups whole wheat flour

Dissolve the yeast in the warm water in a large bowl. Stir in the honey and let stand until foamy, about 10 minutes. Then add the yogurt, salt, and rye flour. Beat well, then slowly add enough of the whole wheat flour to work the dough. Knead 5 to 7 minutes, working in more whole wheat flour as necessary.

Place in a large bowl, cover, let rise until double (about 1 1/2 hours). Punch down, shape into three loaves, and place in 9 x 5 loaf pans. Let rise until almost double, about 1 hour. Bake at 350° for 45 to 50 minutes.

TROPICAL COFFEE CAKE

This light, quick coffee cake is flavored with pineapple and has a delicious, crunchy topping. If you want to make the cake in a conventional fashion, combine the liquid ingredients, and then stir in the sifted dry ingredients. I am not sure it makes a great deal of difference. You can use pineapple yogurt, or stir 2 tablespoons pineapple jam or drained crushed canned pineapple into plain yogurt.

1 1/2 cups flour	• Topping •
1/2 cup sugar	1 cup coconut
2 teaspoons baking powder	1/3 cup brown sugar
1/2 teaspoon salt	1 teaspoon cinnamon
1 cup pineapple yogurt	
1/2 cup oil	
2 eggs	

Grease a 9-inch square or 11 x 7 pan. In a large bowl blend the cake ingredients. Beat 3 minutes at medium speed. Pour into the prepared pan. In a small bowl combine the topping and sprinkle over the batter. Bake at 350° 35 to 40 minutes or until the cake tests done. Makes 9 to 12 squares.

TURKISH YOGURT CAKE

This is an authentic recipe.

1 cup sugar (white or brown)	1 1/2 teaspoon baking powder
1/3 cup melted margarine *or* oil	1/2 teaspoon salt
3 eggs	1 teaspoon vanilla *or* the juice
1/2 cup yogurt	of 1 lemon
3 tablespoons cold water	1/2 cup raisins
1 1/2 cup flour	flour for dredging

Beat the sugar and shortening, add the eggs, one at a time, beating well. Add the yogurt (diluted with the water; if your yogurt is thin, make it 2 tablespoons) alternately with the sifted dry ingredients, starting and ending with the dry ingredients and beating well after each addition. Add vanilla or lemon juice (lemon juice is better) and the raisins which you have mixed with a little flour. Pour into a greased 9 x 5 loaf pan and bake at 375° for 45 minutes. Do not overbeat or overcook.

☆☆☆ RASPBERRY RING

This is a good tea cake, slightly drier than the previous one. If you have left-over candied peel from your Christmas fruitcakes, add it, chopped finely and mixed with a small amount of flour, to this cake.

2 cups flour	1 cup brown sugar
1 teaspoon baking soda	1 egg
1/2 teaspoon baking powder	1 teaspoon vanilla
1/4 teaspoon salt	1 cup raspberry *or* plain yogurt
1/2 cup butter/margarine	

Grease an 8-cup tube pan. Sift the dry ingredients. Cream the butter with the sugar until fluffy. Beat in the egg and vanilla.

Stir in the flour mixture, alternately with the yogurt until just blended. Bake at 350° for 50 minutes. Cool 10 minutes, turn out on a rack, and sprinkle with 10X sugar.

Other recipes using:
   Yogurt: Avocado Soup; Blender Borscht (Beets); cucumber recipes; Egg-plant Bake; Twelfth-Day Pancakes (Eggnog); Bulgur and Garbanzos (Grains); Granola-Yogurt Bread; Orange Marmalade Tea Loaf (Jams, Jellies, Marmalades); Yogurt-Cottage Cheese Spread (Parsley); Minted Pea Soup; Creamed Spinach; Zucchini Deluxe, Zucchini and Cottage Cheese Bread (Zucchini); Mock Mayon-naise (see the Appendix).
   Lemon Yogurt: Chicken Salad with Yogurt; Slim Pineapple Ring.
   Rice pudding can be made with flavored yogurt.

Zucchini

I have picked and sorted and selected the very best of my zucchini recipes.
You can always freeze zucchini, either blanched for two minutes, or grated raw
(I freeze this in 2-cup amounts in order to make bread).

☆☆☆ ZUCCHINI DELUXE

You may vary the amounts in this recipe without any problems. This dish
is wonderful by itself, or with any braised chicken or veal dish, or with baked
ham. The last time I served it to some French friends, along with Beefsteak
Pizza Style (under Tomatoes); it made a wonderful meal.

5 cups (about) cooked brown rice	1/2 teaspoon salt
salt	1 egg, beaten
1 teaspoon paprika	2 tablespoons chopped chives *or*
1/3 cup toasted sesame seeds	green onions
5 cups zucchini, in cubes	topping (whole wheat bread
2 cups plain yogurt	crumbs, crumbled wheat cereal)
2 tablespoons oil	butter
1/3 cup shredded cheese (cheddar,	
gruyère)	

Stir some salt and the paprika into the cooked rice, then mix in the sesame
seeds. Spread this mixture in the bottom of a large casserole or an 11 x 9 baking dish. Arrange the zucchini pieces (or slices) over the rice. Set aside.

In a small saucepan, combine the yogurt, oil, grated cheese, and salt. Cook
over low heat, stirring, just until the cheese melts. Remove from the heat and
whisk in the beaten egg and the chives. Pour this sauce over the zucchini, top
with crumbs.

Bake 375° until the crumbs are browned and the squash is tender but still
firm. This takes about 35 to 40 minutes. Serves 8.

RICE CASSEROLE ITALIANO

One of those wonderful mixtures that you can vary to suit your taste.

2 cups sliced zucchini	1/8 teaspoon pepper
1/2 pound lean ground beef	1 cup cooked rice
1/2 cup chopped onions	1/2 cup tomato sauce
1/2 clove garlic, crushed	1/2 cup cottage cheese
1/2 teaspoon salt	1 egg, beaten
1/2 teaspoon basil	1/2 cup shredded cheddar
1/4 teaspoon oregano	

Parboil the zucchini in salted water about 3 minutes; drain well. Sauté the ground meat, onions, garlic, and seasonings until the onions are transparent. Stir in the rice and tomato sauce.

Blend the cottage cheese and egg. Arrange half of the zucchini slices in a shallow 1-quart casserole. Spoon the rice-meat mixture on top. Spread the cottage cheese over this mixture. Top with remaining zucchini and sprinkle with the cheese. Bake at 350° for 20 to 25 minutes, or until hot and bubbly. Serves 4.

PASTA AND ZUCCHINI

This is a pasta sauce without tomatoes. You can serve it over hot, drained pasta, or over any hot grains, or folded inside crepes.

3 tablespoons butter	zucchini, young, sliced in rounds
3 tablespoons flour	oil
1 1/2 cups scalded milk	garlic and onion
	parmesan

Melt the butter, stir in the flour until smooth. Add the milk, and whisk over medium heat until the sauce thickens. Sauté the sliced zucchini in a little oil, with some garlic or onion, until just tender. Stir the cooked zucchini into the sauce, add cheese to taste, and your sauce is ready. If it is too thick, add a little more milk.

OPEN-FACED ZUCCHINI OMELETTE

This type of omelette is called a frittata and is popular in southern Europe. This makes a nice luncheon or supper dish with hot crusty bread. In Italy it often is served cold, cut in cubes, as part of the Italian *antipasto*.

6 eggs, beaten	1 teaspoon salt
1 tablespoon cream *or* rich milk	1/8 teaspoon pepper
1 tablespoon softened butter	2 cups finely chopped zucchini
2 tablespoons grated parmesan	1 green pepper, chopped
several drops hot pepper seasoning	2 tablespoons olive oil
or hot sauce *or* worcestershire	

Combine the eggs, cream, butter, parmesan, and seasonings. Beat until well blended. Preheat the oven to 350°. Sauté the zucchini and green pepper in the oil in a large oven-proof skillet until soft, about 5 minutes. Stir in the egg mixture, stir gently, and cook for 2 minutes, or until the eggs are just set on the bottom.

Put the skillet in the preheated oven for 4 to 5 minutes until the top of the eggs are set. Cut in wedges to serve. Serves 4.

◆

These stuffed zucchini dishes can be served as appetizers, as vegetables, or as main dishes, depending on the heartiness of the appetites and the stuffing used. Prepare the shells by cutting the squash in half lengthwise and parboiling in some salted water for 8 to 10 minutes (depending on size). If your zucchini is large, you may have to cut it in quarters; then when you bake the shells, fit the quarters together. I have done this and it works fine; some of the filling drips out, but the whole dish is somewhat drippy anyway, so just scoop it up and pile it back on. I have to confess that I have eaten much stuffed zucchini cold the next day for lunch; sprinkle on some good vinaigrette dressing, add a few tomato wedges, and you have a wonderful and unusual salad.

☆☆☆ ZUCCHINI BOATS

This recipe is somewhat vague. Do not be put off by this, just try it, use your imagination, and I guarantee you will have a perfectly delicious result.

medium zucchini	spaghetti sauce
minced onion	parmesan cheese
chopped mushrooms	cheddar cheese, cut in cubes
butter	

After the zucchini are parboiled, scoop out the inside and cut into cubes (the bigger the zucchini, the bigger the boat). Meanwhile sauté the minced onion and mushrooms together until tender. Mix them in with the cubed zucchini and the cheddar. Then mix in the spaghetti sauce. Heap this mixture into the shells, sprinkle the tops generously with the parmesan cheese.

Place on a shallow baking dish and bake at 375° until lightly browned and thoroughly heated. This takes about 20 minutes. Of course, you eat the whole thing.

If you prefer, you can put the mushroom-onion-zucchini-cheddar mixture into the shells and pour the spaghetti sauce over the top. These can be frozen before they are baked; thaw for an hour or so before cooking.

SOYBEANS AND RICE BOATS

Another super-healthy vegetarian dish. Be sure to allow time for preparation of the various parts.

1 cup dried soybeans	1/2 cup chopped green onions
3 cups cold water	1/2 cup chopped parsley
1 teaspoon salt	1/4 teaspoon pepper
4 medium zucchini	2 tablespoons margarine
2 cups cooked brown rice	3/4 cup wheat germ

Rinse soybeans, cover with cold water, and let stand overnight at room temperature. Then bring them to a boil, stir in the salt. Cover and simmer about 3 hours. They still won't be tender, but don't worry. Drain them and reserve the liquid.

Parboil the squash, drain, scoop out the seeds with a spoon. Measure 3/4 cup of the soybean liquid into the blender, add the soybeans, and whirl at high speed until the mixture is very smooth.

Combine the soybean purée, rice, onions, parsley, and pepper in a bowl. Arrange the zucchini in a shallow baking dish; fill the shells with the soybean mixture. Melt the margarine, stir in the wheat germ, and cook several minutes. Then sprinkle over the filling.

Bake at 375° for 15 minutes, or until topping is golden and the shells are heated through.

SPINACH-STUFFED ZUCCHINI

If you have fresh spinach or Swiss chard in your garden, do use it in this recipe.

6 small zucchini (1 1/2 pounds)	1 teaspoon Italian herbs
1 10-ounce package frozen	1 teaspoon salt
chopped spinach	1/4 teaspoon pepper
1/2 cup minced green onions	2 tablespoons dry bread crumbs
1 clove garlic, minced	4 tablespoons grated parmesan,
2 tablespoons olive oil	divided
	2 tablespoons butter

Scoop out the pulp from the zucchini halves and chop coarsely. Cook the spinach, drain, squeeze out as much liquid as possible. Sauté the onions and garlic in the oil until soft. Add the spinach, zucchini pulp, herbs, salt, pepper, bread crumbs, and 2 tablespoons of the cheese. Mix well.

Heat the oven to 350°. Place the zucchini shells in a baking dish and stuff with the spinach mixture. Melt the butter and drizzle over the top. Sprinkle with remaining cheese. Bake 30 minutes. Serve hot or at room temperature. Serves 6.

ZUCCHINI-TUNA-CHEESE SALAD

Raw zucchini makes a wonderful addition to any mixed green salad; slices of young zucchini are a lovely base for your cocktail spread or as a garnish to a salad plate. This salad is colorful and hearty, a perfect late summer meal.

6 small zucchini	1 tablespoon lemon juice
2 cups ripe cherry tomatoes	4 tablespoons olive oil
1 small red onion, thinly sliced	1 clove garlic, mashed
1/4 teaspoon salt	1 cup mozzarella, cut in dices
1/4 teaspoon pepper	1/2 can tuna, drained
1 1/2 tablespoons red wine vinegar	

Cut zucchini in half lengthwise, then crosswise in 1/2-inch slices, into a large salad bowl. Add tomatoes, onion, salt, and pepper.

Combine the vinegar, lemon juice, oil, and garlic in a small jar with a lid. Shake until well blended and pour over the salad. Toss gently. Garnish the top with cheese, flaked tuna, and, if you like, black ripe olives. Serves 6.

◆

EVERGREEN ZUCCHINI

Another simple dish, with a lovely combination of flavors, not to mention shades of green.

4 pounds zucchini	4 tablespoons minced green onions
1 cup water	1/2 teaspoon freshly grated lemon
2 teaspoons salt	peel
4 tablespoons butter	3 tablespoons fresh lemon juice
	1 cup minced parsley

Use small zucchini and slice them in 3/8-inch cartwheels. Cook, covered, in salted water for about 8 minutes, or until tender but crisp. Drain (save the liquid for your soup pot). Meanwhile, melt the butter in a saucepan, stir in the onion (use some green tops), lemon peel and juice. Add the parsley to the zucchini, then pour the heated sauce over. Toss lightly to mix thoroughly. Serves 8.

☆☆☆ PUFFED-UP ZUCCHINI

This is very elegant and goes well with most main dishes.

4 cups chopped zucchini	1/4 teaspoon salt
1 cup chopped onion	1/8 teaspoon pepper
1/4 cup water	1 tablespoon horseradish
3 tablespoons butter/margarine,	1 egg, slightly beaten
divided	1 cup coarse cracker crumbs

Combine the zucchini, onion, and water and cook, covered, until tender (this takes about 10 minutes). Drain and mash.

Then stir in 2 tablespoons butter/margarine, and the remaining ingredients except the crumbs. (Incidentally, I have never put horseradish in this dish, because I never have any in the house. Try 2 teaspoons worcestershire sauce if you have the same problem.) Pour into a 1-quart baking dish.

Melt the remaining butter and toss the cracker crumbs with it. Spread over the zucchini mixture. Bake at 350° for 30 minutes or until hot and browned. Serves 6.

Variation: Substitute chopped broccoli for the zucchini.

ZUCCHINI AND CARROTS

I like zucchini in combination with other vegetables. The following recipes are very simply prepared, and all involve the stir-and-steam method of preparation.

2 tablespoons oil	5 carrots, thinly sliced (2 cups)
1 small onion, quartered and sliced	1/3 cup parmesan cheese
1 1/2 pounds zucchini, in slices	2 tablespoons chopped parsley
(about 4 cups)	salt and pepper to taste

Heat the oil in a large skillet and sauté the onion over low heat about 5 minutes. Add zucchini and stir-fry for 5 minutes. Stir in the carrots, cover, and cook 10 minutes, or until tender. Remove from heat, stir in the cheese and parsley. Cover and let stand 5 minutes. Season. Serves 4 to 6.

FESTIVE ZUCCHINI

2 tablespoons oil	1/4 teaspoon salt
1/2 cup chopped onion	1/8 teaspoon pepper
4 cups sliced zucchini	1 tablespoon chopped pimiento
1 cup thinly sliced green pepper	seasoned bread cubes

In a large skillet, sauté the onion in the oil until tender. Stir in zucchini, green pepper, salt, and pepper. Cover and cook over medium heat for 10 minutes, or until zucchini is tender. Serve garnished with chopped pimiento and bread cubes. Serves 6.

ZUCCHINI AND TOMATOES

1 pound zucchini, sliced thinly	2 medium tomatoes, peeled and
2 tablespoons olive oil	diced
1 tablespoon chopped green onions	dash garlic salt or powder
	pepper to taste

Sauté the zucchini in the hot oil until lightly browned, stirring briskly. Add onions, tomatoes, and seasonings. Cover and simmer 5 to 10 minutes. Serves 4.

◆

ZUCCHINI SOUP BASE

Here is what you can do with those zucchinis that grew too big when your back was turned. I make enormous quantities of this soup, and we eat it all winter long from the freezer.

3 pounds or more zucchini
1 1/2 cups water
2 envelopes instant chicken broth

1 medium onion, cut up
1/2 clove garlic, minced, *or*
1/4 teaspoon garlic powder

Wash the zucchini, cut it in pieces. Combine with remaining ingredients and boil until tender. Purée in the blender until smooth. Adjust the seasoning. You can reheat the mixture to simmering before you freeze it. I never do. Freeze in pint containers.

To serve: Defrost the soup base and dilute with milk or half-and-half. Garnish with grated parmesan, crumbled bacon, seasoned croutons. This soup can also be served cold, garnished with a dollop of plain yogurt or dairy sour cream and some chopped chives.

ZUCCHINI PICKLES

Another way to use up the abundance from the garden. These pickles are easy to make.

1 quart wine vinegar
2 cups sugar
3 tablespoons salt
2 teaspoons celery seed
2 teaspoons ground tumeric

1 teaspoon dry mustard
5 pounds zucchini (5 to 6 inches
   long), cut into 1/4-inch slices
4 cups thinly sliced onions

Combine the vinegar, sugar, salt, and seasonings in a saucepan; bring to a boil. Pour over the zucchini and onions; let stand for 1 hour, stirring occasionally. Then bring the mixture to a boil and simmer 3 minutes. Continue simmering while quickly packing one hot sterilized jar at a time. Fill to within 1/2-inch of the top, making sure the vinegar solution covers the vegetables. Seal each jar at once. Process 5 minutes. Makes 6 to 7 pints.

ZUCCHINI COOKIES

1 cup grated zucchini	1/4 cup wheat germ
1/2 cup honey	1/2 teaspoon baking soda
1/4 cup oil	1/2 teaspoon cinnamon
1 egg, beaten	1/4 teaspoon nutmeg
1/4 cup flour	1/4 teaspoon salt
2/3 cup whole wheat flour	1/2 teaspoon lemon juice

Mix the honey and oil. Add the egg, then the zucchini. In another bowl, mix the dry ingredients. Combine the dry with the wet ingredients. Add the lemon juice. Drop by teaspoonsful on cookie sheets. Bake at 350° for 10 to 15 minutes. Makes about 2 dozen.

ZUCCHINI AND COTTAGE CHEESE BREAD

This is a tasty, savory bread that is wonderful with cold meats, sliced cheese, or a summer salad.

2 tablespoons yeast	1 cup grated zucchini
1/2 cup warm water	3/4 cup cottage cheese
2 1/2 cups white flour	3/4 cup plain yogurt
1 cup graham flour	3 tablespoons chopped chives *or*
2 teaspoons salt	green onions, minced

Dissolve the yeast in the warm water. Combine with the remaining ingredients. Add enough flour to make the dough easy to handle. Knead about 8 minutes, working in more flour if necessary. Cover and let rise until double, about 1 1/2 hours. Punch down, shape into a loaf, put in a 9 x 5 loaf pan. Let rise until double. Bake at 375° for 45 minutes.

☆☆☆ ZUCCHINI BREAD

I have done a lot of experimenting with zucchini bread recipes and altered many versions. This is the best of all.

3 eggs	1/2 cup wheat germ
1 cup brown sugar	1 cup whole wheat flour
1/4 cup white sugar	1/2 teaspoon salt
2/3 cup vegetable oil	1 teaspoon baking soda
2 cups grated zucchini	1/2 teaspoon baking powder
2 teaspoons vanilla	3 teaspoons cinnamon
1 1/2 cups white flour	1 cup chopped dates *or* raisins

Beat the eggs well, then add the sugars, oil, zucchini, and vanilla. Combine all the dry ingredients, then add them to the wet. Stir well, and add the dates (you can also add 1/2 cup chopped walnuts, if you wish). Bake in two 9 x 5 loaf pans, for one hour, or 3 smaller 7 1/2 x 3 1/2 pans for about 50 minutes.

Other recipes using zucchini: Ratatouille Niçoise (Eggplant); Chicken Zucchini Flips; Calabacitas (Corn); Lamb Provençal Style; Super Minestrone, Tuna and Spinach-Noodle Salad (Noodles & Pasta); Potato Ratatouille; Ricotta-Zucchini Stuffing.

Appendix

Included here are several recipes for basic combinations that are needed in a number of recipes throughout this collection. Instead of repeating them, I give them once here. And because I find such information useful and helpful (especially when we are trying to use what we have), I have given also a list of equivalents and substitutions, a table of measurements, and a guide to baking pan sizes and capacities.

Basic Recipes

BISCUIT MIX

Yes, you can purchase it, if you like. Yes, it is expensive and it often is not very fresh. Yes, you can make it very easily.

8 cups flour	3 teaspoons salt
5 tablespoons plus 1 teaspoon baking powder	1 cup shortening

Sift the dry ingredients together into a large bowl. Then cut in the shortening (make sure you use shortening—or 2 sticks margarine—that does not require refrigeration). Mix together with a fork or your fingers until crumbly.

Store in tightly covered containers. Makes 12 cups.

QUANTITY PIE CRUST

I am not very good at making pie crust, but this recipe is a winner. It never fails, and I like the idea of cutting off what I need, when I need it.

5 cups flour	1 egg
1 teaspoon salt	2 tablespoons vinegar
1 pound lard	water

Mix the flour and salt, cut in the lard. Beat the egg with a fork in an 8-ounce cup. Add the vinegar and fill to the top with water. Add this to the flour mixture and blend well. Wrap in plastic wrap and chill 24 hours. Let stand at room temperature for a half hour before use (I often forget this, it doesn't seem to matter much). Cut off as much as you need and store the rest. It will keep about two weeks in the refrigerator. It can be frozen. Makes about 6 shells.

GRAHAM CRACKER CRUST

1 1/2 cups graham cracker crust	4 tablespoons melted butter
3 tablespoons 10X sugar	

Combine well with a fork. Press into a 9-inch pie plate. Chill until needed. Or bake right away, about 10 minutes at 375°.

CREAM SAUCE

2 tablespoons butter/margarine	1 cup milk
2 tablespoons flour	salt and pepper

Melt the butter over low heat; stir in the flour and cook until it sizzles, about 2 minutes. Whisk in the milk (heated, if you want the sauce to cook faster), and cook, stirring or whisking constantly, until the sauce thickens and boils. Cook several minutes. Add salt and pepper to taste. This makes a medium cream sauce; to make a light sauce, reduce the butter and flour to 1 tablespoon each. If you need a really thick sauce, increase them to 3 tablespoons each.

◆

BOILED DRESSING

1/3 cup sugar
1 tablespoon flour
1/2 teaspoon salt

1/2 teaspoon dry mustard
1 egg
1/2 cup white vinegar mixed with
1/4 cup water

Mix the sugar, flour, salt, and mustard in a small saucepan. Add the egg and beat it in well; then slowly stir in the vinegar-water mixture. (I must confess this recipe also calls for 2 tablespoons melted butter, and if the spirit moves you, by all means add it at this point. I *never* have.) Cook until boiling, stirring constantly (if you have a whisk, this is the time to use it), boil two minutes, still stirring. Strain into a jar, cool, cover, and refrigerate. This dressing will keep for more than a month.

MOCK MAYONNAISE

1/2 cup plain yogurt
1 egg yolk, raw
1 egg yolk, cooked and sieved
salt and pepper to taste

1 teaspoon Dijon mustard
1 teaspoon lemon juice
honey to taste
2 green onions, minced

Mix it all together. The cooked egg yolk is optional, in my view; it does add substance and color to the dressing. You can also season it with a small amount of instant vegetable soup powder. I prefer this dressing to mayonnaise. So would any dieter (it is about 20 calories per tablespoon).

VINAIGRETTE DRESSING

1 cup olive oil
1/2 cup vinegar (garlic, tarragon,
    wine)
salt and pepper to taste

dried salad herbs
1/2 teaspoon dried *or*
    Dijon mustard

Combine all the ingredients in a jar with a tight lid and shake well. Makes about 1 1/2 cups. You can add a crushed garlic clove, if you like.

PASTA SALAD DRESSING

1/2 cup safflower *or* sunflower oil
1/4 cup white vinegar
3 tablespoons lemon *or* lime juice
2 cloves garlic, mashed

1/2 teaspoon honey
1 tablespoon plain yogurt
1 teaspoon Dijon mustard
1/4 teaspoon salt
pepper

Put everything in a covered jar and shake well. Keep refrigerated. Makes about 1 1/4 cups.

CONFECTIONERS' SUGAR GLAZE

Combine 1 cup 10X sugar, 1/2 teaspoon vanilla, and 2 to 3 tablespoons milk in a small bowl. Beat until smooth.

HONEY GLAZE

Beat together 2 1/2 cups 10X sugar, 1 tablespoon honey, and 2 tablespoons milk.

LEMON GLAZE

Blend 1 cup 10X sugar with enough lemon juice to make a spreading consistency.

LIGHT BUTTER FROSTING

Combine 1 1/2 cups 10X sugar, 1 tablespoon soft butter, 1/4 teaspoon vanilla, a dash of salt, and 2 tablespoons milk or light cream. Beat until smooth. If too thick, add more milk; if too thin, more sugar.

ORANGE GLAZE

Combine 1 cup 10X sugar and 1 teaspoon orange peel. Add gradually 1 tablespoon orange juice or orange juice concentrate, and only enough to make a spreading consistency.

CINNAMON TOPPING

Mix together with a fork or your fingers 1/2 teaspoon cinnamon, 1/4 cup finely chopped nuts, 1/4 cup brown or white sugar.

STREUSEL TOPPING

Put the following ingredients in a bowl and work with your fingers until crumbly: 2 tablespoons soft butter, 1/2 cup brown sugar, 1/4 cup flour, and 1 teaspoon cinnamon.

FLUFFY FROSTING

This recipe makes a generous frosting for the tops and sides of two 9-inch layers. Cut it in half for a one-layer, smaller cake.

2 cups 10X sugar	1/2 teaspoon cream of tartar
6 tablespoons hot water	1/8 teaspoon salt
2 egg whites	1 teaspoon vanilla

Measure the sugar into a saucepan and stir in the hot water. Cover and boil until the sugar is dissolved (this takes only a minute or so). Put the egg white, cream of tartar, and salt in a mixing bowl. Beat slightly. Slowly add the hot syrup, beating. Turn the mixer to medium-high for 2 minutes, then to high speed for 2 minutes more, or until the frosting is the right consistency to spread. Add the vanilla while beating.

LEMON SAUCE

I am including this recipe, because I consider a good lemon dessert sauce to be an essential part of a cook's repertory. Also I find that a good recipe is hard to find.

1/2 cup sugar	2 tablespoons butter
1 tablespoon cornstarch	1 teaspoon lemon grated rind
pinch salt	3 tablespoons lemon juice
1 cup boiling water	

Combine the sugar, cornstarch, salt; gradually stir in the water. Boil, stirring constantly, about 5 minutes, or until sauce is thickened and clear. Stir in the remaining ingredients.

If you prefer, substitute 1/3 cup honey for the sugar, adding it along with the boiling water.

CIDER SAUCE

This sauce is very good on pancakes, puddings, and gingerbread.

1 cup sugar	2 tablespoons lemon juice
2 tablespoons cornstarch	2 tablespoons butter
2 cups apple cider	

Combine the sugar, cornstarch, cider, and lemon juice. Bring to a boil, stirring, and boil 2 minutes. Cool slightly and blend in the butter. Serve warm.

Substitutions and Equivalents

1 tablespoon cornstarch 1 tablespoon potato flour	2 tablespoons flour
1 teaspoon baking powder	1/2 teaspoon cream of tartar plus 1/4 teaspoon baking soda
1 ounce chocolate	3 tablespoons cocoa plus 1 1/2 teaspoons fat

1 cup milk	1/2 cup evaporated milk plus 1/2 cup
	    water
	1/3 cup instant dry milk plus liquid to
	    make 1 cup

1 cup soured milk or buttermilk	1 tablespoon vinegar or lemon juice plus sweet milk to make 1 cup
1 cup dairy sour cream	1 tablespoon lemon juice plus evaporated milk to make 1 cup
1 whole egg	2 egg yolks plus 1 tablespoon water
1 cup molasses or corn syrup	1 cup honey
1 cup sugar	1 cup honey plus 1/2 teaspoon soda; (reduce liquid in recipe by 1/4 cup)
1 teaspoon dry herbs	1 tablespoon minced fresh herbs
1 medium lemon	1 teaspoon grated rind and 2 tablespoons lemon juice
1 medium apple	1 cup sliced apples
1 medium potato	1 cup sliced potatoes

(I pass on the raw rice-cooked rice equivalents—there is too much variation among brands and kinds of rice.)

Basic Measures

DRY

3 teaspoons	1 tablespoon
4 tablespoons	1/4 cup
5 tablespoons plus 1 teaspoon	1/3 cup
8 tablespoons	1/2 cup
10 tablespoons plus 2 teaspoons	2/3 cup
12 tablespoons	3/4 cup
16 tablespoons	1 cup

LIQUID

2 tablespoons	1 liquid ounce
1 jigger	1 1/2 liquid ounces
1 cup	1/2 pint
2 cups	1 pint
4 cups	1 quart
4 cups plus 3 1/3 tablespoons	1 liter
4 quarts	1 gallon

SOLID

1 stick butter or margarine	1/2 cup
	8 tablespoons
1/2 stick butter or margarine	1/4 cup
	4 tablespoons

Baking Pans

Common kitchen pans to use as baking dishes

4-cup baking dish (1-quart)

9-inch pie plate
8-inch round layer-cake pan
7 1/2 x 3 1/2-inch loaf pan

6-cup baking dish (1 1/2-quart)

8 or 9-inch layer-cake pan
10-inch pie plate

8-cup baking dish (2-quart)

8-inch square pan
11 x 7-inch baking pan
9 x 5-inch loaf pan

10-cup baking dish (2 1/2-quart)

9-inch square pan
11 x 8-inch baking pan

12-cup baking dish (3-quart)

13 x 8-inch glass pan
13 x 9-inch metal baking pan
14 x 10 baking pan
15 x 10 baking pan

Special pans and their capacities

7 1/2-inch Bundt pan   6 cups
9-inch Bundt pan   9 cups
9-inch tube pan   12 cups
10-inch tube pan   18 cups
8 1/2-inch ring mold   4 1/2 cups
9 1/4-inch ring mold   8 cups

Index

Appetizers
Baked Liver Pâté, 203
Barbeque Hot Dogs, 184
Cereal-Cheese Mounds, 89
Cheese Rounds, 89
Cucumbers in Yogurt, 131
Dry Roasted Nuts, 215
Guacamole, 21
Ham Squares, 176
Ham Tartines, 177
Leeks Vinaigrette, 191
Melons as, 206
Mushroom-Stuffed Toma-
  toes, 310
Oeuf en gelée, 333
Party Meat Balls, 37
Potato skins, baked, x
Stuffed Mushrooms, 210
Sunflower Cottage Cheese
  Crisps, 117
See also Snacks; Spreads
  and Dips

Baking pans, xii; capacities, 362
Basic Granola, 166
Beverages
Apple Flip, 307
Apricot-Orange Tea, 307
Banana Cocktail, 28
Cantaloupe Cocktail, 207
Cranberry Tea, 307
Grape Juice, 175
  Raw, 175
Rhubarb Tea, 276
Rum Iced Coffee, 111
Tea with Milk, 306
Tea Punch, 307
Tomato Cocktail, 309
Tomato Juice, 309
Yogurt Swirl, 341
Watermelon Juice, 207
Biscuit Mix, 354
Breads, Quick
Apple Fruit Loaf, 7
Apple-Nut, 7
Applesauce, 9
Apricot Walnut, 14
Banana, 23
  -Carrot Tea, 23
  Nut, 22
Blueberry Orange, 44
Boston Brown, 56
Cardamom, 9
Cheese
  Buttermilk, 90
  Fast, 90

Corn, 290
  Applesauce, 8
  Coconut, 107
  Spicy Raisin, 144
Cranberry Orange Nut, 125
Dark Orange Raisin, 270
Date-Nut, 139
Fruit-Nut, 9
Gingerbread, 60
Golden Fruit, 14
Holiday, 145
Lemon, 199
Marmalade Tea Loaf, 185
Molasses Brown, 80
Peach, 230
Pear, 237
Pineapple Pecan Loaf, 245
Pumpkin
  Classic, 262
  -Mincemeat, 263
  Sherry, 262
Soda
  Oatmeal, 55
  White, 55
  Whole Wheat, 55
Sweet Potato, 263
Zucchini, 353
See also Coffee Cakes; Muf-
  fins; Pancakes; Rolls and
  Buns
Breads, Yeast
Butter Batter, 56
Dill Casserole, 117
Dill Pickle, 135
Graham-Buttermilk, 57
Grain, 165
Granola-Yogurt, 170
Hearty Breakfast, 84
Hearty Onion, 225
Hearty Yogurt, 341
Oatmeal, 85
Pumpkin, 262
Refrigerator Potato, 260
Rice, 279
Triple Healthy, 260
Whole Wheat Healthy, 260
Zucchini and Cottage Cheese,
  352
See also Rolls and Buns

Cakes
Apple Harvest, 2
Applesauce, 9
Banana-Applesauce, 26
Banana Cake Jamaica, 25
Banana-Carob, 26
Blueberry, 45

Boiled Raisin, 269
Buttermilk Pound, 61
Carrot-Pineapple, 72
Chocolate, 61
Cranberry Upside-Down, 126
Coconut Pound, 106
Cookie Crumb, 67
Currant, 138
Economy Cocoa, 293
Gingerbread, 60
Graham Cracker, 247
Honey and Spice Cupcakes,
  10
Honey, 308
Maple Pecan, 288
Old Fashioned Carrot, 74
Orange-Cranberry, 167
Orange-Date-Nut, 62
Passover, 27
Peach Upside-Down, 231
Pflaumenkuchen, 250
Plum, 251
Poppy Seed, 338
Raspberry Ring, 343
Raisin Peanut Butter Tea, 269
Rhubarb, 272
Snacking, 120
Sour Cream, 288
Spice, 287
Spiced Torte, 293
Sponge, 150
  Wine, 337
Swiss Carrot, 73
Turkish Yogurt, 342
Wheatena Cupcakes, 285
See also Coffee Cakes;
  Desserts
Candies and Confections
Candied Grapefruit, 172
Caramel Nut Fudge, 289
Coffee Fudge, 112
Honey Divinity, 154
Krokant, 216
Moon Balls, 169
Ricotta Bonbons, 285
Snowballs, 142
Spiced Nuts, 216
Sugared Pecans, 216
Casseroles and Baked Dishes
Cheese
  Cheese and Macaroni Bake,
    92
  Noodle Surprise, 213
  Saturday Night Casserole,
    92

Fish
  Baked Fish Creole, 161
  Baked Fish and Nuts, 160
  Fish Florentine, 296
  Tuna Noodle Casserole, 322
  Tuna Romanoff, 118
Meat
  Baked Macaroni with Ricotta, 284
  Beef Casserole, 119
  Beef Casserole with Almonds, 78
  Beef Pot Pie, 36
  Hamburger and Noodles Stroganoff, 334
  Johnny Margetti, 318
  Rice Casserole Italiano, 345
  Scalloped Cauliflower and Ham, 76
  Schinken Makkaroni, 180
  Veal Casserole, 329
Poultry
  Baked Chicken with *Fines Herbes,* 332
  Chicken and Noodle Divan, 103
  Chicken Tetrazzini, 156
  Turkey Ham Bake, 325
Casseroles
Vegetable
  Barley Casserole, 164
  Beans-Celery-Bulgur Casserole, 29
  Broccoli-Noodle Bake, 53
  Bulgur and Celery au Gratin, 79
  Cottage Cheese Potatoes, 119
  Crusted Cauliflower, 77
  Eggplant Bake, 147
  Eggplant and Macaroni, 214
  Green Bean Casserole, 30
  Herbed Spinach Bake, 297
  Lima Beans in Casserole, 196
  Mexican Casserole, 282
  P and P Casserole, 240
  Scalloped Potatoes with Gruyere, 257
  Soybean Casserole, 196
  Super Pie, 197
  Zucchini Deluxe, 344
Coffee Cakes
  Apple Streusel, 291
  Apricot Kuchen, 17
  Blueberry Buckle, 45
  Eggnog Kuchen, 143
  Orange-Coconut, 107
  Pineapple Ring, 182
  Quick Breakfast Cake, 292
  Sour Cream, 286
  Spicy Raisin Corn Bread, 144

Topsy-Turvy Coffee Ring, 58
  Tropical, 342
Cookies
Bars and Squares
  Almond Snowcap, 153
  Apple Brownies, 5
  Applesauce Fudge, 11
  Applesauce Spice, 11
  Apricot, 16
  Apricot-Pineapple, 15
  Butterscotch Chewy, 82
  Carrot Brownies, 75
  Cashew-Caramel, 222
  Cheesecake, 128
  Coconut Lemon, 109
  Date Brownies, 142
  Energy Fruit, 271
  Festive Raisin, 270
  Fruit Nut, 186
  Gatos, 182
  German Cream Cheese Brownies, 127
  Granola, 168
  Honey Oatmeal Chews, 108
  Norwegian Almond, 222
  Oatmeal Date, 141
  Oatmeal Spice, 86
  Pineapple-Graham, 244
  Raisin Toffee, 82
  Saucepan Brownies, 168
  Three-Layer, 109
Drop
  Apple, 6
  Banana Oatmeal, 28
  Crunchy Granola, 169
  Crunchy Jumble, 81
  Currant, 150
  Forest Ranger, 81
  Frosted Carrot, 74
  Golden, 305
  Hermits, 169
Macaroons
  Almond, 153
  Coconut, 110
  Corn Flake, 153
  Nut, 221
  Molasses, 112
  Oatmeal Saucers, 10
  Old-Fashioned Sour Cream, 287
  Peanut Date, 140
  Rice Krispies, 83
  Sesame-Oatmeal, 86
  Sour Cream Chocolate, 287
  Spicy Fruit, 292
  Toffee, 81
  Zucchini, 352
Shaped
  Butter, 151
  Cereal Date, 141
  Nut Crescents, 221

Vanilla-Nut Icebox, 220
  Viennese Rounds, 220
Cooking terms, ix
Cracked Wheat Cereal, 83
Cream, to sour, 286
Crepes
  Chicken-Zucchini Flips, 102
  with Ham, 178
  Spinach Roulade, 296
Crunchy Granola, 167
Crusts, for Pies
  Cereal Crumb, 83
  Cornmeal Pastry, 36
  Cracker Crumb, 91
  Dessert, 83
  Graham Cracker, 355
  Quantity Pie Crust, 355
Curry Dishes
  condiments for, 189, 324
  Bean and Peanut, 195
  Cream of Corn Soup, 113
  Lamb, 188
  Pear Salad, 236
  Rice Salad, 278
  Turkey, 324
  Tuna, 322
  Tuna Squares, 277
  Veal, 330

Desserts
  Austrian Wine Cream, 337
Cheese Cakes
  Peaches and Cream Cake, 128
  Pumpkin, 266
  Skinny, 121
  Chestnut Torte, 98
Frozen
  Frosty Melon Balls, 206
  Grapefruit Sherbet, 172
  Lush Slush, 28
  Orange Layer Dessert, 66
Fruit Combinations
  Apple-Plum Compote, 249
  Cantaloupe and Blackberries, 42
  Cantaloupe Fruit Cups, 206
  Melon Supreme, 206
  Sliced Oranges in Wine, 227
  Stewed pears, 235
  Stewed plums, 248
  See also Freezing, Salads
Fruits, baked
  Apple Nut Torte, 2
  Baked Apples, 1
  in wine, 336
  Baked Cherry Pudding, 95
  Blackberry Birds Nest, 43
  Blackberry Roll, 42
  Blueberry Grunt, 46
  Blueberry Slump, 46

Blueberry Streusel Pudding, 47
Buttery Apple Squares, 5
Cherry Torte, 95
Concord Grape Kuchen, 174
Cranberry Apple Crisp, 125
Date Pudding Cake, 140
Honeyed Fruit Crumble, 3
Peach Cobbler, 232
Peach Macaroon, 232
Plum-Apricot Party Dessert, 249
Plum-Crumb Pudding, 250
Raisin Apple Betty, 268
Rhubaba, 274
Rhubarb Crisp, 274
Gâteau aux Noisettes, 219
Huguenot Torte, 1
Linzertorte, 219
Meringues, 153
Molded
  Apricot Bavarian Cream, 13
  Chestnut Mousse, 98
  Chocolate Bavarian, 157
  Coffee Jelly, 111
    with Brandy, 111
    with Sherry, 111
  Hexenschnee, 12
  Lemon Bisque, 157
  Mai Tai Mold, 247
  Melon in Chablis, 336
  Orange and Lemon Jelly, 336
  Peanut Mousse, 158
  Pineapple Snow Pudding, 152
  Pumpkin Molds with Mince-meat Sauce, 264
  Rhubarb Ring with Straw-berries, 275
Poire à la belle Héléne, 235
Trifle, 66
See also Cakes; Pancakes; Pies; Puddings; Sauces; Top-pings
Dressings
  for poultry, *see* Stuffings
  for salads, *see* Salad Dressings
Dumplings, cheese, 313
Duxelles, 208

Flour
  kinds of, xi
  substitutions for, 360
Freezing
  Blueberries, 44
  Cranberries, 121
  Currants, 136
  Peaches, 230
  Pears, 235
  Plums, 248
  Red Raspberries, 47

Strawberries, 47
  suitable items for, xi
Fritters
  Corn, 155
  Spinach, 295

Frostings and Glazes
  Buttermilk Glaze, 72
  Confectioners' Sugar Glaze, 357
  Cream Cheese Frosting, 130
  Fluffy Frosting, 358
  Fudge Frosting, 62
  Honey Glaze, 357
  Jelly Frosting, 183
  Lemon Glaze, 357
  Light Butter Frosting, 357
  Orange Glaze, 358
  Pineapple, 247
  Ricotta Frosting, 285
Gazpacho, 310
Golden Granola, 166
Guacamole, 21

Hash, 325
Herbs, x, xi, 360
  how to chop, 228

Ingredients to save, ix-x

Jams and Conserves
  Apricot-Orange Jam, 17
  Carrot Marmalade, 184
  Cranberry Butter, 123
  Cranberry-Strawberry Jam, 123
  Currant and Raspberry Jam, 136
  Heavenly Jam, 175
  Orange Marmalade, 185
  Peach Marmalade, 184
  Pear Butter, 237
  Pear "Honey," 237
  Pineapple Preserves, 246
  Plum Conserve, 251
  Raw Pear Conserve, 238
  Rhubarb Conserve, 276
  Rhubarb Pineapple Jam, 275
  Strawberry Jam. 48
Jellies
  how to make, 41
  Black Raspberry, 41
  Currant, 137
  Grape, 174
  Paradise, 7
  Peach, 234
  see also Desserts, Molded
Johnny Margetti, 318

Kasha, 163
  with carrots, 68

Loaves
  Meat and Fish
    Curried Tuna Squares, 277
    Italian Meat, 317
    Meat, 317

Swiss, 93
Veal, 331
Vegetable
  Garbanzo and Pineapple, 194
  Kasha, 163
  Lentil, 196
  Vegetable Nut, 217
  Vegetable Nut Roast, 51
  Walnut Lentil, 217
Lumberman's Mush, 84

Main Dishes
  Basic Pilaf, 162
  Eggs
    Eggs Foo Yong, 149
    Eggs in Onion Sauce, 225
    Piperade, 312
    Saturday Night Casserole, 92
    see also Omelettes; Quiches; Soufflés
  Fish
    Baked Fish Creole, 161
    Baked Fish and Nuts, 160
    Curried Tuna Squares, 277
    Fish Florentine, 296
    Fish Timbales, 160
    Tuna Curry, 322
    Tuna Marengo, 323
    Tuna Romanoff, 118
    Tuna Noodle Casserole, 322
  Meat
    Asparagus Roulades, 18
    Bacon Chive Rice, 277
    Baked Macaroni with Ri-cotta, 284
    Barbecued Beef Burgers, 37
    Beef Casserole, 119
      with Almonds, 78
    Beef Encore, 35
    Beef Pot Pie, 36
    Beefsteak Pizza Style, 315
    Boeuf Bourguignon, 334
    Boeuf Choufleur, 243
    Braised Veal, 333
    Chinese Pork, 252
      and Vegetables, 253
    Curried Lamb, 188
    Demi-Cassoulet, 188
    English Pork Hash, 254
    Ground Beef with Lentils, 195
    Hamburger and Noodles Stroganoff, 334
    Ham-Corn Bread Ring, 180
    Ham Kabobs with Swiss, 179
    Ham Roll-Ups, 179
    Italian Meat Loaf, 317
    Johnny Margetti, 318
    Lamb Provencal Style, 189
    Lamb Terrapin, 187

Meat-Fried Noodles, 35
Meat Loaf, 317
Party Meat Balls, 37
Perciatelli alla Napoletana, 314
Pork-Peas-Rice, 253
Pork and Raisins, 254
Pork Shoulder with Peppers, 242
Pot au Feu, 190
Rice Casserole Italiano, 345
Rice Pizza, 279
Scalloped Cauliflower and Ham, 76
Schinken Makkaroni, 180
Sherry Pork Chops with Fruit, 335
Skillet Lamb Shanks, 335
Swiss Loaf, 93
Veal Casserole, 329
Veal Curry, 330
Veal Fricassee, 155
Veal Loaf, 331
Veal Paprika, 330
Poultry
Baked Chicken with *Fines Herbes,* 332
Chicken Cacciatore, 314
Chicken Cranberry à l'Orientale, 100
Chicken Dijon, 332
Chicken Hawaiian, 246
Chicken Livers Marsala, 204
Chicken Livers, Sweet-Sour, 205
Chicken Livers in Wine Sauce, 204
Chicken and Noodle Divan, 103
Chicken Stroganoff, 101
Chicken Tetrazzini, 156
Dilled Chicken-Tomato Skillet, 313
Turkey Cantonese, 324
Turkey Ham Bake, 325
Turkey Hash, 325
Walnut Chicken, 101
Vegetables
Broccoli-Noodle Bake, 53
Bulgur and Celery au Gratin, 79
Bulgur and Garbanzos, 164
Cheese Custard in Squash Shells, 300
Fettucine with Egg Sauce, 214
Mexican Casserole, 282
Pasta and Zucchini, 345
Soybean Casserole, 196
Soybeans and Rice Boats, 347

Stuffed Peppers, 242
Super Pie, 197
Tomatoes with Cheese Dumplings, 313
Three-Bean Loaf, 30
Vegetable Nut Roast, 51
Zucchini Boats, 346
Zucchini Deluxe, 344
see also Crepes; Omelettes; Quiches; Salads; Soufflés
Marinades, 33, 54, 191
Measures, basic, 361
Meat juices, x
Meringues, 153
Milk, sour, as substitute for sweet, 290
Muffins
Apple Oatmeal, 289
Banana Bran, 24
Banana Orange, 24
Bran, 80
Cranberry, 124
Fresh Pumpkin, 263
Granola, 170
Ham, 178
Orange, 227
Streusel, 186
Omelettes
how to make, 148
Eggplant, 148
Herbed, 228
Mushroom-Stuffed, 209
Open-Faced Zucchini, 346
Tomato, with Herbs, 312
Tuna, 319
Pancakes
Apple, 6
Banana, 25
Holiday Latkes, 118
Oatmeal, 291
Sweet Potato, 305
Twelfth-Day, 145
Wheat Germ Buttermilk, 58
See also Crepes
Pâtes, *see* Spreads and Dips
Pickles and Relishes
Almond Cranberry Sauce, 122
Cranberry Relish, 122
Dill Pickles I, 134
Dill Pickles II, 134
Overnight Fresh Pickles, 134
Pear Chutney, 238
Pepper Relish, 243
Watermelon Pickle, 207
Zucchini Pickles, 351
See also Jams and Conserves
Pie Crusts, *see* Crusts, for Pies
Pies and Pie Fillings
Angel Pecan, 151
Apricot-Apple, 4
Apricot Filling, 15

Blueberry, 44
Buttermilk Raisin, 60
Butter Pecan Chiffon, 158
Coconut Custard, 106
Cream Cheese, 129
German Cherry, 94
Grape Pie, 173
Holiday Eggnog, 144
Lemon Revel, 199
Meatless Pear Mincemeat, 238
Pear, 235
Pecan, 265
Chocolate, 218
Pumpkin, 265
Praline Apple, 4
Pumpkin Chiffon, 265
Pumpkin-Rum, 264
Rhubarb Strawberry, 273
Soda Cracker, 151
Sour Cream Raisin, 269
Winter Pear Walnut, 236
Pilaf
how to make, 162
variations, 162
Piperade, 312
Portable Breakfast, 85
Procedures, xii
Puddings
Apricot Kisel, 13
Bread
Apple, 50
Chocolate, 49
Lemon, 50
Old Fashioned, 49
Pumpkin, 267
Rhubarb, 273
Steamed, 50
Chestnut, 99
Custard
Apples in, 3
Caramel Apple, 4
Cherry, 94
Coffee, 111
Colonial Apple, 12
Mocha, 111
Pumpkin, 266
Wild Fruit, 43
Rice, 280
Honey Date, 280
Sweet Potato, 281
Rote Gruetze, 136
Sponge
Lemon, 198
Orange, 227
Peach, 233
Sweet Potato, 304
Quiches
variations, 91
Cheese and Bacon, 91
Ham and Corn, 181
Liver-Mushroom, 91

Spinach Ricotta Tart, 283
Vegetable, 91

Relishes, *see* Pickles and Relishes
Rolls and Buns
Biscuit Mix, 354
Butterscotch Buns, 24
Coconut Crescents, 108
Corn Rolls, 57
Currant Scones, 138
Golden Onion Rolls, 226
Hot Cross Buns, 137
Potato Puff Rolls, 259
Pumpkin Scones, 264
Whole Wheat and Cottage
    Cheese Rolls, 116
See also Muffins

Salad Dressings
Boiled, 356
Buttermilk, 59
Garlic, 297
Honey Cream, 119
Lemon Garlic, 59
Lemon-Mustard, 71
Parsley, 59
Pineapple, 72
Mayonnaise, 65
Mock Mayonnaise, 356
Pasta Salad, 357
Ricotta, 284
Tomato-Yogurt, 340
Vinaigrette, 356
Yogurt Garlic, 340
Yogurt-Nut, 341
Salads
Fruit
    Avocado and Grapefruit, 21
    Cantaloupe Fruit Cups, 206
    My Favorite, 124
Main Dish
    Chicken-Pineapple Buffet,
        104
    Chicken, with Yogurt, 105
    Crunchy Tuna, 320
    Curried Pear, 236
    Curried Rice, 278
    Fleischsalat, 35
    Fresh Spinach, with Giblets,
        205
    Fruited Chicken, 104
    German Potato, 258
    Ham and Potato, 259
    Hot Turkey, 326
    Indian Melon, 103
    Macaroni and Chicken, 213
    Mushroom Turkey, 326
    Salade Nicoise, 321
    Tuna, 319
      and Spinach-Noodle, 212
    Vegetable Mold, 320
    Zucchini-Cheese, 348

Molded
    Beet Perfection, 39
    Cucumber-Lemon, 131
    Fruit, 124
    Grapefruit Aspic, 172
    Grapefruit Jelly with Sherry,
        171
    Ham Mousse, 177
    Oeuf en gelée, 333
    Orange-Pineapple, 120
    Parsleyed Ham, 177
    Slim Pineapple Ring, 245
    Spinach Salad Ring, 298
    Tuna Vegetable, 320
    Rice, 278
    Tabouli, 228

Salads
Vegetable
    Bean and Egg, 32
    Beet and Potato, 39
    Broccoli in Marinade, 54
    Carrot, 71
    Cucumber-Bean, 132
    Cucumbers in Yogurt, 131
    Fresh spinach, 297
    Green Bean and Mushroom,
        33
    Health, 72
    Healthy, 65
    Hungarian Cucumber Salad,
        131
    Marinated Bean and Chestnut,
        33
    Mixed, 38
    Oriental, 65
    Parsley, 228
    Three Bean, 193
    Spinach and Mushroom, 298
Sandwiches
    Open Tomato-Bacon-Cheese,
        311
    Turkey Pita, 328
    See also Spreads and Dips
Sauces
    for Desserts
        Almond Cranberry, 122
        Butterscotch, 156
        Cherry, 96
        Chestnut, 99
        Cider, 359
        Fruit Syrup, ix-x
        Lemon, 359
        Mincemeat, 264
        Orange, 27
        Pineapple-Orange, 246
        Pineapple, 248
        Rich Chocolate, 156
        Rum Raisin, 271
        Vanilla, 45
        Weinschaum, 337
        See also Toppings

for Meat, Pasta, Vegetables
    chicken, for spaghetti, 102
    Cream, 355
    Parsley Butter, 228
    Spaghetti, 102, 214, 302, 309,
        313, 315, 323, 345
    Tomato, 31, 148, 309, 313,
        316
Skillet/Dutch Oven Dishes
    Basic Pilaf, 162
    Eggs Foo Yong, 149
    Fish
        Tuna Curry, 322
        Tuna Marengo, 322
    Fried Apples, 1
    Golden Oats, 163
    Kasha, 163
    Meat
        Bacon Chive Rice, 277
        Beef Encore, 35
        Beefsteak Pizza Style, 315
        Boeuf Bourguignon, 334
        Boeuf Choufleur, 243
        Braised Veal, 333
        Chicken Livers Marsala, 204
        Chicken Livers, Sweet-Sour,
            205
        Chicken Livers in Wine
            Sauce, 204
        Chinese Pork, 252
            and Vegetables, 253
        Demi-Cassoulet, 188
        Dilled Chicken-Tomato
            Skillet, 313
        English Pork Hash, 254
        Lamb Provencal Style, 189
        Lamb Terrapin, 187
        Meat-Fried Noodles, 35
        Perciatelli alla Napoletana,
            314
        Pork and Raisins, 254
        Pork-Peas-Rice, 253
        Pork Shoulder with Peppers,
            242
        Sherry Pork Chops with
            Fruit, 335
        Skillet Lamb Shanks, 335
        Veal Fricassee, 155
        Veal Paprika, 330
    Poultry
        Chicken Cacciatore, 314
        Chicken Cranberry à l'Orien-
            tale, 100
        Chicken Dijon, 332
        Chicken Hawaiian, 246
        Chicken Livers Marsala, 204
        Chicken Livers, Sweet-Sour,
            205
        Chicken Livers in Wine
            Sauce, 204
        Chicken Stroganoff, 101

Curried Turkey, 324
Turkey Cantonese, 324
Turkey Hash, 325
Walnut Chicken, 101
Vegetable
    Bulgur and Garbanzos, 164
    Eggs in Onion Sauce, 225
    Fettucine with Egg Sauce,
        214
    Hungarian Noodles and Peas,
        240
    Pasta and Zucchini, 345
    Peanut Brown Rice, 218
    Piperade, 312
    Venetian Rice, 239
Snacks
    Dry Roasted Nuts, 215
    Portable Breakfast, 85
    Spiced Nuts, 216
    Sugared Pecans, 216
    Sunflower Cottage Cheese
        Crisps, 117
Soufflés
    Icelandic, 160
    Potato Parmesan, 258
    Squash, 299
Soups
    Avocado, 20
    and Tomato, 20
    Basic, 192
    Blender Borscht, 40
    Carrot-Orange, 71
    Carrot and Rice, 70
    Cheese, 91
    Cold Cucumber, 133
    Chilled Tomato, 318
    Cream of Broccoli, 52
    Cream of Cucumber, 132
    Cream of Tomato, 311
    Curried Cream of Corn, 113
    Danish Beet, 40
    Dinner Chowder, 255
    Fish, 159
    Fresh Pea, 241
    Gazpacho, 310
    German Potato, 255
    Hot Dog, 34
    Leek and Potato, 191
    Leftover Salad, x
    Minted Pea, 240
    Mushroom, 209
    Onion Purée, 223
    Pot au Feu, 190
    Puréed Vegetable, x
    Quick Lima Bean, 200
    Squash, 302
    Slim Asparagus, 294
    Slim Spinach, 294
    Super Minestrone, 212
    Turkey, 327
    Vegetable, 190

Winter Borscht, 64
Yogurt-Barley, 339
Yogurt-Spinach, 340
Zucchini Base, 351
Spaghetti
    sauces for, 102, 214, 302,
        309, 313, 315, 323, 345
    See also Noodles and Pasta
Spaghetti squash, 302
Spreads and Dips
    Beer-Cheese Spread, 88
    Blender Pâté, 204
    Duxelles, 208
    Eggplant Dip, 147
    Guacamole, 21
    Mock Goose-Liver Pâté, 202
    Sherry-Cheese Spread, 88
    Skinny Pâté, 203
    Tuna-Dill Spread, 321
    Yogurt-Cottage Cheese
        Spread, 228
    Yogurt-Garlic Sauce, 340
Stuffings
    for Poultry
        Apricot, 16
        Chestnut, 97
        Duxelles, 208
        Oatmeal, 87
        Ricotta Zucchini, 282
    for Vegetables (peppers,
        squash, tomatoes), 148,
        208, 301
Substitutions and Equivalents,
    360
Sugar
    kinds of, xi
    substitutes for, 360

Tabouli, 228
Timbales
    Asparagus, 19
    Fish, 160
Toppings, for Desserts
    Brandied Apricots and Rai-
        sins, 15
    Cinnamon, 358
    Crunch, 87
    Easy Peach, 233
    Fruited Date Sauce, 183
    Hot Applesauce, 8
    Meatless Pear Mincemeat,
        238
    Peach, 230
    Pear "Honey," 237
    Streusel, 358
    Three Fruit, 183
    See also Sauces, for Dessert
Trifle, 66

Vegetables
    baked
        Asparagus Supreme, 19

Carrots and Apples, 68
Cucumbers Mornay, 133
Hubbard Squash with Pine-
    apple, 302
Stuffed Squash, 301
Carrot Ring, 69
Cheese Custard in Squash
    Shells, 300
Corn-Cheese Casserole, 114
Corn Pudding, 114
Eggplant with Cheese, 147
Italian Broccoli Casserole,
    54
Leeks au gratin, 192
Mushrooms Baked in Foil,
    210
Puffed-Up Zucchini, 349
Spicy Sweet Potatoes, 303
Spinach Ricotta Tart, 283
Stuffed Eggplant, 148
Stuffed Mushrooms, 210
Swedish Potatoes, 257
Sweet Potato Puff, 304
Broccoli Sauté, 53
Choufleur aux Oeufs, 76
Combinations
    Almond Vegetables Man-
        darin, 32
    Carrots and Kasha, 68
    Calabacitas, 115
    Evergreen Zucchini, 349
    Festive Zucchini, 350
    Leipziger Allerei, 201
    Mushroom-Stuffed Toma-
        toes 310
    Potato Ratatouille, 256
    Ratatouille Nicoise, 146
    Soybeans and Rice Boats,
        347
    Spinach-Stuffed Zucchini,
        348
    Succotash, 200
    Zucchini Boats, 346
    Zucchini and Carrots, 350
    Zucchini and Tomatoes,
        350
    Fried Tomatoes, 311
In fritters and patties
    Corn Fritters, 115
    Pecan Patties, 51
    Spinach Fritters, 295
    Sunburgers, 70
    Green Beans with Dill, 31
    Hot Cabbage Salad, 64
    Hot Cucumbers, 133
    Lima Beans with Tarragon,
        201
    Potato Polenta, 256
in Sauce
    Boiled Chestnuts, 97

Braised Celery, 78
California Carrots, 69
Creamed Spinach, 295
Green Beans in Tomato
    Sauce, 31
Leeks Vinaigrette, 191
Mushrooms and Cream,
    211
Onions in Madeira Cream,
    224
Princeton Beets, 39
Red Cabbage, Sweet-Sour,
    63
Sweet and Sour Onions,
    224
in Soup, x
Spinach Roulade, 296
Stir-Fried Cucumbers, 133
See also Casseroles, Loaves,
    Omelettes, Quiches, Sal-
    ads, Soufflés, Timbales,
    and under individual
    vegetables

Yeast, kinds of, xi